Flexible Systems Management

Series editor

Sushil
Department of Management Studies
Indian Institute of Technology Delhi
New Delhi, Delhi
India

Editorial Board

Gerhard Chroust, Institute for Telekooperation, Johannes Kepler University Linz, Austria
Julia Connell, University of Newcastle, Newcastle, NSW, Australia
Stuart Evans, Integrated Innovation Institute, Carnegie Mellon University, USA
Takao Fujiwara, Toyohashi University of Technology, Toyohashi, Aichi, Japan
Mike C. Jackson OBE, University of Hull, UK
Rashmi Jain, Montclair State University, Montclair, NJ, USA
Ramaraj Palanisamy, St. Francis Xavier University, Antigonish, NS, Canada
Edward A. Stohr, Stevens Institute of Technology, NJ, USA

The main objective of this series on Flexible Systems Management is to provide a rich collection of research as well as practice based contributions, from different contexts, that can serve as reference material in this upcoming area. Some of these books will be published in association with 'Global Institute of Flexible Systems Management'. It will help in cross-fertilizing ideas from different perspectives of flexibility so as to consolidate and enrich the paradigm of flexible systems management. The audience for the volumes under this series includes researchers, management students/teachers, and practitioners interested in exploring various facets of flexibility research and practice. The series features five types of books:

- Post conference volumes containing peer reviewed high quality research papers around a theme and clustered in sub-themes that can act as good reference material.
- Contributed thematic volumes based on invited papers from leading professionals, from academia as well practicing world, containing state of the art on an emerging theme.
- Research monographs based on research work making a comprehensive contribution to the body of knowledge.
- Books based on novel frameworks and methodologies covering new developments that are well tested and ready for wider application in research as well as practice.
- Business practices and case based books documenting flexibility practices, strategies, and systems in real life organizations.

The series covers multiple perspectives of flexible systems management; some leading ones, inter alia, are:

- Holistic management of organizational paradoxes with systemic flexibility: including various connotations such as ambidexterity, adaptability, responsiveness, openness, customization, localization, agility, vitality, sustainability, etc.
- Business agility infused by new information and communication technologies: including volatile and virtual business, developments in information and communication technologies generating IT agility such as cloud computing, social networking, knowledge based systems, search technologies, mobile transactions, business continuity, disaster recovery, etc.
- Managing innovation, strategic change and risk: including strategic change, confluence of continuity and change, strategic flexibility, strategy execution, innovation in products/services, processes, management practices, and strategies, business dynamics, business uncertainty and associated risk, etc.
- Flexibility in various operations for achieving business excellence: including organizational flexibility, financial flexibility, manufacturing flexibility, information systems flexibility, marketing flexibility, operational and supply chain flexibility, technology management flexibility, flexibility in business excellence/maturity models, etc.

More information about this series at http://www.springer.com/series/10780

Sanjay Dhir · Sushil
Editors

Flexible Strategies in VUCA Markets

 Springer

Editors
Sanjay Dhir
Indian Institute of Technology Delhi
New Delhi, Delhi, India

Sushil
Indian Institute of Technology Delhi
New Delhi, Delhi, India

ISSN 2199-8493 ISSN 2199-8507 (electronic)
Flexible Systems Management
ISBN 978-981-10-8925-1 ISBN 978-981-10-8926-8 (eBook)
https://doi.org/10.1007/978-981-10-8926-8

Library of Congress Control Number: 2018939930

© Springer Nature Singapore Pte Ltd. 2018
This work is subject to copyright. All rights are reserved by the Publisher, whether the whole or part of the material is concerned, specifically the rights of translation, reprinting, reuse of illustrations, recitation, broadcasting, reproduction on microfilms or in any other physical way, and transmission or information storage and retrieval, electronic adaptation, computer software, or by similar or dissimilar methodology now known or hereafter developed.
The use of general descriptive names, registered names, trademarks, service marks, etc. in this publication does not imply, even in the absence of a specific statement, that such names are exempt from the relevant protective laws and regulations and therefore free for general use.
The publisher, the authors and the editors are safe to assume that the advice and information in this book are believed to be true and accurate at the date of publication. Neither the publisher nor the authors or the editors give a warranty, express or implied, with respect to the material contained herein or for any errors or omissions that may have been made. The publisher remains neutral with regard to jurisdictional claims in published maps and institutional affiliations.

Printed on acid-free paper

This Springer imprint is published by the registered company Springer Nature Singapore Pte Ltd. part of Springer Nature
The registered company address is: 152 Beach Road, #21-01/04 Gateway East, Singapore 189721, Singapore

Preface

Volatility, uncertainty, complexity, and ambiguity (VUCA) strategies were introduced by the US Army War College to define the result of the cold war that was characterized by more volatile, uncertain, complex, and ambiguous multilateral world (Kinsinger and Walch 2012). Across many industries, a rising tide of volatility, uncertainty, and business complexity is stirring markets and changing the nature of competition (Doheny et al. 2012). Corporate firms are not being run as usual. CEOs are dealing with immense VUCA in their decision-making process (Gehrke and Claes 2017). Strategic flexibility in VUCA markets is a compulsion for business leaders for sustaining the advantage in market and attaining a clear vision amidst the chaos (Sushil 2017). Business leaders who stay focused and are aware of external volatility as the prevalent characteristic will be the winners. Business leaders will lose if they are not flexible in this VUCA world and lock themselves into fixed positions (Horney et al. 2010). Globalization has created opportunities on the one hand as it has introduced threats on the other. The stubborn global recession has blunted repeated bursts of optimism for the return to a path of prosperity (Bennett and Lemoine 2014). The global challenge of digesting technological advancements that impact industry, as well as the consequences of demographic shifts in the workforce, has enhanced the competitive pressure on the leaders and strategic flexibility, and thus becomes utmost essential and necessary for firms to succeed in this new normal (Horney and O'Shea 2015). Recognizing and then addressing the myriad factors that can threaten organizational performance is not getting any easier (Lawrence 2013). It is a VUCA world, after all. In this scenario, companies have been obliged to prepare their structures, cultures, and management methods to compete in this volatile, uncertain, complex, and ambiguous environment we have had to live in.

The chapters in this book were selected from papers presented at the "International Conference on Strategies in Volatile and Uncertain Environment for Emerging Markets" held at Indian Institute of Technology Delhi during July 14–15, 2017. The conference aimed to encourage discussions about research and strategies for addressing uncertainty and the opportunities created by changes in the emerging markets. We invited empirical/conceptual/working research papers and also case studies/models for the conference. The conference was able to attract contributions from top universities and institutions across the world and India. The conference received 245 research papers from various countries. Research papers were subjected to stringent peer review. With an acceptance rate of 52%, finally 128 papers were presented at the conference that were again reviewed and organized in the form of this edited volume. This volume is intended to serve as a valuable reference material in the area of flexibility in VUCA markets. The selected chapters cover a variety of issues concerning the theme of VUCA markets and are organized into following four parts:

I. Innovation in VUCA Markets
II. People and Processes in VUCA Markets
III. Financial Management in VUCA Markets
IV. Leadership and Strategies in VUCA Markets

Part I on the topic of innovation in VUCA markets incorporates five chapters. Chapter 1 is by Kumbhat and Sushil and is titled *Development Stages and Scaling Issues of Startups*. The chapter has proposed a development model with multiple dimensions for early-stage start-ups. The comprehensively presented framework enables quantitative identification of development stages. Also, the framework spots imbalance in particular development dimensions and puts forward remedies for the same. Chapter 2 in this part is *Flourishing Innovation Through Organizational Initiatives: An Analytical Study* by Chaubey and Sahoo. The link between organizational initiative and innovation with respect to competitiveness is explored in this chapter for the automobile industry. Mediation by employee creativity has been integrated and a conceptual model developed to have a methodological approach toward organizational innovation. The results substantiate the role of initiatives for creative engagement and sustaining in heavy competition. Chapter 3, *Patent Landscape for Indian Biopharmaceutical Sector: A Strategic Insight*, by Lahiry and Rangarajan throws light on the patent landscape at the firm level. Usage of a variety of patent indicators and multiple factor-based analysis has resulted in a thorough understanding of the role of patents in shaping Indian bio-pharmaceutical sector, the premise of this study. Chapter 4, *Geographical Clustering and Quality of Subsidiary Innovation in a Developing Economy*, is an effort to understand the impact of clustering on quality of subsidiary innovation, particularly in a developing country like India. Written by Betaraya, Nasim and Mukhopadhyay, it is based on the comparison of patent data of two semiconductor design companies in India and reflects on clustering as a moderator in the impacts of subsidiary age, internal network, and local knowledge spillover on innovation quality. The last chapter of this part, *Corporate Governance and Innovation*, is written by Sharma, Jhunjhunwala and Sharda. This chapter looks into the role of corporate governance in encouraging R&D activities in firms. The presence of independent directors was found to be pivotal in the decision-making of firm, especially through their active participation in board meetings.

Part II, comprising of five chapters, contains discussions on the people and processes in VUCA markets. The first of these, *Disability Inclusion*, identifies factors which facilitate successful inclusion of disabled people. These insights, by Heera and Maini, are relevant for stakeholders designing effective inclusion policies for under-represented diverse workforce. The next chapter, *Effective Policing in a VUCA Environment: Lessons from a Dark Network*, interestingly uses a case study approach to identify the effective counter-strategies for Maoists. Rich insights by Gupta and Gupta are provided about Maoists' organizational design and peoples practices which sustain them in a VUCA environment. This chapter, thus, makes important contributions to theory and practice. Chapter 8, *Effect of Gender on Job Satisfaction Among Academicians*, deals with whether the gender of academicians affects the job satisfaction level of university academicians. The study by Sachar has been conducted in public and private universities and identifies certain factors, which, further analyzed, reveal higher satisfaction among female teachers. Chapter 9, *Trainer Engagement Versus Trainer Turnover Ratio*, focuses on reduction of trainer turnover ratio in the Indian training institutes. The root underlying causes have been identified by Prasad, Sekar, Bharani and Vignesh, and various improvement measures were evaluated by an audit. The study thus contributes to reduce the employee attrition rate in the technical training department, and the same can be horizontally deployed to serve as standards for other institutions. The last chapter of the second part, *Supply Chain Strategies to Sustain Economic and Customer Uncertainties*, is written by Sinha and Dey. The chapter is purposed to establish a system dynamics model for studying economic volatility and customer's buying behavior impacts on supply chain of passenger car firms. Supply chain managers can carry out policy experimentation using this framework. The study also addresses the economic instabilities coupled with changing customer preferences.

Part III deals with financial management in VUCA markets, and comprises of four chapters. Chapter 11, *Probing Time-Varying Conditional Correlation Between Crude Oil and Sensex*, is written by Siddiqui and Gaur. It studies the co-movement of crude oil prices and volatility spillover affect on stock market and USD–INR rate of exchange. The Sensex is found to have a significant cross-volatility spillover impact on USD/INR and other exchange rates. This study, due to its significant practical implications, is particularly helpful for portfolio managers. Chapter 12 is titled *Corporate Strategies: Evidence from Indian Cross-Border Acquisitions* and authored by Jain, Kashiramka and Jain. The short-run performance of Indian firms doing cross-border acquisitions is examined in this chapter. Significantly positive but abnormal returns are indicated. This is a modest addition to the extant literature on cross-border acquisitions. *Strategies for Formulating Financial Stability Criterion to Face Challenge of Uncertainties into Energy Sector* is Chap. 13 and written by Ghosh. The financial stability of an electricity utility system is analyzed in a short- and long-term perspective by evaluating tier performance. The chapter also reflects on the role of technology diffusion as a catalyst in restoring organizations' stability. The last chapter of this part is Chap. 14, *Impact of Open Offers on Shareholders' Wealth*, written by Verma and Mittal. This chapter has focused on 31 open offers announced in India during the period 2015–2017. Excessive abnormal returns were found to occur in the phase post-announcement which reaffirms the prior literature. The learning enables shareholders' understanding of generating significant returns.

The last part, i.e., Part IV, includes last five chapters of the book and deals with leadership and strategies in emerging markets. Chapter 15—*Leadership Styles in the VUCA World, Through the Eyes of Gen-Z*—is written by Dabke. It studies the leadership dynamics of Gen Y managers by assessing how emotional intelligence and transformational leadership styles are linked. The results are from the perspective of Gen Z followers' expectations. Chapter 16 is on *Leadership in VUCA Environment* by Chawla and Lenka. It has studied two different leadership styles, transformational and resonant, in terms of suitability for the higher education institutes' survival in VUCA world. The results indicate higher impact of resonant leadership and the comparative differences among the two styles, which can be used by academicians to achieve higher forms of leadership. Chapter 17, *Why Do Small Brands Decline? A Perspective on Indian Apparel Market*, is by Arora and Banerjee. The reasons driving decline of small brands in clothing segment is reflected upon in this chapter. The reasons covered are diverse and range from inappropriate marketing programs to quality and price issues. Relevant recommendations are made for entrepreneurs and managers for enhanced understanding of Indian branded apparel market. Chapter 18 is *Non-tariff Barriers on International Trade Flows in India* by Kumar and Arora. The chapter determines the linkage between non-tariff barriers and international trade barriers. Most of the identified factors were found to have a positive influence on trade generation. Hindrances to trade creation are also discussed, thus providing a holistic understanding in addition to its practicality due to being based on primary data. The last chapter of Part IV is Chap. 19, *Employer Brand and Its External Perspective*, by Sharma and Prasad. This chapter deals with various dimensions of employer brand that attracts the potential employees in IT sector. The exploratory and conclusive nature of research makes a relevant addition to the existing literature. Eight clubbed dimensions presented add to the understanding of employer brand in Indian context.

In summary, the various chapters in this book illustrate the concept of VUCA in the context of emerging markets. As many of the authors point out, concepts of volatility and uncertainty have long been at the heart of many of the core paradigms used in strategic management to understand competitive advantage as well as flexibility in organizational boundaries. Increase in the levels and types of uncertainty potentially has important implications for the durability of firm advantages, the way firms learn and adapt, approaches for managing innovation and knowledge, and the attractiveness of different strategies and organizational models. The edited book is intended to provide a conceptual framework of "flexibility in volatile, uncertain, complex, and ambiguous markets" supported by research projects/case applications and models in various related areas. Given the range of topics, contexts, and methods used to analyze the integration of flexibility across VUCA markets, it is expected that this volume will be a useful addition to the literature on the topic as well as a practical resource for practitioners. In general, it is anticipated that this edited volume on *Flexible Strategies in VUCA Markets* will provide a useful resource for a variety of audiences such as: management students and researchers, practicing business managers, consultants, professional institutions, and corporate organizations.

Finally, we would like to thank all of the authors and reviewers who helped to bring this volume to a reality. In particular, we would like to thank Rejani Raghu, Veethica Smriti, and Nakul Parameswar who effectively communicated with the authors and reviewers as well as helped to format the final manuscript.

New Delhi, India
Sanjay Dhir
Sushil

References

Bennett, N., & Lemoine, G. J. (2014). What a difference a word makes: Understanding threats to performance in a VUCA world. *Business Horizons, 57*(3), 311–317.

Doheny, M., Nagali, V., & Weig, F. (2012). Agile operations for volatile times. *McKinsey Quarterly, 3*, 126–131.

Gehrke, B., & Claes, M. T. (2017). Leadership and global understanding. In *Leadership today* (pp. 371–385). Springer International Publishing.

Horney, N., & O'Shea, T. (2015). *Focused, fast and flexible: Creating agility advantage in a VUCA World*. BookBaby.

Horney, N., Pasmore, B., & O'Shea, T. (2010). Leadership agility: A business imperative for a VUCA World. *People and Strategy, 33*(4), 32.

Kinsinger, P., & Walch, K. (2012, July 9). Living and leading in a VUCA World. *Thunderbird University*.

Lawrence, K. (2013). Developing leaders in a VUCA Environment. *UNC Executive Development*, 1–15.

Sushil. (2017). Small steps for a giant leap: Flexible organization. *Global Journal of Flexible Systems Management, 18*(4), 273–274.

Contents

Part I Innovation in VUCA Markets

1 Development Stages and Scaling Issues of Startups 3
  Abhishek Kumbhat and Sushil

2 Flourishing Innovation Through Organizational Initiatives:
  An Analytical Study 17
  Akriti Chaubey and Chandan Kumar Sahoo

3 Patent Landscape for Indian Biopharmaceutical Sector:
  A Strategic Insight 31
  Sutopa Lahiry and K. Rangarajan

4 Geographical Clustering and Quality of Subsidiary Innovation in
  a Developing Economy 49
  Dixit Manjunatha Betaraya, Saboohi Nasim and Joy Mukhopadhyay

5 Corporate Governance and Innovation 63
  J. P. Sharma, Shital Jhunjhunwala and Shweta Sharda

Part II People and Processes in VUCA Markets

6 Disability Inclusion 79
  Sonali Heera and Arti Maini

7 Effective Policing in a VUCA Environment: Lessons
  from a Dark Network 89
  Dhruv Gupta and Vishal Gupta

8 Effect of Gender on Job Satisfaction Among Academicians 113
  Dimpy Sachar

9 Trainer Engagement Versus Trainer Turnover Ratio 125
  N. Karuppanna Prasad, K. Sekar, G. Srirekha Bharani and B. Vignesh

10	Supply Chain Strategies to Sustain Economic and Customer Uncertainties	139

Deepankar Sinha and Debasri Dey

Part III Financial Management in VUCA Markets

11	Probing Time-Varying Conditional Correlation Between Crude Oil and Sensex	157

Saif Siddiqui and Arushi Gaur

12	Corporate Strategies: Evidence from Indian Cross-Border Acquisitions	167

Samta Jain, Smita Kashiramka and P. K. Jain

13	Strategies for Formulating Financial Stability Criterion to Face Challenge of Uncertainties into Energy Sector	177

Nirmalendunath Ghosh

14	Impact of Open Offers on Shareholders' Wealth	187

Rajit Verma and Anil K. Mittal

Part IV Leadership and Strategies in VUCA Markets

15	Leadership Styles in the VUCA World, Through the Eyes of Gen-Z	201

Deepika Dabke

16	Leadership in VUCA Environment	213

Saniya Chawla and Usha Lenka

17	Why Do Small Brands Decline? A Perspective on Indian Apparel Market	225

Naveen Arora and Neelotpaul Banerjee

18	Non-tariff Barriers on International Trade Flows in India	235

Sanjay Kumar and Falguni Arora

19	Employer Brand and Its External Perspective	251

Ruchika Sharma and Asha Prasad

Index	269

Editors and Contributors

About the Editors

Sanjay Dhir is an Assistant Professor in the area of strategic management at the Department of Management Studies (DMS), Indian Institute of Technology Delhi (IIT Delhi), where he is also the faculty coordinator for placements, and the Director of GIFT School of Strategic Alliances Management. He is a Fellow (Ph.D.) of the Indian Institute of Management (IIM) Lucknow and worked at Mahindra and Mahindra Ltd. (Automotive), R&D Department, Nasik, India, for 3 years. He has published several research papers in leading international journals, including case studies at Richard Ivey School of Business, Western Ontario, jointly distributed by Ivey and Harvard Business School. His research papers have been presented at and published as proceedings of several prestigious academic conferences, such as those of the Academy of Management (AoM), Academy of International Business (AIB), Strategic Management Society (SMS), Southern Management Association (SMA), International Simulation Conference of India (ISCI, IIT Mumbai), and Strategic Management Forum (SMF, IIM Lucknow). His major areas of interest are strategic management, joint ventures, innovation management, management of change and transformation, implementation strategy and international strategy. He is a coordinator of the stakeholders' engagement cell at IIT Delhi, associate editor of the *Global Journal of Flexible Systems Management* (Springer), and editor of the e-journal *Global Journal of Business Excellence*, which aims to create and enhance business excellence practices in Asia and the Pacific.

Sushil is Abdulaziz Alsagar Chair Professor (professor of Strategic, Flexible Systems, and Technology Management), and Chair of Strategic Management Group at the Department of Management Studies, Indian Institute of Technology (IIT) Delhi. He has served as a visiting professor and has delivered seminars in several leading universities, including Kyoto University, University of Minnesota, Stevens Institute of Technology, University of Lethbridge, Alberta, and Université

Paris 1 Panthéon-Sorbonne. He has published about 20 books in the areas of flexibility, strategy, systems thinking, and technology management and over 300 papers in various refereed journals and conferences. He has pioneered the area of "flexible systems management" and made original contributions to the field in the form of interpretive approaches in management. He is the founder editor-in-chief of the *Global Journal of Flexible Systems Management* and serves on the editorial boards of leading international journals. In addition, he is the founder president of the professional body "Global Institute of Flexible Systems Management." He has acted as consultant to both governmental and industrial organizations and has served as an independent director on the boards of RINL (Rashtriya Ispat Nigam Ltd., a Government of India Public Sector Enterprise under the Ministry of Steel) and HSCC (Hospital Services Consultancy Corporation Limited, a Government of India Enterprise under the Ministry of Health and Family Welfare).

Contributors

Falguni Arora Kirori Mal College, University of Delhi, Delhi, New Delhi, India

Naveen Arora National Institute of Technology, Durgapur, West Bengal, India

Neelotpaul Banerjee National Institute of Technology, Durgapur, West Bengal, India

Dixit Manjunatha Betaraya Intel India Technology Pvt. Ltd., Bengaluru, India; Research Scholar, Aligarh Muslim University, Aligarh, India

Akriti Chaubey School of Management, National Institute of Technology, Rourkela, Odisha, India

Saniya Chawla Jagannath International Management School, Kalkaji, New Delhi, India

Deepika Dabke ICFAI Business School, Mumbai, India

Debasri Dey City College of Commerce and Business Administration, Kolkata, India; Department of MCA and BCA, IGNOU Regional Centre Kolkata, Kolkata, India; NMIS, Mumbai, India

Arushi Gaur Centre for Management Studies, Jamia Millia Islamia—A Central University, Delhi, New Delhi, India

Nirmalendunath Ghosh West Bengal State Electricity Board (WBSEB), Kolkata, India

Dhruv Gupta New Raipur, Chhattisgarh, India

Vishal Gupta Organizational Behaviour Area, Indian Institute of Management, Ahmedabad, Gujarat, India

Sonali Heera School of Business, Shri Mata Vaishno Devi University, Kakryal, Jammu and Kashmir, India

P. K. Jain Department of Management Studies, Indian Institute of Technology Delhi, New Delhi, India

Samta Jain Department of Management Studies, Indian Institute of Technology Delhi, New Delhi, India

Shital Jhunjhunwala Faculty of Commerce and Business Studies, Delhi School of Economics, University of Delhi, Delhi, India

N. Karuppanna Prasad HR and ES-IE, Jindal Steel and Power Ltd., Raigarh, India

Smita Kashiramka Department of Management Studies, Indian Institute of Technology Delhi, New Delhi, India

Sanjay Kumar Deloitte India, Delhi, New Delhi, India

Abhishek Kumbhat Department of Management Studies, Indian Institute of Technology Delhi, New Delhi, India; Skilrock Technologies Pvt. Ltd., Gurugram, India

Sutopa Lahiry Indian Institute of Foreign Trade, Kolkata, India

Usha Lenka Indian Institute of Technology Roorkee, Roorkee, Uttarakhand, India

Arti Maini School of Business, Shri Mata Vaishno Devi University, Kakryal, Jammu and Kashmir, India

Anil K. Mittal Kurukshetra University, Kurukshetra, India

Joy Mukhopadhyay ThinkCorp Consultancy Services, Bengaluru, India

Saboohi Nasim Department of Business Administration, Aligarh Muslim University, Aligarh, India

Asha Prasad B.I.T, Mesra, Ranchi, India; B.I.T (Off Campus), Noida, India

K. Rangarajan Strategic Management, Centre for MSME Studies, Indian Institute of Foreign Trade, Kolkata, India

Dimpy Sachar Delhi Institute of Advanced Studies (Affiliated to G.G.S.I.P.U.), Delhi, India

Chandan Kumar Sahoo School of Management, National Institute of Technology, Rourkela, Odisha, India

K. Sekar Department of Mechanical Engineering, National Institute of Technology, Calicut, India

Shweta Sharda Department of Commerce, Indraprastha College for Women, University of Delhi, Delhi, India

J. P. Sharma Department of Commerce, Delhi School of Economics, University of Delhi, Delhi, India

Ruchika Sharma B.I.T, Mesra, Ranchi, India; VIPS, Delhi, India; GGSIPU, Delhi, India

Saif Siddiqui Centre for Management Studies, Jamia Millia Islamia—A Central University, Delhi, New Delhi, India

Deepankar Sinha IIFT, Kolkata, India

G. Srirekha Bharani HR and ES-IE, Jindal Steel and Power Ltd., Raigarh, India

Rajit Verma Chitkara University, Rajpura, India

B. Vignesh Hinduja Tech, Chennai, India

Part I
Innovation in VUCA Markets

Chapter 1
Development Stages and Scaling Issues of Startups

Abhishek Kumbhat and Sushil

Abstract Startups are living organisms, especially early-stage startups operate under conditions of extreme uncertainty in search of right product–market fit. As the challenges and opportunities in each development stage are different, understanding of development stages will not only aid an entrepreneur in anticipating challenges and being prepared but also assist an investor to set right expectation from the startup. Over its lifespan, a startup develops across interdependent dimensions like organization objectives, customer, product, finance, business model, revenues, team, and organization culture. Most of the researchers have proposed models of startups by measuring growth over only one dimension. However, in current business landscape, none of the growth dimensions can be ignored. This chapter proposes a multi-dimensional development model for early-stage startups and explains attributes of each dimension for well-defined development stages. This chapter also presents a comprehensive yet simple framework for quantitatively identifying development stage of a startup. While evaluating numerous startups across the globe, the framework also helps to identify unbalanced development of the startup for a particular dimension and proposes respective remedial measures.

Keywords Development stages · Early-stage startups · Entrepreneurship
Startup lifecycle stages · Unbalanced scaling

A. Kumbhat (✉) · Sushil
Department of Management Studies, Indian Institute of Technology Delhi,
Vishwakarma Bhawan, Shaheed Jeet Singh Marg, New Delhi, India
e-mail: akumbhat@gmail.com

Sushil
e-mail: sushil@dms.iitd.ac.in; profsushil@gmail.com

A. Kumbhat
Skilrock Technologies Pvt. Ltd., Gurugram, India

1.1 Introduction

Study of development stages of an organization has been of deep interest for researchers, especially to understand the way companies evolve over different phases. This understanding aids in anticipating challenges and being prepared for requirements at different phases for the organization. Beyond this, it helps the entrepreneurs to evaluate various government policies for their business.

Beyond the usage of understanding of development stages to address forthcoming challenges for entrepreneurs, understanding of development stages of a startup is also quite beneficial for investors. Every investor sets an expectation from the startup based on the current stage of the organization; for example, the investor will not expect a large portfolio of clients from an early-stage startup; rather, he will expect an MVP or product–market fit testing.

Understanding of development stages is also important to evaluate the need of right success factors of a startup because as a business moves from one stage to another, the need and importance of the factors change (Churchill and Lewis 1983). For example, founder's own capability and level of motivation are highly important at early stages, while the focus shifts to founder's ability to delegate at later stages.

1.2 Prior Art

Researchers have developed a number of models over decades to define stages of corporate growth. Initially, it started at the time of industrial era of manufacturing units, whereby McGuire (1963), while expanding the work of economic growth (Rostow 1960), proposed five stages of economic development: traditional small company, planning for growth, takeoff from existing conditions, drive to professional management, and mass production.

Steinmetz (1969) focused beyond just economic growth and having management styles as pivot for development stages; he proposed that to survive, small businesses must move through four stages of growth. These stages include direct supervision (owner as manager), supervised supervision (owner as administrator), indirect control (owner to delegate), and divisional organization structure.

Christensen and Scott (1964) proposed three development stages of organizational complexity with evolving product–market relationships. These organizational complexities included single unit with no specialized functions, single unit with marketing and finance as specialized functions, and independently running multiple operating units.

Five-stage corporate evolution model, as proposed by Greiner (1972), takes a company from one phase to another by a revolution or crisis, and each of such evolutionary phases is characterized by a particular managerial style to address a dominant management problem faced by the company in the phase.

1 Development Stages and Scaling Issues of Startups

The earlier development stage models were characterizing growth stages fairly in numbers of annual sales; these models critically ignored complexities associated with early stages of startups. Churchill and Lewis (1983) addressed this gap by a new five-stage model, whereby each stage was characterized by five management factors: managerial style, organizational structure, extent of formal systems, major strategic goals, and the owner's involvement in the business. This comprehensive model of small business growth not only addressed the early-stage challenges but also proposed alternate paths an organization may take at different stages and possible outcomes of success and failure in each stage.

With sudden growth in startup ecosystem, commencing from early years of the twenty-first century, some of the researchers proposed startup development models aligned with product development stages—product conceptualization, product development, beta testing, and product launch. However, Blank (2006) suggested that the product development models were not correctly describing the startup development stages as these models focused more on execution than learning and more on product than customer, thus resulted in all execution aligned with product development cycle. Therefore, Blank (2006) proposed customer development model, in contrast to product development models. Focusing on understanding of customer needs, the customer development model of Blank (2006) included stages like customer discovery, customer validation, customer creation, and customer building.

Marmer (2012) proposed "Marmer development stages," adapting the customer development model of Blank (2006), and reinforced it with hard data. In addition, the Marmer stages are product-centric compared to Blank (2006) being company-centric. Marmer stages also defined development stages for late-stage startups as well—including sustenance and renewal stages. Sawhney (2014) gave a different perspective to startup development keeping a focus on scale as opposed to startup, resulting in a five-facet growth phase of a startup, which defines a transformation model for a startup from a growing organization to a grown-up organization.

1.3 Why New Model Required

Startups are living and developing organisms, and these develop across various interdependent dimensions—some of them are internal to the organization (like team, organization culture), while others are external or peripheral to the organization (like customers, revenues, funding). Therefore, the study of development stages of startups should certainly consider all dimensions; however, most of the researchers have proposed development stages model of startups which are governed by measuring growth over single dimension. Churchill and Lewis (1983) proposed a multi-dimensional development stage model of startup, but that model was also restricted to dimensions only internal to the organization, and it was silent about dimensions peripheral or external (customers and revenues) to a startup. Especially in the current competitive business environment and complex economic landscape, none of the growth dimensions of a startup can be ignored (Dhir 2016).

More so, in the recent times of startup growth, investors have gone beyond just providing finances (Khanra and Dhir 2017). They help startups leverage their network as well as provide multi-dimensional mentorship. Therefore, evaluating the startup development stages from multi-dimensional perspective becomes more important and helps the investors to identify right dimensions to focus on. In addition, while talking about multi-dimensional stages for a comprehensive model, it is important to maintain the simplicity of the model. Thus, a new model is being proposed.

While early-stage startups are designed to search for product–market fit under conditions of extreme uncertainty, late-stage startups are designed to search for a repeatable and scalable business model and then scale into large companies designed to execute under conditions of higher certainty (The Startup Genome Report 2012). Considering the difference between landscapes of operational environment of early- and late-stage startups, it is important to look into development stages of early-stage startups completely in isolation. With the surge in startup economy and ecosystem thereby, the survival of early-stage startups and growth thereof becomes absolute critical for this ecosystem to survive and therefore this chapter focuses only for the study of development stages of early-stage startups.

1.4 Proposed Stages

This chapter proposes study of development stages across various dimensions categorized as the ones which are internal to the organization or the others which are peripheral or external to the organization. These dimensions include organization objective, customer, product, finance, business model, revenues, team, and organization culture. While considering only early-stage startups, this chapter proposes four development stages of the organization whereby the organization grows across the dimensions. This chapter explains the attributes of each dimension in each development stage, for an evaluator to characterize the startup in either of the development stage.

1.4.1 Stage #1—Discovery

Objective

- *Discover Value Proposition*: Startup is focused on validating whether it is solving a meaningful problem and whether anybody would hypothetically be interested in solution of the said problem (Do people need it? Does the market understand it?).

- *Discover Competitive Landscape*: Has anybody else tried to solve a similar problem and what solution was proposed earlier? Did earlier instance succeed or fail? How does it differentiate its problem definition and solution from earlier instances?
- *Discover Customers:* Going and talking to prospective customers and asking whether they feel the same problem; is it a problem worth addressing and identifying how are they addressing the problem now (observe than just listen).
- *Discover Solution*: Going to the drawing board to check if earlier prototype (MVP) can solve the problem better.
- *Discover Growth*: Can it grow?

Customer

- Many prospective customer interviews are being conducted.
- Startup should be putting initial feelers out into the community and connecting with people.

Product

- Value proposition is found.
- It is working on developing a minimum viable product (MVP) that will enable surveying the market and getting a sense of the project's acceptance.

Finance

- Founding team may join an accelerator or incubator.
- No formal funding, small funds through self-funding or from friends and family.
- First set of mentors and advisors come on board.

Business Model

- Only outline of Business plan is prepared.

Revenues

- No revenue.

Team

- Founding team is formed.
- One or more founder members work for no salary. Realistically, founders do not need to quit the job at this stage.
- No formal employees hired.

Organization Culture

- No organization culture exists.

1.4.2 Stage #2—Validation

Objective

- Startup validates product–market fit: whether people are interested in its solution through the exchange of money or attention.

Product

- Solution moves from MVP (being hypothetical solutions) to a deployable solution with refined core features.
- It takes action to protect intellectual property rights associated with the solution, if any (search and file patents).
- Implements basic metrics and analytics to monitor customer behavior.

Customer

- First paying customers are onboard.
- It is adding initial customer growth path.

Finance

- It starts with small funding from friends and family, along with options of crowdfunding and seed funding.
- It may continue with deep incubators.

Business Model

- Finalized comprehensive business plan is ready.
- A legal entity and business name is incorporated.

Revenues

- Minimal initial revenues from first paying customers.
- This revenue is just to validate the business model.

Team

- Founders leave the jobs and join the startup on full time.
- First key employees are hired.

Organization Culture

- Casual and informal.
- Do whatever it takes to deliver.

1.4.3 Stage #3—Efficiency/Refinement

Objective

- Startup focuses on to refine and be efficient in—What and how entrepreneurs do.
- Startup focuses on to refine and be efficient in—Processes to head for a lean organization (cut the fat out of it and add value).
- Startup focuses on to refine and be efficient in—Business model and customer acquisition model.
- Startup focuses on being ready to scale.
- It analyzes characteristics and variables of everything around the startup (market, clients, etc.) to refine the business model that adjusts best to the environment. This analysis is done based on various market studies, advice from experts and investors.

Product

- Value proposition is refined.
- Products/services are matured.

Customers

- It has sufficient number of paying customers to prove the business model (but not as a market leader).
- It has established repeatable customer acquisition process.

Finance

- It becomes investor-backed startup that runs through Series A/Series B—formal mid–large-scale funding.

Business Model

- It is ready to scale the business to be a market leader.
- Large market opportunity is validated.

Revenues

- It has established and stable revenues, and these revenues are enough to validate the business model and confirm the scalability of the same.

Team

- Founder still leads the team.
- Team size may be around 20–200 employees.

Organization Culture

- Organization culture transforms from informal to formal.
- With this size of organization (especially in terms of people count), the casual and informal "do what it takes to deliver" culture becomes chaotic and ineffective. The startup starts defining proper culture, training, product management, processes, and procedures (i.e., writing the HR manual, sales comp plan, expense reports, branding guidelines).

1.4.4 Stage #4—Scale/Grow

Objective

- Aggressive growth—Having established a product and market fit, validated business model, and established revenues, startup must be focusing on growth through aggressive customer acquisition.
- It is transforming from Opportunistic to Strategist, Projects to Products, Ownership to Partnership, People to Process, and Relationship to Brands (Sawhney 2014).
- It is under transition from an entrepreneurial high speed and risk style to one of planning, management, and fine-tuning of operations.

Customer

- Massive customer acquisition is taking place—quickly, aggressively, efficiently, and smartly.

Product

- Optional—Complementary product/modules are added—through self-effort or partnership.

Finance

- It offers low-risk investment option to investors, having delivered confidence that on investment of $X in resources/product/marketing/sales will generate $Y revenues.
- It is exploring options for growth like an IPO, being acquired by large organization or acquiring small competitive companies.

Business Model

- Business model is expanded to address large opportunity—typically beyond local geographies.
- Internationalization is being evaluated as the way to grow.

Revenues

- Growing revenues.

Team

- First Executive Hired (Other than founders)—Professional management is on-board to manage transformation.

Organization Culture

- Establishment of departments and process implementation is in progress.
- Having repeatable processes in place, key performance indicators for processes are implemented.
- Focusing on cost optimization, i.e., growing in sustainable manner.

1.5 Identify the Development Stage of a Startup

A startup, as a continuously developing organism, develops along all interdependent dimensions as proposed above. And therefore, the progress of the startup is measured based on the development stage across various dimensions. This chapter presents a tool for identifying development stage of a startup, through a multi-dimensional evaluation process.

(a) A Likert scale is defined for each of the proposed dimensions, as in Table 1.1, whereby each value of Likert scale corresponds to one of the four development stages.
(b) A startup under evaluation is scored over the proposed Likert scale for each dimension.
(c) An average score is calculated through the scores of all dimensions.
(d) A balanced development across all dimensions (same score for all dimensions) maximizes startup's speed of growth, whereas an unbalanced development of one or more dimensions compared to that of other dimension leads to serious challenges. While on a practical case, a number of startups can be found having unbalanced development across dimensions; however, the amount of deviation reflects the unbalanced nature of the startup across specific dimension. Therefore, the value of average score reflects the development stage of the organization, like

   a. Average score between 1.0 and 1.5: Discovery Stage
   b. Average score between 1.5 and 2.5: Validation Stage
   c. Average score between 2.5 and 3.5: Refinement Stage
   d. Average score between 3.5 and 4.0: Growth Stage

Table 1.1 Development stages

Dimension	Development stages			
	Discovery (1)	Validation (2)	Refinement (3)	Growth (4)
Objective	Problem definition and customer discovery (1)	People interested in the solution as exchange of money or attention (2)	Refined—business model, customer acquisition model and processes (3)	Transforming from Opportunistic to Strategist, People to Process, and Relationship to Brands. Transition from high speed and risk style to well-managed operations (4)
Product	Defined value proposition. MVP for better prospecting (1)	First level of deployable solution (2)	Refined value proposition, product matured (3)	Complementary product/modules added (4)
Customer	No real customer; discovery through interviews with prospective customers (1)	First paying customer (2)	Sufficient number of paying customers and has established repeatable customer acquisition process (3)	Aggressive customer acquisition (4)
Finance	No formal funding (1)	Formal funding started through crowdfunding or seed funding (2)	Mid–large-scale funding through Series A/B funding (3)	Low-risk investment option for investors for defined ROI (4)
Business model	Business plan outline only (1)	Business plan finalization (2)	Large market opportunity identified with proven business model (3)	Expanded to address large opportunity—going beyond local geographies (4)
Revenues	No revenues (1)	Minimal initial revenues (2)	Enough revenues to validate the business model-established revenues (3)	Growing revenues (4)
Team	Only founding team; no employees (1)	Founders on full time; few key employees (2)	Founder still leads the team; team size from 20 to 200 employees (3)	First executive hired for professional management (4)
Organization culture	Does not exist (1)	Casual approach—"Do what it takes to deliver" (2)	Refine from informal to formal organization culture and processes (3)	Established departments and processes (4)

1 Development Stages and Scaling Issues of Startups

Table 1.2 Response summary

S. No.	Industry	Location (City)	Average score	Dev. stage	Std deviation
1	Food Tech	Tier 3, India	2.00	Validation	0.71
2	IT Services	Tier 3, India	1.25	Discovery	0.43
3	Real Estate Tech	Tier 2, India	2.25	Validation	0.83
4	Device Hardware	Tier 1, China	2.25	Validation	0.66
5	Travel Tech	Tier 1, India	2.63	Refinement	0.48
6	Travel Tech	Tier 1, India	2.25	Validation	0.43
7	Training	Tier 1, India	1.75	Validation	0.66
8	IT Services	Tier 2, India	2.75	Refinement	0.83
9	Payments Tech	Tier 1, UK	3.38	Refinement	0.70

Higher values of the score for a dimension than the average score reflects premature scaling of the organization for the dimension. In the contrary, it shows less maturity of the dimension.

1.6 Case Studies

During the study, a number of early-stage startups across the globe have been evaluated for their development stages. This evaluation exercise has been conducted through primary research done by obtaining an expert opinion from people associated with early-stage startups across the globe (India, China, and the UK). This expert opinion is collected through an online questionnaire, followed by detailed discussion on the subject matter. Responses received are summarized as in Table 1.2 (startup name and specific details are kept anonymous) and following observations are made:

(a) None of the startup under observation demonstrated a perfect development across all dimensions.
(b) Difference in scores of each dimension as compared to average score reflects unbalanced development for the dimension.
(c) Standard deviation value also reflects overall unbalanced development for the startup.

1.7 Key Considerations and Challenges for Practical Implementation

At times, practitioners of the startup ecosystem face different challenges than envisaged in academics. While the proposed multi-dimensional development stage model is comprehensive enough to address common practical challenges, following are the additional key considerations and challenges for practical implementation of the proposed model.

(a) The proposed development stages model of a startup depicts a linear growth of a startup from one stage to another. However, on a practical note, most of the startups end up into an iterative cycle of maturing business model and associated technology, thus pivoting the startup. That means that a startup may iterate between Discovery and Validation Stage, till its last pivot, and then once the business model and associated technology mature, the startup moves to the Refinement Stage. From the perspective of development stage evaluation of a startup, typically the last pivot is considered as the reference point; however, on a practical note, the startup would have an impact of earlier pivots through parameters like the team, brand value, and finances generated during earlier pivots.

(b) Beyond the development stage and scaling analysis of a startup, the time taken by a startup takes to reach to a development stage and the time duration for which a startup remains in a particular development stage have a reasonable impact on the overall success and growth of the startup. While in most of the cases, this time duration can be standardized based on various factors like offering a new or existing product or service to a market and sales cycle of product or service based on ticket size, industry being served and target market (B2B, B2C, etc.). However, a particular startup can take shorter or longer time duration than standard expected time duration, based on the actual effort put by the founding team during early stage of the startup, count and frequency of pivots, the startup passed through before maturing business model and associated technology (being in Refinement Stage).

(c) Every startup remains in a particular development stage for a defined period of time, and this chapter demonstrates attributes of each dimension while a startup being in a development stage. However, from a practical standpoint, it is important to define entry and exit points of each development stage, whereas one of the dimensions attributes to a different development stage than another dimension. This issue has been addressed by mean scores and standard deviation methodology.

(d) The proposed development stage model is restricted to early development stages of the independent ventures, till these are typically considered as so-called startups. However, the proposed model can be extended to late-stage startups as well as new ventures of large corporates by extending similar attributes to proposed dimensions.

(e) The proposed development stage model should also consider the role of mentors and investors (beyond just financial investment) for the growth of a startup. Mishra and Jain (2014) and Deepali et al. (2017) describe the role of mentors for successful entrepreneurship and how an entrepreneur can select the best mentor to assist the right path for growth.

1.8 Conclusion

In conclusion, this chapter proposes four development stages for an early-stage startup, expressing the growth of the startup as predefined attribute values of all dimensions. Also, the proposed multi-dimensional development stages model helps identify whether an organization is leading to an unbalanced development across a dimension. To bridge the gap between academics and practice, this chapter also illustrates key challenges for practical implementation of the proposed model.

References

Blank, S. G. (2006). *The four steps to the epiphany: Successful strategies for products that win.* S.l.: Caffepress.
Christensen, C. R., & Scott, B. R. (1964). *Review of course activities.* Lausanne: IMEDE.
Churchill, N. C., & Lewis V. L. (1983). The five stages of small business growth. *Entrepreneurial Management Magazine—Harvard Business Review,* May, 1983.
Dhir, S. (2016). Practice-oriented insights on creative problem solving. *Journal of Management & Public Policy, 7*(2).
Deepali, Jain, S. K., & Chaudhary, H. (2017). Quest for effective mentors: A way of mentoring potential entrepreneurs successfully. *Global Journal of Flexible Systems Management, 18*(2), 99–109.
Greiner, L. E. (1972). Evolution and revolution as organizations growth. *Harvard Business Review,* July–August 1972, 37–46.
Khanra, S., & Dhir, S. (2017). Creating value in small-cap firms by mitigating risks of market volatility. *Vision, 21*(4), 350–355.
Marmer, M. (2012). *Stages of the startup lifecycle,* Retrieved May 13, 2017, from https://blog.compass.co/pagesmarmer-stages/.
McGuire, J. W. (1963). *Factors affecting the growth of manufacturing firms.* Seattle: Bureau of Business Research, University of Washington.
Mishra, D., & Jain, S. K. (2014). Flexibility and sustainability of mentorship model for entrepreneurship development: An exploratory study. In M. K. Nandakumar, Sanjay Jharkharia & Abhilash S. Nair (Eds.), *Flexible Systems Management: Organizational flexibility and competitiveness* (25–39). New Delhi: Springer.
Rostow, W. W. (1960). *The stages of economic growth.* London: Cambridge University Press.
Sawhney, M. (2014). *Built to scale.* Retrieved May 13, 2017, from http://www.kellogg.northwestern.edu/news_articles/2014/03102014-sawhney-middle-markets.aspx.
Startup Genome Report. (2012). *Startup genome report: Premature scaling,* v 1.2 (edited March 2012).
Steinmetz, L. L. (1969). Critical stages of small business growth. *Business Horizons, 12*(1), 29–36. https://doi.org/10.1016/0007-6813(69)90107-4.

Chapter 2
Flourishing Innovation Through Organizational Initiatives: An Analytical Study

Akriti Chaubey and Chandan Kumar Sahoo

Abstract Today survival of any organization depends on its innovative efforts in process, management, and product. Several studies have been conducted by researchers, focusing on enhancing creative ability of an individual and flaring organizational innovation, but significantly less work has been done on boosting organizational initiative as an input which addresses the influence of it on increasing creative instinct of an individual and innovation at the organizational level. Pertaining to the harsher reality of competition, the study explores the association between organizational initiative and organizational innovation, focusing on the mediating effect of employee creativity. The study examined 250 valid responses of employees working in private automobile units. The ideation of the hypothesized research model illustrates that employee creativity partially mediates the association between organizational initiatives and organizational innovation. The integral mediating effect of employee creativity signifies that the organization should show optimism toward employee encouragement, training, and challenges to enhance creative instinct within an individual. This convenient form allows managers to take corrective action for fostering innovation in its product and service by augmenting individual's creative approach. A model was developed, which may provide the practitioners a conceptual framework while developing a methodical approach toward organizational innovation.

Keywords Creativity · Innovation · Organizational initiatives · Structural model

---

A. Chaubey (✉) · C. K. Sahoo
School of Management, National Institute of Technology, Rourkela, Odisha, India
e-mail: akritichaubey25@gmail.com

C. K. Sahoo
e-mail: sahooc@nitrkl.ac.in

© Springer Nature Singapore Pte Ltd. 2018
S. Dhir and Sushil (eds.), *Flexible Strategies in VUCA Markets*,
Flexible Systems Management, https://doi.org/10.1007/978-981-10-8926-8_2

2.1 Introduction

Recent advances in the Indian business scenario have made India a hot spot for many investors (Dhir and Sushil 2017). India has been ranked as the fastest and strongest growing major economy of the world. Globalization and economic reforms have changed the business scenario since 1991. Subsequently, with recent developments in technology and increasing business firms, the competition has grown by manifold (Dhir and Dhir 2017). Taking into concern, the prevailing business environment of any organization where changes occur in an abrupt and hasty fashion, survival and growth are considered to be two major concerns (Bishwas 2015). The human asset of an organization requires continuous encouragement for cultivating new ideas. Ideas are the roots for germination of creative ability. Creativity and innovation go hand in hand. Creativity is the fabrication of novel and valuable ideas of an individual; however, organizational innovation is the fruitful execution of original ideas in an organization (Amabile 1988). According to economist Schumpeter, 1947 "Innovation is the novelty in how value is created and distributed, It could be new products and services, but it could also be new ways of producing products, or novel ways of organizing firms and industries." Studies on innovation have suggested that innovation as an effective competitive strategy for a business and put forward that it is influenced by the environment in which it functions (Barney 2001; Tsai and Yang 2013). Innovation has a significant optimistic effect on business performance (Prajogo and Ahmed 2007). Creativity and innovation encourage newer outlook to problem-solving approaches and help in resolving critical organizational problems. The role of HR is to make sure that the employees develop the creative confidence, self-assurance, and ability to turn up with creative ideas, and encourage them to try out those ideas. Hence, by attracting, retaining innovative people and continually improving their skills help an organization to gain competitive advantage.

2.2 Relevance of the Study

At present, the global business market is becoming more and more complex, intricately networked and impenetrable; there is no such organization which does not profess the concept of creativity and innovation to remain competitive. According to Ernst and Young (2016), India provides an immense possibility to the Indian automobile industry for innovation and creating new solutions. The Research & Development (R&D) culture provides a breeding ground for innovation to both India's and international organizations. India houses some units focusing on innovation, which helps automobile companies to develop world-class sophisticated, innovative products to serve the demand of the fast-growing market.

In today's dynamic industrial scenario, a bigger difficult task for current managers is to proficiently and efficiently develop and enhance the organizational innovative capabilities by using employee's strengths (Dhir et al. 2016). To attain such objectives, employees should organize their intellectual capabilities so that an effective organizational change occurs by professing their creativity to action (Alirezaei and Tavalaei 2008). By lacking innovation, organizations merely not only fail on opportunities but also in its capacity to run a more effective and efficient organization. Researchers claim that creativity plays a considerable role for organization's longer sustenance since it empowers the organizations to stay competitive in a wider and dynamic milieu and attains a competitive advantage position (Beheshtifar and Kamani-Fard 2013). Creativity has a significant, decisive effect on the organization's competitive advantage by maintaining a culture of the cooperative network by carrying out research and development work (Chesbrough 2003).

2.3 Objectives of the Research

In the existing literature, there is an evidence of relationship and the effect of different antecedents of creativity leading to employees' creative potential. There have been substantially less or nil empirical traces which are diagnosed concentrating on the impact of organizational initiatives (training, organizational encouragement, and perpetual challenging) on employee creativity.

This research gap of empirical evidence in Indian automobile industry led us to ponder upon the following research questions to conduct the study in a more systematic way:

RQ 1 Is there any significant relationship between organizational initiatives and employee creativity?
RQ 2 Does employee creativity help in enhancing organizational innovation?
RQ 3 Does organizational initiative measures have any impact on organizational innovation?
RQ 4 Does employee creativity act as a significant mediator between organizational initiatives and organizational innovation?

The objectives of the current study are the following:

- To investigate the relationship between organizational initiatives, employee creativity and organizational innovation in the Indian automobile industry.
- To examine the mediating role of employee creativity to strengthen the liaison between organizational initiatives and organizational innovation.

2.4 Theoretical Background and Hypotheses Development

2.4.1 Training and Employee Creativity

Training mainly relates to a scheduled attempt made by an organization to aid the process of skill learning related to job proficiencies. Training boosts employees' competency which is critical to upsurge creative thought procedures and provides prospects that enrich task domain proficiency (Lau and Ngo 2004). Training not only enhances the capacity of the employee but also hones their thinking ability and creativity so as to take an enhanced decision in time and most dynamic fashion (Dewett 2006). Training improves self-efficacy and results in loftier performance on the job, by supplanting the traditional weedy practices by efficient and effective work-related exercises. Training programs groom employees and help an organization to make better use of their human resources to gain competitive advantage (Elnaga and Imran 2013). Several organizations adopt creativity training in an endeavor to develop the innovative capabilities of their employees (Birdi et al. 2012). According to empirical studies done by Rickards and De Cock (1994) and Basadur et al. (1990), training employees with creative thought process gave rise to progressive changes in employee's attitude toward the sub-dimension of divergent thinking. Epstein et al. (2008), in their study in Philadelphia, noted that the city manager, the director of human resources, and other city officials imputed innumerous positive changes that were noticed after creativity training. It was observed that employees were more prompt to share novel ideas, and managers appeared to be more receptive to hear them. Creative researcher like Bharadwaj and Menon (2002) comprehends from their study that there exists a positive association between training for the enhancement of employee creativity and performance of the organization.

2.4.2 Organizational Encouragement and Employee Creativity

Organizational encouragement is the wisdom that top management boosts, supports, identifies creative work, and there are instruments for equal consideration of new ideas. According to Amabile et al. (1996), there exists several facets which are perceived as broadly functional within an organization for the encouragement of its employees, which are embodiment of idea creation with associated risk, systematic, and unbiased assessment of ideas, apprehension of creativity with reward (Cummings 1965), the fluidity and collectivism of idea throughout the entire firm management, participative management, and decision-making (Kanter 1983) which are important aspects of organizational encouragement. Researchers have found that risk appetite of an organization provokes employee to come up with unique ideas (Dewett 2006, 2007; Neves and Eisenberger 2014). It is evident from previous studies that an extrinsic reward helps employees to bloom their creative performance (Zhou et al. 2011).

2.4.3 Perpetual Challenging and Employee Creativity

In the year 2000, Constantine Andriopoulos and Andy Lowe propagated grounded theory on perpetual challenging as a procedure for increasing organizational creativity, focusing on its need due to emerging trends in a global era such as technology, unpredictable clients, change and higher employees' expectations. They defined perpetual challenging as "the ways through which creative organizations enrich their employees' internal effort to perceive every single project as a new creative encounter so that their contribution is maximized and an innovative solution can arise." Andriopoulos and Lowe (2000) described four components of perpetual challenging which are adventuring, overt confronting, portfolioing and opportunising. Adventuring involves a procedure encouraging individuals to tour uncertainty, which will help them in generating innovative solutions. Over confronting mentions about the voluntary work-oriented debates among employees so that their creative thinking capabilities are completely exploited. Portfolioing is an approach where employees with creative instincts are encouraged to get engrossed in various ranges of projects. Opportunising weaves the process through which employees with creative capability are identified and are involved in projects. Sternberg and Lubart (1991) strongly asserted that management executives must allow the messiness to exist. Amabile (1997) has emphasized the importance of challenging work, which states reconciling creative employees with their assignments, based on their skills and interests, which in turn enhances their motivation toward work.

2.4.4 Employee Creativity and Organizational Innovation

The basic lexical unit of the English word "creativity" originates from the Latin term "creō" which means "to create, make." Historically, researchers, scientist, philosophers, psychologists, sociologists, educators in their respective fields carried out studies to analyze the concept of creativity and its related relationship. The idea of creativity has been interpreted differently by several authors and is ever changing. Employee creativity is construed as creating of both new and useful ideas by an individual or group (Zhou and Shalley 2003). The word innovation has its roots from the Latin term "innovare," which means, "to make something new." Theoretically, innovation is defined as a method of converting opportunity into ideas and implementing these ideas throughout an organization (Flynn et al. 2003; Bishwas 2015). The precursor to any firm's innovation is its employee creativity (Hon 2012; Scott and Bruce 1994). Nevertheless, innovation and creativity have been explained more concisely in different studies wherein creativity and innovation are considered two inseparable integral parts of a process, which create an environment that lets employee, generate newer ideas and of the course of introducing newer solutions that work in a better way (Parameswar et al. 2017).

Combining these two inseparable entities of the same construct lets organization to become more innovative (Anderson 2014). An organization relies heavily on innovation and creativity to survive against the competitors (Wang and Ma 2013). The conception of creativity in an organization enables it to succeed among its competitors along with other entities like research and development (Urbancova 2013). Through creativity, an organization not only achieves competitive advantage, but empowers itself to compete and sustain for the long term. Teodorescu et al. (2015) found out that the accomplishment of an organization depends on its encouragement of employee creativity as it fosters organizational innovation, i.e., employee creativity directs to organizational innovation.

On the basis of the above discussions relating to the existing literature, we have proposed the following hypotheses and a research model.

H1 *Organizational initiatives have a positive impact on flourishing employee creativity.*
H2 *Employee creativity has a significant impact on organizational innovation.*
H3 *There is a significant relationship between organizational initiatives and organizational innovation.*
H4 *Employee creativity will mediate the association between organizational initiatives and organizational innovation.*

2.5 Research Methodology

2.5.1 Sampling and Data Collection

The research study focuses on an exploratory survey which attempts to measure the interaction between crucial elements of an organizational initiative (IN), employee creativity (EC), and organizational innovation (OI). A sampling frame of four-wheeler automobile manufacturing and R&D units in the southern part of India was destined for the study. The target population constituted of technocrats, production managers, design engineers, and R&D professionals. Stratified and random sampling technique was adopted. 346 questionnaires were circulated out of which only 250 valid questionnaires were received, resulting in the response rate of 72.25%. The study constituted about 65% of male and 35% of female respondents. Respondents of the age 20–30 years comprised of 56%, whereas 31–40 years aged were 24% and successively 41–50 years were 12%, and 51–60 years constituted 8%. Major respondents were R&D managers (52%), design engineers (28%), production managers (13%), and CAD engineers (7%). 5–10 years' work experience holder constituted 62% shadowed by 0–5 years (22%), 11–15 (8%), 16–20 years (6%), and above 20 years (2%).

2.5.2 Measurement Scales

The questionnaire consisted of three measurement scales that were adapted after research of the existing literature. Training scale comprised of six items (self-developed for this study), whereas organizational encouragement scale consisted of six items (Amabile et al. 1996). Five items scale for perpetual challenging (self-developed for this study). A ten items measure of employee creativity (Torrance 1963; Tierney et al. 1999; Zhang and Bartol 2010) and ten items scale of organizational innovation (Camison and Villar-López 2014; Bolívar-Ramos et al. 2012) were developed for the study. Items in the questionnaire consisted of five-point Likert scale with ranges of strongly agree, i.e., 5 to strongly disagree, i.e., 1.

2.5.3 Sampling Approach

Employees of an organization are distinctive in nature that is why the study was personalized to fit each of the organization's best. Participation was approved with the help of appointments and prior approval via electronic media from the organization. We visited the automobile manufacturing organizations to collect the responses. Participants were assured that there were no right or wrong answers and that their responses would remain anonymous.

2.5.4 Data Analysis

The data was analyzed using exploratory factor analysis (EFA) method with the help of IBM SPSS version 20. Subsequently, AMOS 20 was used to develop a model which confirms the association among the variables of the research.

2.6 Results and Discussion

2.6.1 Preliminary Analysis

Table 2.1 consists of descriptive statistics, reliabilities data, and inter-correlation matrix. Cronbach's alpha ranges from 0.897 to 0.922.

Dimension reduction was carried so as to extract the relevant factors that specify the role of EC in the automobile industry. The value of Kaiser–Meyer–Oklin (KMO) is reported as 0.900. Out of 37 items, 18 items was extracted through principal component analysis using varimax rotation method: eight items for IN, five items for OI, and five items for EC which is depicted in Table 2.2. Loaded

Table 2.1 Descriptive and correlation results

Variables	Items	Mean	SD	α	IN	EC	OI
Organizational initiative (IN)	17	3.62	0.67	0.922	1.000		
Employee creativity (EC)	10	3.58	0.72	0.897	0.428**	1.000	
Organizational innovation (OI)	10	3.72	0.69	0.910	0.472**	0.616**	1.000

**$p < 0.01$

Table 2.2 Measurement model results

Construct	Items	Standardized estimates	AVE	CR	p value
IN	TR1	0.706	0.506	0.891	0.000
	TR3	0.796			0.000
	OE3	0.737			0.000
	TR2	0.725			0.000
	OE1	0.744			0.000
	PC5	0.598			0.000
	PC4	0.682			0.000
	OE6	0.684			0.000
OI	OI5	0.904	0.542	0.855	0.000
	OI3	0.872			0.000
	OI4	0.816			0.000
	OI6	0.877			0.000
	OI1	0.768			0.000
EC	EC4	0.718	0.720	0.928	0.000
	EC3	0.675			0.000
	EC2	0.795			0.000
	EC5	0.792			0.000
	EC9	0.694			0.000

items commonalities ranged from 54 to 83%. The three extracted factors in total explained 65.86% of the overall variation in the sample.

2.6.2 Test for Measurement Model

Confirmatory factor analysis (CFA) was used to estimate the convergent validity, discriminant validity, and goodness of fit statistics. Convergent validity indicators comprises of factor loadings (standardized estimates), average variance extracted (AVE), and composite reliability (CR) which are given in Table 2.2. The constructs were found to be distinctive. Results concluded that reliability estimates and measurement model analysis are significant (Table 2.3).

Table 2.3 Discriminant validity

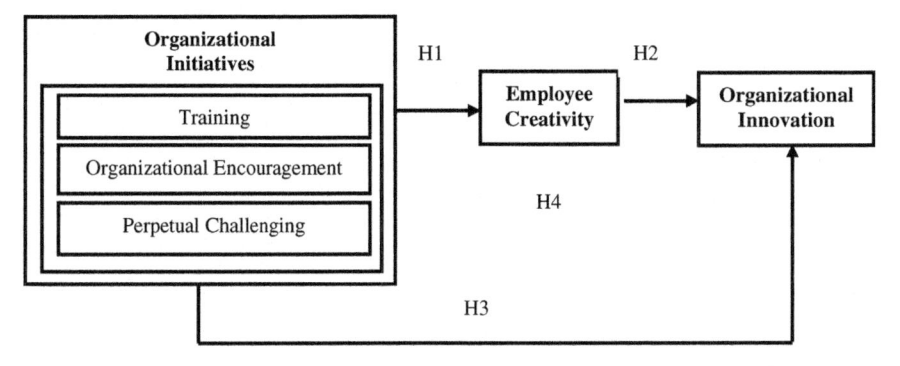

	OI	IN	EC
OI	0.849		
IN	0.395	0.711	
EC	0.523	0.478	0.736

Fig. 2.1 Hypothesized conceptual model

2.6.3 Test of the Structural Model

The structural model is shown in Fig. 2.1. All the fitness indexes indicated that the hypothesized model has a good fitness with the data (χ^2 [130] = 256.551, $p < 0.001$; $\chi^2/df = 1.973$; RMSEA = 0.063, NFI = 0.908, IFI = 0.952, TLI = 0.944, CFI = 0.952). Above results show that IN made a direct impact on OI besides the mediating influence of EC.

2.6.4 Evaluation of the Mediating Effect of EC

Table 2.4 depicts the path estimates between the constructs which suggests that all are significant. Data in Table 2.5 shows that the indirect effect is 0.216 which is substantial while direct effect is 0.195 which is relatively less significant confirming the partial mediation effect of EC on OI. Figure 2.2 portrays the entire model with path coefficients for the mediating role of EC among IN and OI. Thus, from the above discussions, we conclude the establishment of hypothesis 4.

Table 2.4 Inferences are drawn on hypotheses

Hypotheses	Relationship	Beta coefficient	p value	Result
H1	IN → EC	0.478	***	Accepted
H2	EC → OI	0.434	***	Accepted
H3	IN → OI	0.395	***	Accepted

Table 2.5 Total, direct, and indirect effect results

Relationships	OI → IN		p value
Total effects	0.411		***
Direct effects	0.195		***
Indirect effect	0.216		***
Test for mediation		Partial	

Fig. 2.2 Structural model of mediation

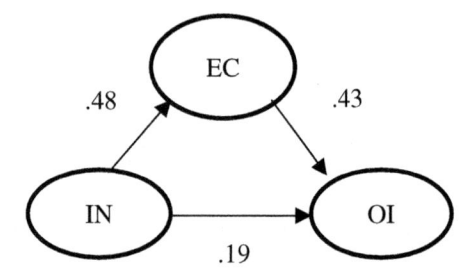

2.7 Managerial Implications

The results of the present study demonstrate that employee creativity catalyzes organizational initiatives toward organizational innovation as a mediating entity. Thus, the current findings establish a threefold relationship between organizational initiatives, employee creativity, and organizational innovation. Managers should emphasize on encouraging employee creativity through initiatives within the organization that foster creative thought process resulting in idea creation. Employees should be given freedom to take risks and come up with innovative ideas. Employees should be made able to feel the sense of openness in the organization. The organization should conduct training session so that employees' competencies get refined. Perpetual challenge provokes individuals for brainstorming and thinks differently due to job complexity. Thus, the study adds to the literature the mediating effect of employee creativity (Gong et al. 2009) and the impact it on organizational innovation (Somech and Drach-Zahavy 2011; Dul and Ceylan 2014). The study yields a conceptual framework for the managers in strategic planning and implementation of initiatives that encourage innovative capabilities of the executives within the organizations. The results also substantiate the idea that R&D managers, designers, and product development managers' get encouraged through organizational initiatives for creative engagement in an organization to sustain heavy competition in the automobile industry.

2.8 Conclusion

The study shows that organizational initiatives have a deterministic effect on organizational innovation. Organizational initiatives for employee encouragement, training, and perpetual challenges create an environment for comprehending employee creativity, which leads to organizational innovation. When activities relating to the organizational initiatives are strategically implemented within an organization, then it systematically empowers employee creativity for delivering innovation in product and services within the organization. Without proper organization support, these driving factors of innovation do not provide efficient results. The outcome of such oblivion makes organization fail to the harsh competitiveness. This research attempted to summarize the substantial impact of the organizational initiative on organizational innovation wherein creativeness among employee makes organization sustainable. The symbiotic relationships among the three crucial aspects of organization survival facing harsher competition are an important key to its sustainability through standardization of an organizational initiative.

References

Alirezaei, A., & Tavalaei, R. (2008). Innovation in the organizations. *Journal of Managing Human Resources in the Oil & Gas Industry, 2*(3), 69–70.

Amabile, T. M. (1988). A model of creativity and innovation in organizations. *Research in Organizational Behavior, 10*(1), 123–167.

Amabile, T. M. (1997). Motivating creativity in organizations: On doing what you love and loving what you do. *California Management Review, 40*(1), 39–58.

Amabile, T. M., Conti, R., Coon, H., Lazenby, J., & Herron, M. (1996). Assessing the work environment for creativity. *Academy of Management Journal, 39*(5), 1154–1184.

Anderson, D. M. (2014). Introduction. In *Leveraging* (pp. 3–34). Springer International Publishing.

Andriopoulos, C., & Lowe, A. (2000). Enhancing organizational creativity: The process of perpetual challenging. *Management Decision, 38*(10), 734–742.

Barney, J. B. (2001). Resource-based theories of competitive advantage: A ten-year retrospective on the resource-based view. *Journal of Management, 27*(6), 643–650.

Basadur, M., Graen, G., & Wakabayashi, M. (1990). Identifying individual differences in creative problem solving style. *The Journal of Creative Behavior, 24*(2), 111–131.

Beheshtifar, M., & Kamani-Fard, F. B. (2013). Organizational creativity: A substantial factor to growth. *International Journal of Academic Research in Business and Social Sciences, 3*(3), 98.

Bharadwaj, R., & Menon, M. B. (2002). *Inventing selves: The sex workers' movement in Kerala and the reception of the film Susanna*. Ernakulam: Sacred Heart College.

Birdi, K., Leach, D., & Magadley, W. (2012). Evaluating the impact of TRIZ creativity training: An organizational field study. *R&D Management, 42*(4), 315–326.

Bishwas, S. K. (2015). Achieving organization vitality through innovation and flexibility: An empirical study. *Global Journal of Flexible Systems Management, 16*(2), 145–156.

Bolívar-Ramos, M. T., García-Morales, V. J., & García-Sánchez, E. (2012). Technological distinctive competencies and organizational learning: Effects on organizational innovation to improve firm performance. *Journal of Engineering and Technology Management, 29*(3), 331–357.

Camisón, C., & Villar-López, A. (2014). Organizational innovation as an enabler of technological innovation capabilities and firm performance. *Journal of Business Research, 67*(1), 2891–2902.

Chesbrough, H. (2003). The logic of open innovation: Managing intellectual property. *California Management Review, 45*(3), 33–58.

Cummings, L. (1965). Organizational climates for creativity. *Academy of Management Journal, 8*(3), 220–227.

Dewett, T. (2006). Exploring the role of risk in employee creativity. *The Journal of Creative Behavior, 40*(1), 27–45.

Dewett, T. (2007). Linking intrinsic motivation, risk taking, and employee creativity in an R&D environment. *R&D Management, 37*(3), 197–208.

Dhir, S., & Sushil. (2017). Flexibility in modification and termination of cross-border joint ventures. *Global Journal of Flexible Systems Management, 18*(2), 139–151.

Dhir, S., & Dhir, S. (2017). Adoption of open-source software versus proprietary software: An exploratory study. *Strategic Change, 26*(4), 363–371.

Dhir, S., Mahajan, V., & Bhal, K. T. (2016). Himbunkar: Turnaround of a social public sector enterprise. *South Asian Journal of Management, 23*(4), 175.

Dul, J., & Ceylan, C. (2014). The impact of a creativity-supporting work environment on a firm's product innovation performance. *Journal of Product Innovation Management, 31*(6), 1254–1267.

Elnaga, A., & Imran, A. (2013). The effect of training on employee performance. *European Journal of Business and Management, 5*(4), 137–147.

Epstein, R., Schmidt, S. M., & Warfel, R. (2008). Measuring and training creativity competencies: Validation of a new test. *Creativity Research Journal, 20*(1), 7–12.

Ernst and Young. (2016). *EY India Sustainability Report 2016—EY*. Retrieved October 6, 2016 from http://www.ey.com/in/en/about-us/corporate-responsibility/ey-india-sustainability-report-2016.

Flynn, M., Dooley, L., O'sullivan, D., & Cormican, K. (2003). Idea management for organizational innovation. *International Journal of Innovation Management, 7*(04), 417–442.

Gong, Y., Huang, J. C., & Farh, J. L. (2009). Employee learning orientation transformational leadership, and employee creativity: The mediating role of employee creative self-efficacy. *Academy of Management Journal, 52*(4), 765–778.

Hon, A. H. (2012). Shaping environments conductive to creativity: The role of intrinsic motivation. *Cornell Hospitality Quarterly, 53*(1), 53–64.

Kanter, R. M. (1983). Frontiers for strategic human resource planning and management. *Human Resource Management, 22*(1–2), 9–21.

Lau, C. M., & Ngo, H. Y. (2004). The HR system, organizational culture, and product innovation. *International Business Review, 13*(6), 685–703.

Neves, P., & Eisenberger, R. (2014). Perceived organizational support and risk taking. *Journal of Managerial Psychology, 29*(2), 187–205.

Parameswar, N., Dhir, S., & Dhir, S. (2017). Banking on innovation, innovation in banking at ICICI bank. *Global Business and Organizational Excellence, 36*(2), 6–16.

Prajogo, D. I., & Ahmed, P. K. (2007). The Relationships between quality, innovation and business performance: An empirical study. *International Journal of Business Performance Management, 9*(4), 380–405.

Rickards, T., & De Cock, C. (1994). Creativity in MS/OR: Training for creativity—Findings in a European Context. *Interfaces, 24*(6), 59–65.

Scott, S. G., & Bruce, R. A. (1994). Determinants of innovative behavior: A path model of individual innovation in the workplace. *Academy of Management Journal, 37*(3), 580–607.

Somech, A., & Drach-Zahavy, A. (2011). Translating team creativity to innovation implementation: The role of team composition and climate for innovation. *Journal of Management, 39*(3), 684–708.

Sternberg, R. J., & Lubart, T. I. (1991). An investment theory of creativity and its development. *Human Development, 34*(1), 1–31.

Teodorescu, N., Stăncioiu, A. F., Răvar, A. S., & Botoş, A. (2015). Creativity and innovation-sources of competitive advantage in the value chain of tourism enterprises. *Theoretical and Applied Economics, 22*(1), 35–48.

Tierney, P., Farmer, S. M., & Graen, G. B. (1999). An examination of leadership and employee creativity: The relevance of traits and relationships. *Personnel Psychology, 52*(3), 591–620.

Torrance, E. P. (1963). The creative personality and the ideal pupil. *Teachers College Record, 65*(3), 220–226.

Tsai, K. H., & Yang, S. Y. (2013). Firm innovativeness and business performance: The joint moderating effects of market turbulence and competition. *Industrial Marketing Management, 42*(8), 1279–1294.

Urbancova, H. (2013). Competitive advantage achievement through innovation and knowledge. *Journal of Competitiveness, 5*(1), 82–96.

Wang, G., & Ma, X. (2013). The effect of psychological climate for innovation on salespeople's creativity and turnover intention. *Journal of Personal Selling & Sales Management, 33*(4), 373–387.

Zhang, X., & Bartol, K. M. (2010). Linking empowering leadership and employee creativity: The influence of psychological empowerment, intrinsic motivation, and creative process engagement. *Academy of Management Journal, 53*(1), 107–128.

Zhou, J., & Shalley, C. E. (2003). Research on employee creativity: A critical review and directions for future research. In *Research in personnel and human resources management* (pp. 165–217). Emerald Group Publishing Limited.

Zhou, Y., Zhang, Y., & Montoro-Sánchez, Á. (2011). Utilitarianism or romanticism: The effect of rewards on employees' innovative behaviour. *International Journal of Manpower, 32*(1), 81–98.

Chapter 3
Patent Landscape for Indian Biopharmaceutical Sector: A Strategic Insight

Sutopa Lahiry and K. Rangarajan

Abstract The emergence of the biopharmaceutical companies has led to transformation in the procedures of drug discovery within the firms and emergence of the whole organization within the industry. Patents are the most important form of intellectual property protection for these companies. The patent cliff from 2015 to 2020 is significant as it signals an opportunity for growth. Since 2005, with the new patent regime in India the competition in the domestic market has increased. This chapter aims to understand the patent landscape for biopharmaceutical companies by conducting a firm-level study. The overall industry analysis is not within the scope. The period for study was chosen from 2005 to 2015, and it provided a snapshot of the patent situation of these companies. The methodology adopted for the study required framing the research questions, defining objectives, identifying search strategy from the free patent databases and analysing the results of the search. An open source tool called "The Lens" was used for analysis. A variety of patent indicators (like date, jurisdictions, classification, document type, publications and infringements) were used to draw patent statistics. This was analysed based on number of factors like—publications by year, coverage by jurisdictions, relationship among technologies, economic and technical utility and patents being an indicator of innovation.

Keywords Patents · Patent landscape · Strategy

S. Lahiry (✉)
Indian Institute of Foreign Trade, Kolkata, India
e-mail: sutopa_phd13@iift.edu; sutopalahiry@gmail.com

K. Rangarajan
Strategic Management, Centre for MSME Studies, Indian Institute
of Foreign Trade, Kolkata, India
e-mail: head_kol@iift.edu; rangarajan@iift.edu

© Springer Nature Singapore Pte Ltd. 2018
S. Dhir and Sushil (eds.), *Flexible Strategies in VUCA Markets*,
Flexible Systems Management, https://doi.org/10.1007/978-981-10-8926-8_3

3.1 Introduction

As the global biopharma industry dynamically unfurls, the prescription drug market today is witnessing a growing trend of the biotechnology-based products. The development of the biopharmaceutical industry can be traced since the 1970s with the coming of "molecular biology evolution". As these new biopharmaceutical companies emerged, their research and innovation have become their fundamental competitive asset. They have led to a radical transformation of the procedures of drug discovery within firms and emergence of the whole organization within the pharma industry. It needs to be mentioned here that the favourable patenting regime in developed countries had contributed heavily to the development of this industry.[1] Thus, the clearly defined intellectual property rights play an important role in this industry. Patents have emerged as the most important form of intellectual property protection for them.

For a company in biopharmaceutical industry, both product and process patents are important. This is because both these types of patents are its "lifeblood". However, when we look at the role of patents in this industry there is an element of uniqueness like the parent pharmaceutical sector (Dhir and Dhir 2017). First, the medicines are usually protected by fewer patents when compared to other products (e.g. smartphones). Second, the effective patent life is 12 years for the biopharmaceutical products. This is much shorter as compared to the products in other industries. Third, twice the level of investment per patent is needed when compared to other products because of the financial investments and the efforts that are needed in research and development are huge. Sometimes the new medicines could take more than a decade and are there could be a lot of regulatory compliance needs. Fourth, most of the R&D in the active biopharmaceutical companies indicates that patents are "very" or "somewhat" important to the sector and only 4% of companies in other industries viewed patents as "very" or "somewhat" important to their business.[2] Thus, this can be safely concluded that because of the uniqueness in the industry patents could possibly be used as a strategy for the companies of this industry.

3.2 Patents and Indian Biopharmaceutical Industry: The Story so Far

To understand the trajectory of events which had led to the growth in the generic medicine sector in India we would need to look back. To begin with, it is required to trace the journey of India's patent regime. The Patent Act of 1970 lacked protection in form of product patents. This significantly had impacted the multinational

---

[1]Sterzi (2010).
[2]Grayson (2015).

pharmaceutical companies and they were reluctant to invest in India. But this absence of product patent regime helped the development of reverse engineering expertise for drugs which were patentable as products outside India. Thus, it helped to usher in a rapid growth in the generic medicine sector by developing relatively much less expensive versions for a number of patented drugs. And for these generic drugs, the processes were patented for the domestic market. Eventually, once the patents in the international markets expired the Indian drug industry moved out globally more aggressively with their expertise generic drugs.

i. With the reintroduction of the product patents in 2005 as part of India's obligations under the WTO TRIPS Agreement, India's patent legislation included provisions for both products and processes in pharmaceutical inventions. The minimum term for which the patents had to be granted was 20 years. Further with the coming of TRIPS-related obligations and commitments, the Patents Act was further amended to provide for the exclusive marketing rights (EMRs). They also helped to create a system for the lock-in the patent applications. This is a period of five years or until the patent is granted or rejected (whichever happens earlier). With this product, patents came into the Indian patent proved to be a boost for multinational companies which had been previously reluctant to invest due to the absence of product patent protection. This new patent regime also resulted in increased competition in the domestic market.[3] The Indian biopharmaceutical companies have reoriented their strategies to not just meet the new challenges but as well to leverage on the opportunities arising from the implementation of this new patent regime.[4]

It needs to be mentioned here that this industry itself has approached its own patent cliff. A blockbuster product in the pharmaceutical industry is a product for which the sales are expected to exceed 1 billion USD per year. The term patent cliff refers to the phenomenon when for a certain group of blockbuster products which capture high percentage of the market, there is an overlap with the patent expiration dates and there is an abrupt drop in sales. This causes an increase in competition in the off-patent markets for many of these big-selling products.[5,6,7]

The patent cliff now, i.e. from 2015 to 2020, is more significant when compared to five years earlier. This is because the patents for branded drugs worth US $92 billion are expected expire. This will obviously mean an increase in the size of the opportunity landscape for the Indian biopharmaceutical companies. For a global biopharmaceutical firm, as they tend to focus on the drug discovery and development value chain there are three distinct stages which are involved. They are

---

[3]Zacharias and Farias (2002).
[4]Khan and Nasim (2016).
[5]Dr. Reddy's (2016).
[6]Löfgren (2007).
[7]Calo-Fernandez and Martínez-Hurtado (2012).

research and development (R&D), clinical trials and manufacture.[8] These are elaborated as below.

i. Research and development (R&D)—The aim of this phase is to discover new drugs. It usually requires considerable quantities of particular molecules for the experiment and a contract research organization (CRO) which could provide the target and even customized molecules.
ii. Clinical trials—In the second phase, a drug typically is sent for clinical trials. It helps to determine if it can deliver consistently, for a large target population, without causing any toxicity or major side effects. Here as well, a CRO might be required to find the patients, work with hospitals and doctors and to manage the data.
iii. Manufacturing—In the third phase, after the drug is tested and approved for production in bulk as per the set formula and the process. This is the most price competitive of the three phases.

The Indian biopharmaceutical multinationals have large-scale manufacturing plants. Their growing R&D capabilities have helped them become major suppliers of Active Pharmaceutical Ingredients (APIs). This enables them to manufacture generic drugs across both developed and developing countries. The patents which are due to expire fuel in further growth opportunities in the sector and could be a factor to explain the changing dynamics of this industry.

3.3 Literature Review

The objective of the literature survey for this chapter was to identify the primary sources for which the secondary, tertiary and non-documentary sources were determined. The "snow ball" method was used by identifying recent papers (primary source), tracking back from references of recent papers and the cross-references which lead to earlier publications.

Primary source of literature reviewed for the chapter was the *WIPO Manual on Open Source Tools for Patent Analytics* (http://www.wipo.int/publications/en/details.jsp?id=4168) and *Patent Landscape Reports by Other Organizations published by WIPO* (http://www.wipo.int/patentscope/en/programs/patent_landscapes/plrdb.html). Further in addition to the above, the research reports, conference proceedings, official publications, patents analysis documents (as enumerated in the references) were studied in detail to obtain the relevant cross-disciplinary information.

---

[8]Kalegaonkar et al. (2008).

3.4 Objectives of the Study

This is a firm-level study for the companies in the biopharmaceutical industry in India which are the major players in the industry. The objectives of this study are threefold. First to identify the key players in the Indian biopharmaceutical industry and to understand the trend in their patent filing activities. Second, the findings from this study may offer concrete facts in relation to the IP strategy for these biopharma companies (like—assessment of patent filings; overview of the trends in relation to patent protection; the technology focus for these companies seeking patent protection.). Third, as these firms aim to use patent as a strategic lever in their growth story, a few sample case based on publically available data could help to understand through the academic lenses as to how a company could use patents in its strategy.

The methodology for the study included developing research questions, within a set of defined objectives. This was followed by identifying a search strategy and analysing the search results and the obtained and gathered business intelligence. Substantial searches were conducted using free patent database namely— PATENTSCOPE, Espacenet, Google Patents. The best patent searches are iterative. Different search were used because the search strings are processed differently by different tools since each tool works slightly differently. Any good search begins by developing a clear description of the subject of the search and therefore the search string is to be carefully designed.[9]

The period for study was chosen for the timeframe for the patents filed from 1 January 2005 to 1 January 2015. This followed building of patent landscapes using a software tool—The Lens (https://www.lens.org/lens/search). This is an open global cyberinfrastructure tool to make the innovation system more efficient and fair, more transparent and inclusive.[10] The results obtained were categorized into different levels and were further worked upon to derive useful inputs for analysis.

3.5 Methodology of Study

3.5.1 Analysing the Patent Statistics—The Indicators

Patents help to protect inventions developed by firms, institutions or individuals. The journey from invention to innovation requires further entrepreneurial efforts to develop, manufacture and market it.[11] The patent office grants or rejects the application-based examination of the filed application. Some of the indicators commonly used for analysing the patent statistics are mostly used for national-level

---

[9]Ellen Krabbe (2017).
[10]WIPO (2016).
[11]The Measurement of Scientific and Technological Activities Using Patent Data as Science and Technology Indicators (1994).

analysis. These indicators, as is described below, can be tailored to analyse the company-level data as well. These patent indicators have been utilized to analyse the patent statistics for the select companies.

- *Date*—In most patent offices, the legal and procedural delay for publishing an application is 18 months after the priority date. The indicators like date for patent filing/date for patent grant/the data for the patent families based on the priority (first filing) date/technology indicators which are based on the publication date, can be used for analysis.[12]
- *Jurisdictions*—There are differences in patent systems at the national level for accommodating different national interests and needs. When a company files a patent, it does decide on the particular jurisdiction depending on some primarily considerations like—how many countries would the company want patents in and whether or not the company wishes to delay costs.[13] There are concrete evidences that those patented inventions are more valued in the financial markets where patents are obtained in more than one jurisdictions.[14]
- *Classification*—The co-classifications among the patents enable at understanding the relationships among technologies at different levels of aggregation.[15]
- *Document type/Publications*—Analysis of these indicators serve as the indicators of the firm's patent quality, which is the indicator of technological and economic value for the company.[16] The strength of accumulated forward citations after the publication of the patent gives an insight into the technological and business impact of the patent for the firm. This helps to understand if patents are applied for to merely build an elaborate portfolio or for the protection of real inventions.
- *Patent infringements*—The general trend shows that the biotech/pharma has the highest median damages awards when it comes to patent infringement.[17] Thus in this industry, the number of patent infringement cases that a company has provides an understanding about nature of patents owned by the firm as the cost and complexity of these trials is too high.
- *Patent family size*—Patents families are patents which are related to each other by one or several common priorities and are filed in several countries. A particular patent family size has an associated economic value. Large international patent families have been found to be particularly more valuable.[18]
- *Innovation indicators*—Patents are one of the main indicators used to assess the productivity of innovation systems. The changes in R&D expenditure for the

---

[12]WIPO (2008).
[13]Raffoul and Brion (2011).
[14]Hall et al. (2007).
[15]Leydesdorff (2008).
[16]Squicciarini et al. (2013).
[17]PwC (2016).
[18]Squicciarini et al. (2013).

firms over time and the number of patents obtained does give an insight into the innovation policy of the firm.[19]

3.5.2 Identifying the Key Players

India is a home to many pharmaceutical companies which manufacture generic medicines and many of them have already established their footprint in global markets. With the patent cliff being very prominent in the pharmaceutical industry from 2015 to 2020, these companies are carving their growth trajectory and emerging as independent biopharmaceutical companies. For the purpose of this study, the following companies are considered which are the leaders (based on market capitalization) in the generic pharmaceuticals for the reference year of 2015. However, it may be mentioned here that the overall industry analysis is not covered within the scope of this study.

- Aurobindo Pharma—It is a Hyderabad-based company. The company is into manufacturing of generic pharmaceuticals and active pharmaceutical ingredients (APIs). In 2015, the company had incurred Rs. 3465.5 million towards R&D expenses, which was around 2.86% of their net revenue. Till March 2015, the company had filed for 594 patent applications with various authorities and of these 87 patents had been approved. The company predicts the expenses R&D might go up to 5–6% of their sales in the next couple of years.[20,21]
- Biocon Ltd.—It is a Bengaluru-based company. The company specializes in the manufacturing of generic active pharmaceutical ingredients (APIs) and biosimilar insulins. For the year 2015, Biocon's R&D expenditure touched Rs. 1735 million, which was an increase of 29% over previous year. The R&D expenditure was 5.29% of finished goods sales. Till March 2015, the company had 1150+ patent applications which had been filed globally and of these 530 + patents had been granted. It had subsidiaries—Syngene, which conducted research for third-party clients for drug discovery and development and Clinigene, which explored opportunities for clinical research. The company estimated their R&D spending to be 12–15% of their biopharmaceuticals segment revenues in the coming years.[22,23]
- Dr. Reddy's Laboratories—It is headquartered at Hyderabad. In the year 2015, the company's R&D expenses grew by 41% to Rs. 17,450 million and accounted for 11.8% of their sales. Aurigene is the biotech arm of the company,

---

[19]Dechezleprêtre et al. (2017).
[20]Aurobindo Pharma Ltd. (2015).
[21]Aurobindo Pharma (2016).
[22]Biocon Ltd. (2015).
[23]Biocon Ltd. (2016).

and it is a wholly owned independent subsidiary of Dr. Reddy's Laboratories. In May 2015, Aurigene had 130+ patents and had out licensed multiple early stage and three late-stage programs. The cost involved in handling the patent litigation as well as their unexpected loss of the patent challenge affected the company's plans to start a generic medicine business in the USA.[24,25,26]

- Sun Pharma—It is headquartered in Mumbai. It is involved in the manufacturing and selling of the pharmaceutical formulations and active pharmaceutical ingredients (APIs). With the acquisition of Ranbaxy in 2014, it has become the largest pharma company in India. It is the fifth largest specialty generic company globally. In 2015, its R&D expenditure was Rs. 19,600 million, which increased 7.2% over the previous year. For 2015, the total R&D expenditure was 11.8% of total turnover and R&D expense as a percentage of net sales was 19.6%. Till March 2015, the company had submitted 1598 patent applications and 951 patents granted.[27]
- Lupin Limited—it is based in Mumbai. It is a pharmaceutical company which majorly manufactures generics, speciality and API. The company is a global player in the drugs like anti-TB, anti-infective and cardiovascular. It also is prominently present in the areas of diabetes, anti-inflammatory and respiratory therapy. Its R&D expenditure in 2015 was Rs. 37,358 million which was 8.9% of net sales for the year. The company had filed 2197 patents on March 2015.[28]

The patenting activity for the select biopharma companies is captured in this section. Then the results are analysed based on the patent statistics obtained from the patent indicators (as described above). Further, at the very onset of the study to understand how patents can play an important role as a strategic factor for a company, we can see two well evident examples. These examples can prove the role of patents for obtaining competitive advantage for these companies in the biopharmaceutical industry which would become more promised with time. The first is the use of patents in case of its insulin development and manufacturing by Biocon. The second example is the loss of biopharmaceutical generic business of Dr. Reddy's laboratories to Pfizer.

---

[24]Wikipedia (2017).
[25]Dr. Reddy's (2015).
[26]Dr. Reddy's (2016).
[27]Sun Pharmaceuticals (2015).
[28]Lupin Ltd. (2015).

3.6 The Patent Landscape Report

3.6.1 Based on Publications by Year

A comparison was sought about the number of documents that got "published" (not the number of patents filed) for the companies on a year-on-year basis for 8 years (2006–2014). The analysis uses "date" as an indicator to obtain the patent statistics. The linear trend line drawn over the period of analysis shows the comparison with the number of patents filed by these companies over the period of time. Further, in the graph below over the years it shows, the companies differ in their pace of filing patents. Biocon is maintaining a steady pace and the company files at a constant rate, while Aurobindo Pharma is showing a declining trend. The other three companies (Dr. Reddy's, Lupin and Sunpharma) are as well continuously rising. It needs to be mentioned here that the slope for Lupin Ltd. is highest, thus indicating a rapid rise in the number of patents published (Fig. 3.1).

3.6.2 Based on Patent Coverage for the Various Jurisdictions

The graph below uses "jurisdictions" as an indicator to obtain the patent statistics. When the patents of the select biopharma companies were analysed for their patent filing patterns, there emerged a very interesting fact for all the companies. In spite of them having their R&D centres in India, the number of patents filed in India is relatively low (nearly negligible) compared to patents the company files abroad.

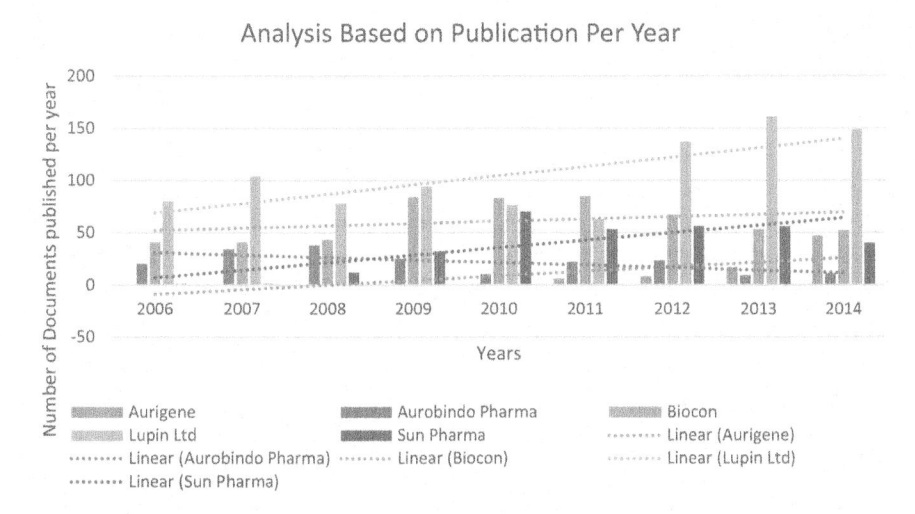

Fig. 3.1 Analysis based on publication per year

Analysis Based on Jurisdiction

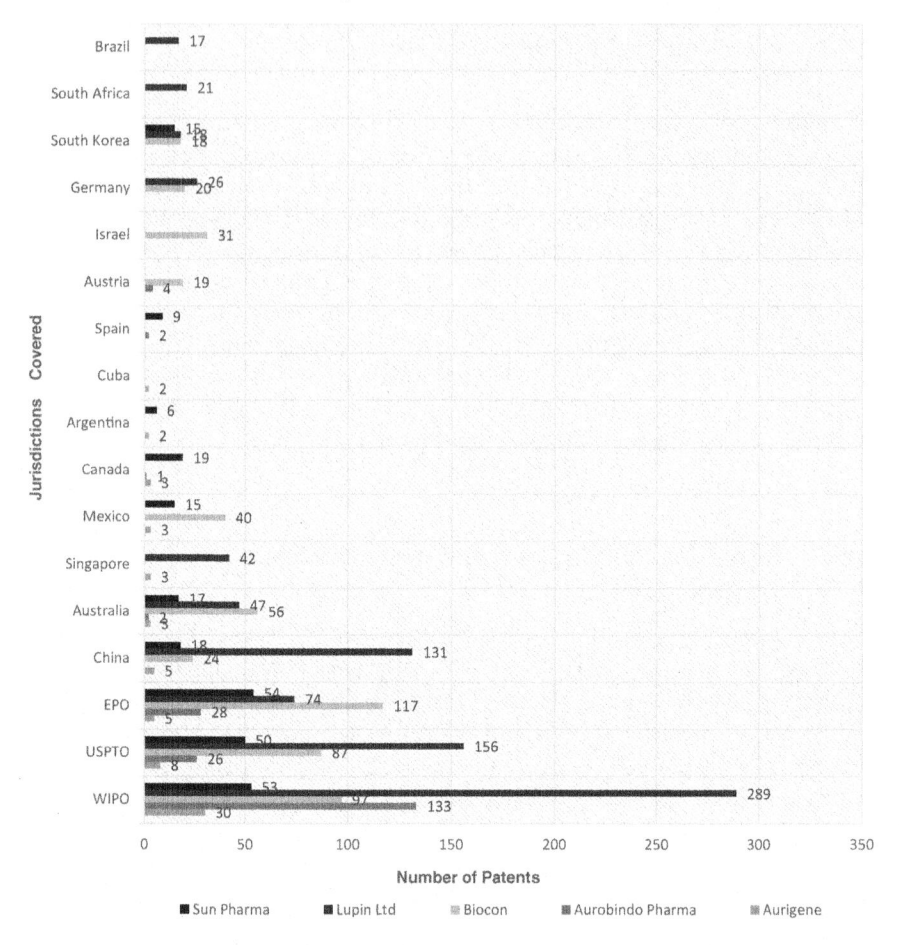

Fig. 3.2 Analysis based on jurisdiction

Further, it is observed that there is a growing focus by these companies towards the South American countries like Brazil, Cuba and Argentina. It is also observed that unlike other four companies, Biocon has more number of patents in the EPO than USPTO or WIPO, this also indicates that their focus market is Europe (Fig. 3.2).

3.6.3 Based on the Relationship Among Technologies

Patent classifications are commonly used to find patents in patent searching and to group patents in patent landscaping. A classification is applicable to the patent

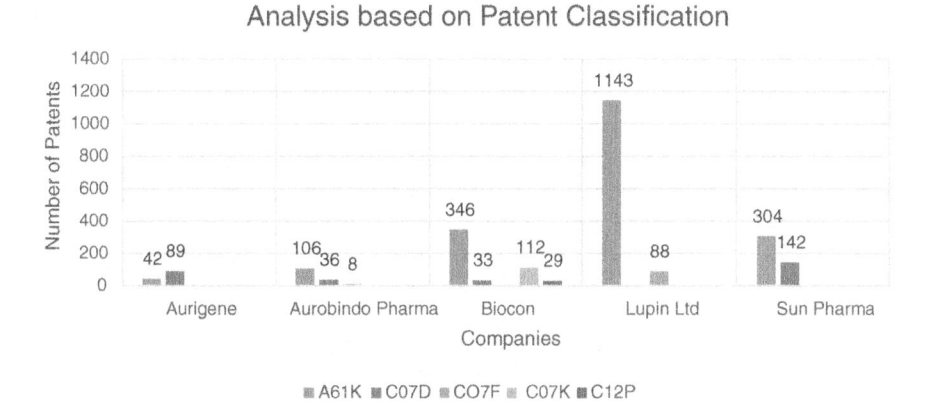

3 Patent Landscape for Indian Biopharmaceutical Sector ...

Fig. 3.3 Analysis based on patent classification

application or other document at the most detailed level and is also applicable to its contents. The indicator of patent "classification" by the various patent databases is used here, to obtain the patent statistics. The top CPC classification of EPO and IPC classification of WIPO were analysed for the firms. This helped to ascertain the technical areas in which these companies are actively filing patents.

The biopharmaceutical companies file their patents in 2 main categories—A: Human Necessities and C: Chemistry and Metallurgy. Further in these categories, the groups in focus are: A61K (1941 Patents) and C07D (300 Patents) and they account for 90% of the patents filed in the industry. As well, a further comparison indicated that the companies are selective their groups, for example Lupin Ltd., files most of its patents in A61K group, while companies like Biocon do their patent filing under the different various classes (Fig. 3.3).

Classification group	Description
A61K	Preparations for medical, dental or toilet purposes
C07D	Heterocyclic compounds
CO7F	Acyclic, carbocyclic or heterocyclic compounds containing elements other than carbon, hydrogen, halogen, oxygen, nitrogen, sulphur, selenium or tellurium
C07K	Peptides
C12P	Fermentation or enzyme-using processes to synthesize a desired chemical compound or composition or to separate optical isomers from a racemic mixture

3.6.4 Based on the Economic and Technical Utility of Patent

There are three patent indicators used here to obtain the patent statistics are—the document type (in the Lens database), the publication In PubMed for citation and the patent infringement. Based on the first type of indicator, *The Lens* organizes its collection by twelve different document types as shown in the graph below. We find that while Lupin has filed maximum number of patent applications, the most number of patents are granted to Biocon. The search reports type of document indicates the relevance of the documents identified by the patent examiner. It is seen here that Lupin has most number of patent searches followed by Biocon (Fig. 3.4).

The second type of indicator used is publications in PubMed. PubMed is a free search engine for accessing database of references and abstracts on life sciences and biomedical publications. Patent documents are another important information source, though they are considerably less accessible. The number of patents for a company indexed in PubMed could mean the impact the patents have in furthering research and invention. The graph below shows the maximum reference for Biocon patents, in the timeframe. This is followed by Lupin Ltd. and Aurigene (Dr. Reddy's Laboratory). It may be noted that although Sun Pharma has a lot of patents which are filed and granted but its patents are not referenced much in PubMed (Fig. 3.5).

The third indicator used is number of infringement cases. As identified from the annual reports of the five companies, all the other four companies have patent infringement cases against them except for Biocon Ltd. The strategy for generic

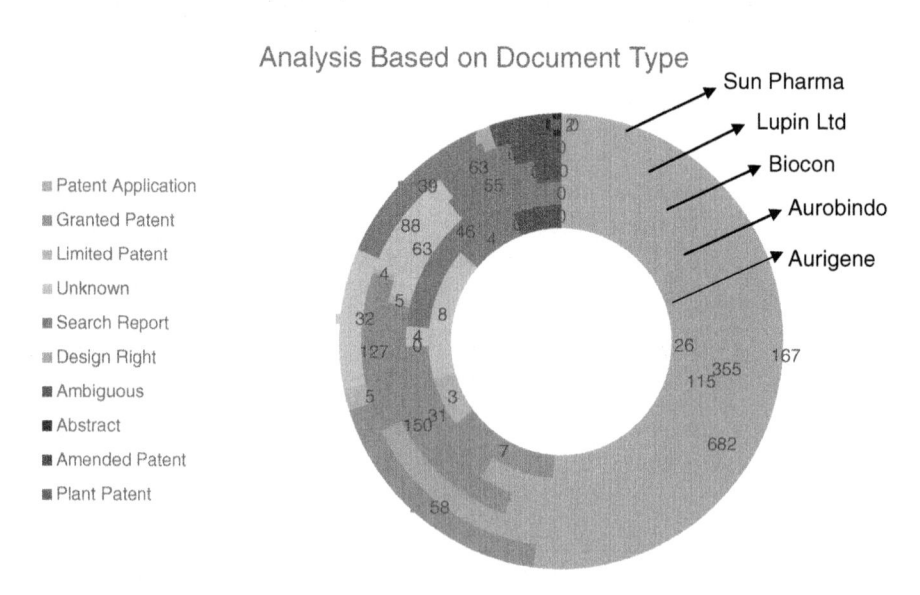

Fig. 3.4 Analysis based on document type

3 Patent Landscape for Indian Biopharmaceutical Sector ...

Number of Documents in PubMed

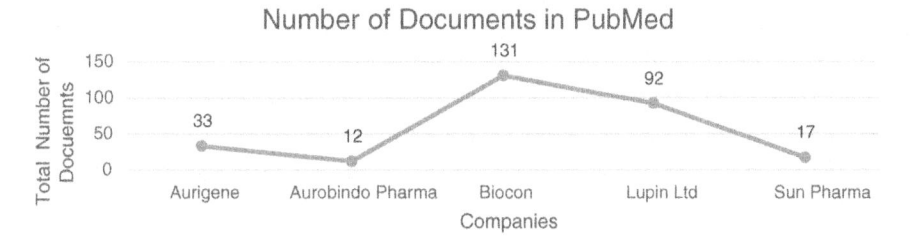

Aurigene: 33; Aurobindo Pharma: 12; Biocon: 131; Lupin Ltd: 92; Sun Pharma: 17

Fig. 3.5 Number of documents in PubMed

business for Dr. Reddy's Laboratories received a severe setback when Dr. Reddy's Laboratory lost the patent challenge in the infringement case to Pfizer.[29]

The case of process patents in the field of biopharmaceuticals are rapidly in rise in India. These processes are mostly directed towards manufacture of drug. However, it needs to be noted here that proving the infringement of such a process patent is a significant challenge, because there is no way to conclusively determine the process used by the defendant for manufacture of identical final product.[30] It is estimated that Indian companies and individuals have more number of pharmaceutical patent infringement cases where even the IP owning generic companies could file suits against other generic pharma companies.[31]

3.6.5 Based on Patent as an Indicator of Innovation

To assess the productivity of innovation systems, patents could be one of the main indicators. The graphs below show for the reference year of 2015, the R&D expense as a percentage of net sales. As well the number of patents filed and granted for the selected companies were analysed as obtained from their annual reports for 2014–2015. On comparing these two graphs, we find that while the R&D expenditure for Sun Pharma is the highest, the highest number of Patents are filed by Lupin Ltd. (Figs. 3.6 and 3.7).

---

[29]Wikipedia (2017), Dr. Reddy's (2015).
[30]Srinivasamani (2015).
[31]Rathod (2016).

Patent as an indicator of innovation for the company - 1

[Chart showing R&D expense as a percentage of net sales for the year 2015:
- Dr. Reddy's: 11.80%
- Aurobindo Pharma: 2.86%
- Biocon: 5.29%
- Lupin Ltd: 8.90%
- Sun Pharma: 19.60%]

Fig. 3.6 Patent as an indicator of innovation for the Company—1

Patent as an indicator of innovation for the company - 2

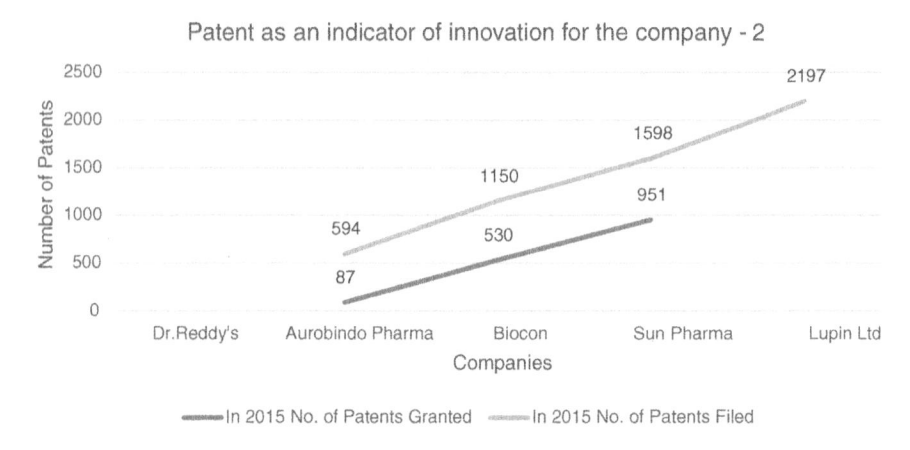

[Chart showing Number of Patents by Company:
- Dr. Reddy's: 87 granted, 594 filed
- Aurobindo Pharma: (data)
- Biocon: 530, 1150
- Sun Pharma: 951, 1598
- Lupin Ltd: 2197
Legend: In 2015 No. of Patents Granted / In 2015 No. of Patents Filed]

Fig. 3.7 Patent as an Indicator of Innovation for the Company—2

3.7 Discussions

The patent landscape for companies in the industry which are the leaders in market capitalization when analysed provided six concrete points of analysis. First, it is found that the companies are aware of the use of patents as a strategic lever in their business. The publications of patents per year for the companies are in general on rise. This could possibly indicate that the R&D capabilities for these companies are strong. The companies are expecting a rise in their R&D activities and are conscious about building a patent portfolio. Second, a distinct fact to be noted is that although the companies have their R&D centres in India they concentrate on filing patents in other jurisdictions. This could thus possibly signal a loss of revenue for India from its R&D. Third, it is observed that there is a growing focus of these companies towards filing of patents in the South American countries. This can signal their expansion tendencies of these companies in these new geographies. Fourth, the results can be analysed for the quality of patents as well. A patent's quality can be ascertained by a number of factors and opinions on the meaning of patent quality are diverse and ambiguous. However, the impact of citations per patent does for sure affect the market value of patents.[32] To understand how the productivity of innovation systems can be assessed through patents, the patent citations were analysed. Based on the analysis, it is found that the patents for only two of the five companies (Lupin and Biocon) have scored high in utility for the parameter considered. Fifth, while filing the patents, the focus is on the technical groups: A61K (Preparations for medical, dental or toilet purposes) and C07D (heterocyclic compounds), which contain multiple subclasses. Sixth, study also brings out that the R&D expenditures for these companies when mapped do not evidence that maximum spending can guarantee quality or quantity of patents.

As mentioned above, the role of patents in shaping the industry's future can be understood, through two evident examples—first is the case of Biocon and second the case of Dr. Reddy's. These are elaborated as below.

Biocon developed the world's first Pichia-based recombinant human insulin called INSUGEN®. Today it is a leader in human insulin production and manufacturing. In words of Ms. Kiran Mazumdar-Shaw: *"We noticed that most of the patented processes used e-coli and bakers' yeast. At Biocon we had expertise in another sort of yeast, and had already licensed the IP for it from a small company in the US. So the way was clear... We started making our own insulin using Pichia yeast. This was a new and unique process, which wasn't covered by any of the existing patents"*. The next example that could be considered here is the loss of generic medicines business by Dr. Reddy's Laboratory to Pfizer. This had happened because of losing the patent challenge in the infringement case. These two examples could provide convincing case study when explored further for enriching the academic literature.

3.8 Conclusion

The Indian biopharma companies, which have mastered the generic pharmaceutical markets, are poised for big growth which is augured by the launch of new products in the present patent cliff (from 2015 to 2020). With the increased number of patents due to expire in developed markets and increased penetration of medicines to happen in the emerging markets the role of patents in this industry is thus expected to increase and might even be a cause of its changing dynamics. The fully integrated biopharmaceutical companies as they emerge in India, the country has a strong potential to become a hub for global biopharma innovations. This would mean a leading role in collaborative research and the patents here would prove to be a strategic lever for these biopharmaceutical companies in this industry. These research-intensive companies would create their intellectual property (IP) wealth for obtaining sustainable competitive advantage.

---

[32]Hall et al. (2005).

References

Aurobindo Pharma. (2016). *Annual Report 2016*. Hyderabad: Aurobindo Pharma.
Aurobindo Pharma Ltd. (2015). *Driving sustainable growth—Annual Report 2014–15*. Hyderabad: Aurobindo Pharma Ltd.
Biocon. (2016). *Biocon about us page*. Retrieved November 28, 2016, from http://www.biocon.com/biocon_aboutus.asp.
Biocon. (2016). *History*. Retrieved November 27, 2016, from http://www.biocon.com/biocon_aboutus_history.asp.
Biocon Ltd. (2015). *Exclusively inclusive—Annual Report 2015*. Bangalore: Biocon Ltd.
Biocon Ltd. (2016). *Credibly capable—Annual Report 2016*. Bangalore: Biocon Limited. Retrieved from http://www.biocon.com/docs/Biocon_AR_2016_Consolidated_AR.pdf.
Building Foundations of IP. (2016). Retrieved from http://www.wipo.int/ipadvantage/en/details.jsp?id=2602.
Calo-Fernandez, B., & Martínez-Hurtado, J. L. (2012). Biosimilars: Company strategies to capture value from the Pharmaceuticals. Retrieved from www.mdpi.com/journal/pharmaceuticals.
Dechezleprêtre, A., Ménière, Y., & Mohnen, M. (2017, March). International patent families: From application strategies to statistical indicators. *LSE Research Online: March 2017*. Retrieved from http://eprints.lse.ac.uk/69486/7/Dechezlepretre_International%20patent%20families%20published_2017.pdf.
Dhir, S. (2016). Practice-oriented insights on creative problem solving. *Journal of Management & Public Policy, 7*(2).
Dhir, S., & Dhir, S. (2017). Adoption of open-source software versus proprietary software: An exploratory study. *Strategic Change, 26*(4), 363–371.
Dhir, S., & Dhir, S. (2015). Diversification: Literature review and issues. *Strategic Change, 24*(6), 569–588.
Dhir, S., & Mital, A. (2013). Value creation on bilateral cross-border joint ventures: Evidence from India. *Strategic Change, 22*(5–6), 307–326.
Dr. Reddy's. (2015). *Annual Report 2014–15*. Hyderabad: Dr. Reddy's.
Dr. Reddy's. (2016). *Annual Report 2015–2016*. Hyderabad: Dr. Reddy's.
Economic Times. (2016). Time for India to be innovator nation in bio-pharmaceuticals: Expert, PTI. New Delhi: Press Trust of India. Retrieved from http://economictimes.indiatimes.com/small-biz/startups/time-for-india-to-be-innovator-nation-in-bio-pharmaceuticals-expert/articleshow/52532569.cms.
Ellen Krabbe, S. S. (2017). *Patent searching using free search tools*. Intellectual Property Owner's Association.
Grayson, M. (2015). *PhRMA*. Retrieved May 6, 2017, from http://catalyst.phrma.org/5-reasons-why-biopharmaceutical-patents-are-different.
Hall, B. H., Jaffe, A., & Trajtenberg, M. (2005, January 01). Market value and patent citations. *Rand Journal of Economics*. Retrieved from http://eml.berkeley.edu/~bhhall/papers/HallJaffeTrajtenberg03.pdf.
Hall, B. H., Thoma, G., & Torrisi, S. (2007, September). *The market value of patents and R&D: Evidence from European firms*. Cambridge, MA: National Bureau of Economic Research.
Kalegaonkar, A., Locke, R., & Lehrich, J. (2008, November 4). Biocon India Group. *MIT Sloan Management Review*, 08–081. Retrieved from https://mitsloan.mit.edu/LearningEdge/CaseDocs/08-081%20Biocon%20India%20Group%20Case.pdf.
Khan, S. A., & Nasim, S. (2016). Impact of product patent regime on pharmaceutical companies in India. In C. J. Sushil (Ed.), *Flexible work organizations: The challenges of capacity building in Asia, flexible systems management*. New Delhi: Springer.
Leydesdorff, L. (2008). Patent classifications as indicators of intellectual organization. *Journal of the Association for Information Science & Technology, 59*(10). Retrieved from http://www.leydesdorff.net/wipo06/wipo06.pdf.

Löfgren, H. (2007). The global biopharma industry and the rise of Indian drug multinationals: Implications for Australian generics policy. *Australian and New Zealand Health Policy, v.4* (PMC1896171), PMC1896171. Retrieved from https://www.ncbi.nlm.nih.gov/pmc/articles/PMC1896171/.

Lupin Ltd. (2015). *Annual Report 2014–2015.* Lupin Ltd.

PwC. (2016). *2016 Patent litigation study are we at an.* USA: PwC. Retrieved from https://www.pwc.com/us/en/forensic-services/publications/assets/2016-pwc-patent-litigation-study.pdf.

Raffoul, N., & Brion, A. (2011, December). Reasons for patent protection and cost-effective patent filing options for SMEs. *Technology Innovation Management Review.* Retrieved from https://timreview.ca/article/505.

Rathod, S. K. (2016). Injunctions in Indian pharmaceutical patent injunctions in Indian pharmaceutical patent. Retrieved from https://papers.ssrn.com/sol3/papers.cfm?abstract_id=2758327.

Squicciarini, M., Dernis, H., & Criscuolo, C. (2013, June). Measuring patent quality—Indicators of technological and economic value. In *OECD science, technology and industry working papers* (p. 69). Retrieved from http://www.oecd-ilibrary.org/science-and-technology/measuring-patent-quality_5k4522wkw1r8-en.

Srinivasamani, V. (2015). *Process patent litigation in pharma sector—An overview.* Lakshmikumaran & Sridharan. Retrieved from http://www.lakshmisri.com/News-and-Publications/Publications/Articles/IPR/process-patent-litigation-in-pharma-sector-an-overview.

Sterzi, L. O. (2010). *Comparative study of the use of patents in different industries.* Milano: KITeS-Bocconi University.

Sun Pharmaceuticals. (2015). *Annual Report 2014–2015.* Sun Pharmaceutical.

The Measurement of Scientific and Technological Activities using Patent Data as Science and Technology Indicators. (1994). Paris: Organisation for Economic Co-Operation and Development. Retrieved from https://www.oecd.org/sti/inno/2095942.pdf.

WHO. (2016). *Insulin patent profile.* WHO, Retrieved from http://apps.who.int/medicinedocs/documents/s22481en/s22481en.pdf.

Wikipedia. (2017). Dr. Reddy's Laboratories.

WIPO. (2008). *World patent report: A statistical review—2008 edition.* WIPO. Retrieved from http://www.wipo.int/ipstats/en/statistics/patents/wipo_pub_931.html.

WIPO. (2015). *Guidelines for preparing patent landscape reports.* Retrieved May 2017, from http://www.wipo.int/edocs/pubdocs/en/wipo_pub_946.pdf.

WIPO. (2016). *Patent databases: The lens.* Retrieved from https://poldham.github.io/lens/.

WIPO. (n.d.). *Innovating India's pharmaceutical industry.* Retrieved May 10, 2017, from http://www.wipo.int/ipadvantage/en/details.jsp?id=2659.

Zacharias, N., & Farias, S. (2002). *Patents and the Indian pharmaceutical industry.* Mumbai: Business Briefing: Pharmatech.

Chapter 4
Geographical Clustering and Quality of Subsidiary Innovation in a Developing Economy

Dixit Manjunatha Betaraya, Saboohi Nasim and Joy Mukhopadhyay

Abstract Clustering has been found to have a positive impact on firm innovation and performance across the world. Clustering leads to local knowledge spillover which is vital to innovation. This chapter attempts to study the impact of clustering on the quality of subsidiary innovation in a developing country context of India. Comparing the patent data of two semiconductor design subsidiaries located in India, this chapter analyzes the moderating effect of clustering on the relationship between subsidiary age, local knowledge spillover, internal networks and the quality of subsidiary innovation. Being located in a cluster is found to have a positive impact on the quality of innovation. Clustering has also been found to positively moderate the impact of subsidiary age and internal network on the quality of innovation, while it has been found to have no moderating impact of local knowledge spillover on the quality of subsidiary innovation.

Keywords Geographical clustering · Innovation · Internal networks
Local knowledge spillover · Multinational · Subsidiary

D. M. Betaraya (✉)
Intel India Technology Pvt. Ltd., Bengaluru, India
e-mail: dixit.m.betaraya@gmail.com

D. M. Betaraya
Research Scholar, Aligarh Muslim University, Aligarh, India

S. Nasim
Department of Business Administration, Aligarh Muslim University, Aligarh, India
e-mail: saboohinasim@gmail.com

J. Mukhopadhyay
ThinkCorp Consultancy Services, Bengaluru, India
e-mail: joymukh@yahoo.com

© Springer Nature Singapore Pte Ltd. 2018
S. Dhir and Sushil (eds.), *Flexible Strategies in VUCA Markets*,
Flexible Systems Management, https://doi.org/10.1007/978-981-10-8926-8_4

4.1 Introduction

While researchers have come up with varying definitions for clusters, most of them agree that *"a cluster is a group of firms from the same or related industry located in the same or near geographic locations"* (Mudambi and Swift 2012). Firms located in clusters have shown to innovate more and perform better (Baptista and Swann 1998; Poon et al. 2013) due to availability of specialized resources and local knowledge spillovers (Griliches 1991).

The seminal paper by Dunning (1998) emphasized the importance of location in the overall multinational enterprise (MNE) strategy. The availability of specialized resources and local knowledge spillovers makes location a critical vector in MNE strategy. It has been shown that MNEs establishing subsidiaries with the objective of competence-seeking need to be closely embedded in the local networks of the host country (Birkinshaw and Hood 1998; Andersson and Forsgren 2000; Foss and Pedersen 2002; Cantwell and Mudambi 2005). In other words, MNEs need to become "insiders" from being "outsiders" to be able to tap the unique knowledge available in the host country (Cantwell and Mudambi 2011). To become insiders, MNEs prefer to locate their subsidiaries within a cluster.

One of the prime reasons for knowledge-seeking MNEs to locate subsidiaries across the world is to access the unique knowledge available in those locations. Combining the external knowledge along with its internal knowledge and processes makes the MNE highly innovative and provides them with distinct competitive advantage. Knowledge required for technological innovation is deemed to be highly tacit in nature (Mudambi and Swift 2012; Dhir and Dhir 2017) which is transferred through informal communication (Saxenian and Hsu 2001) locally (Jaffe 1986; Acs et al. 1992; Jaffe et al. 1993; Almeida and Kogut 1999). Considering that specialized knowledge spillover occurs locally, we expect MNE subsidiaries located in clusters to be more innovative as compared to the ones located outside the cluster.

There are two contradictory theories that attempt to explain innovation in MNEs located in clusters. The "physical attraction" thesis recognizes that MNEs have the best chance to be innovative by locating within the cluster due to valuable knowledge flows which occur through development of local relationships (Cantwell and Mudambi 2011). On the contrary, the "oligopolistic deterrence" thesis proposes that innovative MNEs should stay away from technology clusters. Since these MNEs already are innovative, it is deemed that the losses from outward knowledge spillover to competitors are likely to be higher than the inward knowledge gain from them (Shaver and Flyer 2000).

Prior studies on geographical clustering and innovation have focused on subsidiaries located in developed countries where local institutions are advanced and mature. There is a need to study the impact of geographical clustering on subsidiary innovation from a developing country context lens (like India) where institutions are under developed, but foreign direct investments have been increasing in the past decade (UNCTAD 2014). Moving away from using country as a proxy for locational choice, recent studies have started recognizing the importance of regions or clusters and their influence on innovation (Cantwell and Iammarino 2000; Cantwell and Piscitello 2005; Poon et al. 2013; Vanhaverbeke et al. 2013; Dhir 2016). However, more researches need to be done to explain the subnational influence on subsidiary innovation especially from a developing country context.

This study proposes to fill the above gaps. In the context of India which is a developing country, we attempt to answer the following research questions:

- Does locating within cluster lead to higher quality of subsidiary innovation?
- Does geographical clustering positively moderate the relationship between subsidiary age and quality of subsidiary innovation?
- Does geographical clustering positively moderate the effect of local knowledge spillover on quality of subsidiary innovation?
- Does geographical clustering negatively moderate the effect of internal networks on the quality of subsidiary innovation?

Using patent data, we attempt to answer the above research questions by conducting a comparative study of two semiconductor design subsidiaries located in India. By understanding the role of technological clusters on subsidiary innovation in a developing country context, this chapter adds to the growing body of knowledge of MNEs and geographical clustering of innovation. This study also helps to extend and confirm (or contradict) findings from previous studies about the impact of geographical clustering on the quality of subsidiary innovation from a developing country context. The rest of the chapter is organized as follows. In Sect. 4.2, we discuss the theory of cluster and local knowledge spillovers. Hypotheses around the three research questions stated above are formulated. Section 4.3 details the data and methodology used, while Sect. 4.4 shows the results and finally, Sect. 4.5 presents concluding remarks and limitations of the study.

4.2 Literature Review: Geographic Clusters and Innovation

Research asserts that innovation is highly clustered (Jaffe et al. 1993; Audretsch and Feldman 1996; Keller 2002; Cantwell and Piscitello 2007) due to three reasons. First, the presence of firms within the same industry in geography leads to specialization externalities and intra-industry knowledge spillovers. Second, the presence of firms in related industries in the same geography leads to diversity externalities and inter-industry knowledge spillovers. Finally, the presence of scientific laboratories or universities in the same geography contributes to science and technology spillovers (Cantwell and Piscitello 2005).

Higher levels of tacit knowledge considered essential for valuable innovations (Mudambi and Swift 2012) are highly contextual and extremely difficult to code and require frequent and direct contact for transmission (Audretsch 1998; Cantwell and Santangelo 1999; Saxenian and Hsu 2001; Sorenson et al. 2006) through social networks (Agrawal et al. 2008). Thus, firms located within the knowledge cluster have an advantage to tap into tacit knowledge and thus have been found to innovate faster and more than the firms located outside (Baptista and Swann 1998; Poon et al. 2013).

Recent theory on multinational enterprises (MNEs) has popularized the notion of MNE as a globally distributed innovation network (Frost 2001; Almeida and Phene 2004) that sources, assimilates, and integrates knowledge across the world to generate innovation (Hedlund 1994; Ghoshal and Bartlett 1988). Thus, MNEs looking to source knowledge through their subsidiaries would prefer to locate it in a cluster to take advantage of strong knowledge networks.

There are a number of counter arguments put forth by researchers on the negative impact of clusters on innovation. It is hypothesized that knowledge spillovers occur within a cluster due to labor poaching (Fosfuri and Rønde 2004). Labor poaching leads to competition for R&D resources within a cluster and is found to suppress innovation (Alsleben 2005). Also, high-value knowledge is protected through legal means, and only least valuable knowledge has been found to be available for free (Geroski 1995). It is also argued that due to continuous knowledge spillovers, highly innovative firms within a cluster experience a net loss in knowledge due to higher outflows as compared to inflows (Mudambi and Swift 2012).

4.2.1 Hypotheses

4.2.1.1 Geographical Clusters and Subsidiary Innovation

The physical attraction thesis (Cantwell and Mudambi 2011) asserts the formation of closed innovation system which locks out firms located outside the cluster. R&D activities and innovative firms are found to be clustered due to the spatial dependency of knowledge spillovers (Feldman 1994; Audretsch and Feldman 1996). As a result, firms within a technological cluster have been found to have higher number of patents and patent citations (Jaffe et al. 1993; Zucker et al. 2002). Thus, knowledge-seeking MNEs would like to establish their subsidiaries within those clusters.

Combining the existence of high-value knowledge in host country clusters and the positive influence this knowledge can potentially have on subsidiary innovation, we hypothesize the following:

Hypothesis 1: Subsidiaries located within the host country cluster produce higher quality of innovation as compared to subsidiaries located outside.

Firm experience is associated with learning-by-doing (Parameswar et al. 2017). Learning-by-doing is expected to increase over time due to improvement in organizational competencies. Thus, firm experience is expected to have a positive impact on the quality of innovation. On the contrary, firm experience can lead to organizational inertia. Organizational inertia inhibits firms from making radical changes in structure and strategy which may be required to adapt to external environmental changes (Balasubramanian and Lee 2008).

We argue that subsidiaries located within a geographical cluster can gain experience and learn faster due to the locational advantage. Given the competition for resources and technology, we also believe that firms located within a cluster have to be more dynamic and will adapt to external changes faster than those located outside the cluster.

Based on the above arguments, we hypothesize the following:

Hypothesis 2: Geographical clustering positively moderates the relationship between subsidiary age and the quality of innovation.

4.2.1.2 Geographical Clustering, Local Knowledge Spillovers and Subsidiary Innovation

Firms involved in R&D activity rely heavily on skilled human resources. These skilled human resources are the primary medium of knowledge spillovers in industries which rely heavily on R&D. Higher the skill of the knowledge resources, more important is the knowledge spillover associated with them. Hence, geographical clusters which house such skilled workers are expected to have higher knowledge spillovers which in turn are expected to positively contribute to firms located in that cluster (Audretsch and Feldman 1996).

Given the observations by past research that R&D knowledge spillover is high within a cluster and skilled labor contributes to the propagation of knowledge within a cluster, we hypothesize the following:

Hypothesis 3: Geographical clustering positively moderates the relationship between local knowledge spillovers and quality of subsidiary innovation.

4.2.1.3 Internal Networks and Subsidiary Innovation

The oligopolistic deterrence thesis (Shaver and Flyer 2000) argues that firms with superior technologies, human capital, training programs, suppliers, or distributors will minimally benefit from access to competition due to higher knowledge outflows as compared to knowledge inflow. While agglomeration may facilitate hiring skilled R&D workers from competitors, there is also a threat of losing them to competition. Thus, there is very little motivation for large and dominant MNCs to locate their subsidiaries within a technology cluster. The absence of agglomeration externalities leads the subsidiary to lean heavily on its internal network (Vidyarthi and Singh 2011). The capacity of the subsidiary to absorb incoming knowledge will lead to higher internal knowledge flows (Gupta and Govindarajan 2000).

Based on the above discussion, we hypothesize the following:

Hypothesis 4: Geographic clustering negatively moderates the relationship of internal network to subsidiary innovation quality.

4.3 Data and Methods

4.3.1 Research Setting

The hypotheses are tested in the context of two semiconductor design subsidiaries located in India. The industry has an international character of knowledge development which requires sourcing of knowledge through the subsidiaries and proliferating it throughout the MNC (Almeida 1996). In the Indian context, semiconductor design industry is found to be more advanced than China based on the number of design leads and the number and size of specialized design teams (Fuller 2014).

4.3.2 Sample

Our sample consists of two companies, one located within the technology cluster of Bangalore and another located in the National Capital Region (NCR) of Delhi which is outside the technology cluster. The company located within the cluster (will be called as Company A) is a subsidiary of a large US MNC, and the company located outside the cluster (henceforth referred to as Company B) is the subsidiary of a large EU MNC. Every patent granted to the two companies by the US Patent Office (USPTO) in the time period 2001–2010 with at least one inventor located in India is analyzed. Subsidiary patent is the unit of analysis. The number of observations in the ten-year period for Company A was 372 and for Company B was 175, bringing the total number of observations to 547.

4.3.3 Patents and Patent Citations

Patenting in the US system is done by every major semiconductor design company since USA is a major design, manufacturing, and market for semiconductor devices (Phene and Almeida 2008). While patents as a measure of innovation look attractive, there are some limitations in doing so. First, patents represent only codified knowledge and not tacit knowledge. However, researchers have pointed out that codified knowledge and tacit knowledge are closely linked and complementary (Mowery et al. 1996). Second, not all technological innovations may be patented since patenting is a strategic choice of the MNC. However, the characteristics of the semiconductor design industry encourage firms to patent, and every firm is found to have a very healthy patent portfolio (Almeida 1996). Despite the limitations, patents have been used by researchers to capture innovations and knowledge flows (Jaffe 1986; Jaffe et al. 1993; Almeida 1996; Almeida and Phene 2004; Phene and Almeida 2008).

4.3.4 Variable Operationalization

The variables included in the analysis and their operationalization are described below.

4.3.4.1 Dependent Variable

The dependent variable—quality of subsidiary innovation—was built by examining the patent portfolio of the two companies and the number of citations received by the portfolio between the years 2001–2010

Quality of Subsidiary Innovation (QSI) Trajtenberg (1990) has demonstrated that the importance of an innovation can be studied through patent citations. This measure was constructed by considering the total citations received by each of the patents granted between the years 2001–2010.

4.3.4.2 Independent Variables

Local Knowledge Spillover (LKS) One of the important ways of local knowledge spillover within a cluster in a high-technology sector like semiconductors is through mobility of technology workers (Almeida and Kogut 1999; Fosfuri and Rønde 2004). LKS is calculated by dividing the local inventors by the total inventors for each patent.

Internal Network (INW) The strength of internal network for each patent is measured as the ratio of the number of international inventors to the total number of inventors. Higher the number of international inventors, stronger is the internal network.

Geographical Clustering (GC) Geographical clustering is defined as a categorical variable. For all the patents filed by Company A, GC is sent to IN, and for all the patents filed by Company B, GC is set to OUT.

4.3.4.3 Control Variables

R&D Intensity (RDI) RDI is calculated by dividing the MNC R&D spending by net sales. R&D spending and net sales data are directly from the annual reports for the year t-3 as a proxy for subsidiary R&D intensity.

Subsidiary Age (SA) Subsidiary age for each of the patent is computed by subtracting the subsidiary establishment year from the patent filing year and taking a natural log of it.

4.3.5 Methods

Poisson model is typically suggested for analyzing patents which has count data. However, overdispersion in such data due to the presence of a large number of zero counts (patent citations) leads to underestimation of standard errors and inflation of significance levels (Phene and Almeida 2008). A chi-square goodness-of-fit value of 5747.46 with a p-value of 0.00 was obtained for the quality of innovation. The high and significant value of chi-square indicates overdispersion and suggests that the Poisson model is not suitable for our analysis. To correct the presence of over dispersion, negative binomial regression model (Almeida and Phene 2004; Phene and Almeida 2008) is used for analysis.

4.4 Results

Descriptive statistics for the number of citations are tabulated in Table 4.1. Median number of citations is six for the company located in the cluster, while it is five for the company located outside the cluster. This suggests that foreign subsidiaries of semiconductor MNCs located in India have a limited capability to generate quality innovations.

The variable inflation factor (VIF) for all the factors in a negative binomial regression model was checked and found to be less than five. The highest value of VIF was 1.46 for INW which indicates very low levels of collinearity among the explanatory variables.

Our findings are presented in Table 4.2. Model 1 is the baseline model. Models 2, 3, 4 and 5 incorporate the effect of geographical clustering, moderating effect of

Table 4.1 Descriptive statistics of citation count

	Within cluster	Outside cluster
No. of patents	372	175
Min. no. of citations	0	0
Max. no. of citations	202	87
Mean (no. of citations)	10.95	7.93
Median (no. of citations)	6	5
Variance	278.42	123.56

Table 4.2 Quality of subsidiary innovation: negative binomial regression

	Hypothesis	Model 1	Model 2	Model 3	Model 4	Model 5	Full model
Direct effects							
GC (OUT)	H1	−0.226* (0.114)	−0.353** (0.108)	2.947 (2.004)	−0.297 (0.194)	−0.217§ (0.119)	4.316* (2.041)
LKS		0.297* (0.14)			0.153 (0.156)		0.569** (0.185)
INW		0.588* (0.243)				0.462* (0.228)	0.953*** (0.272)
Indirect effects							
SA × GC (OUT)	H2			−1.249§ (0.756)			−1.521* (0.761)
LKS × GC (OUT)	H3				−0.092 (0.261)		−0.64* (0.281)
INW × GC (OUT)	H4					−1.649* (0.699)	−2.296** (0.734)
Control variables							
SA		−1.964*** (0.298)	−2.093*** (0.298)	−1.844*** (0.343)	−2.108*** (0.299)	−2.02*** (0.299)	−1.725*** (0.34)
RDI		−0.005 (0.01)	−0.003 (0.01)	0.002 (0.011)	−0.002 (0.011)	−0.008 (0.011)	−0.001 (0.011)
Wald statistic		52.5***	66.4***	71.1***	67.2***	70.5***	84.4***

$N = 547$; standard errors in parentheses; §$p < 0.1$, *$p < 0.05$, **$p < 0.01$, ***$p < 0.001$; dependent variable: quality of subsidiary innovation

geographical clustering on subsidiary age, local knowledge spillover, and internal network, respectively. Model 6 is the comprehensive model which incorporates the effect of all the explanatory and control variables. Wald statistic values indicate that adding more independent variables contributes to increased explanatory power.

Based on Model 2, we conclude that Hypothesis 1 is supported indicating that geographical clustering has a positive impact on the quality of innovation. Hypothesis 2 is weakly supported in Model 3 and strongly supported in full model which indicates that subsidiaries located within the cluster tend to produce higher quality of innovation faster than the ones located outside the cluster. Hypothesis 3 is not supported which indicates that subsidiaries located within clusters do not appear to benefit from local knowledge spillovers occurring due to expert resource movement. Model 5 and full model support Hypothesis 4 but in opposite direction. This means that stronger internal networks are built with subsidiaries located within cluster.

Of the control variables, subsidiary age has a negative impact on the quality of innovation. This is in line with the findings of earlier studies (Balasubramanian and Lee 2008; Sørensen and Stuart 2000) indicating the existence of inertia. R&D intensity does not seem to have any impact on the quality of innovation.

4.5 Discussion

The primary contribution of our study is to provide a clearer picture about the impact of geographical clustering on the quality of subsidiary innovation. The results of our study throw up some intuitive and non-intuitive findings.

Our study confirms the finding that the subsidiary located within a cluster produces higher quality of innovation as compared to the one located outside. This supports the finding of earlier studies which assert that technological innovation is geographical clustered (Jaffe et al. 1993; Audretsch and Feldman 1996; Keller 2002) even in a developing economy like India. From a theoretical standpoint, the results of this study appear to support the physical attraction thesis (Cantwell and Mudambi 2011).

There are two non-intuitive results obtained from this study. First, geographical clustering does not positively moderate the impact of local resources (which are a proxy for local knowledge spillover) on the quality of subsidiary innovation. There are a couple of possible explanations for this result. Since the subsidiary was one of the first one to be established within the cluster, it may not have benefitted much from the inward labor movement. It could also be that the free knowledge available within the cluster could be of limited use to generate quality innovation (Geroski 1995; Zucker et al. 1998).

The second non-intuitive result is the negative moderating effect of geographical clustering on the relationship between internal network and quality of subsidiary innovation. This relationship suggests that internal networks are strong in a subsidiary located within the cluster. Given the fact that the subsidiary located within the network produces high quality of innovation, we posit that it has higher absorptive capability. Higher absorptive capability is one of the perquisite for higher internal knowledge flows (Gupta and Govindarajan 2000).

4.6 Conclusion

Though our study highlights a number of interesting findings regarding the influence of geographical clustering on the quality of subsidiary innovation, it has several limitations. Caution is suggested in interpreting the results while providing opportunity for future research. First, the sample for study is limited to two semiconductor design subsidiaries located in India. It is recommended to extend this study to other high-technology industries like pharmaceuticals, automobile with focus on other emerging markets like China, Brazil. The sample used in this study is a convenience sample and may not truly represent the population. Thus, the findings of this study may not be directly translated to the population of the semiconductor design firms in an emerging market.

Second, only citation of patents is used as indicator for quality of innovation. It is understood that there are other forms and indicators of innovation like new products, process, and centers of excellence. As a future study, it is recommended to comprehend broader innovation capabilities through a research survey instrument.

Finally, we have used the availability of local resources as a proxy for local knowledge spillovers. While it is a good indicator, we acknowledge that it is a partial one. Knowledge acquired through interactions with suppliers, customer, R&D laboratories, and universities is not captured by this study. Future research can focus on these sources of local knowledge spillover and examine its impact on the quality of subsidiary innovation.

References

Acs, Z. J., Audretsch, D. B., & Feldman, M. P. (1992). Real effects of academic research: Comment. *The American Economic Review, 82*(1), 363–367.
Agrawal, A., Kapur, D., & McHale, J. (2008). How do spatial and social proximity influence knowledge flows? Evidence from patent data. *Journal of Urban Economics, 64*(2), 258–269.
Almeida, P. (1996). Knowledge sourcing by foreign multinationals: Patent citation analysis in the U.S. semiconductor industry. *Strategic Management Journal*, 155–165.
Almeida, P., & Kogut, B. (1999). Localization of knowledge and the mobility of engineers in regional networks. *Management Science, 45*(7), 905–917.
Almeida, P., & Phene, A. (2004). Subsidiaries and knowledge creation: The influence of the MNC and host country on innovation. *Strategic Management Journal, 25*(8/9), 847.
Alsleben, C. (2005). The downside of knowledge spillovers: An explanation for the dispersion of high-tech industries. *Journal of Economics, 84*(3), 217–248.

Andersson, U., & Forsgren, M. (2000). In search of centre of excellence: Network embeddedness and subsidiary roles in multinational corporations. *MIR. Management International Review, 40*(4), 329–350.

Audretsch, B. (1998). Agglomeration and the location of innovative activity. *Oxford Review of Economic Policy, 14*(2), 18–29.

Audretsch, D. B., & Feldman, M. P. (1996). R&D spillovers and the geography of innovation and production. *The American Economic Review, 86*(3), 630–640.

Balasubramanian, N., & Lee, J. (2008). Firm age and innovation. *Industrial and Corporate Change, 17*(5), 1019–1047.

Baptista, R., & Swann, P. (1998). Do firms in clusters innovate more? *Research Policy, 27*(5), 525–540.

Birkinshaw, J., & Hood, N. (1998). Multinational subsidiary evolution: Capability and charter change in foreign-owned subsidiary companies. *Academy of Management Review, 23*(4), 773–795.

Cantwell, J. A., & Mudambi, R. (2011). Physical attraction and the geography of knowledge sourcing in multinational enterprises. *Global Strategy Journal, 1*(3–4), 206–232.

Cantwell, J., & Iammarino, S. (2000). Multinational corporations and the location of technological innovation in the UK regions. *Regional Studies, 34*(4), 317–332.

Cantwell, J., & Mudambi, R. (2005). MNE competence-creating subsidiary mandates. *Strategic Management Journal, 26*(12), 1109–1128.

Cantwell, J., & Piscitello, L. (2005). Recent location of foreign-owned research and development activities by large multinational corporations in the European regions: The role of spillovers and externalities. *Regional Studies, 39*(1), 1–16.

Cantwell, J., & Piscitello, L. (2007). Attraction and deterrence in the location of foreign-owned R&D activities: The role of positive and negative spillovers. *International Journal of Technological Learning, Innovation and Development, 1*(1), 83–111.

Cantwell, J., & Santangelo, G. D. (1999). The frontier of international technology networks: Sourcing abroad the most highly tacit capabilities. *Information Economics and Policy, 11*(1), 101–123.

Dhir, S. (2016). Global competitiveness of informal economy organizations. In *Flexible work organizations* (pp. 209–224). India: Springer.

Dhir, S., & Dhir, S. (2017). Adoption of open-source software versus proprietary software: An exploratory study. *Strategic Change, 26*(4), 363–371.

Dunning, J. H. (1998). Location and the multinational enterprise: A neglected factor? *Journal of International Business Studies, 29*(1), 45–66.

Feldman, M. P. (1994). The university and economic development: The case of Johns Hopkins University and baltimore. *Economic Development Quarterly, 8*(1), 67–76.

Fosfuri, A., & Rønde, T. (2004). High-tech clusters, technology spillovers, and trade secret laws. *International Journal of Industrial Organization, 22*(1), 45–65.

Foss, N. J., & Pedersen, T. (2002). Transferring knowledge in MNCs: The role of sources of subsidiary knowledge and organizational context. *Journal of International Management, 8*(1), 49–67.

Frost, T. S. (2001). The geographic sources of foreign subsidiaries' innovations. *Strategic Management Journal, 22*(2), 101–123.

Fuller, D. B. (2014). Chip design in China and India: Multinationals, industry structure and development outcomes in the integrated circuit industry. *Technological Forecasting and Social Change, 81*(1), 1–10.

Geroski, P. A. (1995). Markets for technology: Knowledge, innovation and appropriability. In P. Stoneman (Ed.), *Handbook of the economics of innovation and technological change* (pp. 90–131). Oxford: Blackwell Publishers.

Ghoshal, S., & Bartlett, C. A. (1988). Creation, adoption, and diffusion of innovations by subsidiaries of multinational corporations. *Journal of International Business Studies, 19*(3), 365–388.

Griliches, Z. (1991) *The search for R&D spillovers* (Working Paper No. 3768), Cambridge (MA): National Bureau of Economic Research. https://doi.org/10.3386/w3768.

Gupta, A. K., & Govindarajan, V. (2000). Knowledge flows within multinational corporations. *Strategic Management Journal, 21*(4), 473–496.

Hedlund, G. (1994). A model of knowledge management and the N-form corporation. *Strategic Management Journal, 15*(S2), 73–90.

Jaffe, A. (1986). Technological opportunity and spillovers of R&D: Evidence from firms' patents, profits, and market value. *American Economic Review, 76*(5), 984–1001.

Jaffe, A. B., Trajtenberg, M., & Henderson, R. (1993). Geographic localization of knowledge spillovers as evidenced by patent citations. *The Quarterly Journal of Economics, 108*(3), 577–598.

Keller, W. (2002). Geographic Localization of international technology diffusion. *The American Economic Review, 92*(1), 120–142.

Mowery, D. C., Oxley, J. E., & Silverman, B. S. (1996). Strategic alliances and interfirm knowledge transfer. *Strategic Management Journal, 17*, 77–91.

Mudambi, R., & Swift, T. (2012). Multinational enterprises and the geographical clustering of innovation. *Industry and Innovation, 19*(1), 1–21.

Parameswar, N., Dhir, S., & Dhir, S. (2017). Banking on innovation, innovation in banking at ICICI bank. *Global Business and Organizational Excellence, 36*(2), 6–16.

Phene, A., & Almeida, P. (2008). Innovation in multinational subsidiaries: The role of knowledge assimilation and subsidiary capabilities. *Journal of International Business Studies, 39*(5), 901–919.

Poon, J. P. H., Kedron, P., & Bagchi-Sen, S. (2013). Do foreign subsidiaries innovate and perform better in a cluster? A spatial analysis of Japanese subsidiaries in the US. *Applied Geography, 44*, 33–42. https://doi.org/10.1016/j.apgeog.2013.07.007.

Saxenian, A., & Hsu, J.-Y. (2001). The Silicon Valley-Hsinchu connection: Technical communities and industrial upgrading. *Industrial and Corporate Change, 10*(4), 893–920.

Shaver, J. M., & Flyer, F. (2000). Agglomeration economies, firm heterogeneity, and foreign direct investment in the United States. *Strategic Management Journal, 21*(12), 1175–1193.

Sørensen, J. B., & Stuart, T. E. (2000). Aging, obsolescence, and organizational innovation. *Administrative Science Quarterly, 45*(1), 81–112.

Sorenson, O., Rivkin, J. W., & Fleming, L. (2006). Complexity, networks and knowledge flow. *Research Policy, 35*(7), 994–1017.

Trajtenberg, M. (1990). *Economic analysis of product innovation: The case of CT scanners* (Vol. 160). London: Harvard University Press.

UNCTAD (2014) *World Investment Report 2014*.

Vanhaverbeke, W., Du, J., & Zedtwitz, M. von. (2013). Managing open innovation in multinational enterprises: Combining open innovation and R&D globalization literature. In *World scientific book chapters* (pp. 213–233). World Scientific Publishing Co. Pte. Ltd. Retrieved from https://ideas.repec.org/h/wsi/wschap/9781783262816_0009.html.

Vidyarthi, R., & Singh, D. (2011). Clustering value drivers of indian telecom customers—Pathway for effective strategy formulation. *Global Journal of Flexible Systems Management, 12*(3&4), 53–64.

Zucker, L. G., Darby, M. R., & Armstrong, J. S. (2002). Commercializing knowledge: University science, knowledge capture, and firm performance in biotechnology. *Management Science, 48*(1), 138–153.

Zucker, L. G., Darby, M. R., & Brewer, M. B. (1998). Intellectual human capital and the birth of U.S. biotechnology enterprises. *The American Economic Review, 88*(1), 290–306.

Chapter 5
Corporate Governance and Innovation

J. P. Sharma, Shital Jhunjhunwala and Shweta Sharda

Abstract Innovation is the key source of growth and sustainability of a nation as it determines the competitive performance of country as well as firms. The innovation activities carried out by the corporate sector in India are the outcome of strategic investment decisions made by top management. Directors play pivotal role in innovation with the greatest power to select Research & Development project and evaluate its effectiveness, which is crucial for efficient utilization of resources. However, the uncertainty in the expected results of Research & Development activities makes the attitude of manager towards risk an important determinant in corporate innovation. The board may deviate towards short-term investments to reduce risks associated with long-term Research & Development investments; thus, their decisions need to be monitored through corporate governance oversight mechanisms. The chapter examines the role of corporate governance in enhancing the level of Research & Development activities in firms, and it was found that the role of independent director is pivotal in the decision-making of firm, especially through their active participation in board meetings.

Keywords Board · Corporate governance · Innovation · Research & Development

---

J. P. Sharma
Department of Commerce, Delhi School of Economics,
University of Delhi, Delhi, India
e-mail: jaiprakash2509@gmail.com

S. Jhunjhunwala
Faculty of Commerce and Business Studies,
Delhi School of Economics, University of Delhi, Delhi, India
e-mail: casjhunjhunwala@gmail.com

S. Sharda (✉)
Department of Commerce, Indraprastha College for Women,
University of Delhi, Delhi, India
e-mail: ssharda@ip.du.ac.in

© Springer Nature Singapore Pte Ltd. 2018
S. Dhir and Sushil (eds.), *Flexible Strategies in VUCA Markets*,
Flexible Systems Management, https://doi.org/10.1007/978-981-10-8926-8_5

5.1 Introduction

Innovation is characterized by novelty in ideas, products and services, encouraged due to fierce rivalry among firms in order to survive in the market. India is emerging as innovation hub with initiatives to foster research in all the sectors ranging from automobiles, pharmaceuticals, IT services, consumer goods to the essentials like drinking water, health, education, utilities. UNCTAD's Investment Report—2005 defines Research & Development as follows: "R&D is only one component of innovation activities, but it represents the most developed, widely available and internationally comparable statistical indicator of industrial innovation activities". The report refers to an OECD study and states that R&D (also called research and experimental development) comprises creative work "undertaken on a systematic basis in order to increase the stock of knowledge, including knowledge of man, culture and society, and the use of this stock of knowledge to devise new applications".[1] R&D spending of a particular country has been used by many organizations (World Bank 2007; World Economic Forum 2008) to measure the competitiveness of countries.[2] The entry of multinational companies with large R&D centres and foreign investment in India are contributing towards the innovative activities in India. The technological edge is important for India to be at the forefront in the fiercely competitive international market. The R&D investment is a long-term commitment with uncertainty involved in the expected returns.

The existence of innovative enterprise depends on managers' efficiency in formulating strategies to utilize shareholders' funds efficiently. Firms differ in their innovation investments because allocation of funds is a matter of strategic choice of corporate managers. The investment in R&D does not guarantee returns, thus depending upon the risk-taking attitude of management. Due to the inherent risk involved in R&D spending, managers tend to alter their investment decisions to avoid risks. To address this discrepancy, shareholders want corporation to be governed with oversight mechanisms in order to align manager's interest with their interests (Zahra 1996) to enhance risk-taking with the objective of pursuing innovation. Thus, corporate governance is meant to overcome managerial risk aversion to enhance firm innovativeness.

---

[1]Fourth Report of the Committee to Review Taxation of Development Centres and the IT sector accessed on 08 August 2016 at http://www.taxlawsonline.com/news/Fourth%20Report.pdf.

[2]Bhattacharya, Sujit & Lal, Kashmiri, (2008). Industrial R&D in India: Contemporary Scenario. India, Science and Technology accessed on 10 August 2016 at http://www.nistads.res.in/indiasnt2008/t4industry/t4ind4.htm.

5.2 Literature Review and Hypotheses

Corporate governance plays central role in the process of innovation, where composition of board of directors, independent directors, separating the role of chairman of the board and CEO, regular meetings of directors in the company and participation of directors therein and other practices enhance the strategic decision-making. The board is responsible for making critical strategic decisions, laying the foundation of strong corporate governance and thus firm innovativeness. Since large publicly traded firms incur the major chunk of Research & Development by utilizing shareholders' funds, the role of board of directors in decision-making becomes important for generating long-term returns to shareholders.

Researchers have assessed the effect of corporate governance practices on innovation empirically, particularly focusing on R&D investment levels as a measure of innovation (Lee and O'Neil 2003; Aghion et al. 2009; Munari et al. 2010; Bhat 2010; Bhat et al. 2011; Driver and Guedes 2012, Dhir and Dhir 2017a, b). Firms with weaker governance experience lower innovation and firm value (Atanassov 2013). However, It is proved empirically that the investments in R&D reduced in US companies after the implementation of SOX and that the increase in outside monitoring had a detrimental effect on innovation-related activities (Cohen et al. 2009; Bargeron et al. 2010). The impact of governance on R&D spending has been inconclusive (Hill and Snell 1988; Baysinger et al. 1991; Hoskisson et al. 2002), and there is limited evidence that corporate governance affects innovation performance (Shapiro et al. 2015; Dhir et al. 2014). Corporate governance is considered as a mechanism to ensure successful implementation of R&D project in accordance with shareholder's interest (Wright et al. 2002; Alladi et al. 2015, Dhir and Dhir 2017a, b).

5.2.1 *Innovation*

Research & Development investments are the driving force in innovation; It helps in introduction of new products and processes in the economy. The literature provides strong support for R&D as the proxy for innovation and its relationship with performance. R&D is the building block of innovation (Becker-Blease 2011), and it is the indicator of firm's innovation ability, as it is viewed as input to the innovation process (Griliches 1990; Parameswar et al. 2017) and increasing R&D investment fuels innovation (Griffith et al. 2004). The continuous investments in R&D are prerequisite to remain competitive as It ensures flow of newer products and services into the market (O'Brien 2003).

5.2.2 Board Size

Boards are considered as the source of mitigating the agency problem in the company due to separation of ownership and control. It is believed that there will be timely and faster decision-making in small groups as compared to large group sizes due to inherent problem of coordination and conflicts among the members. There exists negative relationship between board size and corporate performance (Goodstein et al. 1994; Yermack 1996; Alshimmiri 2004; Andres et al. 2005; Garg 2007; Kaur and Gill 2008; Kota and Tomar 2010; Al-Manaseer et al. 2012; Gugnani 2013). As per resource dependency theory, the board of directors is an important resource where large board size provides more number of people in the company with required expertise, knowledge and skills than the smaller boards. This improves the quality of strategic decisions; hence, there exists empirical evidence on positive association between board size and company performance (Pearce and Zahra 1992; Ghosh 2006; Van den Berghe and Levrau 2004; Dwivedi and Jain 2005; Kyereboah-Coleman and Biekpe 2007; Abidin et al. 2009; Jackling and Johl 2009; Varshney et al. 2012).

1. H_A: There exists significant relationship between the size of the board of directors and R&D investment.

5.2.3 Board Independence

Innovative activities involve special knowledge, expertise, exceptional skills and experience where advising and monitoring by external directors is highly valuable resource to improve innovative performance based on their high levels of leadership skills and experiences (Hill and Snell 1988; Lacetera 2001; Chung et al. 2003; Chen and Hsu 2009; Castro et al. 2009; Kim et al. 2009; Faleye et al. 2011). On the contrary, the presence of outside directors is questioned due to major corporate failures, and independent directors have significant negative association with risk in the organization (Driver and Guedes 2012; Ben and Dwivedi 2013; Chang et al. 2015). Faleye et al. (2011) find negative relationship between independent director presence in boards and its committees with innovation in firm.

2. H_B: The proportion of independent directors on the board of directors has positive relationship with Research & Development investment.

5.2.4 Board Leadership

The separation of roles can enhance innovation (Hill and Snell 1988; Lacetera 2001), and duality has negative effect on the innovation activities due to influence of CEO in all the strategic decisions (Kor 2006; Chen and Hsu 2009; Ben and Dwivedi 2013; Chang et al. 2015). It is positive (Hung and Mondejar 2005; Galasso and Simcoe 2011; Driver and Guedes 2012; Hirshleifer et al. 2012). Therefore, the position of CEO and chairman of the board of directors should rest with different individuals to avoid concentration of decision-making with one individual, which would help in evaluation of decisions, impartially leading to improvement in the long-term health of the company.

3. H_C: The separation of CEO and board chairman positions has positive relationship with Research & Development investment.

5.2.5 Board Participation

The successful implementation and generation of returns from innovation investments rests upon the strategic decision-making exercise of top management which takes place during meetings. The time devoted by directors debating on the alternative investment opportunities is crucial for greater scrutiny, required to make thoughtful decision. The active board is particularly relevant for strategic decision-making and hence crucial for better performance (Lipton and Lorsch 1992; Rabi et al. 2010; Alhazaimeh et al. 2014). The above findings were opposed by (Jensen 1993) indicating poor performance due to more number of meetings because It leads to wastage of time in routine matters. The attendance of independent directors is particularly important to exercise their voting rights, and the relevance of conducting board meetings will be futile with the unavailability of required number of directors during their meetings.

4. H_D: The participation of directors in board meetings has positive relationship with Research & Development investment.
5. H_E: The participation of independent directors in board meetings has positive relationship with Research & Development investment.

5.2.6 Board Busyness

The board of directors is considered busy when they sit in the boards of multiple companies that may hinder their participation in the corporate affairs. The busyness of directors negatively affects the performance of company (Jackling and Johl 2009;

Jiraporn et al. 2009). The involvement of directors with multiple companies makes them busy, and their commitment to different firms reduces their time spent in the affairs of the companies (Fich and Shivdasani 2004).

6. H_F: The multiple directorships held by independent directors have positive relationship with Research & Development investment

5.2.7 Age and Leverage

The age of the firm represents years of existence of the firm; the older firms tend to have higher tendency to invest in R&D due to their experience in the market. The debt–equity ratio can limit investments in order to maintain regular cash flows.

7. H_G: Age of a firm is positively related to Research & Development investment.
8. H_H: There is a negative relationship between leverage (debt–equity ratio) and Research & Development investment.

5.3 Research Methodology

To study the effect of corporate governance on R&D investment decisions in firms, R&D intensity is taken as dependent and CG attributes as independent variables in the study.

5.3.1 Dependent Variable: Research & Development Intensity

Thus, R&D ratio is taken as dependent variable, computed as firm's annual R&D expenditures divided by its total assets (Hirshleifer et al. 2012; Zona 2016). R&D ratio is better than absolute amount of R&D expenditure to address the differences in firm size and heteroscedasticity. R&D ratio was transformed by taking log as it had a right-skewed distribution, important to maintain the regression assumptions. The variables are defined in Table 5.1.

To find out the relationship between corporate governance and R&D investment in a firm, the sample is drawn from NIFTY 500 listed on NSE as on 31 March 2016. The NIFTY 500 Index represents about 94% of the free-float market capitalization of the stocks. The final sample is taken for 218 companies after excluding firms which have not incurred R&D expenditure. The data on corporate governance and

5 Corporate Governance and Innovation

Table 5.1 Definition of variables

Variable	Definition
Dependent variable	
R&D intensity	Expenses on Research & Development/Total assets of the firm
Independent variables	
Board size	Total number of directors in the board
Board independence	Percentage of independent directors in the board
Board leadership	Dummy variable 1 if CEO and chairman are different, otherwise 0
Board participation	Average number of meetings attended by the directors in a year
Participation of independent directors	Average number of meetings attended by the independent directors in a year
Busyness of independent directors	Average number of other directorships held by independent directors
Control variables	
Debt/equity	Debt–equity ratio of the firm
Age	Present year—incorporation year

Table 5.2 Descriptive statistics

	N	Min	Max	Mean	Std. Dev.	Skewness
Log R&D intensity	218	−11.32	−1.93	−5.530	1.778	−0.454
Age	218	1	119	45.48	23.17	0.635
Debt-to-equity ratio	218	0.00	2.82	0.3978	0.5261	1.918
Board size	218	7	21	12.94	2.790	0.416
Board independence	218	0.08	0.75	0.4232	0.09661	−0.181
Board leadership	218	0	1	0.59	0.493	−0.376
Independent directors' participation	218	1.80	9.80	4.710	1.412	0.774
Independent directors' busyness	218	0.00	15.67	4.076	2.800	1.123
Board participation	218	1.78	8.00	4.049	1.201	0.833
Valid N	218					

R&D is gathered from *Prowess*, the corporate database of the Centre for Monitoring of the Indian Economy (CMIE).

In order to find the relationship between corporate governance and R&D investment of companies, correlation and multiple regressions are used. The results are presented in Table 5.2.

The descriptive statistics shows that the average proportion of independent board members is 42.32%, average number of directors in a board is 13, average debt–equity ratio is 0.39, average age of firm is 45, on an average directors attended four board meetings where independent directors are seen actively engaged, and independent directors hold four other directorships on an average. Table 5.3 shows that

Table 5.3 Correlation Analysis

			1	2	3	4	5	6	7
1.	Log R&D intensity	Pearson correlation	1						
		Sig. (two-tailed)							
2.	Board size	Pearson correlation	−0.096	1					
		Sig. (two-tailed)	0.159						
3.	Board independence	Pearson correlation	0.159*	−0.064	1				
		Sig. (two-tailed)	0.019	0.348					
4.	Board leadership	Pearson correlation	−0.047	−0.120	−0.014	1			
		Sig. (two-tailed)	0.493	0.078	0.841				
5.	Board participation	Pearson correlation	−0.002	0.163*	0.069	−0.052	1		
		Sig. (two-tailed)	0.976	0.016	0.312	0.446			
6.	Independent directors' participation	Pearson correlation	0.095	−0.098	0.004	0.162*	0.717**	1	
		Sig. (two-tailed)	0.163	0.151	0.957	0.017	0.000		
7.	Independent directors' busyness	Pearson correlation	0.080	−0.144*	0.062	0.167*	−0.069	0.158*	1
		Sig. (two-tailed)	0.237	0.034	0.361	0.014	0.310	0.020	

*Correlation is significant at the 0.05 level (two-tailed)
**Correlation is significant at the 0.01 level (two-tailed)

there exists significant correlation between variables but the correlation coefficients are less than 0.8. Also, variance inflation factors (in the range 1.009–2.650) are below 10 which shows no problem of multicollinearity. The correlation matrix indicates that the R&D ratio has significant relation with proportion of independent directors in board; this suggests exploring this relationship further with the help of regression. With increase in board size, there is significant increase in the participation of directors in meetings to make decisions. Also there is positive correlation between participation of independent directors in board meetings and their busyness; this shows that they perform their duty diligently and do not compromise with their multiple positions (Table 5.4).

An analysis of residuals, plots of the standardized residuals against predicted values, is conducted to test for homoscedasticity, linearity and normality assumptions before conducting multiple regression analysis. The value of R square 45%, shows that relationship is stronger between the observed and predicted values of the dependent variable. R-square shows that 20.3% of the variation in R&D investment is explained by the variation in the explanatory variables. Hypotheses 2 and 5 are accepted, where the average R&D investment of firm with every additional independent directors increases by 272.1% and there is significant increase in average R&D investment by 30.1% for every additional increase in the participation rate of independent directors in board meetings, holding all other variables constant. Hypothesis 8 assumed a negative relationship between leverage and firm's R&D investment is accepted. Hypotheses 1, 3, 4, 6 and 7 are not supported. The presence

5 Corporate Governance and Innovation

Table 5.4 Regression

Model	Unstandardized coefficients		Standardized coefficients	t	Sig.	Collinearity statistics	
	B	Std. Error	Beta			Tolerance	VIF
(Constant)	−5.796	0.884		−6.558	0.000		
Age	−0.007	0.005	−0.088	−1.403	0.162	0.962	1.040
Debt–equity ratio (times)	−1.249	0.210	−0.369	−5.955	0.000	0.991	1.009
Board size size	−0.027	0.042	−0.042	−0.635	0.526	0.866	1.154
Board independence	**2.721**	**1.154**	**0.148**	**2.358**	**0.019**	**0.972**	**1.029**
Board leadership	−0.445	0.236	−0.123	−1.890	0.060	0.895	1.117
Independent directors' participation	**0.301**	**0.127**	**0.239**	**2.376**	**0.018**	**0.377**	**2.650**
Independent directors' busyness	0.020	0.042	0.031	0.473	0.637	0.888	1.126
Board participation	−0.239	0.148	−0.161	−1.612	0.108	0.381	2.625
R	0.450		R-square			0.203	
Adjusted R-square	0.172		F(sig.)			6.634 (0.000)	

Dependent variable: Log R&D intensity
Variables in Bold are significant at 5% level of significance

of independent directors in board and their participation in board meetings are important determinants of R&D investment, as shown by their significance at 1% level. Also the participation of independent directors in board meetings for the purpose of making decisions on R&D expenses is more important as shown by the values of standardized coefficients of beta, rather than just being part of board of directors.

Hypothesis 1, of the study, which assumed significant relationship between board size and R&D investment, is not supported; moreover, the negative beta value shows that the average R&D investment goes down by 2.7% for every additional director in board, *ceteris paribus;* thus, smaller board size is better. Hypothesis 2, which assumed a positive relationship between board independence and R&D investment, is accepted as beta value is positive and statistically significant. The average R&D investment of firm with every additional independent director increases by 272.1%, other variables being constant. Hypotheses 3, which assumed a positive relationship of separate positions of CEO and chairman with R&D investment, is not accepted. The average R&D investment is lower in firms where position of CEO and chairman rests with different individuals by 44.5% as compared to firms having duality. Hypothesis 4, which assumed a positive relationship between participation of directors in board meetings and R&D investment, is not accepted, but Hypothesis 5 stating that there exists positive relationship of participation of independent directors in board meetings with R&D investment is highly significant and accepted at 1% significance level. The coefficient of 0.301 for participation of independent directors in meetings means that there is significant increase in average R&D investment by 30.1% for every additional increase in the participation rate of independent directors in board meetings, holding all other variables constant. Hypothesis 6, which assumed a positive relationship between busyness of independent directors with R&D investment is insignificant. Hypothesis 7 assumed a negative relationship between leverage and firm's R&D investment is accepted, whereas Hypothesis 9 assuming relationship between age and R&D investment is not accepted.

5.4 Conclusion

The presence of independent directors plays pivotal role in enhancing the long-term investments in the company through R&D, thereby building competitive advantage of the firm. The time devoted in meetings to make decisions is required where active involvement of independent directors is crucial, and they can oversee the process of board decision-making and ask questions wherever diversion is seen in the interest of board and stakeholders at large. The evaluation of director's performance as whether they monitor the decisions of management, attend regular meetings and ask frequent questions for protection of shareholder's rights is important for a strong governance system.

The role and responsibility of the independent directors should be strengthened to improve decisions. The guidelines should be framed to make it mandatory for directors, especially independent directors, to attend board meetings regularly and participate in all the discussions with thorough preparations; it will maintain check on the management practices. This will generate a sense of responsibility among the directors as well as management in the company, building high professional standards due to peer pressure. The corporate governance norms should be continually evaluated by the regulators to enforce stringent regulations for its implementation in totality, to ensure compliance with good practices by the Indian companies for sustainable performance.

References

Abidin, Z. Z., Kamal, N. M., & Jusoff, K. (2009). Board structure and corporate performance in Malaysia. *International Journal of Economics and Finance, 1*(1), 150.

Aghion, P., Van Reenen, J., & Zingales, L. (2009). Innovation and institutional ownership, In: CEPR Discussion Paper No. DP7195.

Alhazaimeh, A., Palaniappan, R., & Almsafir, M. (2014). The impact of corporate governance and ownership structure on voluntary disclosure in annual reports among listed Jordanian companies. *Procedia-Social and Behavioral Sciences, 129,* 341–348.

Alladi, A., Pillutla, R.S., & Divi, S. (2015). Stakeholder engagement methodology in the context of innovation management. In Sushil, K. T. Bhal, & S. P. Singh (Eds.), *Managing flexibility: People, process, technology and business* (pp. 223–238). New Delhi: Flexible Systems Management, Springer.

Al-Manaseer, M. F. A., Al-Hindawi, R. M., Al-Dahiyat, M. A., & Sartawi, I. I. (2012). The impact of corporate governance on the performance of Jordanian Banks. *European Journal of Scientific Research, 67*(3), 349–359.

Alshimmiri, T. (2004). Board composition, executive remuneration and corporate performance: The case of REITS. *Corporate Ownership and Control, 2*(1), 104–118.

Atanassov, J. (2013). Corporate governance, non-financial stakeholders, and innovation: Evidence from a natural experiment (June 30, 2013).

Bargeron, L. L., Lehn, K. M., & Zutter, C. J. (2010). Sarbanes-Oxley and corporate risk-taking. *Journal of Accounting and Economics, 49*(1), 34–52.

Baysinger, B. D., Kosnik, R. D., & Turk, T. A. (1991). Effects of board and ownership structure on corporate R&D strategy. *Academy of Management Journal, 34*(1), 205–214.

Becker-Blease, J. (2011). Governance and innovation. *Journal of Corporate Finance, 17*(4), 947–958.

Ben, P. J., & Dwivedi, N. (2013). The role of corporate governance: A hurdle or steroid in the commercialization of innovations? *Indian Journal of Corporate Governance, 6*(1), 18–31.

Bhat, J. S. A. (2010). Managing innovation: Understanding how continuity and change are interlinked. *Global Journal of Flexible Systems Management, 11*(1&2), 63–74.

Bhat, J. S. A., Sushil, & Jain, P. K. (2011). Innovation by harmonizing continuity and change. *Journal of Business Strategy (Emerald), 32*(2), 38–49.

Castro, C. B., La Concha, D., Dominguez, M., Gravel, J. V., & Periñan, M. M. V. (2009). Does the team leverage the board's decisions? *Corporate Governance: An International Review, 17*(6), 744–761.

Chang, C. S., Yu, S. W., & Hung, C. H. (2015). Firm risk and performance: The role of corporate governance. *Review of Managerial Science, 9*(1), 141–173.

Chen, H. L., & Hsu, W. T. (2009). Family ownership, board independence, and R&D investment. *Family Business Review, 22*(4), 347–362.

Chung, K. H., Wright, P., & Kedia, B. (2003). Corporate governance and market valuation of capital and R&D investments. *Review of Financial Economics, 12*(2), 161–172.

Cohen, D., Deys, A., & Lys, T. (2009). The Sarbanes–Oxley Act of 2002: Implications for compensation contracts and managerial risk-taking. In: Working Paper Available at SSRN 1027448.

De Andres, P., Azofra, V., & Lopez, F. (2005). Corporate boards in OECD countries: Size, composition, functioning and effectiveness. *Corporate Governance: An International Review, 13*(2), 197–210.

Dhir, S., & Dhir, S. (2017a). Adoption of open-source software versus proprietary software: An exploratory study. *Strategic Change, 26*(4), 363–371.

Dhir, S., & Dhir, S. (2017b). COMFED: The new challenges of diversification. *Emerald Emerging Markets Case Studies.* https://doi.org/10.1108/EEMCS-09-2016-0188.

Dhir, S., Mital, A., & Chaurasia, S. (2014). Balanced scorecard on top performing Indian firms. *International Journal of Indian Culture and Business Management, 9*(1), 89–100.

Driver, C., & Guedes, M. J. C. (2012). Research and development, cash flow, agency and governance: UK large companies. *Research Policy, 41*(9), 1565–1577.

Dwivedi, N., & Jain, A. K. (2005). Corporate governance and performance of Indian firms: The effect of board size and ownership. *Employee Responsibilities and Rights Journal, 17*(3), 161–172.

Faleye, O., Hoitash, R., & Hoitash, U. (2011). The costs of intense board monitoring. *Journal of Financial Economics, 101*(1), 160–181.

Fich, E. M., & Shivdasani, A. (2004). Are busy boards effective monitors? In ECGI-Finance Working Paper, (55).

Galasso, A., & Simcoe, T. S. (2011). CEO overconfidence and innovation. *Management Science, 57*(8), 1469–1484.

Garg, A. K. (2007). Influence of board size and independence on firm performance: A study of Indian companies. *Vikalpa, 32*(3), 39–60.

Ghosh, S. (2006). Do board characteristics affect corporate performance? Firm-level evidence for India. *Applied Economics Letters, 13*(7), 435–443.

Goodstein, J., Gautam, K., & Boeker, W. (1994). The effects of board size and diversity on strategic change. *Strategic Management Journal, 15*(3), 241–250.

Griffith, R., Redding, S., & Van Reenen, J. (2004). Mapping the two faces of R&D: Productivity growth in a panel of OECD industries. *Review of Economics and Statistics, 86*(4), 883–895.

Griliches, Z. (1990). Patent Statistics as Economic Indicators: A Survey (No. w3301). National Bureau of Economic Research.

Gugnani, R. (2013). Corporate governance and financial performance of Indian firms.

Hill, C. W., & Snell, S. A. (1988). External control, corporate strategy, and firm performance in research-intensive industries. *Strategic Management Journal, 9*(6), 577–590.

Hirshleifer, D., Low, A., & Teoh, S. H. (2012). Are overconfident CEOs better innovators? *Journal of Finance, 67*(4), 1457–1498.

Hoskisson, R. E., Hitt, M. A., Johnson, R. A., & Grossman, W. (2002). Conflicting voices, the effects of institutional ownership heterogeneity and internal governance on corporate innovation strategies. *Academy of Management Journal, 45*(4), 697–716.

Hung, H., & Mondejar, R. (2005). Corporate directors and entrepreneurial innovation an empirical study. *Journal of Entrepreneurship, 14*(2), 117–129.

Jackling, B., & Johl, S. (2009). Board structure and firm performance: Evidence from India's top companies. *Corporate Governance: An International Review, 17*(4), 492–509.

Jensen, M. C. (1993). The modern industrial revolution, exit, and the failure of internal control systems. *The Journal of Finance, 48*(3), 831–880.

Jiraporn, P., Davidson, W. N., DaDalt, P., & Ning, Y. (2009). Too busy to show up? An analysis of directors' absences. *The Quarterly Review of Economics and Finance, 49*(3), 1159–1171.

Kaur, P., & Gill, S. (2008). The effects of ownership structure on corporate governance and performance: An empirical assessment in India, Research Project, NFCG 2007–2008, available at www.nfcgindia.org/pdf/UBS.pdf. Retrieved on March 11, 2011.

Kim, B., Burns, M. L., & Prescott, J. E. (2009). The strategic role of the board: The impact of board structure on top management team strategic action capability. *Corporate Governance: An International Review, 17*(6), 728–743.

Kor, Y. Y. (2006). Direct and interaction effects of top management team and board compositions on R&D investment strategy. *Strategic Management Journal, 27*(11), 1081–1099.

Kota, H. B., & Tomar, S. (2010). Corporate governance practices in Indian firms. *Journal of Management & Organization, 16*(2), 266–279.

Kyereboah-Coleman, A., & Biekpe, N. (2007). On the determinants of board size and its composition: Additional evidence from Ghana. *Journal of Accounting & Organizational Change, 3*(1), 68–77.

Lacetera, N. (2001). Corporate governance and the governance of innovation: The case of pharmaceutical industry. *Journal of Management and Governance, 5*(1), 29–59.

Lee, P. M., & O'neill, H. M. (2003). Ownership structures and R&D investments of US and Japanese firms: Agency and stewardship perspectives. *Academy of Management Journal, 46*(2), 212–225.

Lipton, M., & Lorsch, J. W. (1992). A modest proposal for improved corporate governance. *The Business Lawyer, 48*(1), 59–77.

Munari, F., Oriani, R., & Sobrero, M. (2010). The effects of owner identity and external governance systems on R&D investments: A study of Western European firms. *Research Policy, 39*(8), 1093–1105.

O'Brien, J. P. (2003). The capital structure implications of pursuing a strategy of innovation. *Strategic Management Journal, 24*(5), 415–431.

Parameswar, N., Dhir, S., & Dhir, S. (2017). Banking on innovation, innovation in banking at ICICI bank. *Global Business and Organizational Excellence, 36*(2), 6–16.

Pearce, J. A., & Zahra, S. A. (1992). Board Composition from a strategic contingency perspective. *Journal of Management Studies, 29*(4), 411–438.

Rabi, N. M., Zulkafli, A. H., & Haat, M. H. C. (2010). Corporate governance, innovation investment and firm performance: Evidence from Malaysian public listed companies. *Economia. Seria Management, 13*(2), 225–239.

Shapiro, D., Tang, Y., Wang, M., & Zhang, W. (2015). The effects of corporate governance and ownership on the innovation performance of Chinese SMEs. *Journal of Chinese Economic and Business Studies, 13*(4), 311–335.

Van den Berghe, L. A., & Levrau, A. (2004). Evaluating boards of directors: What constitutes a good corporate board? *Corporate Governance: An International Review, 12*(4), 461–478.

Varshney, P., Kaul, V. K., & Vasal, V. K. (2012). Corporate governance index and firm performance: Empirical evidence from India (July 11, 2012).Available at SSRN: https://ssrn.com/abstract=2103462 or http://dx.doi.org/10.2139/ssrn.2103462.

World Bank. (2007). Unleashing India's innovation: Towards sustainable and inclusive growth. Washington, D.C.: World Bank.

World Economic Forum. (2008). Global Competitiveness Report 2008–09, Geneva.

Wright, P., Kroll, M., & Elenkov, D. (2002). Acquisition returns, increase in firm size, and chief executive officer compensation: The moderating role of monitoring. *Academic Management Journal, 45*(2), 599–608.

Yermack, D. (1996). Higher market valuation of companies with a small board of directors. *Journal of Financial Economics, 40*(2), 185–211.

Zahra, S. A. (1996). Governance, ownership, and corporate entrepreneurship: The moderating impact of industry technological opportunities. *Academy of Management Journal, 39*(6), 1713–1735.

Zona, F. (2016). Agency models in different stages of CEO tenure: The effects of stock options and board independence on R&D investment. *Research Policy, 45*(2), 560–575.

Part II
People and Processes in VUCA Markets

Chapter 6
Disability Inclusion

Sonali Heera and Arti Maini

Abstract In recent times, research on workforce diversity is gaining momentum in the organizational circles. However, inclusion of people with disabilities as 'diverse workforce' has received less attention than other categories of diversity such as gender or race. The purpose of this chapter is to investigate the factors influencing inclusion of people with disabilities at workplace. Using 31 semi-structured interviews of people with disabilities, various factors that facilitate their successful inclusion at workplace were found. Data was analysed thematically, and four themes were identified. Key factors that were identified are 'inclusive pathways in terms of organizational culture' that encourage participation of people with disabilities, need for due 'accommodation', adequate 'job fit' and the vital role of other 'stakeholders'. The insights gained from this chapter hold importance for several stakeholders for designing and implementing strategies, interventions and policies to facilitate effective inclusion of under-represented diverse workforce that is 'people with disabilities'.

Keywords Diversity · Inclusion · Organization · People with disabilities Workforce

6.1 Introduction

Workforce diversity is gaining recognition as a core management concept. The growing literature demonstrates that diverse individuals are productive source of organizational value creation (Kulkarni et al. 2016), who bring compendium of competencies and skills that are difficult to imitate. The term 'workforce diversity'

S. Heera (✉) · A. Maini
School of Business, Shri Mata Vaishno Devi University, Kakryal,
Jammu and Kashmir, India
e-mail: b.sonali24@gmail.com

A. Maini
e-mail: arti.maini@smvdu.ac.in

recognizes that individuals differ on account of several ways, such as age, gender, ethnicity, sexual orientation, religion and disability (Kossek et al. 2005). Recent research provides evidence on inclusion of diverse workforce with a large focus on gender (Shen et al. 2009) and race (Joshi and Roh 2007). However, people with disabilities, one of the highest demographic minorities, continue to be under-represented in organizations (Kulkarni and Rodrigues 2014).

The present chapter outlines organizational factors that influence inclusion of people with disabilities. More specifically, this chapter focuses on in-depth interviews of 31 employees with disabilities across the State of Jammu and Kashmir in India, which has disability rate higher than that of national average (Census 2011). This chapter contributes to the existing literature on disability inclusion in the following ways. Firstly, previous research is centred on ascertaining employers' perspective towards hiring people with disabilities (Zissi et al. 2007) with little focus on perspective of employees' with disabilities on their inclusion. Secondly, this chapter aims to address the call on field research in disability literature as majority of the previous studies are laboratory based (Colella 1996). Thirdly, research on workforce diversity has mainly focused on Western context (Cooke and Saini 2012). As a leading emerging market, India is also facing increasing diversity and inclusion issues (Cooke and Saini 2012; Kulkarni et al. 2016; Dhir et al. 2014). Till date, to our knowledge there are limited studies on disability and inclusion in Indian context (Kulkarni et al. 2016). Finally, the chapter also contributes to the literature on diversity and inclusion by noting how employees with disabilities experience inclusion, a topic having implications for both employers and human resource practitioners. Thus, the focus of this chapter is on identification of factors that facilitate organizational inclusion of people with disabilities.

6.2 Literature Review

Diversity management found its origin as a human resource intervention due to demographic change (Barak 2005) and due to an urge to add business value through equal opportunity management (Dhir and Dhir 2015). Theoretical work on disability, as component of diversity, may have increased after passage of laws which protect people with disabilities against discrimination, but research evidence on 'disability inclusion' is somewhat sparse (Shore et al. 2009). Despite several interventions, aiming at employment integration of people with disabilities, they continue to be overlooked and underutilized in the global economy (Lengnick-Hall et al. 2008). Literature suggests that on attaining employment, many employees with disabilities do not reach their potential or feel included (Kulkarni and Rodrigues 2014) in organizations. This points out to the incongruity between what people with disabilities need for effective integration at workplace and what is offered to them in the organizations.

6.2.1 Inclusion of People with Disabilities

Disability is defined as 'an impairment caused by some bodily functioning' (Confederation of Indian Industry 2009). Globally, there are over one billion people with disabilities of which majority (80%) live in developing countries (WHO 2011). Specifically, there are over 21 million people with disabilities in India (Census 2011) and only 34% are employed. To include this underutilized talent pool, the Government of India has undertaken several steps such as reservation of 3% in vacancies in identified posts within government organizations, including several public sector organizations, and incentives for private sector organizations to encourage hiring of people with disabilities. Despite these initiatives, the organizations in India do not have an understanding of the utilization of people with disabilities and the terms of their inclusion in employment (Confederation of Indian Industry 2009). Therefore, it becomes imperative to understand how people with disabilities experience inclusion on entry in the labour market.

Inclusion, from an individual's perspective, focuses on perceptions and feelings of acceptance amongst diverse workforce. Inclusion has been defined as the 'degree to which an employee is accepted and treated as an insider by others in a work system' (Pelled et al. 1999). Kulkarni and Rodrigues (2014) studied how do top 100 organizations in India communicate their engagement with disability through the annual reports. They found that public sector organizations hire people with disabilities out of institutional pressure (Robert and Harlan 2006) and private sector organizations preferred engaging with disability issues in the form of corporate social responsibility (CSR) activities. A comparative study on India and China explored the initiatives undertaken by multinational organizations to increase workplace inclusion of people with disabilities (Kulkarni et al. 2016). It was found that employers included people with disabilities for harnessing diversity and multistakeholder engagement, including top management, employee groups and other non-governmental organizations. Therefore, previous studies in India, though limited in number, have focused on employers' perspective towards people with disabilities in multinational organizations, yet the studies on employees' perspective on inclusion and influences remain unexplored. Hence, this chapter has been framed to identify the factors that facilitate organizational inclusion of people with disabilities.

6.3 Methodology

This chapter utilizes qualitative research to assess the inclusion experience of people with disabilities. Semi-structured interviews of people with disabilities were conducted to collect the data. Purposive and convenience sampling was used to select respondents that allowed adequate representation and in-depth focus. The data was collected until saturation was reached in responses (Miles and Huberman 1994).

The final sample consisted of 31 respondents of which 19 respondents were males and 12 respondents were females. These respondents from 22 organizations had full-time working experience across six industries. Specifically, seven respondents were from education sector, six respondents were from hospitality sector, five respondents were from health sector, five respondents were from manufacturing, four respondents were from telecommunications, and two respondents were from wholesale trade. Thirty of those interviewed had held more than one job, and there was only one respondent who did not have any previous experience of work. Seventeen respondents were in the age range of 21–40 years, and 14 respondents were of 41–60 years of age. Fifteen respondents were presently employed in public sector, and 16 respondents were employed in private sector. Seventeen respondents had locomotor disability, 12 respondents had visual impairment, and two respondents suffered from intellectual disability.

6.3.1 Data Analysis

Thematic analysis was undertaken on the transcribed data (Strauss and Corbin 1998). The interview transcripts were read and independently coded by both the researchers. Line-by-line coding was done and discussed amongst researchers several times to identify emerging concepts. These concepts were not preconceived or restricted and were identified as they emerged from the existing data. These concepts eventually led to categorization of themes. The thematic analysis was done using spreadsheet taking into consideration the small qualitative data set (Kulkarni 2013).

6.4 Analysis and Results

Respondents, participating in this study, identified several factors (refer Table 6.1) that facilitated their inclusion in their respective workplaces. The findings demonstrate their inclusion experience through data excerpts on organizational factors.

6.4.1 Organizational Culture

Findings indicated that top management commitment plays an integral role in building organizational culture that recognizes diversity and facilitates disability inclusion by entrusting resources to it. Majority of the respondents explained the importance of top management commitment for ensuring a work environment of acceptance and respect for people with disabilities. This complements the prior research where the human resource practitioners lay emphasis on top management

Table 6.1 Organizational factors influencing inclusion of people with disabilities

Theme	Sub-themes	N	Description
Organizational culture	Top management attitude	25	– Positive employer attitude and commitment towards inclusion
	Fair treatment	17	– Equality and non-discrimination in terms of recruitment and benefits
	Policies and practices	15	– Designed formal policies for recruitment and development
	Values and ethos	08	– Acceptance of diversity- and disability-friendly language
Accommodation	Workplace accessibility	22	– Transport and location of workstation and basic amenities
	Built-in environment	12	– Ergonomic design of the organization
	Assistive technologies	04	– Adjustments or investing in equipment or software
	Flexible work schedules	04	– Work timings and leave
Support network	Role of co-worker	19	– Help in job tasks and socialization
	Role of supervisor	15	– Formal and informal support; tolerance and caring
	Human resource and personnel	03	– Guidance and handling concerns
Job fit	Matching skills	15	– Focus on their capability over disability and provide job
	Training and career development	08	– Training for further career development
	Flexibility in job	02	– Allowing for job change after entry or training

commitment for communication of inclusive work environment (Kulkarni et al. 2016). In line, one respondent quoted, *'You know… if the people at the top do not believe in us then the message of non-acceptance flows from business head to the manager… to supervisor… to peon. We will never feel like we belong here… always out of place. Always different… always at mercy'*.

Respondents perceived employers' attitude as one of the most important factors for belonging to an organization. One respondent when referring to positive employer attitude stated that *'[Employer] Sir treats me like I am no different from [Co-worker] which makes me feel good in contrast to my previous organization where I was often given the "other" treatment… you know like I was a burden or something'*.

Organizational practices also have outcomes or consequences for people with disabilities. Another respondent illustrated evidence of this by stating, *'[Organization] has written policies for hiring people with disabilities and another one for non-discrimination… so the acceptance for people like us is high here as compared to other organizations where we, disabled face barrier in gaining entry in organizations, let alone inclusion'*.

6.4.2 Accommodation

The interview excerpts indicate that accommodation, in terms of workplace accessibility, built-in environment, assistive technologies and flexible work schedules, has emerged as a critical factor. Some of the respondents have shared instances when they could not take up certain employment or even had to quit a job because of lack of accommodation in their organization. There are several positive instances that have resulted in their successful workplace inclusion. For example, one respondent with a physical impairment quoted, *'Because of my limitation, I cannot climb stairs. My manager ensured that my work station is on the ground floor also I can access the washrooms easily'*.

Also, accommodation needs vary according to type of disability, and 'one-size-fits-all' approach cannot be applied across different disability types. While people with physical or mobility impairments prefer open workspaces but the same may pose problems for people with visual impairments. A respondent with a visual impairment relied on the technical assistance [software] in the bank to perform his job. The respondent said, *'Honestly, I feel lucky that [organization] has taken the initiative of not just hiring but also accommodating people with visual impairment…'*.

Respondents with severe mobility impairments advocated flexible work schedules which included the facility of working part-time when needed, reduced hours of work, leave benefits.

6.4.3 Support Network

The importance of 'support' from the supervisors, co-workers or human resource officials cannot be neglected for inclusive work environment. Reflecting from their personal accounts, people with disabilities sought support, for specific work tasks, accessing workplace facilities, accommodation and socialization activities. For example, respondents quoted, *'I was scared to even try going to social events thinking people would make fun of me. But my team members encouraged me to go with them and gradually that fear disappeared. Now, I feel like… I am one of them'*.

[Co-worker] often helps in getting signature on the file [work] knowing my mobility limitation. He never says no. He might say 'I will get It done later but never refuses'.

For some of the respondents, the quality of relationship with their immediate supervisor was instrumental in feeling inclusion at workplace. One respondent quoted, *'When I work harder than the others and the supervisor appreciates the effort I have put in by sharing It as a success story… I feel proud, respected and an equal member in the organization'*. Employees working in organizations with dedicated human resource function appeared to feel that they had someone they could easily approach in case of any problem. One respondent recounted, '*... Initially, I felt so lost here, then I spoke to the HR Manager and I realized she is someone I can approach in case of any problem, big or small'*.

6.4.4 Job Fit

While people with disabilities share an equal desire for job as people without disabilities, but they are more hesitant in looking for a job due to fear of not finding a suitable job (Ali et al. 2011). This is reflective of the recognition that job expectations vary depending on the employee skill set, education and training. Some of the respondents expressed satisfaction due to organizational efforts on matching their skills with that of jobs available. One respondent stated, '*I was hired under quota and given a job, I did not specialize in. I have expertise in teaching Urdu language but my job required me to teach science and math to primary school students. I was glad I had a government job but later when there was a vacancy there. My senior official addressed the formal request and I started teaching Urdu which I enjoy the most'*. This indicates that employees were allowed to switch their jobs after recruitment and the available talent was utilized effectively. Respondents who developed disability during employment preferred flexibility in their jobs. A respondent with a muscular-skeletal impairment quoted, '*I developed disability on the job 4 years ago but the organization ensured that I did not quit my job because of my disability. I was given a sitting job of database management in place of my old job of floor supervisor'*.

Participation in training programs or equal promotional opportunities appeared critical to many respondents for developing a sense of belongingness and inclusion in organization. A respondent cited a specific example: '*... there was a workshop on culinary skills in [place] and only two respondents were allowed from each organization. I was sure I would not be considered due to my disability but the moment Mr. [Manager] said... [Respondent's Name]... I think you should go... That is the best appreciation I could have received'*.

Overall, organizational factors, which influence disability inclusion, comprise of specific variables such as top management support in formulation and implementation of inclusive policies, inclusive culture reflective of acceptance and harnessing diversity, accommodation adjustments in the form of workplace accessibility, support network and adequate job matching.

6.5 Conclusion

The purpose of this chapter was to explore the organization-specific factors that influence the inclusion of people with disabilities at workplace. The literature suggests that long-term consequences of disability inclusion can eventually lead to business success (Kulkarni et al. 2016). Thus, understanding the organizational factors that enhance disability inclusion is critical for designing successful interventions and strategies for their effective integration. Bamel et al. (2018) also stated that creation of an organizational climate, that harnesses diverse workforce, can avail the various benefits attached to diversity. Most notably, this chapter confirms the integral role of top management for disability inclusion. Additionally, accommodation, support, also facilitates inclusion. Other theme that emerged from the chapter was the need for ensuring job matching for disability inclusion. Based on these themes, possible policy-, organizational- and individual-level strategies, for inclusion of people with disabilities, have been presented in Table 6.2.

The limitations of the chapter must be noted while interpreting the findings. First, the sample did not include those with hearing or speech impairment owing to researchers' limited communication ability in their language. Further, the focus was only on organization-specific factors that help in experiencing inclusion, overlooking other individual-related dimensions. Also, in future, researchers may collect quantitative data to empirically test the factors of disability inclusion. This chapter has implications for India considering the high disability rate of 2.1% and higher disability incidence of 2.87% in the State of Jammu and Kashmir (Census 2011). These findings offer opportunities to researchers, policy makers and management practitioners to reflect on the organizational factors that influence individual's inclusion experiences. Therefore, factors such as disability inclusive culture, support from organizational members, adequate accommodation and job fit influence the inclusion of people with disabilities at workplace.

Table 6.2 Possible strategies to improve inclusion of people with disabilities in organizations

Policy-Level Strategies
1. Develop partnerships with organizations that help in recruitment of people with disabilities (PWD)
2. Encourage positive societal attitudes towards PWD
3. Develop strict legal regulations in place of existing guidelines
Organization-Level Strategies
4. Develop specific policies that include PWD for hiring and development
5. Disability awareness training or sensitization programs
Individual-Level Strategies
6. Disability Champions who advocate for PWD
7. Encourage PWD to participate right from education to employment

References

Ali, M., Schur, L., & Blanck, M. (2011). What type of jobs do people with disabilities want? *Journal of Occupational Rehabilitation, 21*(2), 199–210.

Bamel, U. K., Paul, H., & Bamel, N. (2018) Managing workplace diversity through organizational climate. In T. P. S. Sushil et al. (Eds.), *Flexibility in resource management. Flexible systems management* (pp. 87–97). Singapore: Springer. https://doi.org/10.1007/978-981-10-4888-3_6.

Barak, M. M. (2005). *Managing diversity: Towards a globally inclusive workplace*. Thousand Oaks, CA: Sage.

Census of India. (2011). http://censusindia.gov.in/pca/searchdata.aspx. Retrieved on the 1st of February, 2016.

Confederation of Indian Industry. (2009). *A values route to business success: The why and how of employing persons with disability*. Bangalore: Diversity and Equal Opportunity Center.

Colella, A. (1996). Organizational socialization of employees with disabilities: Theory and research. In G. R. Ferris (Ed.), *Research in personnel and human resources management* (pp. 351–417). Greenwich, CT: JAI Press.

Cooke, F. L., & Saini, D. S. (2012). Managing diversity in Chinese and Indian organizations: A qualitative study. *Journal of Chinese Human Resources Management, 3*(1), 16–32.

Dhir, S., & Dhir, S. (2015). Diversification: Literature review and issues. *Strategic Change, 24*(6), 569–588.

Dhir, S., Mital, A., & Chaurasia, S. (2014). Balanced scorecard on top performing Indian firms. *International Journal of Indian Culture and Business Management, 9*(1), 89–100.

Joshi, A., & Roh, H. (2007). Context matters: A multilevel framework for work team diversity research. In J. Martocchio (Ed.), *Research in personnel and human resource management* (Vol. 26, pp. 1–48). Greenwich, CT: JAI Press.

Kossek, E. E., Lobel, S. A., & Brown, A. J. (2005). Human resource strategies to manage workforce diversity. In A. M. Konrad, P. Prasad, & J. M. Pringle (Eds.), *Handbook of workplace diversity* (pp. 54–74). Thousand Oaks, CA: Sage.

Kulkarni, M. (2013). Help-seeking behaviors of people with disabilities in the workplace. *Employee Responsibilities and Rights Journal, 25*(1), 41–57.

Kulkarni, M., Boehm, S. A., & Basu, S. (2016). Workplace inclusion of persons with a disability. *Equality, Diversity and Inclusion: An International Journal, 35*(7/8), 397–414.

Kulkarni, M., & Rodrigues, C. (2014). Engagement with disability: Analysis of annual reports of Indian organizations. *The International Journal of Human Resource Management, 25*(11), 1547–1566.

Lengnick-Hall, M. L., Gaunt, P. M., & Kulkarni, M. (2008). Overlooked and underutilized: People with disabilities are an untapped human resource. *Human Resource Management, 47,* 255–273.

Miles, M. B., & Huberman, A. M. (1994). *Qualitative data analysis*. Thousand Oaks: Sage.

Pelled, L. H., Ledford, G. E., & Mohrman, S. A. (1999). Demographic dissimilarity and workplace inclusion. *Journal of Management Studies, 36*(7), 1013–1031.

Robert, P. M., & Harlan, S. L. (2006). Mechanisms of disability discrimination in large bureaucratic organizations: Ascriptive inequalities in the workplace. *The Sociological Quarterly, 47*(4), 599–630.

Shen, J., Chanda, A., D'Netto, B., & Monga, M. (2009). Managing diversity through human resource management: An international perspective and conceptual framework. *The International Journal of Human Resource Management, 20*(2), 235–251.

Shore, L. M., Chung-Herrera, B. G., Dean, M. A., Ehrhart, K. H., Jung, D. I., Randel, A. E., et al. (2009). Diversity in organizations: Where are we now and where are we going? *Human Resource Management Review, 19*(2), 117–133.

Strauss, A., & Corbin, J. (1998) *Basics of qualitative research: Techniques and procedures for developing grounded theory* (2nd ed.). Thousand Oaks, CA: Sage.

World Health Organization (WHO). (2011). *World report on disability: Summary*. WHO/NMH/VIP/11.01. Retrieved from http://www.who.int/disabilities/world_report/2011/report.pdf, on the 1st of April, 2016.

Zissi, A., Rontos, C., Papageorgiou, D., & Pierrakou, C. (2007). Greek employers' attitudes to employing people with disabilities: Effects of the type of disability. *Scandinavian Journal of Disability Research*, 9(1), 14–25.

Chapter 7
Effective Policing in a VUCA Environment: Lessons from a Dark Network

Dhruv Gupta and Vishal Gupta

Abstract In a Volatile, Uncertain, Complex and Ambiguous (VUCA) environment, the dark networks are able to defy the much stronger police forces by successfully addressing these environmental risks, and instead creating these risks for police forces. Using the extended case study method, this study identifies effective counter-strategies by confronting an empirical case of CPI (Maoists), one of India's oldest and most successful dark networks. This study also identifies the organizational changes that need to be adopted by the police forces if they have to defeat the dark networks. We highlight that a direct confrontation is not an efficient answer. Rather, the solution lies in attacking each of the strengths of CPI (Maoists) individually, in an orderly fashion. This case study also provides rich insights into the organizational design and peoples' practices adopted by CPI (Maoists) that minimizes the impact of the VUCA environmental risks and adds to the literature on civil wars and criminal organizations.

Keywords Dark network · Internal security · Organizational design Policing · VUCA

7.1 Introduction

Since the September 2001 terrorist attacks in USA, the developed countries have started fighting the 'dark networks' (a figurative expression used by Milward and Raab 2006, to denote covert and illegal organizations like the terrorist, insurgent and criminal organizations) operating from various developing countries, either

---

D. Gupta (✉)
Police Headquarters, New Raipur, Chhattisgarh, India
e-mail: dhruvgupta0@gmail.com

V. Gupta
Organizational Behaviour Area, Indian Institute of Management,
Ahmedabad, Gujarat, India
e-mail: vishal@iima.ac.in

individually or through military alliances, with the domestic government as a de facto military ally (Gupta and Sriram 2018). However, the success rates of even the strongest militaries are not very encouraging despite having vastly more resources and global sanctions against the terrorists' resources (Freeman 2013; Holmes 2014; Stewart 2014). One popular reason advanced in the media for such a dismal performance is that these security forces (in this paper we concentrate in the police forces only) are working in foreign lands amidst climatic, anthropogenic and information-related disadvantages *vis-a-vis* these dark networks. This puts them at serious disadvantage compared to these dark networks (Sageman 2008).

On the other hand, it is these dark networks that function in a much more hostile environment due to the ever-lurking fear of police action. They thrive by adjusting their organizational structure to the risks posed by the police action. However, the relationship between such environmental risks and organizational structures have not been studied holistically (Bakker et al. 2012; Sushil 2014; Srivastava 2016; Dhir et al. 2016) by the researchers, so far. In this paper, we present a holistic view using the framework of volatility (a dynamically changing social context), uncertainty (missing information), complexity (multiple potentially relevant dimensions) and ambiguity (multiple possible interpretations of available information) risks found in the work environment, popularly known as VUCA risks. Notably, the term VUCA was coined in the 1990s by the US army as it was gearing for the possible asymmetric wars of the next century (Whiteman 1998). They came to acknowledge the possible environmental risks of VUCA that their army may face in future and were drawing plans to thrive in it.

Further, we understand that the dark networks establish a balance between their environment and strengths by addressing the most risky VUCA element first, down to the least risky one. This strategy minimizes the whole effort as certain components facilitate the adoption of solutions to other risks. Besides, as a part of strategy, it is also involved in 'VUCAisation' of the environment (for want of a better term), which increases the VUCA risks for the police forces. For instance, Gupta (2011) highlighted that in the war against terror, wasting the government resources added to own efficiency and demoralization of the police forces by VUCAizing the environment. Yet, there is still a lack of clarity about how exactly a dark network operates, which makes it so successful and resilient, and what lessons are there to be learnt for modern-day management of police forces that work directly against them.

The police organizations being complex, change management needs to take care of two aspects: (1) the changes in the policing environment need to be carefully incorporated to prevent wasteful expenditures that may upset the balance between the resources and the duties expected from the police forces; (2) as every other organization, police departments also have multiple departments that face the VUCA risks in varying proportions and interdepartmental coordination needs to be incorporated in any attempt at organizational redesign (Roberts and Stockport 2009). Therefore, a (holistic) systems approach that incorporates the interconnectedness and dynamicity of the VUCA environment is pertinent for any meaningful redesign of police organization.

On the other hand, though the literature continuously talks of changes in the police organizations, a holistic view of the issue is rarely presented (Ransley and Mazerolle 2009). Consequently, many recommendations are not adopted and efforts are wasted apart from building mistrust between the police officers and the academicians (Rosenbaum 2010). To bridge this gap, we undertake a detailed extended case study of one dark network and add to the literature on 'dark networks' and organizational redesign of police in multiple ways. First, by describing the relationship of a 'dark network' with its environment, this holistic analysis helps to better understand what a dark network does to minimize the impact of VUCA elements within its environment, while simultaneously 'VUCAising' environment for the police forces. Second, this study provides certain clear and precise suggestions to the police forces about how to plan their possible counter-insurgency operations by focusing on the environmental risks presented in the form of high volatility, complexity, uncertainty and ambiguity, by studying the dark networks. Therefore, instead of merely increasing the resources allocated to fighting them, the police forces must instead focus on reducing the environmental risks they face in fighting the dark networks. In effect, in some areas, the ground strategies adopted by the police force may be dramatically different from those adopted by dark networks.

Towards this end, we present a detailed analysis of one dark network called, Communist Party of India (Maoists) [CPI Maoists]. CPI (Maoists) is particularly well suited for this kind of a study because it is the most lethal Naxalite (insurgency) organization in India (and today, the word Naxalites has become synonymous with cadres of CPI (Maoists); and has been thriving (and expanding) since 1967, despite action by police forces. It has caused nearly 45% of all the Naxalite-related deaths since its inception in 2004 (Ministry of Home Affairs, Government of India 2011) and has been called as the 'single largest internal security threat' to the country (PTI 2010). Today, CPI (Maoists) is either covertly or overtly present in more than twenty states of the country, and despite the allocation of more than 100 Central Armed Police Forces (CAPFs) battalions (approximately 102 thousand policemen) and states' police forces, there is no sign of an end to the insurgency (Sharma 2014) and the organization is showing immense resilience.

In summary, the research questions (RQs) for this study can be stated as follows:

RQ1: To identify the organizational changes made by the CPI (Maoists) in their organization that makes them resilient to action by police forces in a VUCA environment.

RQ2: To identify the factors used by the CPI (Maoists) for increasing 'VUCAisation' of the environment for the police forces.

RQ3: To identify the organizational and tactical changes that the police forces can learn from the CPI (Maoists) to minimize the impact of VUCA elements in their environment and increase their operational efficiency.

7.2 Method

This study follows the tradition of in-depth and extended case studies. CPI (Maoists) is a particularly attractive organization for such a case study because it is one of the most prominent and lethal dark networks in India that has flourished for more than fifty years (beginning in 1967). The first step of our data gathering was to develop a comprehensive collection of the literature that was available about the organization. We collected extensive published archival data on CPI (Maoists) over the last five decades. The first author of the study is a serving officer in the Indian Police Service (IPS), one of the elite Indian civil services, and was directly involved in studying as well as countering the insurgency operation in the state of Chhattisgarh, one of the worst insurgency-affected states in India. His serving as an IPS officer helped in collection of documents that are limited in access to the general public. Data was also collected from online sources such as magazine articles, and online books and documents.

To supplement our detailed archival data, we conducted interviews with members of CPI (Maoists) who had either surrendered to the police forces or had been arrested during counter-insurgency operations. Interviews focused on understanding the characteristics and day-to-day functioning of the department or local formation of CPI (Maoists) for which they worked. All the interviews were conducted in face-to-face meetings, and extensive notes were taken. The interviews were recorded and later transcribed verbatim. To confirm the accuracy of our transcriptions, we showed/read out the text of the interviews to the interviewees and asked them to let us know in case there were any changes to be made. Besides, the information was triangulated by verifying the facts with multiple interviewees and also by matching them with facts that have been published in popular press or are present in existing government records. To protect the identity of the interviewees, we present the interviewee quotes with only the initials of the interviewee.

Our methodology uses empirical data gathered through case studies to conceptualize and extend theory. The process undergoes many cycles of iterations between data and theory, directing the research to theoretical concepts and more data. The method consists of two running exchanges: (1) between the literature review and data analysis and (2) between data analysis and data collection. Together, these exchanges can be represented as: literature review ↔ data analysis ↔ data collection (Danneels 2010). The first exchange involves the joint inspection of existing concepts/theories and data. Data analysis points to relevant concepts and theories in the literature, while the literature provides hints to frameworks to aid the interpretation of data. This study started with the literature on organizational design, which after confrontation with the CPI (Maoists) led into the multidisciplinary literature related to shared and distributed leadership, recruitment and selection human resources practices, decision-making and organizational resilience. To prepare the case study of the CPI (Maoists), we studied their historical development and response to the government strategy through a study of their printed documents, media reports including the literature review and interviews from some arrested and surrendered Naxalites. This threefold methodology helped us to firstly verify the strategies and responses of the CPI (Maoists) as it is a covert organization and to corroborate the findings of our study.

7.3 Findings

In order to counter volatility (a dynamically changing social context), uncertainty (missing information), complexity (multiple potentially relevant dimensions) and ambiguity (multiple possible interpretations of available information) [VUCA], CPI (Maoists) has created an organization that is complex and differentiated but integrated, and has a loyal base of human resource. These adaptations provide the organization necessary flexibility and ability to adapt to changing external environment (Srivastava and Sushil 2014). The Naxalites associate with or arouse the grievances of the public (Collier and Hoeffler 2004) to motivate them to join the CPI (Maoists). In Marxist terminology, they aim to become the 'vanguard' of the have-nots. This is easier especially in the Central and Eastern India, which are much poorer, less developed and has a much lesser presence of government institutions, including police forces, as compared to the Western and Southern India. In the following sections, we discuss the organization (leadership, structure, practices and process) that it has adopted to minimize the VUCA-related risks in greater detail below.

7.3.1 Organizational Structure

CPI (Maoists) maintains a large organization to dissipate the police forces and to benefit from the myopia of the police forces that work within the administrative boundaries allocated to them by respective state governments. They operate by attacking in one administrative area while seeking refuge in another. This movement is governed and coordinated by the different regional committees of both their political and military wings. The organizational structure is given in Fig. 7.1.

The political formation is composed of committees headed by the Polit Bureau. Similarly, the military formation is further composed of commands headed by the Central Military Commission (CMC). The Polit Bureau and CMC support the Central Committee. The heads and commanders of every lower-level committee and command are also the members of each immediately higher-level committee and command. This is called as the *three-in-one* principle, and this structure ensures a maximum amount of *democratic centralism* where central leadership open-heartedly seeks opinions on various policies and activities from the lower-level functionaries before adopting a centralized decision. According to NS (an arrested Naxalite), 'In 2006, there were 38 members working for the Central Committee but it is currently down to 21 members due to state intervention.

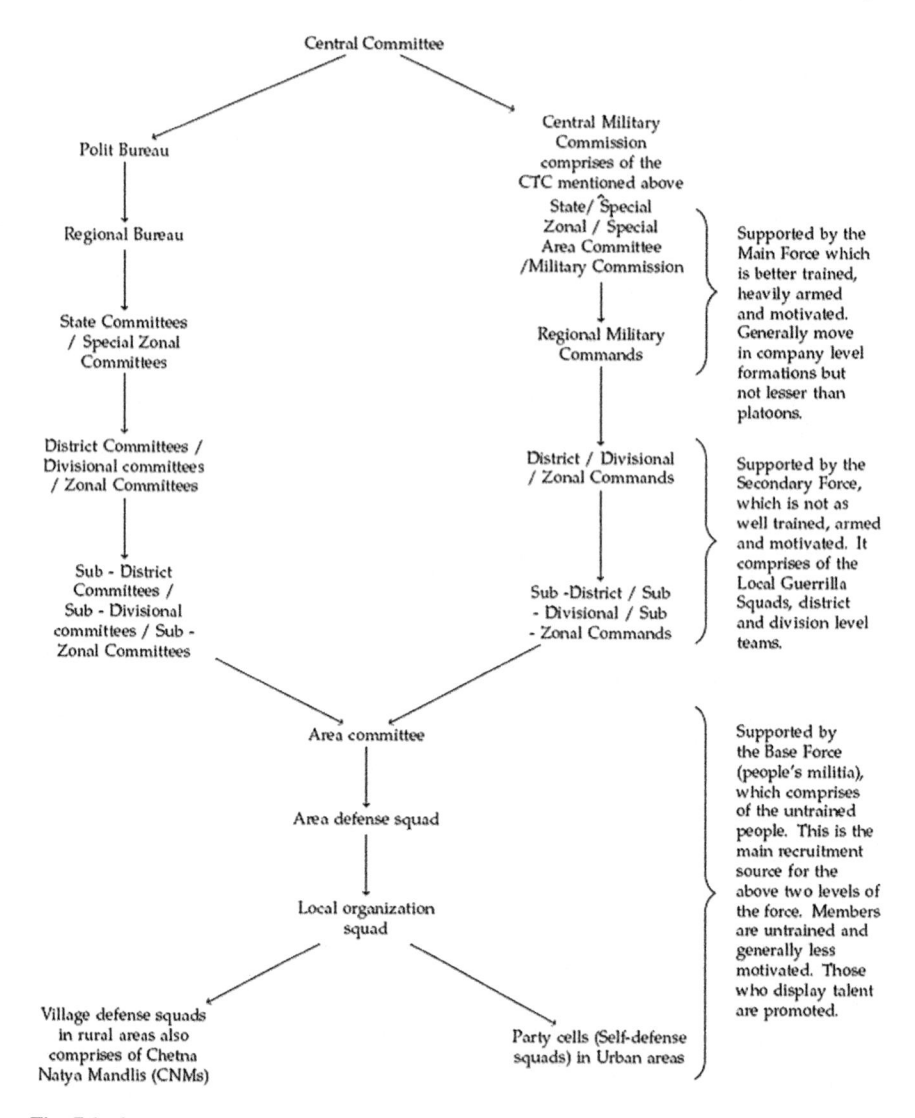

Fig. 7.1 Organizational structure of CPI (Maoists)

The key to minimizing ambiguity is decentralized leadership that constantly keeps evolving to the needs of their organizational sustenance'.

The principle of democreatic centralism works well with the requirements of CPI (Maoists) because its field units operate in isolated areas where it is difficult to monitor the activities of each member. Hence, a decentralized leadership generates a sense of responsibility and reduces the scope for moral hazard, while stringent punishment reduces the scope for adverse selection. 'To promote such decentralized leadership, they are allowed to retain 20%-30% of the revenues extorted and are encouraged to take local-level decisions locally. The higher-level hierarchies coordinate common strategy on topics like area of operations, membership and disciplinary actions where uniformity and transparency across the different smaller units are essential'. (KG, an arrested Naxalite). Such an organizational structure creates a battery of self-motivated leaders who can occupy the positions of current leaders in future. Therefore, it reduces uncertainty in the organization lest the central command is neutralized.

7.3.2 Winning Legitimacy

Towards the process of gaining internal legitimacy, the main strategy and tactics document 'Strategy and Tactics of the Indian Revolution' (internal document of CPI (Maoists)) identifies four fault lines in the Indian society that can be exploited in order to first garner a following amongst people, that can later be developed into a mass base to launch a successful revolution against the government of India in future. These are as follows: (1) contradiction between imperialism and the Indian people; (2) contradiction between feudalism and broad masses; (3) contradiction between capital and labour; and (4) internal contradictions amongst the ruling classes.

These four contradictions are written in the declining order of the number of people affected by each contradiction that the vision document identifies. Amongst these contradictions, it considers the first two contradictions as strategically crucial and peasants as the most exploited class. Therefore, the CPI (Maoists) has formed a combine of the frontal organizations and the cultural wing called as *Chetna Natya Mandalis* (CNM). The frontal organizations investigate the social faults and arouse the public sentiment against the administrative apathy. On the other hand, the CNMs train small groups of members (village defence squads) to perform exciting dramas highlighting the fault lines relevant to the potential audience identified in the village society and seek voluntary recruitment from the people to fight it. For example, such dramas could deal with issues related to day-to-day problems and exploitation at the hands of the moneylenders, forest officials and issues of land and political power that arouse public emotions. Hence, one would also find the local-level fighters or the members of the village defence squads carrying musical instruments along with weapons. Nearly, all of the CPI (Maoists) cadres hailing from rural areas that have been interrogated by the first author attributed their initial association with the organization to the influence of a CNM.

It is interesting to note that the CNMs are composed largely of the local people even though they attract much recruitment. Dramas are performed in the local dialect and local customary setting, raking sentimental issues like maltreatment by the forest guards or policemen, or social stigmas like religious or gender biases that strike a chord with the locals and bring recruits. This helps naxaltes strike a chord with the local villagers and motivates them to join their ranks.

Once the peasantry is prepared for the revolution, a steady stream of recruits is assured as the recruitment makes the locals an enemy of the state. This creates a 'thick crime habitat' (for more details, see Felson 2006) which involves the local families in some way. As many of the young men, women and children are drawn in as recruits, their families have a stake in providing the logistics support to the Naxalites and do not leak their information to the police. Hence, the families provide resources including taxes and food items and act as couriers of the Naxalites.

7.3.3 Military Consolidation

Identification of an area where the CPI (Maoists) can launch a guerrilla war with reasonable success and convert it into a guerrilla base in future is of utmost importance for its success. Such areas are necessarily large and deeply forested hilly tracts contiguous to the regions where the guerrilla bases already exist. Once such a strategic area (geographically disassociated) is identified, social investigation of the different contradictions in the local society (exploitation and oppression) is conducted so as to identify the target groups and the nature of the fault lines and arouse them for revolutionary politics through propaganda, as mentioned above. Where such conditions are weak, secret efforts precede for a sufficient period of time, mainly through the underground peasant organizations. Simultaneously, open organizations work to deepen the political mobilization against feudalism, imperialism and bureaucracy through the CNMs. On the other hand, in the areas where the geographical terrain is extremely favourable, armed form of struggle is adopted from the very beginning with the aim of starting the *Jantana Sarkars* (people's government). This instruction in the document is crucial to our thesis as it shows that if obtaining legitimacy is not important (i.e. it does not cause much volatility to for the police forces) military strategy can be adopted immediately. Consolidation of an area reinforces their legitimacy as worthy successors of the government there.

7.3.4 Strategic Layers of the War

Naxalites have created three strategic stages of the 'protracted people's war'. These stages can be understood as occurring simultaneously in different parts of the country, though the initial conception was to see them inter-temporally where the war evolved from initial stages to the subsequent stages. These stages are: (1) stage of strategic defence; (2) stage of strategic stalemate; and (3) stage of strategic offence. The strategy of strategic defence, also called as the strategy of strategic retreat, is rooted in guerrilla warfare and highlights the tactical principle of 'eating mouthful by mouthful'. This means that the members of the CPI (Maoists) attack when least expected to and cause dismay, dispirit and fatigue amongst the police forces, and retreat in the face of an offence from the police forces. Further, to minimize the loss of the armed cadres and functionaries carrying out the offensive during battle, the CPI (Maoists) uses untrained '*Jan Militia*' in large numbers in the front (as shields) to outnumber the police forces in a Lancaster-type battle (Taylor 1983). Maoists also use people's militia for their knowledge of the terrain. This kind of the warfare is conducted in the guerrilla zones.

Far into the jungles where the CPI (Maoists) holds more ground, they follow the strategy of strategic stalemate. In such areas, called as guerrilla bases, they hold the police forces from advancing. Due to the lower probabilities of successes in battles, the police forces do enter these areas very often. Finally, there is the strategy of strategic offence. In these areas, the police forces are at a gross disadvantage vis-a-vis CPI (Maoists) and rarely do they venture into these areas. In these liberated zones, CPI (Maoists) is running parallel governments called as *Jantana Sarkar* (people's government). They have made systematic efforts in preventing the development initiatives of the government from reaching the local people, in these guerrilla zones and bases. This act is essential for capturing the minds of the people, maintaining their legitimacy and obtaining a regular flow of recruits that includes children and women. This move is also necessary for the sustenance of an organization that does not work on a capital base high enough to challenge the government of India openly through a paid army. For the same reason, the CPI (Maoists) also destroys community assets like schools and hospitals that the government creates in the guerrilla zones and bases and checks people from entering the area.

Figure 7.2 provides a diagrammatic representation of the three strategies. The three strategies intricately support each other. As the guerrilla zone increases in size, so do the guerrilla bases and the liberated areas because the power gradient of the CPI (Maoists) increases at the cost of the government. Conception of these stages is important for the training of the new members, as is the study of the contradictions in the Indian society discussed above.

> There are 8-12 party members in each village and a functioning government called in each group of 5-10 villages, which is called as the *Jantana Sarkar*. Currently, about 120 *Jantana Sarkars* are functional. It performs many duties that include the following: (1) carrying out the welfare activities like education and health; (2) using public labour for agricultural purposes of an individual like tilling the land; (3) levying and collection of taxes; (4) mobilization of people against the police forces and forcing them to inform the *Jantana Sarkar* about any movement of the police forces in the vicinity; (5) forcing half the members of villages to work for the *Jantana Sarkar* by rotation; and (6) procurement and maintenance of ration and other items of daily needs for the party members. (AR, an arrested Naxalite)

> Schools are important because they are also centres of propagation of communist traditions and breaking the sanctions of Hindu religion like forcibly feeding beef. Around 20-30% of the revenues of the CPI (Maoists) are used for education. The people who help in agriculture are paid in kind (providing food to who contribute through labour). Lands are also earmarked for the public distribution to the poorer. However, in practice, their produce is used for feeding the military formations. (NS, an arrested Naxalite)

> The secretary of the local *Jantana Sarkar* is responsible for maintaining the ration stocks for each company, platoon or CNM separately. In some villages pigs, hens and land are also

Guerrilla Base:
Here they hold the ground and recruit. The police informers are few. Incidence of violence is high and major fighting occurs here. Company level formations of the military wing are common. This includes areas like Dandakaranya, N and S Telengana, Nallamalla hills, AoB, Koil - Kaimur area of Jharkhand, Gondia and Gadchiroli in Maharashtra.

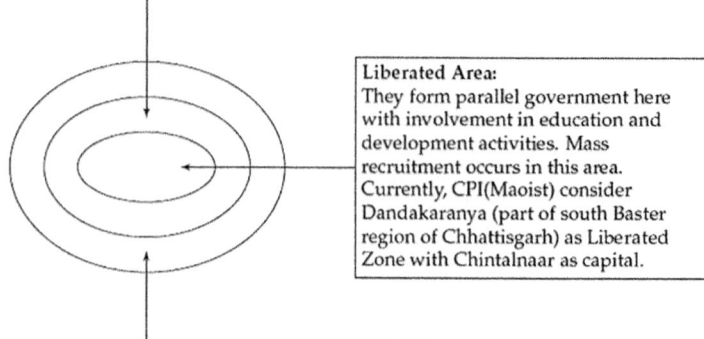

Liberated Area:
They form parallel government here with involvement in education and development activities. Mass recruitment occurs in this area. Currently, CPI(Maoist) consider Dandakaranya (part of south Baster region of Chhattisgarh) as Liberated Zone with Chintalnaar as capital.

Guerrilla Zone:
This is also the zone of mobile warfare. Here, they do not hold the ground but extort and kill both civilians and security forces. The incidence of violence is low on security forces as CPI(Maoists) are weak here. They are not strong enough to oppose development related efforts. Squad and Platoon level formations are common. However, a company may visit for conducting special tasks like attacking a police installation or a VIP.

Fig. 7.2 Strategic layers of war adopted by CPI (Maoists). The contours show that an outer layer protects an inner layer

earmarked for each such organization to prevent friction with the villagers. Yet there would be frictions due to occasional lack of items for a visiting group. Further, the ration is also obtained from the government suppliers supplying free rice to the poor people. Items are also bought through the various functionaries like contractors or teachers on payment. (KG, an arrested Naxalite).

7.3.5 External Networking

External networking is geared towards obtaining political support from other insurgent outfits, inside or outside the country, through alliances of its 'mass organizations' with theirs, which is called the 'Strategic United Front'. Towards this end, the CPI (Maoists) express their solidarity with the Jammu and Kashmir and North-Eastern terrorist groups, calling India as a prison house of many nationalities, as part of their yet to be fulfilled dream of 'Strategic United Front' (SUF) against India. Idea of SUF is conceptualized as a coalition of different ultras working against the country. According to the vision document, the Maoist revolution is currently in the stage of strategic defence and SUF is essential to keep the police forces busy fighting many such groups simultaneously stretched out in different directions of the country. For this purpose, they have frontal organizations active in 20 states. Hence, this would prevent the forces from concentrating and defeating them one at a time. Further, the political pressure from international organizations would also prevent the governments from taking harsh steps against the Naxalites as the state could be projected as working against voiceless tribal/poor population.

> Apart from seeking the support from other insurgent groups working in India, CPI (Maoists) also has close links with Communist parties in other countries. However, many of these relations have not fructified due to internal differences and repression from the police forces. (NS, an arrested Naxalite)

7.3.6 Recruitment Process

The members of CPI (Maoist) are initially inducted at the level of the people's militia in the rural areas, and then depending upon the motivation and skills, they are promoted into the secondary and the main forces and given leadership roles. However, the members are put under strict vigilance (see Table 7.1) before they are inducted formally as members of the organization. Having disloyal people in the organization would not only increase the uncertainty and ambiguity (to be discussed later) for Naxalites but would directly reduce it for the police forces. Therefore, the Naxalites adopt utmost caution in recruiting their members.

Table 7.1 Observation period for different members at CPI (Maoists)

S. No.	Origin	Period of observation[a]
1.	Working class, landless poor peasants and agricultural labourers	6 months
2.	Middle class peasants, petty bourgeoisie and urban middle class	1 year
3.	Other classes and other parties[b]	2 years

[a]May be extended by another 6 months by the next higher committee subject to review by the next higher committee. Zonal/district committee must approve the new membership. SC/state committee finally approves it

[b]Functionaries from other parties are given positions not below that they were bearing in those parties. Their case must be recommended by two party members, one of them being a party member at least for two years and accepted by the next higher committee. Functionaries who have worked at levels higher than the area level or above need to be recommended by two party members one of them being party members at least for five years and must be accepted by the state committee or by the central committee. Non-professional people are not inducted above the area committees

Recruitment is conducted on the basis of class and mass origins and affiliation with the revolutionary ideology as propagated by MLM for all citizens who have attained 16 years of age (though children from the age of 6 years are indoctrinated with revolutionary ideas and are used for fighting). In the urban areas, the voluntary members are admitted as individuals, through a primary party unit that comprises of 3–5 members and is the lowest level unit (according to AS, a surrendered Naxalite). This unit is involved in day-to-day functioning in the local area. Unless two party members who have thorough knowledge about the person recommend, he/she is not considered for the membership. Generally, party members will be admitted from activist groups (mass organizations) working under the guidance of the party unit. The admission to the party is subjected to a secret enquiry and approval of the next higher committee (at least area committee). The admission phase is called as *candidate membership* in which the members are given low-quality work and are put under strict observation. Depending upon the origin of the person, different observation periods are determined. These are listed in Table 7.1.

In the rural areas, things are different because the Naxalites wield much more power. The civilian families are forced to part off with children in fear of massacre of the family. Families often part with the female child as a bargain for the male child. Therefore, women constitute nearly 40% of the force in the army. The party also abducts orphans from villages and grown-up children from orphanages. These children are recruited in *Krantikari Bal Sanghs* (Children's Revolutionary Groups) and are fed with revolutionary ideas in the schools run by the *Jantana Sarkar*. For children between 15 and 22 years, revolutionary ideas are fed in Basic Communist Training Schools (BCTSs). They are also used as child soldiers and spies.

Upon obtaining adulthood, they are recruited as hard core Naxalites in secondary or the main force. This way the Naxalites dominate village after village. Some adults are conscripted from the areas held long by the CPI (Maoist), while others join upon being motivated by the revolutionary ideas. To prevent the attrition, after the entrant is a part of an illegal act, they explain to them that they have committed crime by joining the banned organization and the police would act against them if they decide to join the mainstream.

The urban dwellers can handle more complex tasks and responsibilities like intelligence collection, managing logistics and development of weapons that a countryman cannot. However, in the urban areas the government also has a much stronger presence. Therefore, they work through frontal organizations that create ambiguity in the minds of the police forces regarding the true nature of their work. There are three types of mass organizations in the urban area:

(i) Underground Revolutionary Mass Organizations (linked to the party): these organizations secretly organize mass struggles and propaganda and call for people's war. Such organizations are found at best in semi-urban areas or villages since they can easily be arrested by the police forces.
(ii) Open Revolutionary Mass Organizations: these organizations propagate the politics of new democratic revolution by available legal means to carry on

7 Effective Policing in a VUCA Environment … 101

revolutionary propaganda and agitation. They play an important role in filing litigation against individual members of the police forces to demotivate them and VUCAise the environment; and

(iii) Other Mass Organizations not directly linked to the party: these organizations try to broad base the party by uniting non-party organizations under the common programme. These organizations are also called as frontal organizations and can also be very useful in carrying out activities when open organizations are not allowed to function due to a strict vigil.

These organizations are the main source of urban recruitment into the revolutionary movement. These organizations bring the urban youth into the revolutionary umbrella with the propagation of revolutionary politics and the consolidation of a revolutionary front. The urban youth are valuable since they are more educated. Hence, they act as vital nodes to manage specialized tasks, logistics, propaganda and finances since they are more educated. As an incentive, the educated youth are promoted much faster than their rural counterparts in the hierarchy. However, according to NS (an arrested Naxalite), "the quality of people joining the movement drastically deteriorated since the 1990s (compared to the 1980s). Previously, educated elites used to join the movement but now the uneducated rural and poor people join it." According to AS, 'in the recent years CPI (Maoists) has targeted the urban dwellers who either work in the rural areas as contractors, teachers and doctors. They also have targeted the local rural people who have family members in urban areas to gradually build relationship towards recruitment. Acknowledging the predominantly rural character of the cadres, they are given training in urban areas regarding how to function while visiting these places.

7.3.7 Discipline

In case of any disagreement with the decision of the committee/unit, the member is supposed to remain loyal to carry out the decision and may present her dissenting opinion in any subsequent meeting or may send her opinion to higher committee. If the respective committee fails to solve the problem within six months, she has the right to send her opinion directly to the central committee for consideration. It is, however, the discretion of the committee to decide whether to reopen the matter or not. Same procedure is also followed in sending criticisms considered against any other party member not in her unit to the next higher committee. The punishment periods are shown in Table 7.2.

> According to AS (an arrested Naxalite), "the period of the punishment for the different level of the post holders increases with the capacity. Most importantly, members are killed on the slightest doubt of being a police informer in front of all the other members to signal the importance of secrecy to them. Besides, one major disciplinary issue often raised pertains to behaviour of men towards women. Around 2007–2010, when the CPI (Maoists) was

Table 7.2 Member post and suspension period

Member post	Period of suspension
Central committee	4 years
State committee	3 years
Regional committee	2.5 years
Divisional committee	2 years
Area committee	1 year
Other party member	6 months
Local organizational squad (LOS)	3 months

strong, they overlooked the major complaints of harassment against women. However, in recent days when the cadre strength is declining, and they have to appeal to the shortcoming of the governmental machinery for recruitment, the leadership has become strict and have even demoted erring cadres/leaders."

7.3.8 Differentiation and Integration in Practice

The fighting units are organized into three arms: *Main Force*—this is the main fighting force of the CPI (Maoist), which is best equipped and is trained like a professional army. It comprises of military companies, platoons and special action teams that participate in big operations based on the command of the military commissions or commands. *Secondary Force*—the local/special guerrilla squads and district-/division-level action teams comprise the secondary force. They generally move in squads of 10–12 guerrillas and have fewer weapons than the main force and take on smaller tasks like market raids on policemen with small action teams. Some outstanding members of the secondary force promoted into the main force, and the dress code is green. *Base Force*—this consists of the '*Jan Militia*', which is ill-equipped and does not bear any modern weapons. This force is estimated to be anywhere between 40,000 and 60,000 people (Chhikara 2012). They work at or below the area committee level and are the main source of the recruitment for the secondary and main forces. The base force also plays a crucial role in integration of the main and secondary forces by providing the required logistics and intelligence-related support (according to NS, an arrested Naxalite).

'Functioning of Military Commissions and Commands Coordination of Main, Secondary and Base Forces', an internal document CPI [M-L] and CPI [Maoists], also clarifies their emphasis on differentiation and integration in forces.

> The Militia and the Secondary Forces in an area are required to participate in a variety of tasks such as, intelligence gathering to find out the weaknesses of the enemy, not letting out the news about our forces, working as guides, transporting all kinds of supplies, sentry works, finding out the movements of the enemy and informing the Command immediately about the enemy's situation when the Main Force concentrates in the area to strike the enemy. In addition to the above-mentioned tasks, the Militia and the Secondary Forces shall also sabotage whenever necessary the communication and transport facilities of the enemy.

Such a co-ordination will certainly help the Main Force to concentrate its forces in time and secretly to attack surprisingly on the enemy's weaknesses and annihilate him. By conducting such actions efficiently, the Main Force is able to provide flexibility and protection to the local organizations and committees. The coordination must be such that the Militia and the Secondary Forces shall take up such actions as to frustrate, harass, stop, terrorise and trap the enemy so as to make the major military actions of the Main Force successful.

As mentioned in the quoted text, the CPI (Maoists) differentiates the three components of its fighting forces mentioned-above, taking advantage of the largess of the forests and geographical spread and spreading them into different sub-groups, to create ambiguity and minimize losses from either retaliation or pursuit by police forces. To be more efficient, the CPI (Maoists) integrate these three components. For this purpose, CPI (Maoists) mobilize '*Jan Militia*' that has specialized geographical knowledge, and helps the fighting forces integrate and organize an attack on the individual units of police forces in a Lancaster's version of the guerrilla warfare (see Deitchman 1962; Taylor 1983) and vanish immediately into the vastness of the forests. In other words, the main, secondary and the base forces work largely in tandem and they are integrated through prior communication for an attack. This organizational structure also helps the CPI (Maoists) test the ability of the person on ground before he is promoted into the main fighting secondary and the primary forces. With their unique guerrilla capability derived from ability to camouflage and conceal in the forests, the Naxalites are able to organize spectacular attacks on the police forces. As it is widely known, the police forces draw into a retreat (Kumar 2009, p. 133) after a spectacular attack and the Naxalites have a free run till they recover their morale.

7.4 Discussion

In the previous section, we discussed the organization adjustments that helped CPI (Maoists) sustain and succeed in a highly volatile, uncertain, ambiguous environment. We believe that there are a lot of insights that can be gleamed from the case study of a dark network to understand what needs to be done to make police forces more effective. We have summarized the findings and our suggestions in Table 7.3.

7.4.1 Implications for Theory and Practice

The study makes important contributions to theory and practice. First, we believe that CPI (Maoists) has been successful so far because it has worked in a highly decentralized manner. If the police forces have to succeed against them, then they will need to increase the number of lower-level leaders and give them more control and autonomy for taking ground-level decisions. Training should be aimed at creating lower-level leaders. Therefore, room should be created for the leaders to

Table 7.3 Summary of findings and recommendations

Component	What is it[1]?	What Naxalites do to mitigate it? (*based on the discussion in the chapter*)	What Naxalites do to 'VUCAise' the environment?	What the current position of the police forces (SF)? (*Information witudely available on print and electronic media*)	What the police forces (SF) should do to counter-dark networks[2]?
Volatility	Relatively unstable change; information is available, and the situation is understandable, but change is frequent and sometimes unpredictable	1. Legitimacy to recruitment 2. Occupation and governance of rural areas 3. Attack the police forces to signal their vitality to the businessmen to obtain extortion revenues	It implies minimizing the impact of the random factors and increasing the randomness for the police forces by attacking them when it is least expected to	Police force is lesser than required by the UN norms of 450 per million	1. Increase the police force 2. Build trust with the local public
Uncertainty	A lack of knowledge as to whether an event will have meaningful ramifications; cause and effect are understood, but it is unknown if an event will create significant change	1. Winning loyalty through *Jantana Sarkar* that replicates the government's development activities 2. Fear (through extreme violence, e.g., Kangaroo Courts) 3. Clear and detailed document stating the strategies and tactics of the activities	Obtaining war-related information on police forces by training the local villagers to become their eyes and ears. It also involves preventing the flow of own information by the use of an iron hand. It also includes planting of wrong information and analysing the movement of the police forces for planting ambushes	1. The commands are given from the senior officers 2. Fighting force moves in large numbers, provides a target and reveals the movement (from security base camps to jungles)-related information to the Naxalites 3. Knee-jerk and reactionary policies that often change depending on the public outcry on some incidents	1. Increase the number of small-level leaders to enable leadership to emerge by giving operational freedom (any non-monitorable and unverifiable task should be decentralized to levels that can monitor or verify it) 2. Organizational structure of the police forces should closely match the Naxalites in terms of say

(continued)

7 Effective Policing in a VUCA Environment ...

Table 7.3 (continued)

Component	What is it[1]?	What Naxalites do to mitigate it? (*based on the discussion in the chapter*)	What Naxalites do to 'VUCAise' the environment?	What the current position of the police forces (SF)? (*Information widely available on print and electronic media*)	What the police forces (SF) should do to counter-dark networks[2]?
		4. Many Naxalites adopt same name to prevent identification 5. Minimum use of the mobile phones to prevent electronic surveillance. They use the local people's phones to communicate if they have to 6. Creating 'thick crime habitats'		4. Information on Naxalites is rarely pinpointed, and we rely on chance encounters for success	of the leaders and feedback 3. Creation of small teams will prevent loss of information. Both defensive and offensive tactics are essential in the guerrilla warfare 4. Analysis of the evolution of Naxalites' strategies and resources in the medium term and develop counter-strategies using modern analytical tools 5. Alternative strategies should be developed and discussed threadbare before implementing
Complexity	Many interconnected parts forming an elaborate network of information and procedures; often multiform and convoluted, but not necessarily involving change	1. Geographically based regional committees are formed based on similarity of fault line. Similarly, military and political wings are separate	Benefitting from a complex organizational structure and preventing the police forces from exploiting the fault lines of the Naxalites as the Naxalites exploit those prevailing the society.	1. The geographical units have administrative boundaries 2. High degree of centralization of power kills the initiative at the lower end. Lower-level	1. Interstate and interdepartmental coordination by the use of more central forces along the interstate border areas and coordinating with other civil agencies

(continued)

Table 7.3 (continued)

Component	What is it?[1]	What Naxalites do to mitigate it? (based on the discussion in the chapter)	What Naxalites do to 'VUCAise' the environment?	What the current position of the police forces (SF)? (Information widely available on print and electronic media)	What the police forces (SF) should do to counter-dark networks[2]?
		2. Local-level leaders and who have worked for a long time in the area are provided local-level leadership 3. Lower-level leadership is part of the upper-level decision-making. This provides continuity and ownership 4. Feedback analysis is objective. Even the subordinates are allowed to comment on the actions of the seniors	Towards this goal, the Naxalites commit asymmetric number of attacks in different locations across different states to prevent the police forces from concentrating on one area and cooperating. Similarly, their frontal organizations file cases regarding Human Rights violations by the police forces, corruption and under-spending on development by the government organizations to VUCAise the environment and keep them busy in different areas	leadership does not evolve 3. Coordination is absent between states fighting Naxalites as the intensity faced by them is different	present in there, like the forest department, public works department etc. 2. Increase the local composition of the force leaders to have families for relaxation in free time 3. A leadership development programme is essential to understand the importance of cooperation and coordination between forces 4. Decentralized leadership for operational commanders is essential as they face the risk to life the most and reduce the complexity in decision-making by reducing the layers of decision-makers

(continued)

7 Effective Policing in a VUCA Environment ...   107

Table 7.3 (continued)

Component	What is it?	What Naxalites do to mitigate it? (*based on the discussion in the chapter*)	What Naxalites do to 'VUCAise' the environment?	What the current position of the police forces (SF)? (*Information wilndely available on print and electronic media*)	What the police forces (SF) should do to counter-dark networks[2]?
Ambiguity	A lack of knowledge as to the basic rules of the game; cause and effect are not understood, and there is no precedent for making predictions as to what to expect	Frontal organizations covertly recruiting and demoralizing police forces in the name of Human Rights violations and political freedom	Understanding the cause and effect of own and police forces' strategies, while innovating adequately to prevent the police forces from unravelling the causality and create confusion in their action	1. The police forces are not involved in counter-propaganda 2. The police forces fight the Human Rights cases by themselves; the state does not help them 3. The battle tactics are old and predictable	1. Check for sources for funds, logistics[3] and couriers of these frontal organizations 2. Newer tactical formations must be developed and experienced to maintain surprise amongst Naxalites 3. Each constable with an additional skill will be essential, as it would reduce the burden of the government, especially in rebuilding the war-torn area 4. False propaganda regarding own astrategies would make Naxalite unable to understand the cause and effect of police forces' actions

Note [1]The definitions in Column 2 are based on Bennett and Lemoine (2014)
[2]It may be seen that some of the solutions provided are common to more than one risks as the risks manifest themselves with common symptoms
[3]Gupta (2011) discusses this issue in grreater detail

brainstorm amongst alternative strategies amongst themselves. This would force them to ponder over the alternatives and increase the quality of leadership.

Second, the governments and the police forces need to also spend more resources in advertising their good deeds, policies and the surrender-cum-rehabilitation scheme (specifically emphasized by GU and NS, arrested Naxalites). These steps are essential to manage the public perception for the police forces and reduce the room for the Naxalites to capture public minds.

Also, the government does not involve much in counter-propaganda. Therefore, the government stands vilified in the eyes of the public. The governments must work objectively towards developing public sentiment against the adversary through advertisement and public involvement through debates, fairs and contact programmes. The government should decentralize the governance on the lines of the tribal councils formed in other parts of the country that are backward and predominantly inhabited by the tribal people to develop a feeling of inclusivity.

Third, adequate information regarding the Naxalites is not available with the police forces. Many Naxalites bear the same name to prevent identification. Also, they minimize the use of the mobile phones to prevent electronic surveillance. Often, they use the local villagers' phones to communicate if they have to. Therefore, neither are the police forces able to understand the mind of a Naxalite leader nor are they able to identify their locations. Monitorable warfare tactics like static ambushes should be used for operations where the police forces have information-related disadvantage. Just like the dark networks, the police forces need to bring in an element of surprise in their operations. Therefore, police forces have to refrain from routine operations to prevent the slack. It is also essential that long-range patrols are conducted in small numbers and at irregular intervals.

Besides, it would be better to target the lower- and middle-level Naxalite leaders instead of the top leaders because the CPI (Maoists) has structured its organization to withstand the onslaught of the police forces. They have a built bottom-up organization with decentralized decision-making that withstands the onslaught of the police forces. Therefore, it is not very useful to target the higher-level leaders. Instead, middle-level leaders, who are the crucial link between the ground forces and the top level, are more useful targets for disrupting a dark network.

Fourth, developing a flexible police force is essential for gearing up to the dynamicity of the changing times. For this purpose, each security personnel deployed should be trained in an additional task that may be beneficial for the force or community and that may be completed in the off-duty times. This will reduce the economic burden of the government in sanctioning more forces and help in rotating the police forces between peace and war areas seamlessly.

Fifth, the government must expose the frontal organizations working for the Naxalites by clamping on their financial resources in line with the UN resolutions. In addition, the government must institute an in-house enquiry to screen those allegations of Human Rights violations that are genuine and support ones that are frivolous with legal support to the police forces and discourage those supporting such complaints by legal action. Frontal organizations that file frivolous complaints must also face legal action.

Sixthly, urban areas should be regularly monitored for the Naxalites who might take refuge there.

Finally, this study adds both to the studies on organizational design and countering dark networks. This chapter highlights that from a policy perspective, the emphasis on causality and onset of civil wars (see Blattmann and Miguel 2010) has caused the researchers to overlook an important perspective, the internal organization of dark networks and their dynamic adjustment to various risks emerging from the environment.

7.5 Limitation and Future Directions

The major limitation of this study lies in the single case that was selected given its uniqueness and difficulty in getting access to the details. Besides, due to the limited scope of the study, the CPI (Maoists) cannot be considered as a representative of all types of dark networks. However, it provides a rich description as it has survived and expanded over the last several decades and also adds to the literature. Nonetheless, more evidence must be sought using a larger sample for generalizing the framework's various elements and their mutual relationships. A deeper analysis of the theoretical framework that links up the elements of the dark network to describe its ability to survive in a VUCA world is needed, and Social Network Analysis can also add to this. An in-depth analysis of the trade-off and synergies amongst different aspects of organizational design and organizational strategy is worth studying from both an academician's and a practitioner's perspective.

7.6 Conclusion

In this chapter, we confronted the questions that what makes the CPI (Maoists) thrive in a Volatile, Uncertain, Complex and Ambiguous (VUCA) environment and what could police organizations learn from it. To answer these questions, we present a case study of the CPI (Maoists). The main reason that the CPI (Maoists) has been able to withstand a VUCA environment is that they have structured their organization to address each of these individual components or risks separately, addressing first the most important risk, Volatility. Down to the least important one, but also closely related to it. For instance, the factors that support the military strategy used to reduce the impact of volatility also help in reducing the uncertainty for the CPI (Maoists). Therefore, we understand that the strategy for the police forces also lies in first reducing the volatility-related risks followed by reducing other risks, as reflected in counter-insurgency strategy, tactics and organizational redesign.

References

Bakker, R., Raab, J., & Milward, B. H. (2012). A preliminary theory of dark network resilience. *Journal of Policy Analysis and Management, 31*(1), 33–62.

Bennett, N., & Lemoine, J. (2014). What VUCA really means for you. *Harvard Business Review, 92*(1/2).

Blattmann, C., & Miguel, E. (2010). Civil war. *Journal of Economic Literature, 48*(1), 3–57.

Chhikara, R. (2012) *People's liberation guerrilla army of CPI (Maoist)*. Manekshaw Paper no. 35. New Delhi: Centre for Land Warfare Studies.

Collier, P., & Hoeffler, A. (2004). Greed and grievance in civil war. *Oxford Economic Papers, 56*(4), 563–595.

Danneels, E. (2010). Trying to become a different type of company: Dynamic capability at Smith Corona. *Strategic Management Journal, 32*(1), 1–31.

Deitchman, S. J. (1962). A Lanchester model of guerrilla warfare. *Operations Research, 10*(6), 818–827.

Dhir, S., Mahajan, V., & Bhal, K. T. (2016). Himbunkar: Turnaround of a social public sector enterprise. *South Asian Journal of Management, 23*(4), 175.

Felson, M. (2006). *Crime and nature*. Thousand Oaks, Calif: Sage Publications.

Freeman, C. (2013). Violence in Iraq goes up Despite US Pull out, as Freed Prisoners Rejoin Militias. *Telegraph*, March 16. Available at: http://www.telegraph.co.uk/news/worldnews/middleeast/iraq/9934656/Violence-in-Iraq-goes-up-despite-US-pull-out?-as-freed-prisoners-rejoin-militias.html.

Gupta, D. (2011). Bastar—An asymmetric war. *The Indian Police Journal, LVIII*(2), 38–45.

Gupta, D., & Sriram, K. (2018). Impact of security expenditures in military alliances on violence from non-state actors: Evidence from India, *World Development, 107*, 338–357. ISSN 0305-750X.

Holmes, M. (2014). Inside Iraq: Two Years after U.S. Withdrawal, are Things Worse than Ever? *CNN*, January 15. Available at: http://edition.cnn.com/2014/01/13/world/meast/iraq-anbar-violence-holmes.

Kumar, S. (Ed.). (2009). *India's National Security: Annual review 2009*. New Delhi: Routlledge.

Milward, H. B., & Raab, J. (2006). Dark networks as organizational problems: Elements of a theory. *International Public Management Journal, 9*(3), 333–360.

Ministry of Home Affairs, Frequently Asked Questions on Left Wing Extremism, Available at: http://mha.nic.in/sites/upload_files/mha/files/LWE_FAQS_22012016.pdf. Retrieved on January 07, 2017.

PTI. (2010). Naxalism Biggest Threat to Internal Security: Manmohan. *The Hindu*, May 24. Available at: http://www.thehindu.com/news/national/Naxalism-biggest-threat-to-internal-security-Manmohan/article16302952.ece.

Ransley, G., & Mazerolle, L. (2009). Policing in an era of uncertainty. *Police Practice and Research, 10*(4), 365–381.

Roberts, N., & Stockport, G. J. (2009). Defining strategic flexibility. *Global Journal of Flexible Systems Management, 10*(1), 27–32.

Rosenbaum, D. P. (2010). Police research: Merging the policy and action research traditions. *Police Practice and Research, 11*(2), 144–149.

Sageman, M. (2008). *Leaderless Jihad: Terror networks in the twenty-first century*. Philadelphia: University of Pennsylvania Press.

SATP. (n.d.). *CPI (Maoists): Party Constitution*. Available at: http://www.satp.org/satporgtp/countries/india/maoist/documents/papers/partyconstitution.htm.

SATP. (n.d.). *Strategy and Tactics of Indian Revolution*. Available at: http://www.satp.org/satporgtp/countries/india/maoist/documents/\pape-rs/strategy.htm.

SATP. (n.d.). *Urban Perspective: Our Work in Urban Areas*. Available at: http://www.satp.org/satporgtp/countries/india/maoist/documents/\pape-rs/Urbanperspective.htm.

SATP. (n.d.). *Functioning of Military Commissions and Commands Coordination of Main, Secondary and Base Forces.* Available at: http://www.satp.org/satporgtp/countries/india/maoist/\\documents/pape-rs/Functioning.htm.

Sharma, A. (2014). Fighting biggest national security challenge: Home ministry asks state govts to target top leaders of CPI (Maoist). *The Economic Times,* July 8. Available at: http://articles.economictimes.indiatimes.com/2014-07-08/news/51191483_1_homeministry-home-secretary-anil-goswami-security-challenge.

Srivastava, A., & Sushil. (2014). Adapt: A critical pillar of strategy execution process. In M. K. Nandakumar, Sanjay Jharkharia, & A. S. Nair (Eds.), *Organizational flexibility and competitiveness. Flexible systems management* (pp. 9–24). Springer: New Delhi.

Srivastava, P. (2016). Flexible HR to cater to VUCA times. *Global Journal of Flexible Systems Management, 17*(1), 105–108.

Stewart, P. (2014) U.S. to Keep more Troops in Afghanistan as Violence Spikes. *Reuters,* December 6. Available at: http://www.reuters.com/article/2014/12/06/US-USA-Afghanistan-Military-idUSKBN0JK0GH20141206\#FeJfaQgBeE7P2dpQ.99.

Sushil. (2014). The concept of a flexible enterprise. In Sushil & E. A. Stohr (Eds.), *The flexible enterprise. Flexible systems management* (pp. 3–26). Springer: New Delhi.

Taylor, J. G. (1983) *Lanchaster models of warfare* (2 Vols.). Arlington, VA: Operations Research Society of America, Military Applications Section.

Whiteman, W. E. (1998). *Training and educating army officers for the 21st century, implications for the United States Military Academy.* Fort Belvoir, VA: Defense Technical Information Center.

Chapter 8
Effect of Gender on Job Satisfaction Among Academicians

Dimpy Sachar

Abstract The objective of conducting this research survey is to analyze the effect of gender on different factors affecting the job satisfaction among both public and private university academicians. The research problem undertaken in this study is that whether the gender of academicians affects the job satisfaction level of university academicians. Two public and two private universities of the Delhi and NCR region were taken for conducting this study. The data is primary in nature and is collected by distributing the questionnaire to the respondents. Data was collected from 405 respondents comprising 199 male respondents and 206 female respondents. Research instrument consists of 90 statements, and 11 factors were retrieved from those statements. These factors were named as: Attitude and Behavior of Authorities, Research and Development Facilities, Facilities (i.e. fringe benefits), Attitude and Behavior of Administrative Staff, Attitude and Behavior of Students, Coordination and Cooperation among Co-faculty Members, Technological and Informational Needs, Working Environment Conditions, Academic Environment Conditions, Service Condition Policies, and Compensation. Quantitative data was analyzed using descriptive and inferential statistics. Research findings indicate that the female teachers are more satisfied as compared to the male teachers.

Keywords Academicians · Gender · Job satisfaction · Private university Public university

8.1 Introduction

Education is a dignified profession, and academicians are always appreciated and respected by the society. Teachers are building blocks of society. Teacher plays an important role in shaping student's career. Therefore, the teachers are an important and indispensable element of an education system. Teacher performance depends on

D. Sachar (✉)
Delhi Institute of Advanced Studies (Affiliated to G.G.S.I.P.U.), Delhi, India
e-mail: dimpysachar81@gmail.com

the satisfaction level of teachers. A satisfied teacher can yield desired results, whereas dissatisfied teacher can lead to failures. Job satisfaction is a feeling about the various aspects of the job. Discovering the level of job satisfaction tries to find out which aspect of the job satisfies or dissatisfies the most (Dhir and Dhir 2015). Drago et al. (1992) stated that challenging work, fair rewards, conducive working conditions, and helpful co-workers are the significant factors enhancing the job satisfaction level of employees. Spector (1997) revealed that job satisfaction develops behaviors that can either have a positive or negative impact on organization performance.

8.2 Literature Review

A study conducted by Ivancevich et al. (1990) stated that job satisfaction develops an optimistic or pessimistic attitude of an individual toward his/her job. As per Cribbin (1972), job satisfaction is a pleasure feeling which an employee tries to obtain from his job, organization, peers, and administrative officials. There are different research studies stating the factors influencing the job satisfaction among employees. Whereas, Houston et al. (2006) mentioned in their study that flexibility, responsibility, and job variety develops a sense of satisfaction among employees. Korunka et al. (2003) reveals that role clarity, and job control, Zembylas and Papanastasiou (2005) show that autonomy in decision making, Garrido et al. (2005) proves that financial conditions and the level of autonomy, whereas Stevens et al. (2006) and Dhir and Dhir (2017) mentioned that supportive HR policies are the major factors influencing the job satisfaction level among employees. On the other hand, Nguni et al. (2006) proves that motivational leadership influences job satisfaction among employees. Rhodes et al. (2007) found that harmonious relations with colleagues and participative working conditions, and Luthans et al. (1992) stated that wages and salaries are major factors affecting the job satisfaction level of employees. The study tries to deal with the problem; that is, the gender affects the job satisfaction level of university teachers and also tries to find out the impact of gender on different factors affecting job satisfaction. Several studies revealed that there are some male-dominant culture and societies which does not provide equal employment opportunities and benefits to the female employees in the organization (Dhir et al. 2014). Gender strongly influences the job satisfaction of the employees of the organizations (Bamel et al. 2014). Some of the Asian countries are male-dominant society, and they believe that males should lead and control the command of their families and organization. As per Li and Wang Leung (2001), since many centuries women are exploited, as they are not allowed to speak loudly. Highly qualified women cannot reach to the higher level positions in the organization, whereas Pinar et al. (2011) stated that being female society think that female cannot work for longer durations and not in a position to shift from one place to another. Study of McCuddy et al. (2010) discovered that while working in organizations female employees are getting lesser chances of promotions as compared to their male colleagues. Various researches revealed the effects of gender on job satisfaction, and most studies' results have shown that females were more satisfied. A survey undertaken by Lacy and Sheehan (1997) remarked that there are studies which reported that satisfaction level of male employees is higher as compared to female employees. Research of Cooper and Kelly (1993) reported that there is a significant difference in the job satisfaction level of female head teachers and their male counterparts in secondary and higher education schools. The result reveals that female head teachers are dissatisfied. A study in Botswana showed that male teachers in secondary schools are highly satisfied than their female counterparts (Maphorisa 1997; Bendall-Lyon and Powers 2002; Siu 2002) and found that male employees enjoy better opportunities of advancements in the organization and females are on their least priority. An empirical study of Potter et al. (2001) revealed that the type of school influences significantly the job satisfaction of teachers. They also explored the factors affecting job satisfaction with gender effect. However, Clark (1997) and Poza and Poza (2003) suggested that females are more contented from their jobs as compared to men. On the other hand, Fields and Blum (1997) showed that male and female employees working in the same organization have different levels of self-esteem and job contentment. Study of Iqbal (2012) explored that type of school—public and private—influences the level of self-esteem and job contentment among school teachers. On the contrary, Schuler (1975) reported that females always prefer to work with humble and nice employees as compared to males. On the other hand, male counterparts prefer to take work-related important decisions and like to handle difficult tasks (Bhal and Sharma 2001). Whereas Nash (1985) and Ramayah et al. (2001) found that there is a variation in the factors that affect the job satisfaction level of men and women. On the one hand, men require advancement, job security, rank, type of work, organization, salary, colleagues, facilities, supervision, and duration. On the other hand women prefer type of work, organization, security, colleagues, duration, advancement, supervision, salary, working conditions and facilities. As per Wu Huei-Jane and You-I Wu (2001), it was concluded that female teachers, teachers on director post, less-qualified teachers, and teachers with higher income are highly satisfied with their jobs. Although Lortie (1975), Birmingham (1984), and Galloway et al. (1985) indicate that some studies proved that female teachers are highly satisfied than male teachers, whereas other studies showed that male teachers are highly satisfied as compared to female teachers, and there are studies which reported no relationship between gender and teacher job satisfaction (Hoppock 1935).

8.3 Research Methodology

- *Research Objective*:
    (a) To determine the effect of gender on teacher's job satisfaction.
    (b) To identify which factors affect the job satisfaction of male and female teachers.

(c) To assess the job satisfaction of male and female teachers in public and private universities.

- **Hypothesis** H_0: There is no significant impact of gender on factors affecting job satisfaction among university teachers.
- **Sampling and Sample Size**: For achieving the objectives of the study, an exploratory and descriptive study was conducted followed by the judgmental sampling method. The data was collected from 450 academicians of public and private universities comprising of assistant professors, associate professors, and professors. Forty-five questionnaires were rejected due to the inappropriate information. Only 405 questionnaires were analyzed for the purpose.
- **Survey Instrument**: A well-structured questionnaire was developed after rigorous literature review. Suggestions from experts and statisticians were also solicited to develop an authentic questionnaire.
- **Respondent's Profile**: Almost equal proportion of response rate was received from public and private universities, i.e., 49.4 and 50.6%. Majority of the respondents were from the category of assistant professors, comprising of 63.2%, whereas 22.0 and 14.8% respondents are associate professors and professors. The ratios of male and female respondents were almost equal, i.e., 49.1 and 50.9%. Majority of the respondents (54.1%) were from the age group of 25–35 years, followed by 35.8% (35–45 years) and 10.1% (45 years and above). There were 52.8% of the respondents only having a postgraduate degree and 47.2% respondents acquiring doctoral degree. Relating to experience, 62.2% respondents are having 1–10 years followed by 24.4% (11–20 years), 9.4% (21–30 years), and only 4.0% respondents are having (31 years) teaching experience. Out of total respondents, 81.7% are married and 18.3% are unmarried. 41.7% were from income category of Rs. 30,001–50,000, 24.7% were from Rs. 50,001 to 100,000, 31.1% were from Rs. 100,000 and above, while only 2.5% teachers were from less than Rs. 30,000 category.

8.4 Managerial Implications

From the viewpoint of practical implementations, the findings of the study can be used as guiding principles for public and private universities to sustain or enhance the job satisfaction level of female and male academicians.

8.5 Analysis and Interpretation

The reliability of the scale was assessed by computing the coefficient of alpha (α). The value of the coefficient of alpha (α) was computed as 0.941, which is greater than 0.6. Therefore, this value was considered reliable and acceptable. The result

8 Effect of Gender on Job Satisfaction Among Academicians

Table 8.1 Descriptive statistics

Factors affecting job satisfaction among university teachers	Public university Gender Male mean and (S.D.)	Female mean and (S.D.)	Total mean	Private university Gender Male mean and (S.D.)	Female mean and (S.D.)	Total mean	Cronbach's alpha
Attitude and Behavior of Authorities	**2.93** (1.01)	**3.69** (0.915)	3.38	**2.75** (1.02)	**3.60** (1.11)	3.11	0.956
Research and Development	3.35 (0.909)	3.35 (0.902)	3.35	2.74 (0.949)	2.96 (0.987)	2.83	0.904
Facilities	2.92 (1.16)	3.06 (1.17)	3.00	2.46 (1.14)	2.30 (1.01)	2.39	0.946
Attitude and Behavior of Administrative Staff	**1.93** (0.734)	**1.91** (0.744)	1.92	**1.93** (0.667)	**1.87** (0.641)	1.91	0.872
Attitude and Behavior of Students	2.63 (0.903)	3.34 (0.807)	3.06	2.83 (0.974)	2.94 (1.00)	2.87	0.881
Coordination and Cooperation among Co-faculty Members	2.84 (1.02)	3.27 (0.900)	3.10	**2.90** (1.00)	**3.40** (0.814)	3.11	0.881
Technological and Informational Needs	3.39 (0.934)	3.43 (0.894)	3.41	**3.40** (0.976)	**3.56** (0.978)	3.46	0.964
Working Environment Conditions	**3.34** (1.14)	**3.86** (0.925)	3.65	**2.88** (1.10)	**3.56** (1.11)	3.17	0.954
Academic Environment Conditions	**3.61** (0.765)	**3.65** (0.763)	3.63	3.04 (0.924)	2.88 (0.921)	2.98	0.956
Service Condition Policies	3.27 (0.785)	3.19 (0.864)	3.22	2.91 (1.00)	3.14 (0.862)	3.00	0.958
Compensation	**3.41** (0.949)	**3.70** (0.869)	3.58	**2.86** (1.05)	**3.28** (1.00)	3.04	0.962

Bold values represents the gap in the satisfaction level of male and female teachers on different dimensions indicates that the male teachers in the public universities are satisfied on the dimensions like Academic Environment Conditions (mean = 3.61), Compensation (mean = 3.41), and Working Environment Conditions (mean = 3.34). It is also noticed from Table 8.1 that female teachers in public universities show higher satisfaction as compared to male counterparts on the dimensions like Academic Environment Conditions (mean = 3.65), Compensation (mean = 3.70), and Working Environment Conditions (mean = 3.86). Female teachers in the public universities are also satisfied with the dimension Attitude and Behavior of Authorities (mean = 3.69). Result also reveals that Technological and Informational Needs (mean = 3.40) is the dimension on which the male teachers of private university are likely to be satisfied. Attitude and Behavior of Authorities (mean = 3.60), Coordination and Cooperation among Co-faculty Members (mean = 3.40), Technological and Informational Needs (mean = 3.56), and Working Environment Conditions are the dimensions that satisfy them the most. Male and female teachers of both public and private universities are dissatisfied on the dimension Attitude and Behavior of Administrative Staff with mean values of (1.93 and 1.93) and (1.91 and 1.87). On this front, teachers in both universities believe that noncooperative behavior of administrative staff needs to be taken care of.

8.5.1 Gender of Academicians and Job Satisfaction

In the research study, the primary data is collected from faculty members from public and private universities regarding their perception about different factors affecting their job satisfaction. It is anticipated that the gender of faculty members influences their level of job satisfaction. The gender of the faculty could be either male or female. Independent sample t test is applied to test that gender differences also influence the job satisfaction level. The null hypothesis of independent sample t test and its result are given (Table 8.2).

H_0: There is no significant impact of gender on factors affecting job satisfaction among university teachers.

The result depicts that the t value is less than 5% level of significance in case of the following variables: Attitude and Behavior of Authorities, Research and Development Facilities, Attitude and Behavior of Students, Coordination and Cooperation among Co-faculty Members, Working Environment Conditions, Compensation to the teachers.

Null hypothesis (H_0) is rejected as there is a significant difference among the satisfaction level of faculty members based on gender. The mean value of the items shows that the female faculty members have significant higher job satisfaction as compared to the male faculty members. It could be because of difference in

Table 8.2 Independent sample t test between genders

Variables	Groups	Mean and (S.D.)	t statistic (p value)	Remarks
Attitude and Behavior of Authorities	Male	2.82 (1.017)	8.253 (0.000)	Significant difference exist
	Female	3.65 (1.001)		
Research and Development Facilities	Male	2.99 (0.978)	2.117 (0.035)	Significant difference exist
	Female	3.19 (0.955)		
Fringe benefits to the teachers	Male	2.64 (1.171)	0.858 (0.391)	No significant difference
	Female	2.74 (1.150)		
Attitude and Behavior of Administrative Staff	Male	1.93 (0.693)	0.576 (0.565)	No significant difference
	Female	1.89 (0.701)		
Attitude and Behavior of Students	Male	2.75 (0.949)	4.564 (0.000)	Significant difference exist
	Female	3.17 (0.915)		
Coordination and Cooperation among Co-faculty Members	Male	2.87 (1.010)	4.850 (0.000)	Significant difference exist
	Female	3.33 (0.865)		
Technological and Informational Needs	Male	3.39 (0.957)	0.922 (0.357)	No significant difference
	Female	3.48 (0.930)		
Working Environment Conditions	Male	3.07 (1.139)	6.266 (0.000)	Significant difference exist
	Female	3.74 (1.015)		
Academic Environment	Male	3.27 (0.905)	0.677 (0.499)	No significant difference
	Female	3.33 (0.913)		
Service Condition Policies	Male	3.05 (0.938)	1.319 (0.188)	No significant difference
	Female	3.17 (0.861)		
Compensation to the teachers	Male	3.08 (1.046)	4.477 (0.000)	Significant difference exist
	Female	3.52 (0.946)		

professional values among males and females. The reason could be that the female faculty emphasizes more on the social aspects of a job. As compared to their male counterparts, female teachers like to have work time flexibility and like to be employed part time. Female academicians receiving lesser salaries enjoy same level of job satisfaction. Proper communication and cordial relations with peers are important for female teachers. It was found that for male and female employees, self-respect, commitment, workplace communications, and professional relations are more important. Despite lower salary, slower promotion pace, smaller number of published articles, and higher job stress, the job satisfaction level of female faculty is higher, whereas male faculty considers participating in management decisions, giving directions to subordinates, career, compensation, opportunity for self-expression, dominance in job, and promotion opportunities as more important. With respect to the rest of the variables, such as fringe benefits to the teachers, Attitude and Behavior of Administrative Staff, Technological and Informational Needs, Academic Environment Conditions, and in-service condition policies, no significant difference is found.

8.6 Conclusion

The outcomes of the research determined that the gender directly influences teachers' job satisfaction. It could be because male and female teachers have their own set of preferences. Attitude and Behavior of Authorities, Research and Development Facilities, Attitude and Behavior of Students, Coordination and Cooperation among Co-faculty Members, Working Environment Conditions, and Compensation to the teachers are the factors that affect the job satisfaction of male and female teachers in the universities. Female teachers in both public and private universities are highly satisfied than their male counterparts. There is a dimension Attitude and Behavior of Administrative Staff on which male and female teachers of both public and private universities are dissatisfied. Therefore, universities should believe in maintaining gender parity, where academicians are treated evenly in all aspects. It is advisable to build up an atmosphere where both male and female academicians enjoy same level of independence, are rewarded equally, enjoy equal level of career growth opportunities, give admiration to each other, fulfill their commitments, and maintain harmonious workplace relations.

A primary limitation of the study is that the results generated from the research cannot generalize the responses of population of university teachers, as circumstances in other university environments may differ from the sample that was selected. It is possible that data collected from questionnaires is unable to capture some more aspects of job satisfaction. In this study, the data has been collected from the public and private university teachers at all levels. There is a possibility that respondents may be biased at the time of furnishing their opinions. The two major constraints, time and money, confined the study only to the specified region and sample universities. The above study can be conducted in other universities so as to generalize the findings of the study, and some more relevant factors can be drawn out. In future, the researchers can reassess the opinions of university teachers by taking a larger sample and re-evaluate whether the level of job satisfaction among university teachers is increasing or decreasing. Further studies could be conducted to assess how the job satisfaction level of university teachers improves the performance of public and private universities and performance of their students.

References

Bamel, U. K., Rangnekar, S., & Rastogi, R. (2014). Do gender, position, and organization shape human resource flexibility? In M. K. Nandakumar, S. Jharkharia & A. S. Nair (Eds.), *Organizational flexibility and competitiveness* (pp. 123–134). Flexible systems management. New Delhi: Springer.

Bendall-Lyon, D., & Powers, T. L. (2002). The impact of gender differences on change in satisfaction over time. *Journal of Consumer Marketing, 19*(1), 12–23.

Bhal, K. T., & Sharma, P. (2001). Multiplicity of cognitive frameworks for ethical decision-making: Variability across gender and age groups. *Global Journal of Flexible Systems Management, 2*(2), 1–10.

Birmingham, J. A. (1984). Job satisfaction and burnout among minnesota teachers (stress, morale). *Dissertation Abstracts International, 45*(8), 2318-A.

Clark, L. (1997). Job satisfaction. In L. K. Jones (Ed.), *Encyclopedia of career*.

Cooper, C. L., & Kelly, M. (1993). Occupational stress in head teachers: A national UK study. *British Journal of Educational Psychology, 63*(1), 130–143.

Cribbin, J. J. (1972). *Effective managerial leadership*. New York: American Management Association Inc.

Dhir, S., & Dhir, S. (2015). Diversification: Literature review and issues. *Strategic Change, 24*(6), 569–588.

Dhir, S., & Dhir, S. (2017). COMFED: The new challenges of diversification. *Emerald emerging markets case studies*. https://doi.org/10.1108/EEMCS-09-2016-0188.

Dhir, S., Mital, A., & Chaurasia, S. (2014). Balanced scorecard on top performing Indian firms. *International Journal of Indian Culture and Business Management, 9*(1), 89–100.

Drago, R. W., Wooden, M., & Sloan, J. (1992). *Productive relations? Australian industrial relations and workplace performance*. Sydney: Allen and Unwin.

Fields, L., & Blum, O. (1997). *Self-esteem in employees*. CA: Brooks Publishing Company.

Galloway, D., Boswell, K., Panckhurst, F., Boswell, C., & Green, K. (1985). Sources of satisfaction and dissatisfaction for New Zealand primary school teachers. *Educational Research, 27*(1), 44–51.

Garrido, M. J., Pérez, P., & Antón, C. (2005). Determinants of sales manager job satisfaction. An analysis of Spanish industrial firms. *The International Journal of Human Resource Management, 16*(10), 1934–1954.

Hoppock, R. (1935). *Job satisfaction*. New York: Harper.

Houston, D., Meyer, L. H., & Paewai, S. (2006). Academic staff workloads and job satisfaction: Expectations and values in academe. *Journal of Higher Education Policy and Management, 28*(1), 17–30.

Iqbal (2012). Job satisfaction as related to organizational climate and occupational stress in teachers. *Journal of Behavioral Sciences, 3,* 12–16.

Ivancevich, J. M., Matteson, M. T., & Konopaske, R. (1990). *Organizational behavior and management.* New York, NY: McGraw-Hill.

Korunka, C., Scharitzer, D., Carayon, P., & Sainfort, F. (2003). Employee strain and job satisfaction related to an implementation of quality in a public service organization: A longitudinal study. *Work & Stress, 17*(1), 52–72.

Lacy, F. J., & Sheehan, B. A. (1997). Job satisfaction among academic staff: An international perspective. *Higher Education, 34*(3), 305–322.

Li, L., & Wang Leung, R. (2001). Female managers in Asian hotels: Profile and career challenges. *International Journal of Contemporary Hospitality Management, 13*(4), 189–196.

Lortie, D. C. (1975). *School teacher: A sociological inquiry.*

Luthans, F., Wahl, L. V. K., & Steinhaus, C. S. (1992). The importance of social support for employee commitment: A quantitative and qualitative analysis of bank tellers. *Organization Development Journal, 10*(4), 1–10.

Maphorisa, J. K. (1997). *Job satisfaction of Batswana secondary school teachers* (Unpublished M Ed thesis). University of Botswana.

McCuddy, M., Pinar, M., & Birkan, I. (2010). Gender bias in managing human resources in the Turkish hospitality industry: Is bias impacted by demographic context. *Proceedings of ASBBS, 17*(1), 479–493.

Nash, M. (1985). *Managing organizational performance.* San Francisco, CA: Jossey-Bass.

Nguni, S., Sleegers, P., & Denessen, E. (2006). Transformational and transactional leadership effects on teachers' job satisfaction, organizational commitment, and organizational citizenship behavior in primary schools: The Tanzanian case. *School Effectiveness and School Improvement, 17*(2), 145–177.

Pinar, M., McCuddy, M. K., Birkan, I., & Kozak, M. (2011). Gender diversity in the hospitality industry: An empirical study in Turkey. *International Journal of Hospitality Management, 30*(1), 73–81.

Potter, I., Gosling, O., & Trezesniewski, K. H. (2001). *Self-esteem psychology: The psychology of self-esteem.* Retrieved from http://www.energypsychologyusa.com/selfesteem.html.

Poza, K., & Poza, L. K. (2003). *Psychology and industry today: An introduction to industrial and organizational psychology* (5th ed.). New York: Macmillan Publishing Company.

Ramayah, T., Jantan, M., & Tadisina, S. K. (2001, November) Job satisfaction: Empirical evidence for alternatives to JDI. In *32nd Annual Meeting of Decision Sciences Institute Conference,* Track OB2, San Francisco, USA.

Rhodes, C., Hollinshead, A., & Nevill, A. (2007). Changing times, changing lives: A new look at job satisfaction in two university schools of education located in the English West Midlands. *Research in Post-compulsory Education, 12*(1), 71–89.

Schuler, R. S. (1975). Sex, organizational level, and outcome importance: Where the differences are. *Personnel Psychology, 28*(3), 365–375.

Siu, O. L. (2002). Predictors of job satisfaction and absenteeism in two samples of Hong Kong nurses. *Journal of Advanced Nursing, 40*(2), 218–229.

Spector, P. E. (1997). *Job satisfaction: Application, assessment, causes, and consequences* (Vol. 3). Sage Publications.

Stevens, M. J., Oddou, G., Furuya, N., Bird, A., & Mendenhall, M. (2006). HR factors affecting repatriate job satisfaction and job attachment for Japanese managers. *The International Journal of Human Resource Management, 17*(5), 831–841.

Wu Huei-Jane & Wu You-I (2001). A study on elementary school teachers job satisfaction and its relationship with their social network, job characteristics. *Bulletin of Educational Research, 46*(1), 147–180.

Zembylas, M., & Papanastasiou, E. C. (2005). Modeling teacher empowerment: The role of job satisfaction. *Educational Research and Evaluation, 11*(5), 433–459.

Chapter 9
Trainer Engagement Versus Trainer Turnover Ratio

N. Karuppanna Prasad, K. Sekar, G. Srirekha Bharani and B. Vignesh

Abstract In twenty-first century, the top management in organization was facing the ever-changing marketing condition and was in an urge to pacify the versatile market need to attain a competitive advantage in external market. Organization competitiveness can be attained through continuous practice on competitive strategy known as Total Quality Management (TQM). The TQM in present era had set a path to achieve Total Employee Involvement (TEI) that provides opportunity for operator to involve in teams for solving the recurrence problem using a problem-solving approach. In present context, case narrows down on reducing the trainer turnover ratio in the Indian Training Institute (ITI) that lacks on trainer engagement, motivation and interpersonal trust. To identify the root cause for increase in trainer turnover ratio, the cross-functional teams (CFTs) have been formed that on first hand discuss with Human Resource (HR) team and trainers to identify the vital few reasons that impact turnover ratio as no employee engagement/involvement and ineffective trade-off between the performance and appraisal system in the ITI. The CFTs after data collection and analysis identify and implement the various improvement measures such as design, development of trainer index card, Kaizen/suggestion template, and trainers' key result area (KRA) in the ITI. The CFTs then validate the continuous adherence and sustaince sustenance on aforesaid improvements during the pilot period through peer audit done in the ITI. The audit done during the standardization period of three months had identified the adherence of imperative improvement measure such as trainer

N. Karuppanna Prasad (✉) · G. Srirekha Bharani
HR & ES-IE, Jindal Steel and Power Ltd., Raigarh, India
e-mail: Prasad.karupana@gmail.com; karuppanna.prasad@jspl.com

G. Srirekha Bharani
e-mail: srirekha9900@gmail.com

K. Sekar
Department of Mechanical Engineering, National Institute of Technology, Calicut, India
e-mail: sekar@nitc.ac.in

B. Vignesh
Hinduja Tech, Chennai 600087, India
e-mail: bevicky113@gmail.com

© Springer Nature Singapore Pte Ltd. 2018
S. Dhir and Sushil (eds.), *Flexible Strategies in VUCA Markets*,
Flexible Systems Management, https://doi.org/10.1007/978-981-10-8926-8_9

turnover ratio, employee involvement index, peer audit feedback, customer feedback, new programme or trainer and Kaizen or suggestion scheme. The audit results reveal the improvement in reduction of trainer turnover ratio to 5% from 20% and reduction in overhead cost to 0.5 million from 4 million along with improvement in trainer morale.

Keywords Human resource · KRA · Productivity · Quality · TQM

9.1 Introduction

In twenty-first century, the top management in organization was facing the ever-changing marketing condition and was in an urge to pacify the versatile market need to attain a competitive advantage that will lead to validation on core area (Khanna and Gupta 2014; Chowdhury et al. 2007). The organization competitiveness in domestic and global markets can be achieved and sustained through the practice of competitive strategy known as Total Quality Management (TQM) (Shaukat et al. 2002; Khanna and Gupta 2014; Srinivasan et al. 2016). The TQM is an integrated management philosophy that narrowly tailors on bottom line operator who thrives to satisfy the customer perception with economic of cost (Tang et al. 2010). As defined by Mohanakrishnan (2014) "TQM is the organizational effort on continuous improvement of all process, product and service through overall involvement which result in increased customer satisfaction, loyalty and improved business bottom line". The seven pinnacle enablers for incorporating TQM in organization were top management involvement, quality validation and yardstick, process control, product design, employee learning and development, supplier quality management, customer involvement and satisfaction (Motwani 2001; Chatterjee 2015). The TQM in present era had set a path for attaining a customer delight in upstream by starting with employee involvement and accountability in downstream through creation of knowledge workforce with high qualification and workplace performance (Matzler and Renzl 2006; Soltani et al. 2005). The employee engagement in the organization workplace can be attained through employee learning, employee accountability, teamwork, top management leadership, employee reward and recognition that lead to employee satisfaction and loyalty (Chang et al. 2010). The employee engagement also leads to total employee involvement (TEI) in TQM that provides opportunity for operator to involve in teams for solving the recurrence problem using a problem-solving seven quality control (7QC) tools such as check sheet, Pareto diagram, cause-and-effect diagram, scatter diagram, graph and control chart, histogram and stratification (Ishikawa 1982). The employee in organization applies the 7QC tools through forming of capable work teams such as quality control circle (QCC), supervisor improvement teams (SITs), cross-functional teams (CFTs) and task force (TF) to provide solution for problem by following the seven quality control (QC) story steps (Mohanakrishnan 2014).

In this context, the present chapter narrows down in implementing the QC story approach on reducing the trainer turnover ratio in the Indian Training Institute (ITI). The chapter has been structured by covering the Case Study in Level 2 and Conclusion with Future Scope in Level 3 in the ITI.

9.2 Case Study

The case reported in the present chapter was successfully derived from the ITI located in south India. The ITI is a doyen in the field of training by providing the need-based training for the incoming trainee in three various verticals such as business to business (B to B), business to education (B to E), and business to government (B to G). The training to the incoming trainee was given with the core value of "enter to learn in ITI and exit to perform" in their respective work area aftermath training. The training department wing in ITI comprises of highly capable trainers who have hands-on experience in various vertical specializations such as computer numeric control (CNC), quality system, industrial engineering. In the past three years, ITI had continuously faced customer complaint on quality of training that leads to trainee skill gap in customer end. To identify the reason for quality declination, brainstorming session was held along with top management, Human resource (HR) people from ITI and customers. The minutes of meeting (MOM) reveal existence of deviation in the training session with respect to customer-end requirement on training. The high customer exhaustion cum complaints leads to decline in the bottom line of the ITI over the past three years. The organization ineffectiveness on mishandling the customer pressure leads to highly dissatisfied trainer wing who are day in and out fire by the top management official that end result in an increase trainer turnover ratio that also lead to increase in overhead cost such as alternate trainer recruitment cost, training cost and labour cost for the past three years in the ITI. In this context, current chapter narrows down to identify the core reason for reducing the trainer turnover ratio in ITI through setting up of capable CFT who apply the concept of 7QC tools in the QC story problem-solving approach.

9.2.1 QC Story Problem-Solving Steps

The QC story is the problem-solving approach most endemically used by various working teams in organization such as QCC, SIT, CFT and TF for solving the recurrence problem with high effect, and the reason for occurrence is unknown. The 7 QC story steps were defined as Problem Definition, Data Collection, Data Analysis, Action or Improvement Deployment, Action Taken or Improvement Implementation, Effect of Action and Standardization which are illustrated briefly for reducing the trainer turnover ratio in the ITI.

9.2.1.1 Problem Definition

To identify the decline in trainer turnover ratio, the CFT consists of three members who were formed in the ITI. The CFT on first hand conducted the interview with the HR team members to understand the lack of employee motivation, engagement and interpersonal trust in the ITI to frame the project charter as shown in Table 9.1.

The CFT through exit interview report identify the huge gap between management and training wing that impact the trainer participation in human value chain which may be an imperative reason to increase in the turnover ratio with subsequent increase in the overhead cost for the ITI. The increase in turnover ratio leads to exit of capable trainers from ITI that urges the CFT to perform 360° data collection as a next course of action.

9.2.1.2 Data Collection

The CFT conducts a brainstorming session with the HR team members, top management, training head of the ITI to identify the various reasons that have created a state of oblivion on trainer demotivation, disengagement and non-trustable work environment for the past three years in the ITI. The CFT also performs the verification and validation of past three years' trainer exit interview record available with the HR team members in ITI to identify and stratify the various reasons that were listed down in the attribute check sheet as shown in Table 9.2.

From Table 9.2, CFT identifies that nearly 74 trainers had left the job over the past three years due to trainer disengagement, 67 trainers left the job because of flawed performance appraisal system, and 28 trainers were exited due to no career succession growth and many other valuable reasons. The quantitative data collected

Table 9.1 Project charter for reducing trainer turnover ratio

Project Charter - Trainer turnover ratio
Problem: Increase in trainer turnover ratio in the Indian Training Institute (ITI)
Problem definition: The top management ineffectiveness on trainer involvement cum engagement leads to increase in trainer turnover ratio to 20% in the past three years in the ITI
Reasons for taking up this problem: The reduced trainer turnover ratio and trainer engagement will lead to reduction in recruitment cost, attrition rate, labour cost and with improved trainer capability and bottom line in ITI
Target: To reduce the employee turn over ratio by half in the ITI
Limitation and boundary: Technical training wing
Team members: 3 (Authors, HR)
Tools: Pareto diagram, cause-and-effect diagram, why-why analysis, action plan, trainer involvement index sheet, Kaizen/suggestion sheet, KRA template
Expected customer benefit: Enhance trainee capability after training days that lead to repeated customer training order in the ITI

9 Trainer Engagement Versus Trainer Turnover Ratio

Table 9.2 Attribute check sheet for trainer turnover ratio

S. No.	Reason for increase in turnover ratio	Total	Contribution (%)	Cumulative (%)
1	No trainer disengagement	74	37	37
2	Ineffective trade-off between the performance and appraisal	67	33.5	70.5
3	No career growth	28	14	84.5
4	No top management commitment	18	9	93.5
5	Over workload as not a part of KRA	13	6.5	100
Card total		200		

by the CFT was to be analysed for identifying the imperative reason that highly impacts the trainer turnover ratio in the ITI.

9.2.1.3 Data Analysis

The CFT aftermath data collection from the HR team of the ITI starts analysing the data offline using the two common analysis tools such as Pareto diagram and cause-and-effect diagram. The Pareto diagram was first introduced by the Italian economist by the name Vilfredo Pareto for identifying the problem priority to solve and improve the process by reducing the defect occurrence and variation (Ishikawa 1982). The Pareto diagram works under the thumb rule of 20% of causes are the reason for the 80% of defect occurrence (vital few) and 80% of causes are the reason for the 20% of defect occurrence (trivial many). The Pareto diagram in the ITI is used to identify the priority among the reasons that create high impact on trainer exit that leads to high trainer turnover ratio, and Pareto chart for the current study has been plotted using the Minitab software as shown in Fig. 9.1.

From Fig. 9.1, the CFT identifies the vital few reasons that create a highly dissatisfied trainer workforce were no trainer involvement/engagement that contributes nearly 37% of the total reasons followed by ineffective performance appraisal system that contributes nearly 33.5% in the ITI. The causes were accumulated using "why-why" analysis by asking question on each "why occurrence" to the subject matter experts (SMEs), HR team, top management of the ITI. The answers from shooting of each why questions on key variables list down Level 1 causes cum Level 2 subcauses that were recorded meticulously by the CFT. The collected causes from brainstorming session were stratified based on key variables such as People, Plant, Policy and Procedure (4P) to build the Level 1 type of cause-and-effect diagram as shown in Fig. 9.2.

The CFT further had a discussion with steering committee of experts to isolate the indifferent causes by creating Level 2- and Level 3-type cause-and-effect diagram for bringing in the trainer engagement and creation of robust performance appraisal structure for the trainers in the ITI. In overall, subjective feedback analysis done with

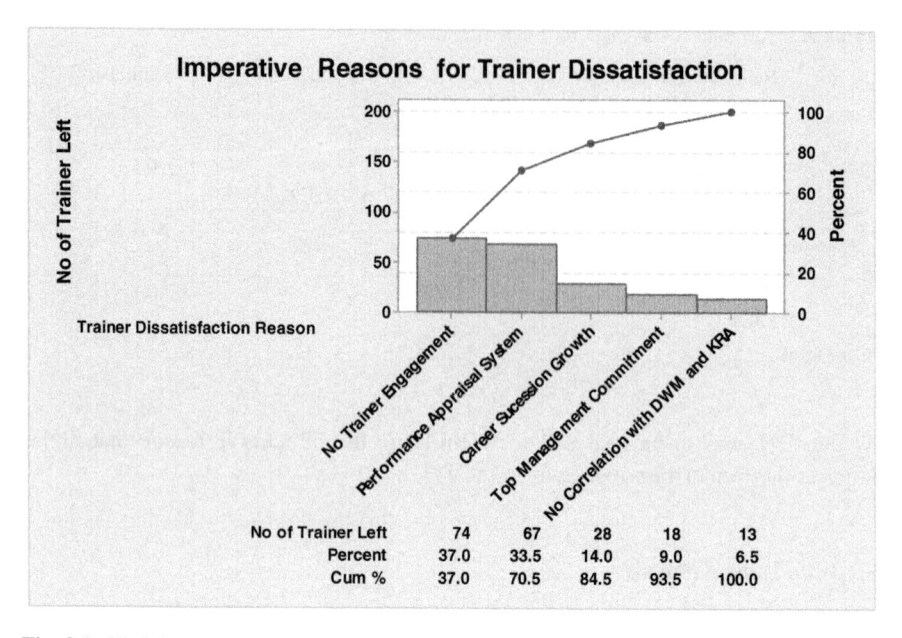

Fig. 9.1 Vital few reasons for trainer turnover ratio increase

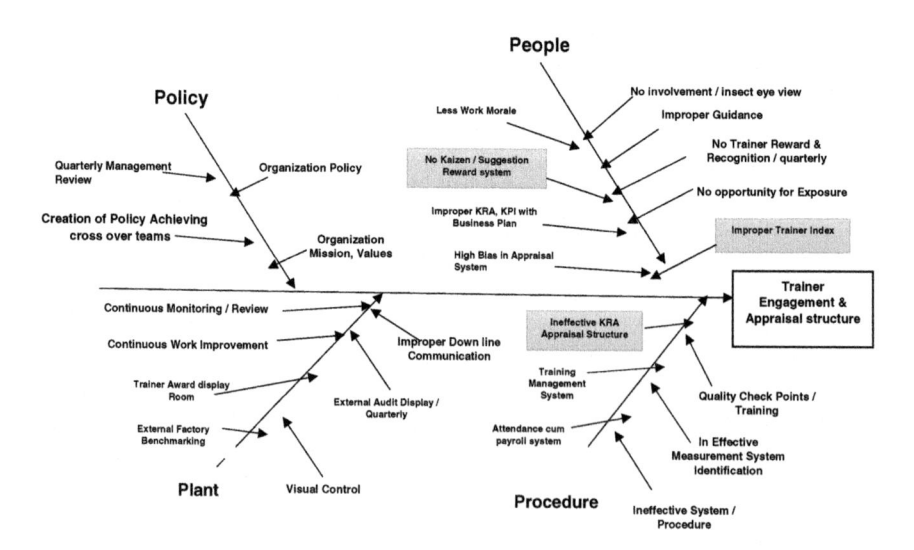

Fig. 9.2 Cause and effect diagram for trainer disengagement and performance appraisal system

steering committee members in various stages leads to identification of last level vital causes that may bring the total quality environment which were unavailability of trainer index card (year till date (YTD)), Kaizen/suggestion scheme for trainers and ineffective key result area (KRA) cum key performance indicator (KPI) appraisal structure. To implement and identify the improvement in pilot basis, the CFT designs, develops and sustains the aforesaid improvement in ITI.

9.2.1.4 Improvement Deployment

The CFT from data analysis and discussion with steering committee experts identify the improvement causes to be deployed as development of trainer index card, trainer Kaizen/suggestion scheme and trainer performance appraisal system. The implementation of suggested improvement in the pilot basis was continuously monitored through the action plan as shown in Table 9.3.

The action plan was developed in the format of 5W1H (What, Why, When, Where, Who and How) for implementing the improvement measure in the training department of the ITI. In first stage of improvement, CFT after discussion with the training department and HR team designs and develops the trainer index card template for adherence as shown in Table 9.4.

In second phase, the CFT had discussion with the HR team to conduct the contest for designing and developing the template for Kaizen/suggestion scheme among trainers. The consensus on selected template from contest was shown in Fig. 9.3. The discussion also concludes that the target for each trainer has been fixed as 4 Kaizen/year and each trainer to provide the breakthrough improvement of

Table 9.3 Action management plan for improving trainer turnover ratio

S. No.	What Root cause	Why	When Date	Where Organization	Who Responsibility	How Improvement solution
1	No trainer index score card (YTD)	Continuous monitoring and recording of trainer performance based on PQCDSM	XXXX	Training department in the Indian Training Institute	XXXX	Design, develop and adherence of trainer index card template
2	No Kaizen/suggestion scheme	The Kaizen/suggestion scheme will improve the morale and provide monetary saving to the ITI	XXXX		XXXX	Kaizen/suggestion template has been designed along with target/year/trainer
3	Ineffective KRA appraisal structure	The trainer to obtain the performance-based pay, review and identify individual performance need every quarterly	XXXX		XXXX	KRA to link with the annual business plan of ITI

Table 9.4 Trainer index card template in ITI

Trainer index card template for FY 2016–17									Month	April
Trainer name	Trainer Id	P (10%)	Q (20%)	C (10%)	D (20%)	S (20%)	M (20%)	Total (100%)	Trainer index (at the end of FY)
XXX	02	5%	3%	6%	6%	12%	2%	34%	–

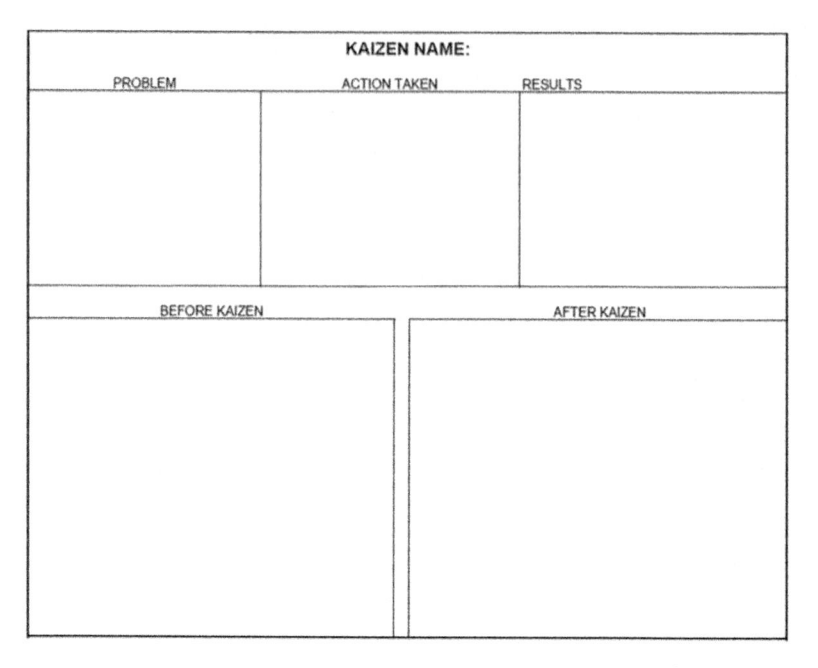

	KAIZEN NAME:	
PROBLEM	ACTION TAKEN	RESULTS
BEFORE KAIZEN		AFTER KAIZEN

Fig. 9.3 Kaizen sheet for trainer idea/thinking in ITI

minimum 1 suggestion/year by involving the trainer through formation of various CFTs in the ITI.

In third phase, implementation on framing of appropriate KRA of performance appraisal system for each trainer was developed. To create an effective KRA, CFT understands the current year annual plan on which the daily work management (DWM) of the trainer has been stratified with respect to productivity (P), quality (Q), cost (C), delivery (D), safety (S) and morale (M). The trainers yearly KRA will be derived from the voice of customer (VOC) based on which the yearly stratification of managing point (MP) for trainer–manager cum checkpoint (CP) for trainer–subordinate has been done. The review will be done on KRA plan versus actual every quarterly through management review meeting (MRM). The KRA template for the sample trainer position in ITI is shown in Table 9.5.

Table 9.5 Trainer KRA in the ITI

Trainer key result area—ITI for FY 2016–17			
Trainer name: XXX		Designation: executive	
Department: XXXX		Grade: L2	
Performance metrics	Action plan	Target	
Productivity (P)	To learn and train new training modules	2 training modules/year
Quality (Q)	Customer training feedback	3–4 (in four point rating scale)
Cost (C)	Organization cost saving	10–20% of department expenses
Delivery (D)	Internal/external audit score	7–10 (average of three audits done per year)
Safety (S)	To identify and correct the unsafe act (UA) and unsafe condition (UC) to achieve zero accident	10—near miss, 5—minor accident, 2—major accident (per year)
Morale (M)	Kaizen/suggestion scheme	4/1 (per year)

The effect of the adherence towards the improvement made in the pilot stage has been standardized for the period of three months.

9.2.1.5 Improvement Implementation

The CFT after having comparative discussion with the HR team, training team and management had framed the trainer index template, Kaizen and trainer KRA performance appraisal template. The pilot implementation of the same in the training department has been done for the period of three months. The adherence of the same is evaluated through conduction of 360° feedback by the CFT who interacts with the HR team, trainer and top management team to identify the objective feedback on the questionnaires as shown in Table 9.6.

From Table 9.6, suggested improvement has been slowly and steadily imbibed by the employee engagement and involvement into the DWM of the training wing in ITI. The period of standardization provides a limelight for the trainers and top management to reach an enhanced pathway to challenge and sustain the present improvement and further improve to reach the world-class standards. The organization improvement during the period of standardization had been validated by CFT to assess the solution effectiveness.

Table 9.6 Improvement adherence action plan

Improvement deployment cum adherence action plan			
Questionnaire	External audit rating	Trainer rating	Top management rating
Is suggestion/Kaizen scheme implemented	Good	Good	Good
Does employee are motivated regularly	Medium	Below medium	Good
Employee KNOWS annual plan/policy	Good	Medium	Good
Is training index card maintain regularly	Medium	Medium	Good
Is KRA review every quarterly	Medium	Medium	Medium

Note The linguistic score is obtained through feedback from external audit team, trainer and top management

9.2.1.6 Effect of Action

The improvement deployment in training department was done for the period of three months. During this period, CFT conducts an audit through 360° feedback interaction with training team, HR team and top management officials on key training criteria such as trainer turnover ratio, employee involvement index, peer audit feedback, customer feedback, new programme/trainer and Kaizen/suggestion scheme that were commonly stratify into productivity (P), quality (Q), cost (C), delivery (D), safety (S) and morale (M) as shown in Table 9.7.

From Table 9.7, audit from peer team identifies the existence of a considerable improvement in key productivity criteria such as reduction in trainer turnover ratio

Table 9.7 PQCDM improvement in ITI

S. No.	Performance metric	Performance measure	Actual	Proposed	Remarks
1	Productivity (P)	Trainer turn over ratio	20%	4%	Organization will have 4–5% attrition/year
		Trainer involvement index score	2	8	Score of 10
2	Quality (Q)	Customer feedback	1	3	Programme quality score max of 4
		Peer audit feedback	1	3	
3	Cost (C)	Overhead cost	4 million	0.5 million	Reduction in training, recruitment cost
4	Delivery (D)	New customer/module trained per year	1	2	New programme/new customer
5	Morale (M)	Kaizen/suggestion	–	4/1	Employee involvement

to 4% that was achieved through trainer engagement, motivation and tangible appraisal structure that subsequently increase the trainer involvement index score from 1 to 8 (Max of 10). The content development cell has been set up who tweaks and standardizes the PPT, material and pedagogy as per the trainee that improves the trainee capability which was assessed through customer feedback score that had improved from 1 to 3 (Max to 4). The continuous sustainability of identification of corrective action during the standardization period reduces the overhead cost to 0.5 from 4 million. The training team through multiskilling had provided the opportunity for the trainer to learn minimum two new modules/year. To create a highly engaged workforce, the Kaizen/suggestion scheme was introduced where each trainer provides at least 4 Kaizen/year and gets involved in providing 1 suggestion/Year. The best Kaizen/suggestion was recognized with suitable rewards that will improve trainer workplace morale.

9.2.1.7 Standardization

The CFT aftermath effective improvement in implementation for the period of three months had identified the change in culture of the trainers who are employed in the ITI through their engagement in work teams to provide suggestion, Kaizen. The top management had also started to perform continuous quarterly review to assess the effectiveness on trainer involvement to identify and improve the gap in their KPI with respect to KRA. The review system was framed in such a manner where the individual trainer will do self-appraisal on their KPI with respect to KRA every quarterly followed by subordinate boss appraisal and skip-level boss appraisal on trainer KPI with respect to KRA in the ITI. The present review system had provided an opportunity for identifying the strength and gap in trainers capability that can be improved by providing the skill-based train the trainers programme which overall embark organization growth and goal. The improvement incorporated in pilot basis has to be standardized continuously in ITI whose adherence will be validated through surprise check by the CFT who interacts with trainers every quarterly to obtain 360° feedback on improvement sustenance. The CFT report will be submitted to the board of directors (BODs) team. To continuously adopt the present improvement visual management system (VMS) had been created with respect to PQCDSM to reveal the key training criteria that will be updated every quarterly by the process data owner in the ITI. The VMS will provide the clear visualization on employee engagement cum performance data every quarterly in the ITI.

9.3 Conclusion

The present research work has been taken in the ITI that lacks on employee engagement, motivation and interpersonal trust among the trainers due to organization ineffectiveness in handling the customer pressure that leads to increase in the employee turnover ratio by 20% that creates an impediment increase in new trainer recruitment cost, trainer training cost and labour cost for the ITI. The CFTs have been formed who validate the present situation using seven QC for data collection, data analysis to identify the reason for unhappiness that were due to no trainer engagement, flawed appraisal system that subsequently increase the trainer turnover ratio. To reduce the turnover ratio, CFTs conducted discussion with the HR team to identify various process level Kaizen such as trainer index template, Kaizen/suggestion template and KRA template that have been implemented successfully and whose adherence cum sustenance have been monitored through 360° feedback system by CFTs. The improvement done in the ITI has improved the morale of trainers and sustaince of same in future days will empower trainers who can create a centre for world-class excellence in training. *Future Scope*: In future, positive improvement leads to reduction in the employee attrition rate in the technical training department. The same can be horizontally deployed to serve as standards for institutions other than ITIs for creating a world-class centre of excellence.

References

Chang, C. C., Chiu, C. M., & Chen, C. A. (2010). The effect of TQM practices on employee satisfaction and loyalty in government. *Total Quality Management and Business Excellence, 21*(12), 1299–1314.

Chatterjee, A. (2015). Organizational excellence through total flexi-quality: People dimension. In Sushil, K. T. Bhal & S. P. Singh (Eds.), *Managing flexibility: People, process, technology and business* (pp. 37–42). Flexible systems management. New Delhi: Springer.

Chowdhury, M., Paul, H., & Das, A. (2007). The impact of top management commitment on total quality management practice: An exploratory study in the Thai garment industry. *Global Journal of Flexible Systems Management, 8*(1–2), 17–30.

Ishikawa, I. (1982). *Guide to quality control*. Tokyo: Asian Productivity Organization.

Khanna, V. K., & Gupta, R. (2014). Comparative study of the impact of competency-based training on 5 "S" and TQM: A case study. *International Journal of Quality and Reliability Management, 31*(3), 238–260.

Matzler, K., & Renzl, B. (2006). The relationship between interpersonal trust, employee satisfaction and employee loyalty. *Total Quality Management, 17*(10), 1261–1271.

Mohanakrishnan, S. (2014). *The way to the practise of total quality management*. Madras: Productivity and Quality Publisher Private Limited.

Motwani, J. (2001). Critical factors and performance measures of TQM. *The TQM Magazine, 13*(4), 292–300.

Shaukat, A. B., Serene, S. L., & Tee, B. M. R. (2002). Relationship between TQM and performance of Singapore companies. *International Journal of Quality and Reliability Management, 19*(4), 356–379.

Soltani, E., Lai, P. C., & Gharneh, N. S. (2005). Breaking through barriers to TQM effectiveness: Lack of commitment of upper-level management. *Total Quality Management and Business Excellence, 16*(8–9), 1009–1021.

Srinivasan, K., Muthu, S., Devadasan, S. R., & Sugumaran, C. (2016). Six sigma through DMAIC phases: A literature review. *International Journal of Productivity and Quality Management, 17*(2), 236–257.

Tang, Z., Chen, X., & Wu, Z. (2010). Using behaviour theory to investigate individual-level determinants of employee involvement in TQM. *Total Quality Management and Business Excellence, 21*(12), 1231–1260.

Chapter 10
Supply Chain Strategies to Sustain Economic and Customer Uncertainties

Deepankar Sinha and Debasri Dey

Abstract Previous research showed that passenger car manufacturing sector gets affected due to economic volatility and customer behavior pattern. In course of economic slowdown, inventory builds up and production rate suffers. While during recovery, backlog increases causing customers to shift brand loyalty. Besides, customer's preference tends to affect the supply chain of a firm too. In passenger car sector, changes in pre-designed models have significant bearing on the lead time. Delay in adopting changes sought by the customers' results in longer production time and obsolescence of inventory. The impact of economic variations on sales of cars has been analyzed through multivariate regression, and the dimensions explaining the customers' buying pattern have been identified through factor analysis of responses obtained from car buyers. The purpose of this chapter is to establish a system dynamics model, to study the effect of economic volatility and customer's buying behavior on supply chain of passenger car firms. The proposed framework will enable supply chain managers to carry out policy experimentation under different volatile situations arising out of exogenous factors. The proposed model is expected to address the major challenge, i.e., when there is economic instability with changing customer preferences.

Keywords Customer's preference · Economic volatility · Factor analysis
Passenger car · System dynamics

D. Sinha
IIFT, Kolkata, India

D. Dey (✉)
City College of Commerce and Business Administration, Kolkata, India
e-mail: debasrichatterjee@gmail.com

D. Dey
Department of MCA, BCA, IGNOU Regional Centre Kolkata, Kolkata, India

D. Dey
NMIS, Mumbai, India

10.1 Introduction

Supply chain decisions are crucial to a firm's success. Several attempts have been made to suggest framework for its decision making. Of these, the most important are the supply chain drivers approach (Chopra and Meindle 2001), systems approach (Van der Velde and Meijer 2003), contingency approach (Mukhtar et al 2009). The primary drivers included production, inventory, transportation, location, and information. Dey and Sinha (2016) suggested an integrated approach towards decision making.

The erratic fluctuations in financial system and economy of the country are referred to as economic volatility (Khanra and Dhir 2017). Economic ups and downs impact negatively on consumer confidence resulting in reduction in buying goods and products (Parameswar et al. 2017). This in turn results in excess inventories and downsizings. This becomes a vicious cycle. People's earnings drop due to loss of jobs and incomes causing reduction in their purchases. This makes economy volatile (NCPERS 2016). Macroeconomic volatility hinders growth. Hnatkovska and Loayza (2005) showed the causality between volatility and growth in GDP. They estimated that increase in the average value of volatility by the value of its standard deviation results in an average loss of growth in GDP. Volatility acts as a major hindrance in economic and social development (Cariolle 2012).

The income growth is measured through the increase in GDP. Gross domestic product (GDP) can be said to be similar to income conceptually. The sale of normal good would increase if incomes increase. This relationship between income growth and normal goods sales may be called income elasticity (State Board of Equalization, Economic Perspective, Summary of Recent Economic Developments, August 2007, Publication 329).

Demiroğlu and Yüncüler (2016) showed that increase in total household expenditure is proportional to rate of change of GDP, calculated over a ten-year-period data. They concluded that the nominal expenses on automobiles have shown faster growth than nominal GDP. Income is a significant factor in decisions on car ownership (Dargay and Gately 1999, 2001). Wu et al. (2014) and Rota et al. (2016) showed S-shaped relationship between per capita income and the vehicle per capita indicating that there exist limits to growth in demand of cars. The demand for cars, with respect to income, is higher at low levels of per capita number of cars compared to the levels that are close to the saturation level (Rota et al. 2016). The saturation point has been estimated as approximately 850 vehicles per 1000 people by IMF (2005). Rota et al. (2016) fit a Gombertz curve and estimated a joint saturation level of 622 vehicles per 1000 inhabitants (based on data from 59 countries). Demiroğlu and Yüncüler (2016) concluded that the relationship between increase in per capita income and the number of passenger vehicles per capita is strong in developing countries compared to the developed countries. Several authors (Kahn 1986; Hamilton and Macauley 1998; Greenspan and Cohen 1999; Eskeland and Feyzioglu 1997; Jacobsen and Van Benthem 2015) have reinforced that income level and the fuel prices are factors of disposal rate of cars. They showed that when fuel price rises people, who can afford, replace their cars with more fuel-efficient versions.

One of the most critical success factors of the automotive industry in the world is that they recognize that customer's preferences are considered as the essential part of the vehicles those are being marketed, purchased, and determined. More and more customers are willing to compensate premiums for vehicles that are produced and operated according to customer's compliant practices. In very recent years, the automotive industries have seen costly product recalls due to faulty airbags, brakes, alternators, electronic systems, and other parts. As a result, the industry, which includes automobile manufacturers, suppliers, and Original Equipment Manufacturers (OEMs), must adhere to strict product quality standards, such as ISO 9001 and ISO/TS 16949. Additionally, businesses operate in a highly competitive environment where customer preferences are constantly evolving and regulatory compliance is always a high priority. Automotive companies also need to ensure product quality, safety, and compliance throughout the supply chain and maintain a level of environment, health and safety performance.

It has been found that the passenger car manufacturing sector in India is also affected by the customer's preference-related uncertainty factor in a large scale, and due to this, production delay is introduced in the system. This in turn accumulates backlog and sometimes also causes the generation of obsolete inventory, to be drained out in near future. Over a period of time passenger car manufacturers have been competing by differentiating their models with as many features possible.

In recent past, Maruti Suzuki announced that it would provide the customers to customize their choices through the "i Create" platform, where customers can opt from 90 customization options in different packages (Naik 2016). Patel et al. (2017) opined that "the product life cycle of cars is shortening. Every four years, you need to upgrade design and technology of a model, while refreshing It with minor changes every four years."

Gunawan and Chandra (2014) in a report on car purchasing patterns in urban India concluded that it may not be correct to assume that car customers have pre-decided choice of model of car. They may change their views at the time of buying. He estimated that three out of five buyers, who were prejudiced, changed their decision at the time of buying. This change in decision is primarily on the type, model, and fuel type. The consumers are influenced by the salesperson, family, and friends. Figure 10.1 summarizes the dimensions and uncertainty in customer buying behavior. It depicts that 44% of consumers changed the preference of the model they decided to buy before reaching the showroom. About 37% changed their brand, and 30% altered their choice of fuel type at the time of buying. There were few, around 13%, who deviated from their pre-decided budget and color.

India is one of fastest growing economies and is set to grow at a rate of 7% or so. The Indian automobile industry is considered as one of the major industries contributing 18.5% (as in 2015–16) to the GDP. However, external factors such as oil price, US Fed rate, policies, and disintegration of EU are likely to pose threat to the

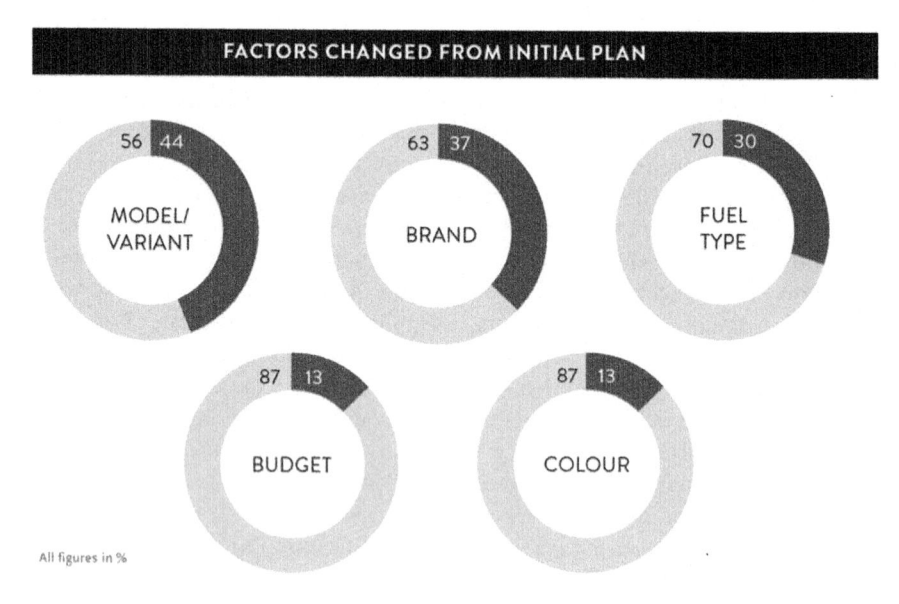

Fig. 10.1 Dimensions and uncertainty in customer buying behavior

economy of the country causing economic upheavals. ESCAP (2017) in their report concluded India's growth rate to hit 7.5% in 2018, but US policies pose risk.

In addition to this the growing consciences among the Indian buyers of small cars, the supply chain decisions are likely to become more complex. So far, literature review shows that very few studies have been done on impact of economic conditions on sales of passenger cars and its consequent effects on supply chain considering the customer's preferences-related uncertainties together. Recent economic downturns factor have left the supply chain managers clueless and take ad hoc decisions.

This chapter is targeted to capture the causality arising out of financial instability and uncertainties' arising out of customer's buying behavior. It proposes to model the cumulative dynamics arising out economic volatility and customer's buying behavior. This chapter proposes use of systems dynamics approach for developing a decision making framework for supply chain managers in passenger car industry.

System dynamics approach, introduced by (Forrester 1961, 1968), enables simulation of policies. It is based on the principles of causality (cause–effect relationships) and feedback control framework to understand the dynamic behavior of the systems (Sushil 1993). According to Senge (1990), any decision should be based on systems thinking. The cause and effect relationships give rise to the dynamic complexity, and the impact of decisions over time is not apparent.

System dynamics study aims at explaining the systems behavior when parameters are changed or policies are revised. Based on the behavior of the system (illustrated through simulation runs using software such as Vensim or Stella or similar), it enables decision makers to change the structure, policies or both for improvement in system's behavior. Coyle (1977) proposed three-layer structure of a firm's operation. The core is the "controller," i.e., the firm's own internal environment over which it has control and influence. The "controller" is surrounded by the "complement" comprising the customers and business partners. In this layer, the firm can only influence but cannot control. The outermost layer is the environment on which the firm can neither influence nor control. A change in the environment comes as a shock, and it is the firms' ability to withstand these shocks. Changes in economy within the country or worldwide and similarly disruption due to natural calamities are examples of environmental shocks.

10.2 Modeling Impact of Economic Volatility and Customer Uncertainty on Supply Chain Management of Passenger Cars

The following two sub-sections, i.e., 10.2.1 and 10.2.2, respectively, describe the concept and basis of modeling the impact of economic volatility and customer uncertainty on supply chain management of passenger cars. The causality has been established based on literature and secondary and primary data analysis.

The integrated model is described in Sect. 10.2.3.

10.2.1 Modeling Impact of Economic Volatility on Supply Chain Management of Passenger Cars

Breakdown in economy in the period 2008–2009 led to the study and explanation of sudden shrinkage in trade and the ways to manage such trade collapse. Authors (Sheffi and Rice 2005; Gunasekaran et al. 2008; Swafford et al. 2006) suggest that firms endeavor to grow, maintain, and develop capabilities required to react to changes arising out of environmental uncertainty (Kurien and Qureshi 2014; Dhir and Mital 2013). At this time, Stevenson and Spring (2007) call for enhancing firms' capability such as flexibility within the organization and across its supply chain partners. This has been reinforced by Christopher (2005) who concluded that firms now compete among their supply chains rather than as individual firms. Thus, supply chain management (SCM) is important to sustain competitiveness (Gunasekaran et al. 2008). Authors have suggested vital recession–recovery strategies for manufacturers to effectually reduce supply chain risks, quickly respond to opportunities associated with the economic recovery, and operate a more efficient and competitive business (Gunasekaran et al. 2016; Dhir et al. 2014). The strategies include strengthening of cash position, rearrange the supply chain to accomplish financial goals, consider a hybrid nearshore/offshore approach and similar. There exists a perception delay among consumers about the recovery of economy, and as a result, they remain covert in spending and exhibit meticulousness on value going into every decision, even when the economy salvages. This will, however, be viewed as an opportunity by successful companies, to create a strategic advantage by realigning their product offerings with the new consumer preferences (Bibhushan et al. 2014).

A statistical analysis (multiple regressions) of sales of passenger cars as dependent variable and economic variables, viz. GDP, WPI, Fuel-Price as independent variables, has been carried out. The results show that sales are sensitive to economic variables such as GDP, WPI, and Fuel-Price. The elasticity has been found to be more than 1. The r^2 was 0.996 indicating the acceptance of the results.

The data has been retrieved from Web sites of RBI (Reserve Bank of India—https://www.rbi.org.in/) and SIAM (Society of Indian Automobile Manufactures www.siamindia.com).

As the result of statistical analysis show that the sales of passenger cars are sensitive to changes in macroeconomic variables, the supply chain management is likely to become vulnerable during economic slowdown when the inventory builds up and production becomes unstable. The macroeconomic phenomena may be said to comprise three stages, namely pre-recovery or slowdown stage, recovery stage, and post-recovery stage. The characteristics of these stages are laid down below.

Pre-recovery stage—The pre-recovery stage is characterized with the state as: Order level = Low, Inventory level = Very High, Production Level = Low and Capacity Utilization = Low. Figure 10.2 illustrates the pre-recovery stage graphically.

Thus, pre-recovery with respect to supply chain can be defined in terms of inventory level, obsolescence, backlog, order levels, and production levels. In pre-recovery, the inventory level expected to be higher, obsolescence is higher, production level is very low, backlog is zero (0), and order level is low. These form the initial condition of the system dynamics model.

Recovery Stage The recovery stage is characterized with the state as: Order level = Increasing, Inventory level = Decreasing, Production Level = Increasing, and Capacity Utilization = Increasing.

Post-Recovery Stage The post-recovery stage is characterized with the state as:

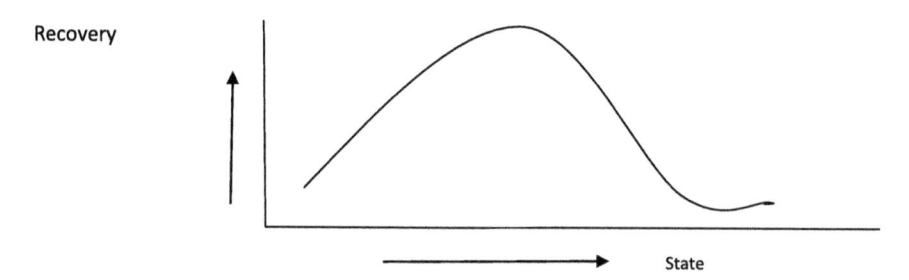

Fig. 10.2 Graph for pre-recovery state

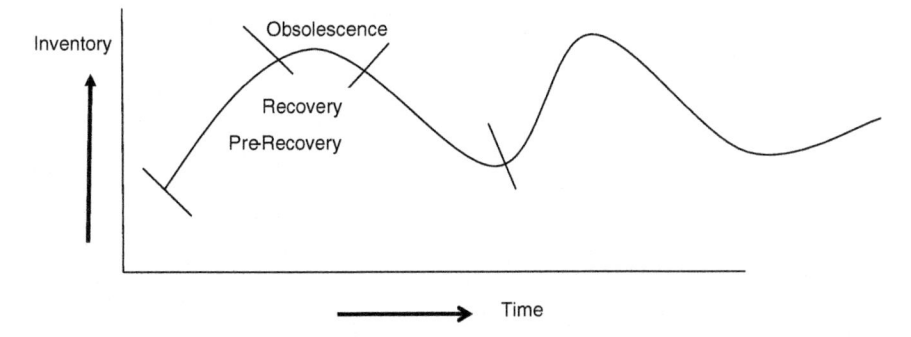

10 Supply Chain Strategies to Sustain Economic and ... 145

Fig. 10.3 Inventory level—recovery versus pre-recovery

Order level = Stabilizing, Inventory level = Optimal, Production Level = Optimal, and Capacity Utilization = Optimal. Figure 10.3 shows the inventory level during different phases of economic cycle.

In order to meet the increase in order level (during the recovery period), depleting the previously held inventory, firm needs to increase the production capacity to meet the rise in demand. Increasing of production capacity will involve some delay due to time taken to install additional capacity. During this delay period, the firm is expected to experience lost sales affecting its credibility. Hence, the firm needs to ramp up production with agile manufacturing approach and resort to outsourcing to meet the upsurge in demand. The extent of ramping up production and outsourcing would depend on the rate of recovery. This leads to construct a causal loop diagram and is shown in Fig. 10.4.

There is a loop that explains the dynamics of the system, viz. backlog–order received loop: The increase in order received will increase backlog. Increase in

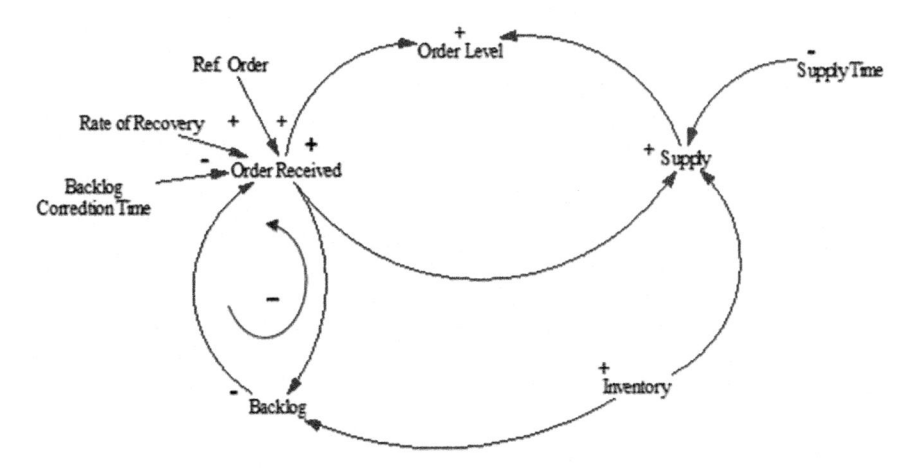

Fig. 10.4 Causal loop diagram showing the economic recovery from downturn

backlog will decrease order received, as this will cause customers to shift brands and models resulting in lost sales, hence a negative loop.

The state of level variable backlog indicates the combined influence of order level and inventory level. If the backlog increases, then it can be concluded that the plant is unable to meet order received from customer. The order level is also dependent on accumulated backlog. If the order level is higher than accumulated inventory level, then backlog will increase, until the rate of production meets the demand. If the rate of recovery is high, then inventory will reduce and may result in increase in backlog resulting in lost sales. During the post-recovery stage, it is expected that the rate of production and inventory level is optimum.

Therefore, it may be concluded that the rate of recovery is likely to affect the order level which in turn affects the inventory and production rates. If these rates have imbalances, it will result in backlog causing order level to fall. Through this causal framework, it has been tried to illustrate that a transition is expected from pre-recovery phase (characterized by high inventory level, low production level, zero backlog, and low order level) to the recovery period where the order level is expected to grow either at steady rate or at slow rate or the recovery may take a downward dip again. During the recovery period, increasing of production capacity will involve some delay due to time taken to install additional capacity. During this delay period, the firm is expected to experience lost sales affecting its credibility. Hence, the firm needs to ramp up production with agile manufacturing approach and resort to outsourcing to meet the upsurge in demand. The extent of ramping up production and outsourcing would depend on the rate of recovery. Simulation of the System dynamics model is expected to aid the supply chain manager in determination of the right production and outsourcing decisions.

10.2.2 Modeling Impact of Customer Behavior on Supply Chain Management of Passenger Cars

A structured questionnaire-based survey among the buyers and potential buyers has been carried out to identify the customer's buying behavior causing uncertainty in supply chain planning. A total number of 165 responses were obtained.

Literature survey showed that there are different perspectives that affect buying behavior. These include exterior look, interior look, and comfort, safety, waiting period, and economy and brand affiliation. The questions were based on these five dimensions. The data so collected has been subjected to:

Rotated–Factor–Analysis to identify the latent dimensions and variables associated with it. The loadings of the variables indicate the impact on the factors. Seven dimensions were obtained from this analysis. Those are listed below:

- **Modernity Dimension** The variables under this factor include External-Modernity of the Design, Uniqueness of Design, and Shininess/smoothness.
- **Anterior view Dimension** The variables under this factor include Front Design, External Color, and Non-Availability of suitable Technical Specification, Overall Interior Design/Look, Adjustable Front-Seats, and Adjustable Head-Rests.
- **Comfort Dimension** The variables under this factor include Leg room, Seat Designs, Boot Space, and Dashboards.
- **Internal Design Factors** The variables under this factor include Design of Light and Blinker, Uniqueness, Internal Modernity of Design, Interior-Color, and Back Design.
- **Economy Dimension** The variables under this factor include After Sale Service, Fuel Efficiency, Price, and Brand Name.
- **Rejection Dimension** The variables under this factor include No Desired Exterior, No Desired Interior, and No Desired color. This factor comprises variables that will lead to rejection of a particular model of a passenger car.
- **Brand Loyalty** The variables under this factor include "The time to wait."

Seven (7) distinct factors having direct or indirect impact of supply chain management of the company required to be factored in the decision making process. Any deviation sought by the buyer with respect to any of the factors or their combination have bearing in the lead time affecting the production rate. Change in production rate will in turn impact inventory, with cascading effect on backlog and customer satisfaction. Figure 10.5 depicts the causal loop diagram incorporating the drivers of the supply chain and the customers' preference affecting the production rate and the order rate (No. of Orders).

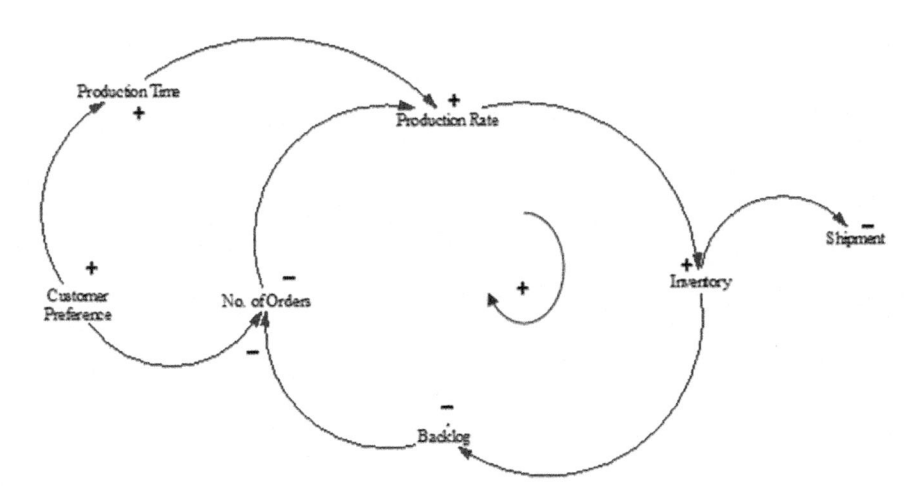

Fig. 10.5 Causal loop diagram considering customer preference

The causal loop diagram shows that there is an interacting loop, i.e., No. of Orders–Production Rate–Inventory–Backlog–No. of Orders loop, indicating that increase in no. of orders leads to increase the production rate which in turn increases the inventory causing the backlog to decrease. However, consumer preference affects the production time which in turn will affect the production rate. If the production rate does not meet the waiting time of customer, the no. of orders (order rate) is likely to be affected. The inventory resulting out of production but not sold will result in obsolescence. This loop is reinforcing or a positive loop.

10.2.3 Modeling the Cumulative Dynamics Arising Out Economic Volatility and Customer Preference: An Integrated Causal Loop Diagram

Interpretation The loop that explains the cumulative dynamics of the system is the "No. of Orders–Production Rate–Inventory" loop, where the exogenous factors, namely the economic uncertainty and the customer preference, impact the no. of orders. The no. of orders in combination with the production time affects the production rate. If number of orders received is beyond the normal rate of orders, then production rate is required to be increased else will impact the inventory which in turn will affect the no. of orders and the cumulative sales of the firm (Fig. 10.6).

The Integrated System Dynamic Model An integrated system dynamic model is constructed and simulated using the Vensim software. Figure 10.7 depicts the model.

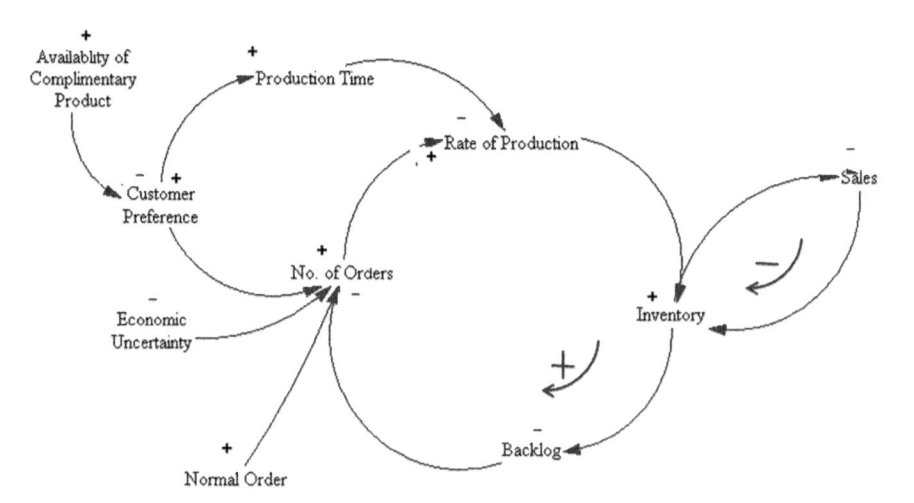

Fig. 10.6 An integrated causal loop diagram

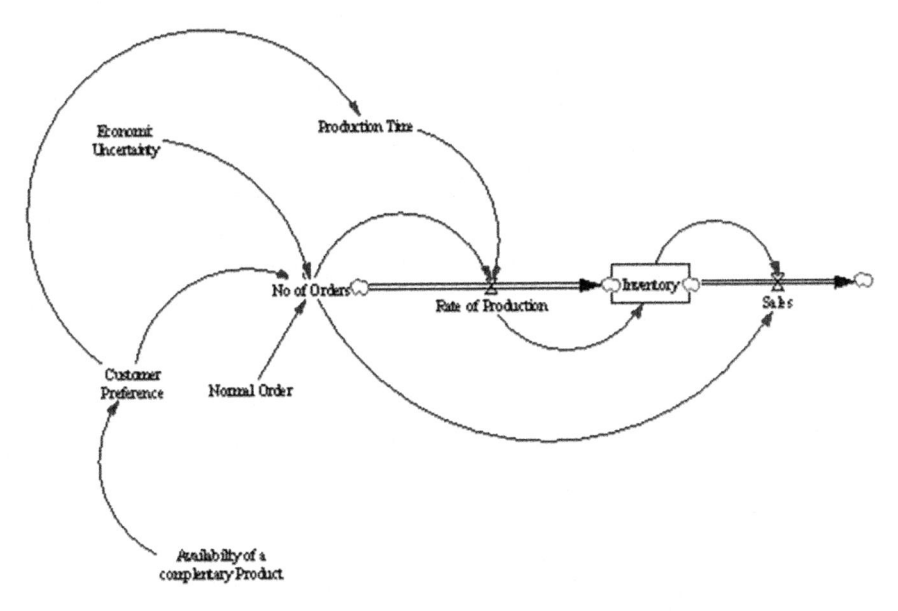

Fig. 10.7 An integrated system dynamic model for passenger car supply chain management system

10.2.3.1 Model Validation and Interpretation

- **Discussion**—Order rate has been considered to be an outcome of interactive effect of economic and customer uncertainty over the normal order rate, meaning that if there are no uncertainty, order rate remains unchanged, with any one of these variables changing order rate will decrease.
- **Result**—After simulating the system dynamics model, the graphical outputs are shown in Figs. 10.8 and 10.9.

10.3 Conclusion

More than a few individual approaches in the perspective of supply chain design, viz. supply chain drivers identification (Chopra and Meindle 2001), systems approach (Van der Velde and Meijer 2003), contingency approach (Mukhtar et al. 2009), have been considered to manage the performance of a supply chain. In this chapter, a holistic approach incorporating these different perspectives has been attempted. The major drivers, namely production and inventory, have been modeled based on systems dynamics approach. System dynamics approach is based on system thinking and is a system approach to problem solving and decision making.

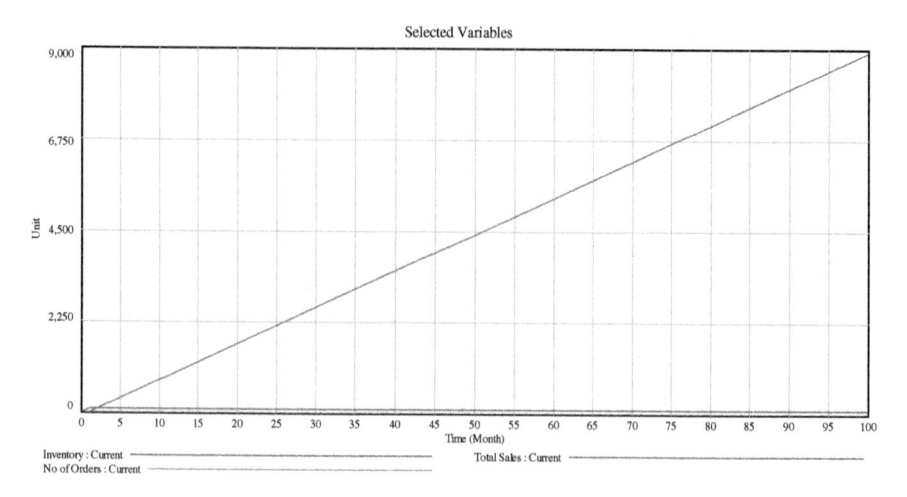

Fig. 10.8 Graph shows order–inventory–sales relationship when there is no uncertainty

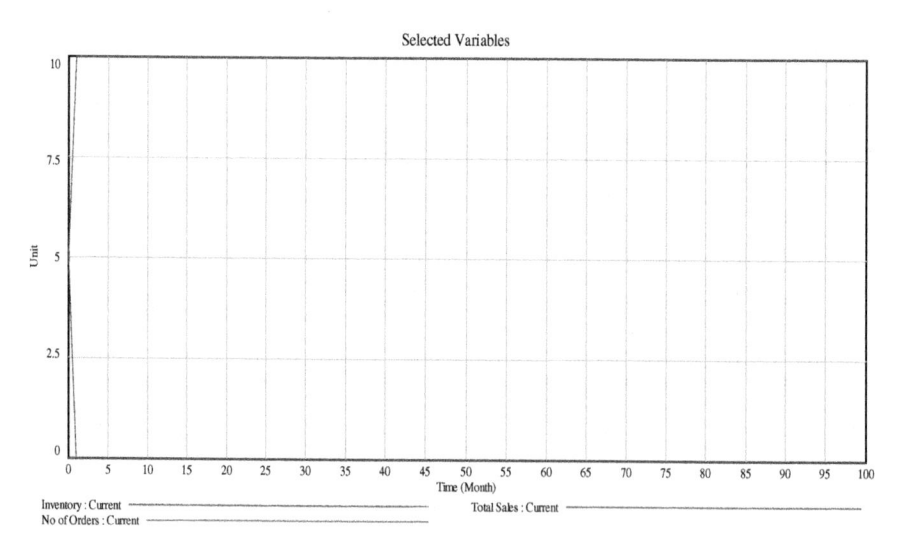

Fig. 10.9 Graph shows order–inventory–sales relationship when there exist both economic and customer's centric uncertainty factors

The factors on which a supply chain of a car is contingent have been identified in this chapter. Two factors, namely economic volatility and customer's behavior, have been factored in the model, and subsequently a system dynamics loop is constructed to explain the cumulative dynamics of supply chain of passenger cars. The economic volatility has been substantiated through statistical analysis. A multiple regression with sales of passenger car as dependent variable and macroeconomic variables, viz. GDP, WPI, and Fuel-Price as independent variables, has been carried out. The results show that sale is sensitive to economic variables such as GDP, WPI, and Fuel-Price. Dimensions of customer buying behavior have been identified through factor analysis of responses obtained through questionnaire survey. The governing loop comprises variables, namely "No. of Orders–Production Rate–Inventory–Backlog–No. of Orders." This is a reinforcing loop explaining the cumulative dynamics arising out of economic volatility and customer preference. The proposed framework will enable supply chain managers to carry out policy experimentation under different volatile situations arising out of exogenous factors. The major challenge lies when there is economic instability with changing customer preferences. The supply chain manager can vary the policy variables under its control, namely ramping up of production rate, decision to change the models to meet customer's requirement, and similar ones. The proposed model is expected to address the major challenge, i.e., when there is economic instability with changing customer preferences.

An integrated system dynamics model incorporating the supplier's uncertainty as well may be taken up as future research work.

References

Bibhushan, Prakash A., & Wadhwa, B. (2014). Supply chain flexibility: Some perceptions. In Sushil & E. A. Stohr (Eds.), *The flexible enterprise*, Flexible Systems Management (pp. 321–331). New Delhi: Springer.

Cariolle, J. (2012). *Measuring macroeconomic volatility applications to export revenue data, 1970–2005, Fondation Pour Les Etudes Et Recherches Sur Le Development International.* Working paper n°I14 "Innovative indicators" series March 2012.

Chopra, S., & Meindl, P. (2001). *Supply chain management: Strategy, planning, and operation* (p. 457). New Jersey: Prentice Hall, Upper Saddle River.

Christopher, M. (2005). *Logistics and supply chain management: Creating value adding networks* (3rd ed.), London, UK: Financial Times Prentice Hall.

Coyle, R. G. (1977). *Management system dynamics*. London: Wiley.

Dargay, J., & Gately, D. (1999). Income's effect on car and vehicle ownership, worldwide: 1960–2015. *Transportation Research. Part A: Policy and Practice, 33*(2).

Dargay, J., & Gately, D. (2001). Modelling global vehicle ownership. In *Proceedings of the Ninth World Conference on Transport Research* (pp. 22–27).

Demiroğlu, U., & Yüncüler, Ç. (2016). Estimating light-vehicle sales in Turkey. *Central Bank Review, 16*(3), 93–108.

Dey, D., & Sinha, D. (2016). System dynamics simulation of a supply chain intelligence model. In A. Dwivedi (Ed.), *Innovative solutions for implementing global supply chains in emerging markets* (pp. 71–83). UK: University of Hull Business School.

Dhir, S., Aniruddha, N. A., & Mital, A. (2014). Alliance network heterogeneity absorptive capacity and innovation performance: A framework for mediation and moderation effects, international. *Journal of Strategic Business Alliances, 3*(2–3), 168–178.

Dhir, S., & Mital, A. (2013). Value creation on bilateral cross-border joint ventures: Evidence from India. *Strategic Change, 22*(5–6), 307–326.

Eskeland, G., & Feyzioglu, T. (1997). Is demand for polluting goods manageable? An econometric study of car ownership and use in Mexico. *Journal of Development Economics, 5*(3), 423–445.

Forrester, J. W. (1961). *Industrial, dynamics* (p. 156). Cambridge, Massachusetts: M.I.T Press.

Forrester, J. W. (1968). *Principals of systems*. Cambridge, Massachusetts: Wright Allen Press.
Greenspan, A., & Cohen, D. (1999). Motor vehicle stocks, scrappage and sales. *The Review of Economics and Statistics, 81*(3), 369–383.
Gunasekaran, A., Dubey, R., & Singh, S. P. (2016). Flexible sustainable supply chain network design: Current trends, opportunities and future. *Global Journal of Flexible Systems Management, 17*(2), 109–112.
Gunasekaran, A., Lai, K. H., & Edwin Cheng, T. C. (2008). Responsive supply chain: A competitive strategy in a networked economy. *Omega, 36*(4), 549–564.
Gunawan, F. E., & Chandra, F. Y. (2014). Optimal averaging time for predicting traffic velocity using floating car data technique for advanced traveler information system. *Procedia-Social and Behavioral Sciences, 138*, 566–575.
Hamilton, B. W., & Macauley, M. K. (1998). *Competition and car longevity*, Working paper.
Hnatkovska, V., & Loayza, N. (2005). Volatility and Growth. In J. Azeinman & B. Pinto (Eds.), *Managing economic volatility and crises*. Cambridge, Mass: Cambridge University Press.
Jacobsen, M. R., & Van Benthem, A. A. (2015). Vehicle scrappage and gasoline policy. *The American Economic Review, 105*(3), 1312–1338.
Kahn, J. A. (1986). Gasoline prices and the used car market: A rational expectations asset price approach. *The Quarterly Journal of Economics, 101*(2), 323–340.
Khanra, S., & Dhir, S. (2017). Creating value in small-cap firms by mitigating risks of market volatility. *Vision, 21*(4), 350–355.
Kurien, G. P., & Qureshi, M. N. (2014). Measurement of flexibility and its benchmarking using data envelopment analysis in supply chains. In M. K. Nandakumar, Sanjay Jharkharia & Abhilash S. Nair (Eds.), *Organizational flexibility and competitiveness*, Flexible Systems Management (pp. 259–272). New Delhi: Springer.
Mukhtar, M., Jailani, N., Abdullah, S., Yahya, Y., & Abdullah, Z. (2009). A framework for analyzing E-supply chains. *European Journal of Scientific Research, 25*(4), 649–662.
Naik, A. (2016). http://auto.ndtv.com/news/maruti-suzuki-vitara-brezza-wins-cnb-viewers-choice-car-of-the-year-2017-163990, May 2, 2017.
Parameswar, N., Dhir, S., & Dhir, S. (2017). Banking on innovation, innovation in banking at ICICI bank. *Global Business and Organizational Excellence, 36*(2), 6–16.
Patel, J., Modi, A., & Paul, J. (2017). Pro-environmental behavior and socio-demographic factors in an emerging market. *Asian Journal of Business Ethics, 6*(2), 189–214.
Rota, M. F., Carcedo, J. M., & García, J. P. (2016). Dual approach for modelling demand saturation levels in the automobile market. The Gompertz curve: Macro versus Micro data. *Investigación Económica, 75*(296), 43–72.
Senge, P. (1990). *The fifth discipline: The art and science of the learning organization*. New York: Currency Doubleday.
Sheffi, Y., & Rice, J. B. (2005). A supply chain view of the resilient enterprise. *MIT Sloan Management Review, 47*(1), 41–48.
Stevenson, M., & Spring, M. (2007). Flexibility from a supply chain perspective: Definition and review. *International Journal of Operations & Production Management, 27*(7), 685–713.
Sushil, (1993). *System dynamics—A practical approach for managerial problems*. New Delhi: Wiley Eastern Ltd.
Swafford, P. M., Ghosh, S., & Murthy, N. (2006). The antecedents of supply chain agility of a firm: Scale development and model testing. *Journal of Operations Management, 24*(2), 170–188.
Van der Velde, L.N. J., & Meijer, B. R. (2003). *A system approach to supply chain design with a multinational for colorant and coatings*. Retieved September 20, 2006 from http://ww.ifm.eng.ca.ac.uk/mcn/pdf_files/part6_5.pdf.
Wu, T., Zhao, H., & Ou, X. (2014). Vehicle ownership analysis based on GDP per Capita in China: 1963–2050. *Sustainability, 6*(8), 4877–4899.

Web References

http://www.ncpers.org/files/Economic%20Volatility%20May%202016.pdf.
http://www.imf.org/external/pubs/ft/weo/2005/01/.
http://auto.ndtv.com/news/maruti-suzuki-vitara-brezza-wins-cnb-viewers-choice-car-of-the-year-2017-1639901.
http://citeseerx.ist.psu.edu/viewdoc/download?doi=10.1.1.966.7208&rep=rep1&type=pdf.
https://www.boe.ca.gov/news/pdf/ep11-07.pdf.
https://www.pressreader.com/india/business-standard/20170328/281500751084423.
https://www.rbi.org.in/.
www.hindustantimes.com/business-newspaper/maruti-brings-democracy-to-car-customisation, October 18, 2016.
www.siamindia.com.

Part III
Financial Management in VUCA Markets

Chapter 11
Probing Time-Varying Conditional Correlation Between Crude Oil and Sensex

Saif Siddiqui and Arushi Gaur

Abstract Change in oil prices may have a different impact on different countries due to various factors such as their relative position as oil importers or exporters, different tax structures. Oil price affects Indian economy. A small rise in oil price leads to an increase in prices of goods and services. It is also affected by the exchange rate and effects stock market too. Here, we propose to study the co-movement of crude oil prices and volatility spillover affect on stock market and USD–INR rate of exchange. Daily data for the period from June 01, 2014 to August 31, 2016 of BSE S&P Sensex (Sensex), prices of crude oil and USD–INR rate of exchange are taken. We used multivariate GARCH model to identify spillover of volatility. Besides, doing descriptive statistics, Unit Root, Johansen Co-integration and correlation test, we also put Granger causality test. Volatility spillover between exchange rate, Sensex and crude oil prices are found to be significant and bidirectional. Affect of crude oil price movement on Sensex is also significant.

Keywords BEKK · Crude oil · DCC · Exchange rate · Stock market

11.1 Introduction

Oil forces world economies. An oil price change may have a different impact on different countries due to various factors such as their relative position as oil importers or exporters, different tax structures.

In context to Asian countries, oil price is the key factor, which affects the inflation. Due to the rising demand of oil in countries such as China and India, and production cuts by OPEC countries, the oil prices rose significantly from 1999 to mid-2008 from $25 to $150 a barrel. On July 2008, it reached its peak of US$147.27 a barrel. But the financial crises of 2007–2008 affected the oil price

---

S. Siddiqui (✉) · A. Gaur
Centre for Management Studies, Jamia Millia Islamia—A
Central University, Jamia Nagar, Delhi, New Delhi 110025, India
e-mail: drsaifsiddiqui@gmail.com

© Springer Nature Singapore Pte Ltd. 2018
S. Dhir and Sushil (eds.), *Flexible Strategies in VUCA Markets*,
Flexible Systems Management, https://doi.org/10.1007/978-981-10-8926-8_11

and underwent a significant decrease after July 11, 2008. In mid of 2014, from a peak of $115 per barrel in June 2014 oil price started falling because of tremendous increase in production of oil in USA, and diminishing demand in other countries. By February 03, 2016 the price of oil was below $30 a barrel which is almost a drop 75% since mid-2014. This change affected the world economies to great extent.

It affected the investment in stock markets. Price of oil affects the whole economy, especially in India due to its high use in transportation. A rise in prices of oil results to a rise in inflation. A high inflation is not good for an economy. The value of a free currency such as Rupee is determined by its demand in the currency market.

Keeping in view this important relationship, here, we propose to study the movement of crude oil prices and volatility spillover affect of stock market and Exchange rate.

11.2 Review of Literature

Jones and Kaul (1996) examined the effect of world stock markets to various shocks in oil prices by future and current changes in cash flows and likely returns. They used the data of four countries, i.e. USA (i.e. from 1947 to 1991), Canada (i.e. from 1960 to 1991), Japan (i.e. from 1970 to 1991) and UK (i.e. from 1962 to 1991). They found negative effect of stock prices of these countries to shocks in prices of oil on real cash flows. Sadorsky (2001) applied multifactor market model and estimated returns of Canadian oil and gas stock prices. Data for the period from April 1983 to April 1999 were used. They found that as the gas and oil sector moves pro-cyclical, it is likely to be less risky than the market. Agnolucci (2009) used returns from the generic light sweet crude oil for period from December 12, 1991 to May 02, 2005. The result concluded that GARCH models outperformed the other models used. Soytas et al. (2009) investigated short- and long-run transmission of information between US dollar–Lira exchange rate, oil prices, Turkish rate of interest and domestic silver and gold spot price. They used data for the period from May 2, 2003 to March 1, 2007. They observed through Granger test that Turkish exchange rate and spot prices of select metals and bond markets would not help to develop a better anticipation of world oil prices in the long run. Kilian and Park (2009), examined the impact of change in prices of oil on stock prices. They used the data from January 1973 to December 2006. They observed that increase in the oil prices due to substantial increase in demand for oil, over concerns of future oil supplies, has a negative impact on stock prices. Narayan and Narayan (2010) studied the period from 2000 to 2008 to analyse the effect of change in prices of oil on stock prices of Vietnam by applying co-integration test. They observed that oil, stock prices and nominal rate of exchange are co-integrated. They also observed that price of oil impact positively the stock prices. Siddiqui and Seth (2011) analysed the data from January 2010 to December 2014 and studied the relationship of the stock price of NSE and world oil prices. They used VAR model. Result confirmed no integration between variables. Basher et al. (2012) proposed and examined structural VAR model to investigate the dynamic relationship of the variables. They studied a period from January 1988 to December 2008 of stock prices, oil production, interest rates, oil price and global real economic activity. It was also observed that prices of oil respond positively to a positive shock to emerging stock market. Ji and Fan (2012) examined the impact of change in crude oil prices on other different markets during 2008 financial crises. They used bivariate EGARCH model to examine volatility spillover. They observed major effect of volatility spillover of crude oil on non-energy commodity market. Batac and Tatlonghar (2013) examined the effect of change in Peso–Dollar exchange rate, money supply on Philippine stock market and price of crude oil. Quarterly data were used from 1992 to 2010. Autoregressive Distributed Lag, Granger causality Test and Johansen Co-integration Test were applied. The results proved a long-run relationship of PESI with other variables. It further provides the existence of a unidirectional causality flowing from the Peso–Dollar rates to Philippine stock market. Creti et al. (2013) investigated the linkages among stock prices and price return of 25 commodities for the period, i.e. from January 2001 to November 2011. They applied GARCH (DCC) model. It was experienced that stock market was highly volatile during crises of 2007–2008. A correlation between stock and commodity market was also observed. Pal et al. (2014) evolved multifractal de-trended cross-correlation analysis. They used the data of gold, Crude oil, Brent crude oil and foreign exchange for the period from January 3, 1995 to August 2013. They found uncorrelated behaviour between oil prices and gold implied that they both are largely dependent on themselves. Siddiqui and Siddiqui (2015) examined the leverage and volatility effect of spot and future indices. GARCH family models were used such as GARCH (1, 1), EGARCH and CGARCH on Indian Multi-Commodity Exchange from November 2005 to March 2015. High persistence of volatility was observed among indices while leverage effect was found in Agricultural spot, Energy Spot and Metal future. Singhal and Ghosh (2016) investigated co-movements of oil and Indian stock market at both sector and aggregate levels. They used the data of Brent crude, BSE Sensex and indices of Automotive, Financial, Energy, Gas, Oil, Industrial and Power from Bombay Stock Exchange (BSE) for the period from January 1, 2006 to February 2015. VAR-DCC-GARCH model was used to study volatility spillover. At aggregate, volatility spillover from oil market to stock market is not significant, but it is at sector level.

11.3 Objectives

Objectives in this chapter are as follows:

1. To ascertain co-integration among price of crude oil, Sensex and exchange rate of USD and INR
2. To assess causality between price of crude oil, Sensex and exchange rate of USD and INR
3. To estimate volatility spillover in price of crude oil, Sensex and exchange rate of USD and INR.

11.4 Hypotheses

In order to meet the objectives, following null hypotheses are proposed:

H_{01} There is no co-integration among price of crude oil, Sensex and exchange rate of USD and INR
H_{02} There is no causality between price of crude oil, Sensex and exchange rate of USD and INR
H_{03} There is no volatility spillover in price of crude oil, Sensex and exchange rate of USD and INR.

11.5 Research Methodology

Research methodology of the study is as follows:

We have taken daily data for the period from June 01, 2014 to August 31, 2016 of USD–INR exchange rate, crude oil prices and Indian BSE S&P Sensex (Sensex). This data were taken from Yahoo Finance. We have also taken historical crude oil prices from Investing.com and exchange rate from the official Website of RBI. We used DCC and BEKK-MGARCH model to forecast volatility spillover, descriptive statistics, Unit Root and co-integration tests. We used Granger causality test for short-term causality.

11.5.1 Descriptive Statistics

With the help of descriptive statistic, we are describing the various features of crude oil price, Sensex and USD–INR exchange rate. Following Table shows the result of descriptive statistics of the variables under study (Table 11.1).

Table 11.1 Descriptive statistics

	Sensex	Crude oil	USD–INR
Mean	0.000234	−0.001480	0.000228
Median	0.000258	−0.002290	8.77E-05
Std. Dev.	0.009581	0.029798	0.003452
Skewness	−0.661160	−0.610070	0.181870
Jarque-Bera	286.596900	2261.178000	13.063080
Probability	0.000000	0.000000	0.001457

Table 11.2 Phillips Perron (PP test)

	At level		At first difference	
	t-Statistic	Prob.*	t-Statistic	Prob.**
Sensex	−2.1704	0.2176	−21.0998	0.0000
USD–INR	−1.4944	0.5359	−22.2617	0.0000
Crude Oil	−2.2251	0.1977	−24.9290	0.0000

* figure is insignificant at 5% level
** figure is significant at 5% level

USD–INR exchange rate is least volatile as its standard deviation is least with 0.3452% however crude oil price is examined to be highest volatile as its standard deviation is 2.9798%. Here Sensex and prices of crude oil are negatively skewed, whereas USD–INR exchange rate is positively skewed. Here in all cases, hypothesis of normality is rejected.

11.5.2 Unit Root

This test is applied for examining the stationarity or non-stationarity of the variables of time series. Table 11.2 shows the result of Unit Root Test.

In Table 11.2, null hypothesis cannot be rejected at level but rejected at first difference, which means that Sensex, USD–INR exchange rate and price of crude oil are non-stationary at levels but after first difference they become stationary.

11.5.3 Johansen Co-integration Test

Further to check the non-existence and existence of co-integration, we applied Johansen Co-integration test. The following Table 11.3 presents the result of the Test.

Here trace statistics is the decisive statistics, beginning with null hypothesis having no co-integrating equation ($r = 0$), proving that there is no co-integration. The trace test statistic (26.38743) is lesser than its critical value, and the value of probability is 0.1175. Therefore, there is no co-integration.

Table 11.3 Johansen Co-integration test

Hypothesized No. of CE(s)	Eigen value	Trace statistic	0.05 Critical value	Prob.
None	0.025598	26.38743	29.79707	0.1175
At most 1	0.012121	12.59219	15.49471	0.1306
At most 2	0.011408	6.104177	8.841466	0.1350

Table 11.4 Granger causality tests

Null hypothesis:	Obs.	F-Statistic	Prob.
USD/INR does not Granger Cause Crude oil	534	0.29539	0.7444
Crude oil does not Granger Cause USD/INR		1.68694	0.1861
Sensex does not Granger Cause Crude oil		0.62775	0.5342
Crude oil does not Granger Cause Sensex		2.51155	0.0821
Sensex does not Granger Cause USD/INR		0.11321	0.8930
USD/INR does not Granger Cause Sensex		0.18331	0.8326

11.5.4 Granger Causality Tests

The Granger causality test is put in Table 11.4, and this test indicates in which direction causality exists between the understudy variables.

The results of the above Table indicate that null hypothesis is rejected in all cases and causality is non-existence between crude oil price, Sensex and USD–INR exchange rate.

11.5.5 DCC-GARCH

The Dynamic Conditional Correlation GARCH belongs to the class "Models of conditional variances and correlations" which was introduced by Engle and Sheppard (2001). In Sensex, USD–INR exchange rate and crude oil prices, the value of probability of ARCH coefficient is not significant; this means there is no short-run volatility among the variables, whereas the probability of GARCH coefficient is significant, which indicates long-run volatility is there among the variables. As per Table 11.5, it is seen that DCC (A) and DCC (B) are not significant. It implies that there is no spillover effect among the variables.

Table 11.5 DCC-GARCH

Variable	Coefficient	Std. error	T-Stat	Significance
Mean (crude oil)	−2.34E-03	1.05E-03	−2.21973	0.0264370
Mean (Sensex)	1.41E-04	5.36E-04	0.26389	0.7918609
Mean (USD/INR)	2.40E-04	1.26E-04	1.90696	0.0565259
C(1)	4.33E-04	2.48E-05	17.48173	0.0000000
C(2)	4.59E-06	1.88E-06	24.38043	0.0000000
C(3)	5.17E-06	8.98E-07	5.76158	0.0000000
A(1)	**0.0880	0.0352	2.49662	0.0125385
A(2)	**0.0509	0.0218	2.33223	0.0196888
A(3)	0.1095	0.0597	1.83584	0.0663819
B(1)	**0.4477	0.0153	29.34182	0.0000000
B(2)	**0.4588	0.019	24.11362	0.0000000
B(3)	**0.4391	0.0385	11.39303	0.0000000
DCC(A)	−1.22E-08	0.0821	−1.48E-07	0.9999999
DCC(B)	0.1971	0.2958	0.66621	0.5052747

**Shows significant at 5%

11.5.6 BEKK-GARCH

It refers to a specific parameterization of multivariate GARCH model. This model examines the long-run and short-run volatility spillover among the variables. In case if diagonal coefficient, the value of probability of ARCH coefficient of crude oil price, Sensex and USD–INR exchange rate (A (1,1), A(2,2), A(3,3)) is less than 5% which means that in short-run past innovation have significant impact on current volatility. Similarly, the probability of GARCH coefficient of crude oil price, Sensex and USD–INR exchange rate B(1,1), B(2,2), B(3,3) is less than 5% which means that in long run also, and past innovations have a significant impact on current volatility.

In case of off-diagonal coefficient, A(1,3) is significant which means that in short-run crude oil price has significant cross-volatility spillover impact on USD–INR exchange rate (Table 11.6).

Similarly, the value of probability of B(2,3) and B(3,2) is also less than 5% (0.00350484, 0.00008323) which means that in long run, Sensex has a significant cross-volatility spillover impact on USD/INR rate, whereas USD–INR rate has also a significant cross-volatility spillover on Sensex in long term.

Table 11.6 BEKK-GARCH

Variable	Coefficients	Std. error	T-Stats	Significance
Mean(crude oil)	−0.002093900	0.000952	−2.19855	0.02790993
Mean (Sensex)	0.000325657	0.000411	0.79207	0.42831858
Mean(USD/INR)	0.000107644	0.000138	0.78104	0.43477928
C(1,1)	−0.007076520	0.001299	−0.54470	0.58596091
C(2,1)	0.000088145	0.003670	0.02402	0.98083706
C(2,2)	0.003862646	0.001950	1.98094	0.04759750
C(3,1)	−0.000955900	0.000541	−1.76624	0.07735486
C(3,2)	0.001196517	0.000335	3.56268	0.00035709
C(3,3)	0.000000710	0.002057	3.47E-05	0.99997233
A(1,1)	**0.308831306	0.041504	7.44103	0.00000000
A(1,2)	−0.03153994	0.020023	−1.57515	0.11522243
A(1,3)	**0.014124721	0.006840	2.06496	0.03892705
A(2,1)	−.14355853	0.109012	−1.31691	0.18786950
A(2,2)	**−0.20988059	0.053590	−3.91638	0.00008989
A(2,3)	0.00454839	0.023030	0.19750	0.84343487
A(3,1)	−0.41866025	0.286322	−1.46220	0.14368648
A(3,2)	−0.25792515	0.145146	−1.77700	0.07556817
A(3,3)	**0.356774853	0.070364	5.07044	0.00000004
B(1,1)	**0.950092035	0.010707	88.7363	0.00000000
B(1,2)	−0.00183477	0.008657	−0.21194	0.83215415
B(1,3)	−0.00199419	0.003276	−0.60868	0.54273600
B(2,1)	0.05781600	0.071571	0.80781	0.41919000
B(2,2)	**0.8532064	0.103430	8.24913	0.00000000
B(2,3)	**−0.101981	0.034929	−2.91960	0.00350484
B(3,1)	−0.239900	0.208600	−1.15040	0.24997900
B(3,2)	**0.558260384	0.141874	3.93490	0.00008323
B(3,3)	**0.77623576	0.069478	11.17230	0.00000000

**Shows significance at 5%

11.6 Conclusion

The key findings of the study are that USD–INR exchange rate is least volatile in comparison with other indices as the standard deviation is least, whereas crude oil price is considered to be highest volatile. The results of co-integration and Granger causality show that in all cases long-term co-movement and short-term causality do not exist between Sensex, price of crude oil and USD–INR exchange rate. There is no multivariate dynamic correlation among the variables as per Multivariate DCC Model. In long run, Sensex has a significant cross-volatility spillover impact on USD/INR exchange rate as well as on the other hand USD/INR exchange rate has also a cross-volatility spillover impact on Sensex in long run.

This study is helpful to all institutional investors, corporate executives, practitioners and portfolio managers may draw an important conclusion from the result of this study while operating in stock markets.

References

Agnolucci, P. (2009). Volatility in crude oil futures: A comparison of the predictive ability of GARCH and implied volatility models. *Energy Economics, 31*(2), 316–321.

Basher, S. A., Haug, A. A., & Sadorsky, P. (2012). Oil prices, exchange rates and emerging stock markets. *Energy Economics, 34*(1), 227–240.

Batac, C., & Tatlonghari, V. (2013). The behavior of exchange rates, crude oil prices, and money supply and their effects on Philippine stock market performance: A cointegration analysis. *Review of Integrative Business and Economics, 2*(2), 60.

Creti, A., Joëts, M., & Mignon, V. (2013). On the links between stock and commodity markets' volatility. *Energy Economics, 37,* 16–28.

Engle, R. F., & Sheppard, K. (2001). *Theoretical and empirical properties of dynamic conditional correlation multivariate GARCH* (No. w8554). National Bureau of Economic Research.

Ji, Q., & Fan, Y. (2012). How does oil price volatility affect non-energy commodity markets? *Applied Energy, 89*(1), 273–280.

Jones, C. M., & Kaul, G. (1996). Oil and the stock markets. *The Journal of Finance, 51*(2), 463–491.

Kilian, L., & Park, C. (2009). The impact of oil price shocks on the US stock market. *International Economic Review, 50*(4), 1267–1287.

Narayan, P., & Narayan, S. (2010). Modeling the impact of oil prices on vietnam's stock prices. *Applied Energy, 87*(1), 356–361.

Pal, M., Rao, P. M., & Manimaran, P. (2014). Multifractal detrended cross-correlation analysis on gold, crude oil and foreign exchange rate time series. *Physica A: Statistical Mechanics and its Applications, 416,* 452–460.

Sadorsky, P. (2001). Risk factors in stock returns of canadian oil and gas companies. *Energy Economics, 23*(1), 17–28.

Siddiqui, S., & Seth, N. (2011). Exploring autocorrelation in NSE and NASDAQ during the recent financial crisis period. *Business Analyst, 32*(1), 101–110.

Siddiqui, S., & Siddiqui, T. A. (2015) *Forecasting volatility in commodity market: Application of select GARCH models.* Available at SSRN: http://ssrn.com/abstract=2583573.

Singhal, S., & Ghosh, S. (2016). Returns and volatility linkages between international crude oil price, metal and other stock indices in india: Evidence from VAR-DCC-GARCH models. *Resources Policy, 50,* 276–288.

Soytas, U., Sari, R., Hammoudeh, S., & Hacihasanoglu, E. (2009). World oil prices, precious metal prices and macroeconomy in Turkey. *Energy Policy, 37*(12), 5557–5566.

Chapter 12
Corporate Strategies: Evidence from Indian Cross-Border Acquisitions

Samta Jain, Smita Kashiramka and P. K. Jain

Abstract Corporate restructuring now constitutes an important component of modern business enterprises to create new synergies to face the competitive environment and changed market conditions. This chapter aims at examining the short-run performance of Indian acquiring firms involved in cross-border acquisitions, a prevalent practice of corporate restructuring. Event study methodology has been employed to assess the magnitude of value creation or destruction of the acquiring companies. The results indicate that Indian firms experience statistically significant positive abnormal returns on the day of the acquisition announcement. Moreover, cumulative average abnormal return (CAAR) comes out to be positive and significant in all multi-day event windows observed. This work is a modest attempt to add to the existing literature on cross-border acquisitions by examining the short-run performance of acquiring firms from an emerging economy.

Keywords Corporate restructuring · Cross-border acquisitions
Emerging economy · Event study · Stock market response

12.1 Introduction

Corporate restructuring constitutes an important strategic component of modern business enterprises. Competition and free trade have become the buzzwords since the liberalization of national capital markets. This requires steady restructuring and reorganization of businesses to generate positive synergies to cope up with the competitive and changing economic conditions.

Restructuring can be executed internally by means of capital budgeting decisions, divestment, demerger, etc., and externally through mergers and acquisitions (M&A), joint venture, strategic alliances (Agrawal et al. 2015). The focus of this

---

S. Jain (✉) · S. Kashiramka · P. K. Jain
Department of Management Studies, Indian Institute of Technology Delhi,
New Delhi, India
e-mail: samtajain.iitd@gmail.com

© Springer Nature Singapore Pte Ltd. 2018
S. Dhir and Sushil (eds.), *Flexible Strategies in VUCA Markets*,
Flexible Systems Management, https://doi.org/10.1007/978-981-10-8926-8_12

chapter is to examine cross-border acquisitions (CBAs), one of the most common forms of corporate restructuring.

CBAs have become an indispensable aspect of corporate strategy for international expansion. The steep increase in volume and value of foreign investments can partly be attributed to economic liberalization, favorable government policies, and tax incentives as well as partly to unprecedented technological advancement and globalization. Fierce competition, highly volatile financial markets, and informed investors have increased the efforts of the companies to deliver superior performance and value creation for their shareholders (Rani et al. 2012). Thus, corporate restructuring (through CBAs) has enabled organizations to be proactive in identifying and responding to various opportunities and challenges, thereby dispensing competitive advantage in the global market.

Cross-border acquisition is an essential business strategy that empowers companies to expand their existing operations to new economies, advance their current skills, and venture into similar markets (Wang and Xie 2009; Bhagat et al. 2011; Rani et al. 2015). Corporate restructuring through unconventional means of international expansion (i.e., CBAs) has the associated benefits of risk diversification (Larsson and Finkelstein 1999; Shimizu et al. 2004), improved scientific prowess, synergy, and integrating benefits of internalization (Shimizu et al. 2004).

In the last two decades, CBAs have become the most preferred mode of entry for developing economies to enter foreign markets (Aulakh 2007; Bhagat et al. 2011). India witnessed an increased share in the global foreign direct investments (FDI) since the government took unprecedented steps to liberalize Indian economy in the early 1990s. Removal of different bureaucratic hurdles and socialist stigma of self-reliance has allowed Indian firms to acquire foreign firms to fulfill their international aspirations (Ahluwalia 2002). This gave a big boost to the Indian corporate sector to pursue overseas acquisitions in order to become globally competitive (Dhir and Mital 2013).

According to UNCTAD (2011), among all emerging economies, India has been vigorously involved in foreign direct investments (FDI). In the decade of 2000, India reported the maximum number of CBAs. Moreover, CBAs constituted the larger part of overseas investments.

These developments have given an impetus to the present research which aims to analyze the impact of acquisition announcement on the equity price of the acquiring firm and to assess if such strategic decisions would be wealth creating or destroying proposition in the short-run.

CBAs by Indian companies are primarily stimulated by the desire to seek key strategic resources including proprietary information, intangible know-how, and distribution channels, etc., which are non-tradable by their very nature; these may not be available in the home country to enhance their competitiveness relative to their domestic counterparts (Gubbi et al. 2010; Dhir and Mital 2012). In CBAs, a concoction of these strategic resources with different regulatory and operational environment of the target nation offers various opportunities and threats leading to wealth creation for acquirers (Mittal and Jain 2012).

Owing to limited bargaining power, multinational firms from emerging countries, such as India, encounter more hurdles not only at the point of entry but during the integration of operations also (Gubbi 2015; Dhir and Sushil 2017). Such acquirers, most likely, always end-up paying higher premiums in overseas acquisition transactions, thereby causing a dent in the wealth of the shareholders (Narayan and Thenmozhi 2014).

For unequivocal understanding, remaining chapter is delineated in the following manner. Section 12.2 presents the review of existing literature and hypothesis of the study. Section 12.3 explains the data, sample, and methods analyzed and explored in the study. Section 12.4 comprised of the results and discussions followed by Sect. 12.5, containing the conclusion derived from the study.

12.2 Literature Review

The extant literature has analyzed the valuation effect of cross-border acquisition announcement on the bidding firms. But findings of these studies have largely remained inconclusive, thereby leaving a gap in the literature which needs to be bridged through further research.

Gubbi et al. (2010) and Rani et al. (2015) have observed statistically significant positive abnormal returns (AR) for the Indian acquirers. Rani et al. (2014) and Duppati and Rao (2015) have provided empirical evidence of positive stock market reaction post-acquisition announcement by Indian companies. In multiple country contexts, Bhagat et al. (2011) have observed significant positive AR of 1.09% on the day of international acquisition announcement by the bidding firms in developing economies while Aybar and Ficici (2009) and Narayan and Thenmozhi (2014) have cited noticeable deterioration in terms of shareholders' wealth of the acquiring companies. Few studies (Cakici et al. 1996; Corhay and Rad 2000; Uddin and Boateng 2009) have examined value implications of overseas acquisitions for the bidding firms from developed capital markets and reported statistically significant negative returns. Some of the authors (Aw and Chatterjee 2004; Conn et al. 2005; Kohli and Mann 2012; Rani et al. 2014) have indicated mixed results while assessing and comparing the wealth effects for the acquirers from both domestic and international acquisitions.

Even though substantial studies exist on CBAs, these have not been able to satisfy the curiosity of various stakeholders, viz. researchers, practitioners, academicians, policymakers, and corporate managers with regard to the short-run performance of this restructuring strategy. Results, in terms of the value of acquiring firms, have largely been inconsistent. Hence, the present study is likely to contribute to the extant literature, as most of the studies are based on samples drawn from developed countries.

12.3 Methodology and Data

12.3.1 Event Study Methodology

Event study methodology has been applied to measure the valuation impact of acquisition announcement on the market valuation of the acquiring firm. As per Mackinlay (1997), the impact of any unexpected corporate event on the valuation of the firm can be quantified by observing changes in its equity price over a relatively short period of time. In this study, acquisition announcement is the event of interest.

The expected (normal) returns have been computed using an estimation period of 90 (−120, −31) days prior to the acquisition event (Bhagat et al. 2011). The abnormal return (AR_{it}) for stock 'i' on day 't' is obtained by deducting the normal return ($E(R_{it})$) from the actual return (R_{it}) earned during the event window.

$$AR_{it} = R_{it} - E(R_{it}) \qquad (12.1)$$

For computing normal returns, market model as suggested by Fama (1976) and applied by Brown and Warner (1985), Rani et al. (2012), Kashiramka and Rao (2014) has been used. It explains how return on stock 'i' varies with the return on market index where the stock is listed as follows:

$$R_{it} = \alpha_i + \beta_i R_{mt} + \varepsilon_{it}, \quad \text{where } t = -120\ldots -31 \qquad (12.2)$$

In the above equation, α_i and β_i are the market model parameters indicating the constant term and market beta of the 'ith' stock, respectively. R_{mt} is the return on market index where the securities are listed (Nifty 500) and ε_{it} is an error term.

The parameters are estimated by regressing security return on the market return using time-series data of the estimation period that excludes and precedes the event window. The estimated parameters are then used in the calculation of abnormal returns during the event window.

$$AR_{it} = R_{it} - (\hat{\alpha} + \hat{\beta} R_{mt}), \quad \text{where } t = -8\ldots +8 \qquad (12.3)$$

The average abnormal return (AAR_t) for each day 't' in the event window is calculated as follows:

$$AAR_t = \frac{1}{N} \sum_{i=1}^{N} AR_{it} \quad \text{where } N \text{ is the number of acquisition events} \qquad (12.4)$$

The cumulative abnormal return (CAR) for each stock 'i' is computed as follows:

$$\mathrm{CAR}_i = \sum_{t=t_1}^{t_2} \mathrm{AR}_{it} \quad (12.5)$$

The cumulative average abnormal return (CAAR) is calculated as:

$$\mathrm{CAAR}_{t1,t2} = \sum_{t1}^{t2} \mathrm{AAR}_t \quad (12.6)$$

Two null hypotheses to be tested are that there are no AAR as well as no CAAR on the acquisition announcement. Further, this study uses one parametric (*t*-test) and one nonparametric (generalized sign test) to test the statistical significance of abnormal returns.

12.3.2 Cross-Sectional t-Test (t)

Brown and Warner (1985) have delineated the process to test the statistical significance of an overall price impact of CBAs. According to them, the test statistic is the ratio of abnormal return on day '*t*' to its estimated standard deviation. The test statistics for AAR on day '*t*' during the event window and CAAR for the event window (t_1, t_2) are computed using the following equations, respectively:

$$t_{\mathrm{AAR}} = \frac{\mathrm{AAR}_t}{\hat{S}(\mathrm{AAR}_t)} \quad (12.7)$$

$$t_{\mathrm{CAAR}} = \frac{\mathrm{CAAR}_t}{\sqrt{t_2 - t_1 + 1}\hat{S}(\mathrm{AAR}_t)} \quad (12.8)$$

where

$$\hat{S}(\mathrm{AAR}_t) = \sqrt{\frac{\sum_{t=-120}^{-31}(\mathrm{AAR}_t - \overline{\mathrm{AAR}_t})^2}{N-2}} \quad (12.9)$$

12.3.3 Generalized Sign Test (Z_G)

The measure suggested by Cowan (1992) relies on the ratio of positive CAR to negative CAR during the event window. The null hypothesis to be tested is that there is no difference in the proportion of positive returns both in the event window and during the estimation period. It is recommended not to accept the null hypothesis when the count of positive CAR in the event window surpasses the count expected in the estimation period. The ratio ($\hat{P}$) of positive CAR in the estimation period (90 days) is estimated as:

$$\hat{P} = \frac{1}{n}\sum_{i=1}^{n}\frac{1}{90}\sum_{t=1}^{90}S_{it} \qquad (12.10)$$

where S_{it} = {1 if $AR_{it} > 0$ or 0 if $AR_{it} <= 0$}

The following statistic has an approximate unit normal distribution with parameter $\hat{p}$:

$$Z_G = \frac{w - n\hat{p}}{\sqrt{n\hat{p}(1-\hat{p})}} \qquad (12.11)$$

where w = number of securities having positive CAR in the event window.

12.3.4 Data and Sample Size

The present study is based on CBAs announced by Indian enterprises during 2013–2015. CNX Nifty 500 constituents have been taken as the subject for the study. Initial data on cross-border deals have been collected from Bloomberg database. Announcement dates have been manually verified from the archives of corporate announcements on the BSE. Stock return data have also been collected from Bloomberg database. Firms, with event windows clean of any confounding effect or contamination of information as defined by Mcwilliams and Siegel (1997), have been the subject of study.

Data description: Sample data points out that most of the CBAs have been executed in the service sector constituting around 64% of total acquisitions; followed by 35% in the Manufacturing sector. Out of a total sample of 58 CBAs, 19 deals were announced in 2013 that increased to 23 and 26 in 2014 and 2015, respectively. Overall, Indian companies are making rigorous efforts to make their presence felt in the global business world.

12.4 Empirical Results

Tables 12.1 and 12.2 contain data related to returns to the shareholder of the acquiring companies which are earned over and above the expected return from CBAs over multi-days event windows. While Table 12.1 indicates results of AAR, CAAR is presented in Table 12.2. Findings of parametric as well as nonparametric tests performed to gauge the statistical significance of returns have also been

Table 12.1 Average abnormal returns (AAR) during 17 (−8, +8) days event window

Event window	AAR value (%)	Positive: negative AAR	t-test	Z_G
−8	0.01	23:35	0.0247	−1.0964
−7	0.20	25:33	0.5481	−0.5701
−6	0.19	29:29	0.7758	0.4824
−5	0.00	24:34	−	−0.8333
−4	0.50	30:28	1.9533***	0.7456
−3	−0.21	24:34	−0.9885	−0.8333
−2	−0.03	23:35	−0.1467	−1.0964
−1	0.41	31:27	1.4457	1.0087
0	0.61	33:25	1.7649***	1.535
1	0.8	33:25	1.7986***	1.535
2	0.13	25:33	0.4282	−0.5701
3	−0.13	23:35	−0.473	−1.0964
4	0.22	30:28	0.5242	0.7456
5	0.05	32:26	0.2066	1.2718
6	−0.03	27:31	−0.0863	−0.0439
7	0.08	26:32	0.2733	−0.307
8	−0.04	26:32	−0.1541	−0.307

*, **, and *** indicate significance at 1, 5, and 10%, respectively

Table 12.2 Cumulative average abnormal returns (CAAR) over multi-days event windows

Event window	CAAR value (%)	Positive: negative CAR	t-test	Z_G
(−1, 1)	1.82	39:19	2.454**	3.1138*
(−2, 2)	1.92	37:21	2.368**	2.5875*
(−5, 5)	2.36	37:21	1.9998**	2.5875*
(−7, 7)	2.80	36:22	1.9214***	2.3244**
(−8, 8)	2.77	35:23	1.634	2.0613**

*, **, and *** indicate significance at 1, 5, and 10%, respectively

reported. Further, it also provides the ratio of positive and negative CAR observed during different event windows.

From Table 12.1, it is evident that on the day of announcement shareholders earn positive AAR of 0.61% and the proportion of stocks with positive returns to negative returns is 33:25; in other words, the majority (57%) of companies experienced positive abnormal returns.

Moreover, results reported in Table 12.2 indicate significant and positive CAAR of 1.82 and 1.92% during event windows of 3 days (−1, +1) and 5 days (−2, +2), respectively. Highest CAAR value of 2.80% has been obtained during the event window of 15 days (−7, +7). Further, CBAs results in value enhancement for the acquiring firms during all event windows, although the rate of abnormal returns begins to decline beyond event window of 15 days (−7, +7). In the event window of 17 days (−8, +8), CAAR is non-negative although statistically insignificant.

The findings support the proposition that CBAs significantly improve the wealth of the acquiring company's shareholders. The results of the chapter are consistent with Bhagat et al. (2011) and Kohli and Mann (2012).

12.5 Conclusion

Providing empirical support to the theoretical framework, this research measures how the capital markets respond to the announcement of CBAs. Short-run stock price performance of 58 CBAs deals from 2013 to 2015 has been examined using event study methodology. Empirical results have indicated considerable non-negative abnormal returns to the acquirers. The results seem to complement various motives of CBAs. Such acquisitions create positive sentiments in the stock market as such resources are not easy to replicate and may take years to develop indigenously.

The study holds enormous significance for the managers of acquiring companies in emerging markets, in general, and India, in particular. They may look at the positive market response in the event window as a signal of shareholders' support to their strategic decision of expanding operations abroad. Strategic and intangible assets obtained through CBAs possess various competitive benefits that may enhance the global competitiveness of domestic companies. Thus, acquirers from emerging markets can proceed with the objective of acquiring strategic assets through CBAs to enhance their all-inclusive competitiveness. Further, the conclusion drawn from the study has the rationale to guide the policymakers in their effort to formulate investor-friendly policies with regard to overseas investments and relevant tax measures.

To gain the holistic view of the impact of cross-border acquisition announcement, the present study can be extended to include other emerging countries which would further strengthen the results; thereby providing more insight to managers and executives in their quest to become a global player along with creating wealth for their shareholders. Further, the present study is limited to the overall impact of the acquisition announcements, a more comprehensive study can be conducted to gauge the effect of various deal-specific factors, namely, the method of payment, acquisition strategy, the percentage of ownership acquired, on the value of the acquiring firm.

References

Agrawal, A., Sushil, & Jain, P. K. (2015). Multiple perspectives of mergers and acquisitions performance. In Sushil & G. Chroust (Eds.), *Flexible Systems Management: Systemic flexibility and business agility* (pp. 385–398). New Delhi: Springer.

Ahluwalia, M. S. (2002). Economic reforms in India since 1991: Has gradualism worked? *Journal of Economic Perspectives, 16*(3), 67–88.

Aulakh, P. S. (2007). Emerging multinationals from developing economies: Motivations, paths and performance, 235–240.

Aw, M. S., & Chatterjee, R. A. (2004). The performance of UK firms acquiring large crossborder and domestic takeover targets. *Applied Financial Economics, 14*(5), 337–349.

Aybar, B., & Ficici, A. (2009). Cross-border acquisitions and firm value: An analysis of emerging-market multinationals. *Journal of International Business Studies, 40*(8), 1317–1338.

Bhagat, S., Malhotra, S., & Zhu, P. (2011). Emerging country cross-border acquisitions: Characteristics, acquirer returns and cross-sectional determinants. *Emerging Markets Review, 12*(3), 250–271.

Brown, S. J., & Warner, J. B. (1985). Using daily stock returns: The case of event studies. *Journal of Financial Economics, 14*(1), 3–31.

Cakici, N., Hessel, C., & Tandon, K. (1996). Foreign acquisitions in the United States: Effect on shareholder wealth of foreign acquiring firms. *Journal of Banking & Finance, 20*(2), 307–3209.

Conn, R. L., Cosh, A., Guest, P. M., & Hughes, A. (2005). The impact on UK acquirers of domestic, cross-border, public and private acquisitions. *Journal of Business Finance & Accounting, 32*(5–6), 815–870.

Corhay, A., & Rad, A. T. (2000). International acquisitions and shareholder wealth: Evidence from the Netherlands. *International Review of Financial Analysis, 9*(2), 163–174.

Cowan, A. R. (1992). Nonparametric event study tests. *Review of Quantitative Finance and Accounting, 2*(4), 343–358.

Dhir, S., & Sushil. (2017). Flexibility in modification and termination of cross-border joint ventures. *Global Journal of Flexible Systems Management, 18*(2), 139–151.

Dhir, S., & Mital, A. (2012). Decision-making for mergers and acquisitions: The role of agency issues and behavioral biases. *Strategic Change, 21*(1–2), 59–69.

Dhir, S., & Mital, A. (2013). Value creation on bilateral cross-border joint ventures: Evidence from India. *Strategic Change, 22*(5–6), 307–326.

Duppati, G. R., & Rao, N. V. (2015). Cross-border mergers and acquisitions: Mature markets vs. emerging markets—With special reference to the USA and India. *Cogent Business & Management, 2*(1).

Fama, E. F. (1976). *Foundations of finance.* New York: Basic Book.

Gubbi, S. R. (2015). Dominate or ally? Bargaining power and control in cross-border acquisitions by Indian firms. *Long Range Planning, 48*(5), 301–316.

Gubbi, S. R., Aulakh, P. S., Ray, S., Sarkar, M., & Chittoor, R. (2010, April). Do international acquisitions by emerging-economy firms create shareholder value? The case of Indian firms. *Journal of International Business Studies, 41*(3), 397–418.

Kashiramka, S., & Rao, N. M. (2014). Shareholders' wealth effects of mergers and acquisitions on acquiring firms in the Indian IT and ITeS sector. *South Asian Journal of Management, 21*(3), 140.

Kohli, R., & Mann, B. J. (2012). Analyzing determinants of value creation in domestic and cross border acquisitions in India. *International Business Review, 21*(6), 998–1016.

Larsson, R., & Finkelstein, S. (1999). Integrating strategic, organizational, and human resource perspectives on mergers and acquisitions: A case survey of synergy realization. *Organization Science, 10*(1), 1–26.

Mackinlay, A. (1997). Event studies in economics and finance. *Journal of Economic Literature, 35*(1), 13–39.

Mcwilliams, A., & Siegel, D. (1997). Event studies in management research: Theoretical and empirical issues. *Academy of Management Journal, 40*(3), 626–657.

Mittal, A., & Jain, P. (2012). Mergers and acquisitions performance system: Integrated framework for strategy formulation and execution using flexible strategy game-card. *Global Journal of Flexible Systems Management, 13*(1), 41–56.

Narayan, P., & Thenmozhi, M. (2014). Do cross-border acquisitions involving emerging market firms create. *Management Decision, 52*(8), 1451–1473.

Rani, N., Yadav, S. S., & Jain, P. K. (2012). The impact of domestic mergers and acquisitions on acquirer shareholders' wealth in India. *Global Journal of Flexible Systems Management, 13*(4), 179–193.

Rani, N., Yadav, S. S., & Jain, P. K. (2014). Impact of domestic and cross-border acquisitions on acquirer shareholders' wealth: Empirical evidence from Indian corporate. *International Journal of Business and Management, 9*(3), 88–110.

Rani, N., Yadav, S. S., & Jain, P. K. (2015). Market response to internationalization strategies: Evidence from Indian cross-border acquisitions. *IIMB Management Review, 27*(2), 80–91.

Shimizu, K., Hitt, M. A., Vaidyanath, D., & Pisano, V. (2004). Theoretical foundations of cross-border mergers and acquisitions: A review of current research and recommendations for the future. *Journal of International Management, 10*(3), 307–353.

Uddin, M., & Boateng, A. (2009). An analysis of short-run performance of cross-border mergers and acquisitions: Evidence from the UK acquiring firms. *Review of Accounting and Finance, 8*(4), 431–453.

UNCTAD (2011). *World Investment Report: Non-Equity Modes of International Production and Development*. New York and Geneva: United Nations

Wang, C., & Xie, F. (2009). Corporate governance transfer and synergistic gains from mergers and acquisitions. *Review of Financial Studies, 22*(2), 829–858.

Chapter 13
Strategies for Formulating Financial Stability Criterion to Face Challenge of Uncertainties into Energy Sector

Nirmalendunath Ghosh

Abstract Uncertainty in financial stability of the organization is expected due to unpredictable energy market on account of diversity in system environment. The paper aims to analyze financial stability of the electricity utility system in the long-term and short-term period due to the impact of economy, weather, and political environment that may drive financial stability to instability or vice versa. And also to justify the role of technology diffusion as catalyst in restoring stability to corroborate the concept with reality by evaluating stability criteria with available data of different state electricity utilities. The analysis framed a mathematical expression linking market price of electricity and earnings per unit of electricity distributed to ascertain financial stability. Then the change in stability is derived by differentiating with different driving dimensions of economy, weather, and policy issues. Finally, evaluating the performance of the state utilities based on available data about their status justifying the concept involved in the analysis. There are changes in stability function from −ve uncertainty to +ve certainty because of the adaptation of technology in the system. Technology diffusion acts as catalyst to save the organization from instability that results in poor performance.

Keywords Economic growth · Electricity utilities financial stability Technology · Uncertainty

13.1 Introduction

Energy market in the country is depended on the availability of natural gas, oil, and fossil fuel and the corresponding price of the resources. Oil and fossil fuel resources availability is quite comfortable while natural gas availability is not enough to meet the demand. Renewable energy is emerging as alternative resources though solar power and wind power are not dependable resources because of

N. Ghosh (✉)
West Bengal State Electricity Board (WBSEB), Kolkata, India
e-mail: nnghosh1@yahoo.co.uk

unpredictable climate in a region. Financial achievement in energy utilities is linked with cost of the fuel. Now fossil fuel dominates 56% of electricity generation and states privileged with coal mines are able to save cost of transportation while the states located far away from coal pits face the burden of transportation cost. Further, quality of fossil fuel determine extent of financial strain to generate electricity. Then economy of the country is responsible for financial stability of the electricity utilities. The growth in industry and agriculture will contribute to state gross domestic product; as the SGDP increased, so the contribution of electricity sector to SGDP will increase if proper planning procedure is followed, then only the electricity utility will have financial stability keeping in view efficiency improvement measures. Therefore, uncertainty in economic growth will cast a shadow of uncertainty in financial stability of electricity utilities; it has been perceived that technology innovation is always coming into play when such situation arises because of urge of innovation to counter the negativity in the growth trend. The development of computer, laser technology has brought significant relief from uncertainty in functioning of different activities that has reduced cost, improved productivity, and manpower. There is always a trend of innovation in developed country to overcome any difficulties that have resulted in series of changes in industrial and agricultural resources, information technology has completely changed the working system that manages the present scenario to meet the challenges of uncertainty in future. The industrial growth is the basic need for sustaining financial stability of electricity utilities; because installed capacity of generating plant can be efficiently utilized to supply bulk power for base load, at the same time, the tariff is quite high to get best earnings per unit of electricity sold. There is a shortcoming in respect of agricultural load because of subsidy in tariff that area of revenue earning creates a void in financial stability. Uncertainty in financial stability is also related to climate of the region. There is possibility of natural disaster that could bring havoc in electrical installations or the drought situation in a region can push a state to overdraw power to meet its high demand resulting in grid failures that may be a reason of financial losses. There may be uncertainty due to fall in demand for weather change when a part of installed capacity will remain out of network, all those developments on the system result in financial losses. Overall effect of these issues is perceived in dynamic change of financial stability. The policy issues at political level also have impact on future uncertainty, for example, this may be policy on revising selling price or assigning more importance on fossil fuel than renewable energy or technology implementation on specific issues in generation, transmission, and distribution or the land acquisition issues for substation, transmission line that involves a large flow of power through grid. The study has discussed all these issues in subsequent sections in different scenario of uncertainty by assigning weightage in respect of resources, economy, climate, and financial effect and policy decision based on present day scenario of the relative dimensions (Ebinger and Vergara 2011).

13.2 Resources and Financial Uncertainty—Innovation Criteria

The availability of resources for electricity generation is an issue of uncertainty for electricity utilities (Parameswar et al. 2017). Fossil fuel fired generation plant is dominating 55% of total electricity production in utilities across the country While hydroelectricity resource shares 25% of total electricity generation. Natural gas is used to some extent in western region of the country. The major issue of uncertainty in hydropower generation is impact of climate on water availability in the region. The adverse climate will affect the water flow in the rivers that will pose a problem in generating power affecting revenue earnings. Fossil fuel fired generating units will be affected by climate change due to change in ambient temperature, pressure and humidity that has impact on generation cycle efficiency and water requirement, obviously that will affect both cost of supply and availability of target output. In case of renewable energy, grid interactive energy system is now in operation across the country that is susceptible to impact of climate change. Solar power, wind power, and biomass generated power are all dependent on climate effect. Temperature increase will affect natural gas-based generating plants for reduction in heat rate and power output. This shortcoming in power generation will affect both revenue and the cost of supply. These dimensions can be related in a mathematical form.

If Sf is financial stability of the organization and R is resource, then

$$\mathbf{Sf} \infty R$$

or

$$\mathbf{Sf} = \varphi.[R], \quad 0.1 < \varphi < 1 \qquad (1)$$

where φ is uncertainty factor that depends on economy, climate, and policy decision. Again, cost of supply of electricity (I) is a variable that need to be managed by forecasting the demand, available fuel resources, and available plant capacity, if cost of supply increases, the financial stability will be uncertain, whereas decline of cost of supply is an indicator of better status of stability. This status depends on information sharing between the stakeholders of utilities. Thus, the mathematical relation can be re-stated as

$$\mathbf{Sf} = \varphi.[R/I] \qquad (2)$$

13.3 Economy and Financial Stability

Sustainable financial stability in electricity utility depends on the economy of the state. Economy of the state is related to growth of industrial sector and agricultural productivity. There is uncertainty in the growth of economic resources due to recession or affected by policy decision on tax and duties or effect of long-term planning that involves forecast of long-term growth of industrial sector commensurate with investment possibilities and agricultural production with capital investment under favorable climate. Electricity utilities similarly develop long-term planning proposal of capacity addition to meet the expected demand commensurate with growth of economy in the projected year. If there is mismatch between growth in industrial sector and the growth of capacity addition, then there will be uncertainty in evacuating power from the generating sources, either there need be shut down of units or the excess power need be dispatched to other areas through grid if there exist such possibilities. Dependence on renewable energy is also uncertain that needs periodical monitoring of expected dispatch of generated power from wind turbine. The wind power generation is mentioned here because there is substantial growth of grid interactive wind power generation in the country. Economy of the country is interrelated with climate of the region. Economic growth is commensurate with monsoon activity across the country. So, uncertainty in demand of electricity is expected with rise and fall of economy. Therefore, financial stability of the system depends on effective planning with technological input in relation with economy and climate of the state.

This concept has been translated in mathematical form as follows

$$\mathbf{Sf} = \varphi . [I(Q - Ql)/Cs] \qquad (3)$$

where Cs is cost of supply, I is earning of utilities, $Q-Ql$ is the electricity supplied, Ql is loss, and φ is proportionality constant termed as uncertainty.

First of all, the correlation between economy in terms of state gross domestic product (SGDP) and the revenue earned by the utilities is analyzed in the following Figs. 13.1, 13.2, and 13.3.

Figures 13.1, 13.2, and 13.3 visualize the variation of state gross domestic product with revenue earning of state utilities in Tamil Nadu, Maharashtra, Karnataka, MP, Maharashtra, Rajasthan, West Bengal and Orissa covering all major utilities with different load and installed plant capacity, but one thing is important to note that revenue variation with SGDP is linearly correlated. Therefore, the concept that the revenue growth is dependent on state economic growth has been justified. This verification of the concept also justifies the concept that uncertainties

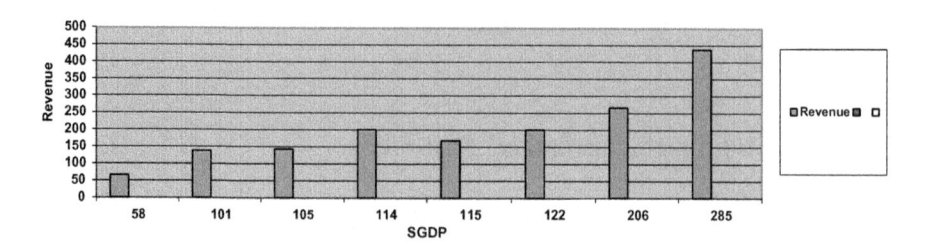

Fig. 13.1 Correlation between SGDP and revenue growth 2012–13

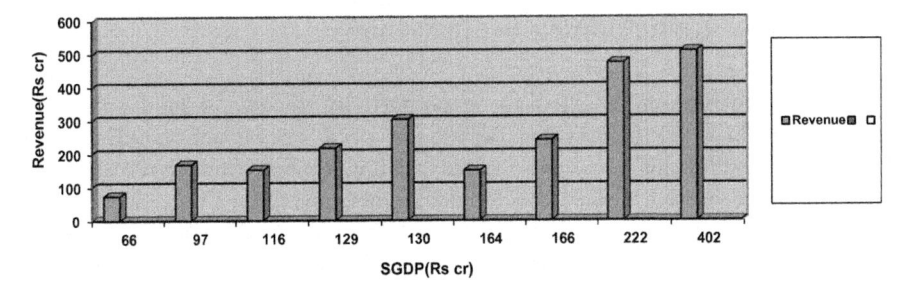

Fig. 13.2 Correlation between SGDP and revenue growth for 2013–14

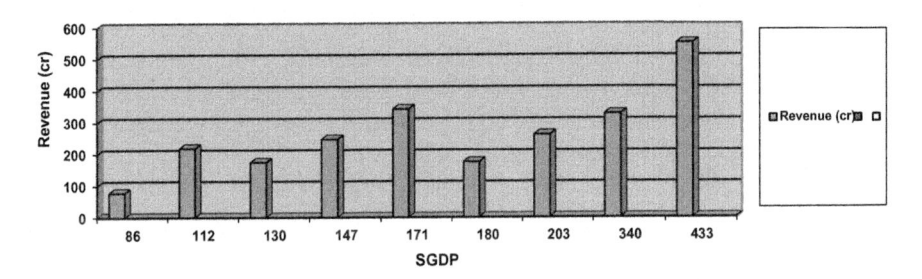

Fig. 13.3 Correlation between SGDP and revenue growth 2014–15. *Source of data* [PFC and data.gov.in]

associated with economic growth due to recession, inflation will also affect revenue, thus affecting financial stability of the system. So far, the study has focused on analysis of the system stability pertaining to climate and economy effect criteria, and next discussion involves on policy issues.

13.4 Policy Issues and Uncertainties

There is state electricity regulatory commission which looks into tariff, performance that act in between state and the utilities. The state utility is under state government; therefore, each of the utilities has their own norms and regulation in operation of the system. Therefore, the decision on the issues of tariff and technology deployment will vary and that will affect the financial stability, but common perception that emerge out of all discussion highlight dependence of financial stability on economic growth of the state. The most important issue is tariff revision commensurate with escalation of fuel cost and cost of operation. The application of this concept is actually depending on policy issues. In many cases, the decision to assign more importance on renewable energy resources with non-renewable energy sources remains unresolved. Therefore, uncertainty in financial stability is expected due to policy issues.

13.5 Innovation Solution to Uncertainty

If the system experience deficiency in productivity, quality of production, and financial attainments, then financial stability of the system is affected. The major issue for consideration is to analyze the performance of sub-systems and then integrating the values to decide how to improve function without impairing existing operational structure. As discussed in the previous section, revenue earnings per unit of energy distributed is varying with SGDP; technology is new idea or a software or hardware which can transform resources to increase productivity with higher efficiency in congruence with growth in SGDP. It has been observed in the previous section that revenue earning of electricity utilities is linearly correlated with SGDP. Moreover, the system is exposed to uncertain characteristics of economy and climate when there is lack of knowledge about future stages of development in those dynamic entities. But advanced technology now has changed the scenario dramatically by long-term forecasting of climate and trend of economy in the country. Technology diffusion in generation of power and efficiency improvement in distribution system will counter negative effects of climate change. Computerization and implementation of information and communication technology in financial work, transmission, and distribution system have dramatically changed the performance in West Bengal, Maharashtra, Karnataka, and Andhra Pradesh states' electricity utilities. There is perceptible string of operation in the function of different sub-systems that need integrated action of technology adaptation to achieve financial stability. Keeping in view, this logic of sustainable financial turnaround and revival of Discom, Ujwal DISCOM Assurance Yojana (UDAY) has been implemented which is adopting technology-based operational strategies. Around 16 states have joined this yojana. Most of the states have achieved improvement in financial achievements except some states like UP. Technology transfer to electricity utilities is possible through different channels of import of software and hardware together with collaboration of institution for skill and knowledge improvement. We can consider these issues as utilities policy decision to adopt as resources. Knowledge base in the utilities needs be enhanced with increasing communication and technology-based operational process (Damelt west 2012).

13.6 Limitation

There is certain limitation about economy growth that may indirectly has effect on financial stability. The different sector of industries is affected by demand pattern variation because of fluctuating market depending on global marketing status. For example, IT industries show a declining trend consequent to the penetration of technology from developed countries or sudden drop in steel in demand that affects financial stability of steel industries. This category-wise effect of economy growth on financial stability has not been discussed.

13.7 Discussion

Now the analysis is focused on explaining the financial stability in light of mathematical relation, and some assumptions are

i. The contribution of electricity sector to state gross domestic product has been considered as growth of electricity sector.
ii. The losses of electricity due to transmission and distribution have been included in the electricity utilization.
iii. Uncertainty factor has been assumed as direct variation with change in economy, weather and policy decision, the proper weightage was assigned to the factor according to the present status of these dimensions in respective state. The logic behind this concept rests on present scenario of state if analyzed with available information of future, then experiencing the challenge of uncertainty in future may be minimized (Fig. 13.4).

The financial stability equation in (1) is further expanded as
Financial stability = ratio of cost of supply and earning per unit of electricity sold

$$\mathbf{Sf} = \varphi * [R * (Q - Ql)/Cs] \qquad (4)$$

Uncertainty factor has been assumed as in Table 13.1.

Uncertainty factor is then determined by permutation and combination of different values assigned to the variables. For example, the economy may be

Fig. 13.4 Block diagram of stability criteria in uncertain situation. *Source* own design

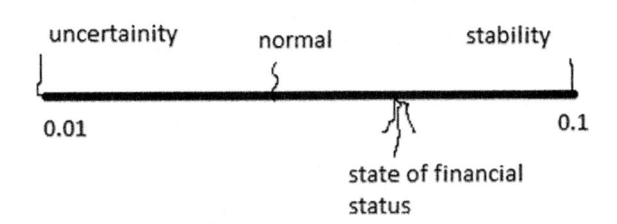

Table 13.1 Uncertainty factor and corresponding dimensions

Dimension	Low	Normal	Extreme
Economy	0.2	0.5	0.9
Climate	0.2	0.5	0.9
Policy/regulation	0.2	0.5	0.9

Source Own design

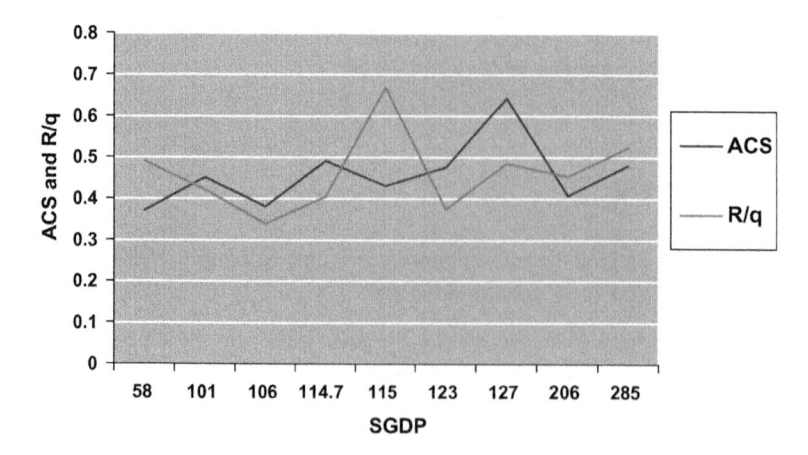

Fig. 13.5 Variation of ACS with SGDP and earning/unit of electricity. *Source of data* PFC and data.gov.in

extremely good and climate may be poor with good policy decision effect, then uncertainty factor is multiplication of weightage values [0.9 * 0.2 * 0.9 = 0.16].

Then the real data of the utilities (PFC, 2016) has been substituted in the equation and the corresponding graph has been plotted (Fig. 13.5).

In determining uncertainty factor, weightage is assumed for each state based on existing economy, climate at state and policy of the utilities.

Option I: economy 0.7; climate 0.9: policy 0.9
Option II: uncertainty factor based on average economy (0.5), average weather 0.5 good policy 0.9
Option III: uncertainty factor based on low economy (0.2), good weather good policy

After substituting real values corresponding to ACS and R/Q, the stability is computed as (Table 13.2):

Table 13.2 Stability index computation

State	Stability index	Option	Uncertainty factor	Average cost of supply	Revenue earning/unit of energy supply
WB	0.07	I	0.58	4.92	0.669
Rajasthan	0.035	II	0.40	3.80	0.339
UP	0.031	II	0.40	4.75	0.375
Karnataka	0.054	I	0.58	4.30	0.405
Tamil Nadu	0.043	I	0.58	6.42	0.485
Orissa	0.018	III	0.14	3.70	0.491
Maharashtra	0.063	I	0.58	4.8	0.524
MP	0.037	II	0.4	4.5	0.421
Gujarat	0.064	I	0.58	4.07	0.454

Source Own design

Table 13.3 Financial stability index of states in order of rank

1	2	3	4	5	6	7	8
West Bengal	Gujarat	Maharashtra	Karnataka	Tamil Nadu	MP	UP	Orissa

Source Own design

Financial stability in order of ranking is as follows (Table 13.3).

The improvement in financial stability can be achieved by diffusion of technology in MP, UP, and Orissa states.

13.8 Conclusion

The study begins with the objective to find the relation between different dimensions and variables involved in achieving financial stability of electricity utilities. For this purpose, the analysis focused on impact of resources, economy and climate and policy issues at different state utilities. Then the correlation between the variables has been justified by graphical analysis. It has been observed that SGDP is linearly varying with revenue earning per unit of electricity distributed by the utilities and climate has impact on stability criteria so also the policy issues. The mathematical expression has been derived for financial stability index to explain the relationship between uncertainty expected due to economy, climate, policy issues and financial attainments comprising of average cost of supply and revenue per unit of electricity supply. Financial stability index is then evaluated by substituting available data of financial attainments of the states as well as assessment of uncertainty factor based on present time status of economy, climate and management policy issues. The study also implies necessity of controlling dynamic stability index that changes from +ve certainty to −ve uncertainty by technology diffusion in the system. The logic behind impact of technology on financial attainments of the utilities has been explained substantiating with evidence of specific states' utilities in innovation solution to uncertainty section that corroborates the findings of evaluated financial stability index of corresponding states in discussion section. The study finally identified the status of financial stability index of the states where technology diffusion is required to achieve '+ve' certainty in financial attainments. The study suggest financial stability criteria is an issue to know the deficiency in the electricity utility in relation to environmental characteristics that can be rectified by appropriate technology adaptation at proper time and right stages. In other words, Financial stability index evaluation for state electricity utilities will be considered as a step to know whether the operational strategy is in right direction, higher the index value, better is financial stability, whereas lower the index value, higher is vulnerability to instability that needs analysis of system performance to find out deficiency for improvement by adaptation of technology-based operation. There is further scope of study in respect impact of category-wise industrial market economy variation on financial stability by segregating contribution of different categories of industries to SGDP as well as generalization of the methodology for finding financial stability criteria to face the challenge of uncertainty.

References

Ebinger, J., & Vergara, W. (2011). *Climate impact on energy system*. Washington, DC: The World Bank Publishers.

Governance Studies at Brooklyn Building an Innovation Based Economy. (2012). Damelt west, Allan Friedman, Walter Valdevia. Retrieved April 16, 2017 from http://www.brooklyn.edu/wp-content/upload/2016.

Parameswar, N., Dhir, S., & Dhir, S. (2017). Banking on innovation, innovation in banking at ICICI bank. *Global Business and Organizational Excellence*, 36(2), 6–16.

Performance Report of State Utilities, Power Finance Corporation. (2016). Retrieved April 20, 2017 from www.pfc.gov.in.

State Gross Domestic Product. (2016). Retrieved from Government of India Data Portal and Retrieved April 10, 2017 from www.data.gov.in.

Chapter 14
Impact of Open Offers on Shareholders' Wealth

Rajit Verma and Anil K. Mittal

Abstract Corporate restructuring is essential for the sustainability and inorganic growth of corporations. Mergers, acquisitions, and takeovers are the prominent strategies, by which companies can restructure their businesses. The chapter focused on 31 large-sized takeover announcements (Open Offers) in India, during the period 2015–2017. The chapter includes only those open offers which have more than Rs. 100 crore payment considerations. For the investigation purpose, standardized event theory was used for the computation of CAARs during the event window of 61 days of selected 24 companies. The study found excessive abnormal returns during the post phase of announcements (0 to +30) as compared to pre-phase of event window (−30 to −1). Further, the findings showed consistent results with the results of prior studies mentioned in the literature. The chapter concluded that shareholders of the target companies can generate excessive returns by rigorously examining the open offer announcements. The chapter also supports the presence of semi-strong form of market efficiency in India.

Keywords Event study · Event window · Open offer · Takeovers

14.1 Introduction

14.1.1 Concept of Open Offer Under SAST[1] 2011

In recent years, open offer has become a prominent tool for corporation takeovers in India. Open offer is an announcement made by an acquiring company to a target

---
[1]*Substantial Acquisition of Shares and Takeovers Regulations.*

R. Verma (✉)
Chitkara University, Rajpura, India
e-mail: rajit.verma@chitkara.edu.in

A. K. Mittal
Kurukshetra University, Kurukshetra, India

© Springer Nature Singapore Pte Ltd. 2018
S. Dhir and Sushil (eds.), *Flexible Strategies in VUCA Markets*,
Flexible Systems Management, https://doi.org/10.1007/978-981-10-8926-8_14

Table 14.1 Threshold limits under open offer (as per SEBI SAST 2011)

Offer size	Voluntary open offer	Mandatory open offer
Minimum offer size	10%	26%
Maximum offer size	Maximum permissible non-public shareholding	Can be entire share capital of target firm

Source www.sebi.gov.in/SAST2011

Table 14.2 Price determination under open offer as per SAST 2011

A	Highest price (negotiated) per share of target firm for any acquisition of shares under the agreement attracting to make a public declaration
B	The volume-weighted average price paid or payable by the acquirers or PAC in the past fifty-two weeks before the open offer announcement date
C	The highest price paid or payable by the acquirer or PAC for any acquisition in the past twenty-six weeks before the open offer announcement date
D	When the shares were frequently traded on the floor of exchange, the volume-weighted average value of the market price of shares for a period of at least 60 trading days immediately before the open offer announcement date
E	When the shares of target firm is not frequently traded on any of the exchange than the open offer manager considers various valuation parameters, such as book value method, similar trading multiple methods

Source www.sebi.gov.in/SAST2011

company's shareholders, in case when acquiring company along with PAC[2] wants to acquire 25% or more holdings in the target firm (SAST 2011). The rationale behind announcing an open offer is to have substantial acquisition of shares, consolidation of holdings, or change in management. Open offer gives advantage to the shareholders to maximize their return by participating in the event. Open Offer has categorized into two parts, i.e., Mandatory Open Offer (where acquiring company's stake is less than 25% in the target company) and Voluntary Open Offer (where acquiring company's stake is more than 25% in the target company). Table 14.1 highlights the threshold limits of open offer size (minimum and maximum) in case of Mandatory Open Offer and Voluntary Open Offer.

14.1.2 Pricing Mechanism of Open Offer

The pricing of Open Offer is the most crucial decision to make it successful. In order to make the open offer more attractive to the shareholders, open offers are made on premium to the market rate. Categories of Open Offers as laid down by SAST 2011 are given in Table 14.2.

---

[2]*Persons acting in Concert.*

Fig. 14.1 Mode of payment consideration under open offer. *Source* www.sebi.gov.in/SAST regulations 2011

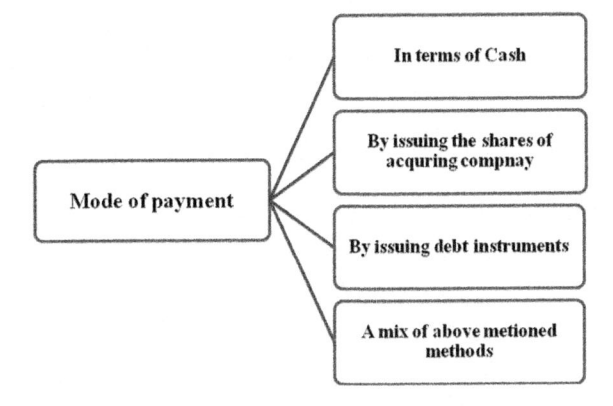

Mode of payment:
- In terms of Cash
- By issuing the shares of acquring compnay
- By issuing debt instruments
- A mix of above metioned methods

14.1.3 Mode of Payment Consideration Under Open Offer

As per Section 9(1) described in SAST 2011, Open Offer price can be paid as given in Fig. 14.1.

14.2 Literature Review

Fama et al. (1969) explored the relationship between the new information available in the stock market and found a significant positive relationship between market behavior and abnormal returns of companies. Thus, the authors concluded that the stock market is efficient enough to absorb the new information during the post-announcement period. Dodd and Ruback (1977), Jensen and Ruback (1983), Bradley et al. (1988), and Jarrell and Poulsen (1989) examined in their respective studies the impact of tender offers in the USA. The studies suggested that the target companies earned significant positive abnormal returns during one month after the announcement date. Brown and Warner (1980) discovered the impact of company-specific events and incidence on the security prices of affected firms. The authors concluded that it is very difficult to stimulate every variation; hence, present study compared various event methodologies rather than giving the best model. Firth (1980), Franks and Harris (1989), and Limmack (1991) analyzed the acquisition and takeover announcements impact on the target companies in the UK. It was found that the shareholders earned substantial gains during and after the announcement date. The attributes of daily stock return data and its impact on event study methodologies were also examined. The study analyzed the autocorrelation in abnormal returns of the data, and the variance based on some special event can be beneficial for the stakeholders Fabozzi et al. (1988) analyzed that the returns of failed tender offers got no other bids in the post-failure year. Datta et al. (1992) explained in their study about wealth creation using M&A announcements in USA. The shareholders of the target companies gained significant returns as they participated in such offers. Singh et al. (1994) analyzed that Open Offer programs do not allow for precise estimate of price movement intensity to measure liquidity effects. Pandey (2001) examined that the open offer announcements and its effect on the share returns of objective firm further it examined the impact of change in control of firm on gains of shareholders (Khanra and Dhir 2017). Bruner (2002) analyzed the effects of takeover announcements on the wealth of shareholders of target companies and found out that such announcements provided abnormal market return to the shareholders. Kothari and Warner (2004) investigated in their working paper on econometrics of event studies about short-horizon methods and long-horizon methods of event studies. The chapter intended to work on long-horizon methods as it has many limitations but short-horizon methods are robust in nature. Agarwal and Bhattacharjea (2006) discussed the effects of regulatory shocks on merger activities in India during 1973–2003. The chapter contained 2253 merger events and categorized into three different phases of regulatory reforms. The chapter concluded that the improvements and amendments in the regulations triggered the merger and acquisition activities in India. Gupta (2006) makes an attempt in his chapter to find the announcement returns for seven subsequent repurchases. He observes a decline in the AAR for -1, 0 and $+1$ days for five companies announcing second repurchase program as compared to first repurchase announcement. Iqbal et al. (2009) provided evidence about the long-run operating and stock performance of UK open offers. Pandey (2001) and Chakraborty (2010) discussed the reaction of takeover announcements on the price movement of the target companies in the short run, i.e., 61 days event window. Pandey analyzed the impact on large-cap companies, and Chakroborty used various parametric and nonparametric tests and apparently they found out that the shareholders can gain significant abnormal return in the short run and not in the long run as they buy and hold for a longer duration. Nangia et al. (2013) examined and empirically tested the excessive earnings generated before and after the announcement date. It was observed that average returns and cumulative average returns of all the sample firms generated negative returns in long run (after event window), but generated positive returns in the short run. Mallikarjunappa and Nayak (2013) discovered the effects of target announcements on the wealth of target firms' shareholders. The chapter used a sample of 227 companies which announced takeovers during the period 1998–2007. The chapter found significant results and results were consistent with prior studies. Rani et al. (2013, 2015) analyzed the abnormal returns on a sample of 623 M&A announcements during 2003–2008. The chapter concluded that shareholders can earn significant abnormal returns in the post-announcement period which is consistent with the prior studies. Ranju and Mallikarjunappa (2017) investigated the impact of acquisition announcements on the shareholders' wealth in India of 349 acquisition announcements during 2005–14. The chapter was concluded that such announcements did not create any value for acquiring company's shareholders rather it was suggested that such acquisition announcements reduced the wealth of the acquiring company's shareholders.

14.3 Research Methodology

14.3.1 Objective

To investigate the impact of open offer size and payment consideration methods on the shareholders' wealth of target companies.

14.3.2 Hypothesis

The null hypothesis states that the cumulative average abnormal return during event window of 61 days is equal to zero.

$$H_0 : CAAR = 0$$

14.3.3 Theoretical Framework

The present chapter intended to employ the standardized event chapter methodology. Event studies originally designed to test the market efficiency. For the present chapter, three things are essential, i.e., estimation window of 120 days (to calculate expected return), event window of 61 days pre- (−30 to −1) and post-phase of event (+1 to +30) and announcement day '0' day (Fig. 14.2).

For the estimation window, ordinary least square regression model (OLS) is used to predict the expected return of the target companies in the event window.

$$(E)R_{it} = \alpha_i + \beta_i R_{mt} + e_{it}$$

R_{it} = stock return of i, α_i = intercept of security i, β_i = slope of security i, R_{mt} = market return

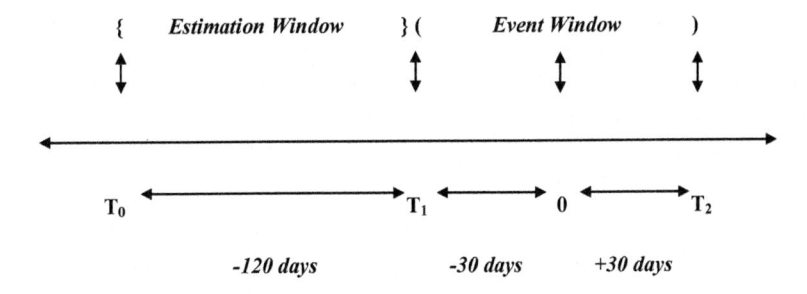

Fig. 14.2 Timeline for estimation window and event window

Further to examine the excessive returns or abnormal returns, the actual returns of the companies are deducted from expected return and Sharpe (1963) market model is used for it.

$$AR_{jt} = R_{jt} - \left(\alpha'_j + \beta'_j R_{mt}\right)$$

Some of the studies which have followed the above model are Dodd and Ruback (1977), Dodd (1980), Dodd and Warner (1983), Dyckman et al. (1984), Brown, and Warner (1980, 1985), and Chatterjee (1986).

The chapter used log returns to evaluate the performance of the target companies using open offer.

Everyday average abnormal returns (AAR_t) for of the event window is calculated as below: $AAR_t = 1/N \left(^n_t \Sigma AR_{it}\right)$.

Cumulative average abnormal returns (CAAR) of the given sample can be computed as:

$$CAAR_{(T_1,T_2)} = \frac{1}{N} \sum_{i=1}^{N} CAR_{i(T_1,T_2)}$$

14.3.4 Sample Selection Criterion

In order to achieve above-stated objectives, the companies are selected on the basis of the following inclusion criteria:

- The chapter examined the wealth effects of target companies' shareholders.
- All the target companies' shares must be traded on the floor of Bombay Stock Exchange (S&P BSE 500) as BSE 500 index is being taken as proxy for the computation of market model and should have sufficient numbers of trading days for the calculation of an estimation window of 120 days. The data should be available for computation for an event window 61 days (30 days before, 0 day being the announcement day, and 30 days after the open offer announcement).
- The chapter included only those open offers which are large in size (above Rs. 100 crore).
- All the multiple announcements such as dividend announcement/buyback announcement/stock split announcements relating to the companies given in the sample if found out would be eliminated for the calculations.

Total 31 companies have announced the open offer which has the value of more than 100 crore rupees during the period April 2015 to March 2017 which were reduced to 24 after using above-mentioned criteria. Table 14.3 revealing the year-wise open offer announcements.

14 Impact of Open Offers on Shareholders' Wealth

Table 14.3 List of large-sized open offer announcements during 2015–2017

Financial Years	Number of open offer announcements (above Rs. 100 crore)	Mode of payment consideration
2014–15	08	Cash
2015–16	10	Cash
2016–17	06	Cash
Total	24	All cash

Source www.sebi.gov.in

14.4 Analysis and Interpretation

The chapter found that for all the 24 large-sized open offers (above 100 crore rupees) during April 2015 to March 2017 has used cash for the payment consideration. In order to investigate the effect of open offer announcements on the price movement of various target companies, the estimation window of 120 days has used to compute the expected returns of the 24 open offers by using the ordinary least square regression (OLS) model. Further to examine the impact of such announcements on the pre-phase and post-phase of the event date, a 61 days event window has been used.

Table 14.4 as mentioned below highlighting the average abnormal returns (AAR) and cumulative abnormal returns (CAAR) of all the target companies mentioned in the sample size during the event window of 61 days.

Table 14.4 Computation of AAR and CAAR of 24 large-sized open offer announcements during the 61 days event window

Days	AAR	CAAR	Days	AAR	CAAR	Days	AAR	CAAR
−30	0.0099	0.0099	−10	0.0065	0.0094	10	−0.0020	0.1162
−29	−0.0048	0.0051	−9	0.0043	0.0137	11	0.0004	0.1167
−28	0.0025	0.0076	−8	−0.0010	0.0127	12	−0.0017	0.1149
−27	0.0000	0.0077	−7	0.0066	0.0193	13	0.0047	0.1196
−26	−0.0086	−0.0010	−6	0.0251	0.0444	14	0.0038	0.1234
−25	−0.0023	−0.0032	−5	0.0067	0.0511	15	−0.0079	0.1155
−24	−0.0004	−0.0037	−4	0.0099	0.0610	16	−0.0045	0.1110
−23	0.0090	0.0054	−3	−0.0001	0.0608	17	0.0044	0.1154
−22	0.0022	0.0075	−2	0.0091	0.0699	18	−0.0001	0.1153
−21	−0.0020	0.0055	−1	0.0117	0.0816	19	−0.0032	0.1121
−20	−0.0056	−0.0001	0	0.0317	0.1133	20	0.0003	0.1123
−19	0.0063	0.0061	1	0.0078	0.1211	21	−0.0028	0.1096
−18	−0.0012	0.0049	2	−0.0200	0.1011	22	−0.0045	0.1051
−17	−0.0079	−0.0030	3	0.0091	0.1103	23	−0.0033	0.1018

(continued)

Table 14.4 (continued)

Days	AAR	CAAR	Days	AAR	CAAR	Days	AAR	CAAR
−16	−0.0042	−0.0072	4	0.0002	0.1105	24	−0.0035	0.0984
−15	−0.0003	−0.0076	5	0.0108	0.1213	25	−0.0054	0.0929
−14	−0.0008	−0.0084	6	0.0030	0.1242	26	0.0083	0.1012
−13	0.0008	−0.0076	7	−0.0003	0.1240	27	−0.0074	0.0938
−12	0.0012	−0.0064	8	0.0000	0.1240	28	0.0003	0.0941
−11	0.0093	0.0029	9	−0.0057	0.1183	29	−0.0004	0.0937
						30	−0.0015	0.0922

Source Authors' computation

The overall results of average abnormal returns (AARs) and cumulative average abnormal returns (CAARs) reflecting that during the pre-phase of open offer announcement, the target firms' shareholders generated only 1–5% CAAR during day −10th to −5th and from day −4th to −1st shareholders generated 6–8% CAAR. On announcement day (0 day), the CAAR of target companies are recorded as 11.33%. During the post-phase of open offer announcement, the highest gain was recorded as 12.34% on the day 14th. After day 14th, the CAAR started declining and reached to 9.22% on the last day of the event window (+30th day). The overall results reflecting that the shareholders of the target companies can generate steady returns which apparently increased the wealth of shareholders of the target companies (Fig. 14.3).

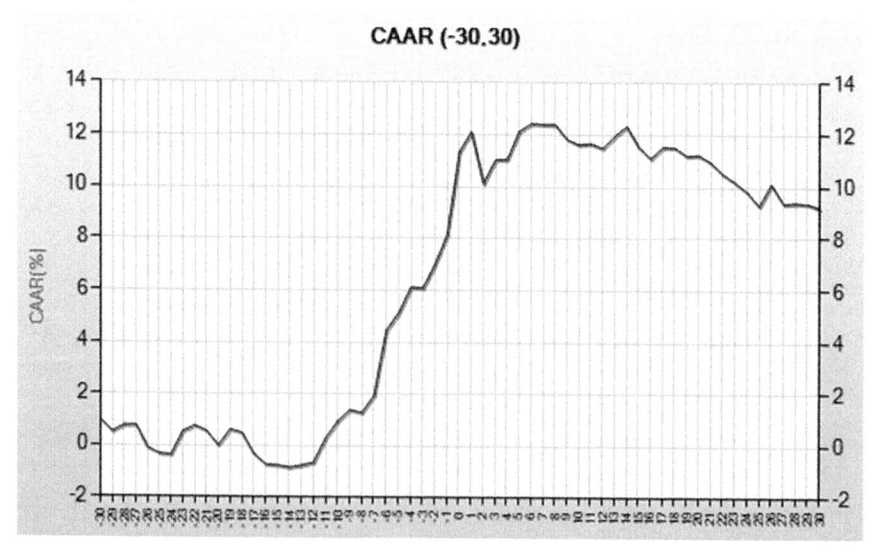

Fig. 14.3 Showing movement of CAAR of large-sized open offers during the event window of 61 days (−30, 0 and +30 days). *Source* Authors' computation

The CAAR results clearly depicting the impact of open offer announcements on the share price performance of target companies. As the pre-phase of the event window showing a gradual decrease in the returns till day −12th but near to the announcement day, i.e., −7th onwards, the target companies' started generating substantial returns. This may happen because either market anticipated this event in advance or there is some leakage of information. Further to examine the significance of these excessive returns, various parametric and nonparametric tools are used. The chapter used 1 and 5% level of significance to test the hypothesis. Table 14.5 mentioned below showing the results of various test statics such as T-test (time series), T-test cross-sectional test, Patell Z-test, BMP test, Corrado rank test, and sign test.

Different test statics has used to examine the significance of announcement effect on the wealth of shareholders in different sub-event windows, i.e., (−30, 30), (−20, 20), (−10, 10), (−5, 5), (−4, 4), (−3, 3), (−2, 2), and (−1, 1). The overall CAAR generated by 24 sample firms was recorded as 9.22% during the main event window of 61 days. The results of tests indicating that the main event window (−30, 30) is showing the positive significant results at a confidence level of 5% using T time series test and at 1% level Patell Z-test showed significant result. Further in sub-event windows as mentioned earlier showed the positive significant results at a confidence level of 1 and 5%. As the CAARs are showing significant results in every event windows and most of the companies showing positive and significant returns, the null hypothesis that CAARs to the target firm's shareholders in response to Open Offer announcements are not statistically different from zero, is rejected.

14.5 Summary of Findings

The chapter investigated the size of open offer and method of payment consideration and its effects on the wealth of shareholders of target companies in India. Following important findings accrued out of chapter:

- The chapter found that of out 31 large-sized open offers (above 100 crore rupees) only 24 open offers used Cash as a method of payment consideration.
- Further, the chapter revealed that all 24 companies who paid more than 100 crore rupees as payment consideration in the cash showed the significant results and found that the companies reacted positively on such open offer announcements. The results showed the significant values which are consistent with the prior studies as mentioned in the literature (Pandey 2001; Mallikarjunappa and Nayak 2013).

Table 14.5 Showing the parametric and nonparametric test statics for the different sub-event windows at different level of significance, i.e., 5 and 1%

Event windows	CAAR	Pos: neg	T-test time series test	Prob.	T-test cross-sectional test	Prob.	Patell Z-test	Prob.	Boehmer et al. test	Prob.	Corrado rank test	Prob.	Sign test	Prob.
(−30…30)	0.0922	13:11	1.8831	0.0597*	1.5143	0.1301	2.4314	0.0015***	1.4159	0.1568	1.0142	0.3105	0.9959	0.31903
(−20…20)	0.1068	14:10	2.6615	0.0078**	2.1274	0.0334*	3.4780	0.0005***	1.7864	0.0740	1.4430	0.1490	1.4070	0.1594
(−10…10)	0.1134	16:08	3.9467	0.0001**	2.6228	0.0087**	4.9237	0.0001***	2.2616	0.0237*	2.0116	0.0443*	2.2293	0.0258*
(−5…5)	0.0769	15:09	3.6980	0.0002**	2.2221	0.0263*	3.5098	0.0004***	1.9573	0.0503*	1.5469	0.1219	1.8182	0.0690
(−4…4)	0.0594	14:10	3.1565	0.0016**	2.1459	0.0319*	2.9662	0.0030***	1.8013	0.0717	1.0749	0.2824	1.4070	0.1594
(−3…3)	0.0493	16:08	2.9730	0.0029**	1.9229	0.0545*	3.2613	0.0011***	1.8414	0.0656	1.4175	0.1563	2.2293	0.0258*
(−2…2)	0.0403	16:08	2.8752	0.0040**	1.6766	0.0936	3.3861	0.0007***	1.7371	0.0824	1.1482	0.2509	2.2293	0.0258*
(−1…1)	0.0512	15:09	4.7134	0.0001**	2.3097	0.0209*	5.6505	0.0001***	2.3614	0.0182*	2.3879	0.0169*	1.8182	0.0690

Source Authors' computation (*at 5% confidence level, **at 1% confidence level)

14.6 Conclusion

The chapter concluded that the Open offer is a prominent tool for the takeover defense. SEBI frequently notifies guidelines for the safeguard of the small investors, and Open offer also provides safeguard to the minority shareholders of the target companies (SAST 2011). Through open offers, shareholders of the target companies can get the advantage by selling the shares to the acquiring company by getting the premium on the share price. Open offer announcements if anticipated well can give abnormal returns to the participants. The chapter gave the significant results about the existence of abnormal returns in the post-phase of event window, when acquiring companies announced such offers in the market.

References

Agarwal, M., & Bhattacharjea, A. (2006). Mergers in India. A response to regulatory shocks. *Emerging Markets Finance and Trade, 42*(3), 46–65.
Bradley, M., Desai, A., & Kim, E. H. (1988). Synergistic gains from corporate acquisitions and their division between the stockholders of target and acquiring firms. *Journal of Financial Economics, 21*(1), 3–40.
Brown, S. J., & Warner, J. B. (1980). Measuring security price performance. *Journal of Financial Economics, 8*(3), 205–258.
Brown, S. J., & Warner, J. B. (1985). Using daily stock returns: The case of event studies. *Journal of Financial Economics, 14*(1), 3–31.
Bruner, R. F. (2002). Does M&A pay? A survey of evidence for the decision-maker. *Journal of Applied Finance, 12*(1), 48–68.
Chakraborty, M. (2010). The wealth effects of takeover announcement for firms in the financial services sector in India. *Journal of Emerging Market Finance, 9*(2), 199–227.
Chatterjee, S. (1986). Types of synergy and economic value: The impact of acquisitions on merging and rival firms. *Strategic Management Journal, 7*(2), 119–139.
Datta, D. K., Pinches, G. E., & Narayanan, V. K. (1992). Factors influencing wealth creation from mergers and acquisitions: A meta-analysis. *Strategic Management Journal, 13*(1), 67–84.
Dodd, P. (1980). Merger proposals, management discretion and stockholder wealth. *Journal of Financial Economics, 8*(2), 105–137.
Dodd, P., & Ruback, R. (1977). Tender offers and stockholder returns: An empirical analysis. *Journal of Financial Economics, 5*(3), 351–373.
Dodd, P., & Warner, J. B. (1983). On corporate governance: A study of proxy contests. *Journal of Financial Economics, 11*(1–4), 401–438.
Dyckman, T., Philbrick, D., & Stephan, J. (1984). A comparison of event study methodologies using daily stock returns: A simulation approach. *Journal of Accounting Research*, 1–30.
Fabozzi, F. J., Ferri, M. G., Fabozzi, T. D., & Tucker, J. (1988). A note on unsuccessful tender offers and stockholder returns. *The Journal of Finance, 43*(5), 1275–1283.
Fama, E. F., Fisher, L., Jensen, M. C., & Roll, R. (1969). The adjustment of stock prices to new information. *International Economic Review, 10*(1), 1–21.
Firth, M. (1980). Takeovers, shareholder returns, and the theory of the firm. *The Quarterly Journal of Economics, 94*(2), 235–260.
Franks, J. R., & Harris, R. S. (1989). Shareholder wealth effects of corporate takeovers: The UK experience 1955–1985. *Journal of Financial Economics, 23*(2), 225–249.

Gupta, A. (2006). Impact of earnings announcements on stock prices: Some empirical evidences from India. *The ICFAI Journal of Applied Finance, 12*(3), 5–13.

Jarrell, G. A., & Poulsen, A. B. (1989). The returns to acquiring firms in tender offers: Evidence from three decades. *Financial Management*, 12–19.

Jensen, M. C., & Ruback, R. S. (1983). The market for corporate control: The scientific evidence. *Journal of Financial Economics, 11*(1–4), 5–50.

Khanra, S., & Dhir, S. (2017). Creating value in small-cap firms by mitigating risks of market volatility. *Vision, 21*(4), 350–355.

Kothari, S. P., & Warner, J. B. (2004). The econometrics of event studies.

Limmack, R. J. (1991). Corporate mergers and shareholder wealth effects: 1977–1986. *Accounting and Business Research, 21*(83), 239–252.

Mallikarjunappa, T., & Nayak, P. (2013). A study of wealth effects of takeover announcements in India on target company shareholders. *Vikalpa, 38*(3), 23–50.

Nangia, V. K., Srinivasa Reddy, K., & Agrawal, R. (2013). Corporate mergers and financial performance: A new assessment of Indian cases. *Nankai Business Review International, 4*(2), 107–129.

Pandey, A. (2001). Takeover announcements, open offers, and shareholders' returns in target firms. *Vikalpa, 26*(3), 19–30.

Patell, J. M. (1976). Corporate forecasts of earnings per share and stock price behavior: Empirical test. *Journal of Accounting Research*, 246–276.

Ranju, P. K., & Mallikarjunappa, T. (2017). Do acquisitions create value for acquirer companies in India? An empirical study. *Indian Journal of Research in Capital Markets, 4*(1), 7–18.

Rani, N., Yadav, S. S., & Jain, P. K. (2013). Market response to the announcement of mergers and acquisitions: An empirical study from India. *Vision, 17*(1), 1–16.

Rani, N., Yadav, S. S., & Jain, P. K. (2015). Innovative mode of financing and abnormal returns to shareholders of Indian acquiring firms. In Sushil & G. Chroust (Eds.), *Systemic flexibility and business agility* (Flexible systems management) (pp. 367–383). Springer: New Delhi.

Sharpe, W. F. (1963). A simplified model for portfolio analysis. *Management Science, 9*(2), 277–293.

Singh, A. K., Zaman, M. A., & Krishnamurti, C. (1994). Liquidity changes associated with open market repurchases. *Financial Management, 23*(1), 47–55.

Further Reading

www.sebi.gov.in/sebi_data/commondocs/acquistionofshares.pdf

Part IV
Leadership and Strategies in VUCA Markets

Chapter 15
Leadership Styles in the VUCA World, Through the Eyes of Gen-Z

Deepika Dabke

Abstract Millennial employees have been a matter of concern and consideration for researchers for more than a decade. Past studies have tried to explore the attributes, values, beliefs and expectations of the millennials and the best mechanism to engage them. The IT industry is currently witnessing an interesting team constellation with Gen-Y employees occupying the team lead roles and Gen-X forming the major workforce that needs to be led for best business outcomes. The current research aims to study the leadership dynamics of Gen-Y managers by assessing relationship between emotional intelligence (EI), as reported by managers and their transformational leadership style as perceived by their Gen-Z followers. Gen-Y managers (194) were administered by the Mayer, Salovey and Caruso Emotional Intelligence Test (MSCEIT). Gen-Z followers were administered by the leadership effectiveness scale and the Multifactor Leadership Questionnaire (MLQ) 5X scale. Results indicated that transformational leadership had a significant positive association with perceived leadership effectiveness. Emotional intelligence and personality did not show a significant relationship with leadership effectiveness. Results have been discussed in the light of Gen-Y leadership patterns and Gen-Z followers' expectations.

Keywords Big Five Personality · Emotional intelligence · Gen-Y Gen-Z · Leadership effectiveness · Transformational leadership

15.1 Introduction

Workplaces have been dynamic places like never before. The world of work has often been described as the VUCA world—(volatile, uncertain, complex and ambiguous). One of the factors that creates greater complexity in this VUCA world and affect leadership models is the existence of multigenerational cohorts

---

D. Dabke (✉)
ICFAI Business School, Mumbai, India
e-mail: deepikadabke@hotmail.com

© Springer Nature Singapore Pte Ltd. 2018
S. Dhir and Sushil (eds.), *Flexible Strategies in VUCA Markets*,
Flexible Systems Management, https://doi.org/10.1007/978-981-10-8926-8_15

(Smola and Sutton 2002; Arsenault 2004; Gladwell et al. 2010). Past research has shown that generation cohorts differ in terms of their beliefs and expectations (Glass 2007), their employee engagement (DeMeuse et al. 2001) and work values (Dabke 2016). Researchers have been keenly studying the dynamics that have emerged due to the presence of the Baby Boomers, Gen-X and the Gen-Y and now the Gen-Z (Broadbridge et al. 2007; Sessa et al. 2007; Ranstad Report 2016). Leadership studies have got a special focus in the past, especially to look at what are the expectations of Gen-Y from their leaders, which are the best models that yield maximum engagement and output from them and ensure their longevity in the organization (Conger et al. 2000; Arsenault 2004; Khanra and Dhir 2017). While this body of research provides a strong foundation to anticipate the behavioural patterns of Gen-Y and explore their working relationships, there is a paucity of studies that aim to ascertain the attributes that make Gen-Y leaders effective. These dynamics become more profound in the Information Technology Enabled Services (ITES), where more and more Gen-Y members are occupying the leadership role and find themselves leading the Gen-Z, who are just a couple of years younger to them. The current chapter is based on data collected from the ITES companies in India to examine whether Gen-Z attribute the same elements to effective leadership as they predecessors or do they look for different attributes that define an effective leader. The study aims to explore this question by focusing on three critical attributes of a leader, namely personality, emotional intelligence of the Gen-Y and transformational leadership and effectiveness as perceived by the Gen-Z followers. The major objective of the study was to examine the association between leadership effectiveness, as perceived by Gen-Z, and emotional intelligence, personality and transformational leadership behaviour of their Gen-Y leaders

15.2 Literature Review

15.2.1 Generation Cohorts

Workplaces witness the interaction between four generations at work, namely the Veterans (1909–1945), Baby Boomers (1946–1964), Generation X (Gen-X) (1965–1985) and Generation Y (Gen-Y) (1986–1984) (Smola and Sutton 2002). Additionally, a new generation has joined the workforce and poses to be the future hope of business, the Generation Z (Gen-Z) (1995–2010). While they may not be too different than the digital natives (Prensky 2001), there are a few differences seen in their work values, preferences and communication patterns (Ranstad Report 2016; Aniruddha and Mital 2014). Studies have also indicated that Gen-Z are more inclined towards in-person communication (Ranstad Report 2016) and are ready to work for managers who develop strong working relationship with colleagues.

15.2.2 Leadership Effectiveness

Leadership may be defined as "a process whereby an individual influences a group of individuals to achieve a common goal" (Northouse 2010, p. 3). Effectiveness has been defined in terms of objective business outcomes, such as unit goals, profit margins, performance goals and subjective outcomes such as subordinate satisfaction, engagement and intention to stay (Gupta and Nagpal 2015). The current study focuses on subjective leadership effectiveness evaluation of Gen-Y by their Gen-Z followers.

15.2.3 Transformational Leadership

Transformational leadership model has been most widely studied and consistently associated with leadership effectiveness (Yammarino and Bass 1990; Avolio and Howell 1992) and emotional intelligence (Gardner and Stough 2002; Palmer et al. 2003). Lowe et al. (1996) have found that in most studies, three transformational leadership behaviours (charisma, individualized consideration and intellectual stimulation) were related to leadership effectiveness. Given the enormous support that the transformational leadership model has gathered over the years (Judge and Piccolo 2004), it is imperative to believe that the same association would be upheld in the context of the Gen-Y leaders and the Gen-Z followers. Thus, hypothesis 1 states:

H1: Transformational Leadership behaviour would have an influence on leadership effectiveness as perceived by Gen-Z followers.

15.2.4 Emotional Intelligence

Salovey and Mayer (1990) define emotional intelligence (EI) as, "the ability to monitor one's own and other's thinking and actions". EI has been shown to be positively associated to leadership effectiveness (Barling et al. 2000; Barbuto and Burbach 2006). These managers inculcate a greater sense of self-esteem in followers and are, thus, considered in a more positive light by subordinates. Considering the previous research, following hypothesis was postulated:

H2: Emotional intelligence would have an influence on leadership effectiveness as perceived by the Gen-Z followers.

```
         Emotional
         Intelligence
                         H1
      Transformational   H2        Leadership
        Leadership                 Effectiveness
                         H3
         Personality
```

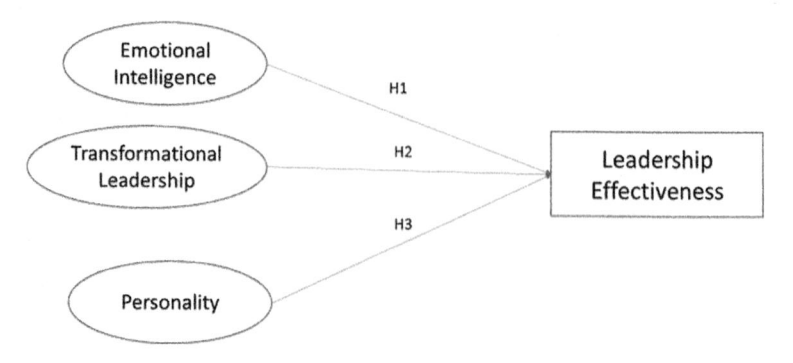

Fig. 15.1 Proposed model of the study. *Source* Author

15.2.5 Big Five Personality

The Big Five Personality taxonomy has been a very popular framework to study leadership-related variables and personality. The association between leadership effectiveness and personality has been mixed and non-conclusive (Costa and McCrae 1992; Judge and Bono 2000; Dhir and Mital 2012). However, It is believed that leadership effectiveness would be dependent on endogenous variables such as personality, as they are stable over period and influence people's cognitive and behavioural patterns consistently.

H3: Personality of the Gen-Y leaders will have an influence on the leadership effectiveness as perceived by the Gen-Z followers.

The proposed model is summarized in Fig. 15.1.

15.3 Methodology

The current research was a quantitative study aimed at exploring the relationship between Gen-Y's perceived leadership effectives and factors such as emotional intelligence, leadership behaviour and Personality

15.3.1 Sample

The sample comprised of 194 Gen-Y employees occupying leadership roles in various ITES organizations. The average age of the Gen-Y leaders was 33.4 years. 63% of the sample was males, and 37% were females. 19% were in the project leader role, 63% were in the team leader role and the remaining 18% occupied some leadership role in the pre-sales function. Average years of experience were 8.7 years. The average age of the Gen-Z followers was 21.7 years. Almost all the 194 Gen-Z were graduates and were in a coder or a developer role. The average work experience was 1.3 years. The current job was the first-ever job for 88% of the respondents. All the followers had been working with the Gen-Y leader for at least 6 months. A total of 250 Gen-Y employees were approached. The final sample size was 194 * 2 sets of response sheets. The response rate was found to be 77.6%.

15.3.2 Research Design and Procedure

The research design was a convenient sample design. Gen-Y leaders were administered by the MSCEIT V.2 test (Mayer 2002) and NEO-FFI (Costa and McCrae 1992). All the Gen-Y leaders selected one Gen-Z follower who had been working with them for at least 6 months. The chose Gen-Z followers were administered by the MLQ 5X as well as leadership effectiveness scales (Kerr et al. 2006) in the form of a Google form.

15.3.3 Measures

- **Emotional Intelligence (EI)**
  EI of participants was measured by the MSCEIT V.2 test (Mayer et al. 2002). The overall EI score was considered for further analysis. The Cronbach's alpha value of the current sample was found to be 0.77.
- **Transformational leadership style**
  Transformational leadership style was measured by the MLQ 5X scale developed by Bass and Avolio (2000). Past research has reported adequate reliabilities (Cronbach's alpha). The MLQ5X, Cronbach's alpha coefficient ranged from 0.71 to 0.93 and was in the acceptable range of 0.70 (Osgood et al. 1956).
- **Leadership effectiveness**
  Perceived leadership effectiveness of subordinates was measured through the nine-item supervisory leadership survey developed by Kerr et al. (2006). The Cronbach's alpha coefficient was found to be 0.87.
- **Personality**
  The Big Five factors as measured by NEO-FFI (NEO-FFI; Costa and McCrae 1992) which comprises 60 answered on a five-point Likert type scale. The Cronbach's alpha scores for the NEO-FFI range from 0.68 (A) to 0.86 (N).

15.3.4 Data Analysis

SPSS (version 20) and AMOS (version 20) were used for the analysis of the data gathered. Reliability coefficients of the scales were measured using SPSS. The proposed model was tested through a Confirmatory Factor Analysis (CFA) technique of the Structured Equation Modelling. To assess how this model represented the data, absolute fit indices such as the $\chi 2$ statistic and the goodness-of-fit index (GFI) as well as incremental fit statistics such as the comparative fit index (CFI) and the root mean square error of approximation (RMSEA) were used. For both GFI and CFI, values >0.95 constitute good fit and values >0.90 acceptable fit. For the RMSEA, it has been suggested that values <0.05 constitute good fit, values in the 0.05–0.08 range acceptable fit, values in the 0.08–0.10 range marginal fit and values >0.10 poor fit (Browne and Cudeck 1993). The SEM output was also used to test the hypotheses exploring the associations between the variables.

15.4 Results

The CFAs showed that the model produced an acceptable fit to the data, $\chi 2$ (50) = 100.185, GFI = 0.916. AGFI = 0.870, CFI = 0.907 and RMSEA = 0.072. The CMIN/DF score was found to be 2.00 indicating that there is a moderately acceptable fit between hypothesized model and sample data. Table 15.1 summarizes the path coefficients obtained and the p values of the variables.

The results have been summarized in Fig. 15.2.

As seen in Table 15.1, leadership effectiveness seemed to be depending on the use of transformational leadership behaviour by Gen-Y. Past research has shown a positive association between Effectiveness perceptions and transformational leadership (Judge and bono 2000; Kerr et al. 2006). The current findings are in line with the past body of knowledge. However, leadership effectiveness failed to show a positive correlation with emotional intelligence. These findings were surprising as past studies have indicated the importance of EI in leadership (Kerr et al. 2006). However, in the current sample, clearly the subordinate's perception of leadership

Table 15.1 Hypothesis testing results

Hypothesis	Estimates	CR.	p values	Results
Leadership effectiveness ← EQ	−0.02	−0.267	0.790	Not supported
Leadership effectiveness ← leadership	0.24	2.097	0.036*	Supported
Leadership effectiveness ← personality	−0.05	−0.451	0.652	Not supported

*$p < 0.05$

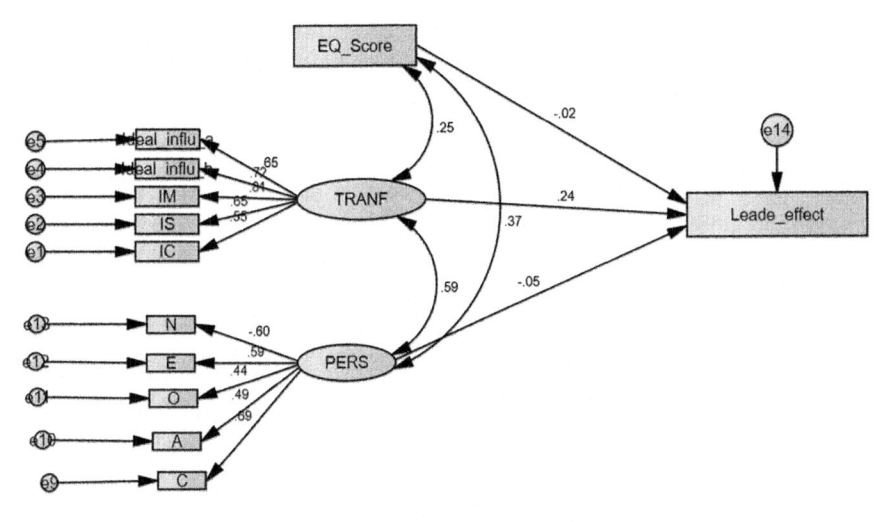

Fig. 15.2 Tested model

effectiveness seems to be a function of factors other than the Gen-Y leader's ability to perceive and deal with emotions in self and others. These findings are in line with the thought process of Antonakis (2004) who suggests that emotional intelligence may not be a critical factor in leadership effectiveness. Finally, leadership effectiveness failed to show any significant correlation with any of the personality variables. The importance of personality in leadership has been systematically studied by Judge and Bono (2000). Past research has had mixed evidence for the role of personality and leadership effectiveness. In a study carried out by Stogdill (1948), there was a lack of evidence for the emergence of any universal trait to leadership effectiveness. In the case of Mann's study (1959), factors other than personality constitute 88% of the explanation of leadership effectiveness. To sum up, the current study found a positive relationship between transformational leadership behaviour and leadership effectiveness.

15.5 Discussion

The current study aimed at assessing factors that contribute to the Gen-Z followers' perception of leadership effectiveness keeping in view the leadership behaviours exhibited by their Gen-Y leaders. Results indicated that leadership effectiveness perceptions were positively associated with leadership behaviour and failed to show significant correlation with emotional intelligence or personality variables.

The current study failed to gather evidence in support of EI and its relationship with Leader effectiveness. In the past, Antonakis (2004) had raised a debate over the importance of EI in leadership role. While critiquing the work of Prati et al. (2003), he had espoused that EI is innate and effective leaders do not need exceptional ability to perceive and mange emotions over and above the normal standards. He was of the opinion that transformational behaviours create a greater affective and behaviour connect with the followers which is far superior for the effectiveness estimations. These findings have been corroborated by other researchers (Schutte et al. 2002; Dabke 2016). Thus, organizations and HR need to be cautious in their over prescription of emotional intelligence as a one-stop solution for better follower management.

Transformational leadership exudes tremendous confidence and creates a sense of common vision (Bass and Avolio 1990) in followers. A leader using transformational style gets followers to question the status quo and encourages them to question their methods and seek ways to improve them (Bass and Avolio 1990). Intellectual stimulation helps the leader encourage the followers to be innovative and creative. These are espousing to be the innate characteristics of the Gen-Z followers (Moorthy 2014). Gen-Z also possesses higher ability to process a great deal of information (Addor 2014). They exhibit entrepreneurial initiate much more than any other generation (Adecco 2015).

15.6 Practical Implications and Recommendations

The study extends the understanding of the Gen-Z and their preferred leadership patterns. "Currently, employee retention and engagement are some of the most critical challenges that organizations face regardless of the company's size, technology and market focus" (Manzoor and Naeem 2011). The current findings throw some light on practices that HR should consider while developing the Gen-Y leaders. The transformational leadership behaviour has been consistently associated with leadership effectiveness and satisfaction. Thus, all followers, irrespective of their generation cohorts, tend to consider transformational behaviours as effective for those in the leadership role. Structured attempts should be made through the Learning and Development initiatives to inculcate the transformational behaviours in leaders. Transformational leadership also improves decision-making and team development (Bass and Avolio 1990). Such behaviours would be a best model to deal with multi-generation workforce. Gen-Y leaders are considered to be somewhat ill prepared to lead the workforce (Randstad Report 2016). Thus, the organization needs to invest in the coaching, mentoring and development of this critical talent. Finally, the results provide a lot of optimism given that leadership effectiveness is associated with leadership behaviour that can be trained and nurtured, rather that EI and personality factors that are innate and to a large extent constant over time. Thus, the organization stands a great chance of creating able leaders to lead the Gen-Z to success

15.7 Limitations and Future Research Avenues

Some limitations of the study and future research directions are as follows:

- One of the major limitations is that the sample is drawn from a specific sector limiting the generalizability to the findings.
- A number of other organization-related variables such as policies, work climate, leader member exchange theory were not considered for this study. A robust research design encompassing a number of exogenous variables affecting leader–follower relationship can also be considered in future.

15.8 Conclusion

Leadership effectiveness is more in the eyes of the follower than in reality. The current study was able to contribute to a better understanding of the leadership expectations of the Gen-Z followers and a peek into the leadership patterns of the Gen-Y leaders. Transformational leadership behaviour has emerged as significant factors that define leadership effectiveness independent of innate factors such as emotional intelligence and Personality.

References

Addor, M. L. (2014). *Generation Z: What is the future of stakeholder engagement?* Retrieved from: http://iei.ncsu.edu/wp-content/uploads/2013/01/GenZStakeholders2.pdf.

Adecco. (2015). *Genertion Z vS millenials*. Available at: http://pages.adeccousa.com/rs/107-IXF-539/images/generation-z-vs-millennials.pdf.

Antonakis, J. (2004). On why "emotional intelligence" will not predict leadership effectiveness beyond IQ or the "big five": An extension and rejoinder. *Organizational Analysis, 12*(2), 171–182.

Arsenault, P. M. (2004). Validating generational differences: A legitimate diversity and leadership issue. *Leadership & Organization Development Journal, 25*(2), 124–141.

Avolio, B. J., & Howell, J. M. (1992). The impact of leader behavior and leader-follower personality match on satisfaction and unit performance. In K. E. Clark & D. R. Campbell (Eds.), *Impact of leadership*. Greensboro, NC: The Center for Creative Leadership.

Barbuto, J. E., & Burbach, M. E. (2006). The emotional intelligence of transformational leaders: A field study of elected officials. *Journal of Social Psychology, 146*(1), 51–64.

Barling, J., Slater, F., & Kelloway, E. K. (2000). Transformational leadership and emotional intelligence. *Leadership and Organization Development Journal, 21*(3), 157–162.

Bass, B. M., & Avolio, B. J. (1990). *Transformational leadership development: Manual for the multifactor leadership questionnaire*. Palo Alto, CA: Consulting Psychologist Press.

Bass, B. M., & Avolio, B. J. (2000). *Effects on platoon readiness of transformational/transactional platoon leadership*. Final Report. Contract DASW01-96K-0008, U.S. Army Research Institute for the Behavioural and Social Sciences, March 2000.

Broadbridge, A. M., Maxwell, G. A., & Ogden, S. M. (2007). 13_2_30: Experiences, perceptions and expectations of retail employment for Generation Y. *Career Development International, 6,* 523–544.

Browne, M. W., & Cudeck, R. (1993). Alternative ways of assessing model fit. In K. A. Bollen & J. S. Long (Eds.), *Testing structural equations models* (pp. 136–162). Newbury Park, CA: Sage.

Conger, J. A., Kanungo, R. N., & Menon, S. T. (2000). Charismatic leadership and follower effects. *Journal of Organizational Behavior, 21*(7), 747–767.

Costa, P. T., Jr., & McCrae, R. R. (1992). *Revised NEO personality inventory (NEO_PI_R) and NEO five-factor inventory (NEO-FFI) professional manual*. Odessa, FL: PAR.

Dabke, D. (2016). Redefining management principles for the "digical" generation. *International Journal of Research in Commerce, Economics & Management, 6*(3), 73–78.

DeMeuse, K. P., Bergmann, T. J., & Lester, S. W. (2001). An investigation of the relational component of the psychological contract across time. *Generation, and Employment Status, Journal of Managerial Issues, 13,* 102–118.

Aniruddha, D. S., & Mital, A. (2014). Alliance network heterogeneity, absorptive capacity and innovation performance: A framework for mediation and moderation effects. *International Journal of Strategic Business Alliances, 3*(2–3), 168–178.

Dhir, S., & Mital, A. (2012). Decision-making for mergers and acquisitions: The role of agency issues and behavioral biases. *Strategic Change, 21*(1–2), 59–69.

Gardner, L., & Stough, C. (2002). Examining the relationship between leadership and emotional intelligence in senior level managers. *Leadership & Organization Development Journal, 23*(2), 68–78.

Gladwell, N. J., Dorwart, C. E., Stone, C. F., & Hammond, C. A. (2010). Importance of and satisfaction with organizational benefits for a multigenerational workforce. *Journal of Park & Recreation Administration, 28*(2), 1–19.

Glass, A. (2007). Understanding generational differences for competitive success. *Industrial and Commercial Training Journal, 39*(2), 98–103.

Gupta, R. K., & Nagpal, S. (2015) Next-generation business excellence model: Integrating flexibility dimension. In Sushil & G. Chroust (Eds.), *Systemic flexibility and business agility, flexible systems management* (pp. 257–270). Springer: New Delhi.

Judge, T., & Bono, J. (2000). Five factor model of personality and transformational leadership. *Journal of Applied Psychology, 85*(5), 751–765.

Judge, T. A., & Piccolo, R. F. (2004). Transformational and transactional leadership: A meta-analytic test of their relative validity. *Journal of Applied Psychology, 89,* 755.

Khanra, S., & Dhir, S. (2017). Creating value in small-cap firms by mitigating risks of marketvolatility. *Vision, 21*(4), 350–355.

Kerr, R., Garvin, J., Heaton, N., & Boyle, E. (2006). Emotional intelligence and leadership effectiveness. *Leadership & Organization Development Journal, 27*(4), 265–279.

Lowe, K. B., Kroeck, K. G., & Sivasubramaniam, N. (1996). Effectiveness correlates of transformation and transactional leadership: A meta-analytic review of the MLQ literature. *Leadership Quarterly, 7,* 385–425.

Mann, R. D. (1959). A review of the relationship between personality and performance in small groups. *Psychological Bulletin, 56,* 241–270.

Manzoor, M., & Naeem, H. (2011). Relationship of organization socialization with organizational commitment and turnover intention: Moderating role of perceived organizational support. *Interdisciplinary Journal of Contemporary Research in Business, 3*(8), 515–529.

Mayer, J. D., Salovey, P., & Caruso, D. R. (2002). *Test User Manual.* Toronto, Canada: MHS.

Moorthy, R. (2014). An empirical study of leadership theory preferences among Gen Y in Malaysia. *Review of Integrative Business and Economics Research, 3*(2), 398–421.

Northouse, P. G. (2010) *Leadership: Theory and practice* (5th ed.) Thousand Oaks, CA: Sage.

Osgood, C. E., Saporta, S., & Nunnally, J. C. (1956). Evaluative assertion analysis. *Litera, 3,* 47–102.

Palmer, B., Gardner, L., & Stough, C. (2003). *The relationship between emotional intelligence, personality and effective leadership*. Paper presented at the 5th Australia Industrial & Organizational Psychology Conference, Melbourne.

Prati, L. M., Douglas, C., Ferris, G. R., Ammeter, A. P., & Buckley, M. R. (2003). Emotional intelligence, leadership effectiveness, and team outcomes. *The International Journal of Organizational Analysis, 11,* 21–30.

Prensky, M. (2001). Digital natives, digital immigrants: Do they really think different? *On the Horizon, 9*(6), 1–6. Retrieved from http://www.marcprensky.com/writing/Prensky%20%20Digital%20Natives,%20Digital%20Immigrants%20-%20Part2.pdf.

Randstad Work Study. (2016*). Gen Z and millennials collide @*. Retrieved from http://experts.randstadusa.com/hubfs/Randstad_GenZ_Millennials_Collide_Report.pdf.

Salovey, P., & Mayer, J. D. (1990). Emotional intelligence. *Imagination, Cognition and Personality, 9*(3), 185–211.

Schutte, N. S., Malouff, J., Simunek, M., Hollander, S., & McKenley, J. (2002). Characteristic emotional intelligence and emotional wellbeing. *Cognition and Emotion, 16,* 769–785.

Sessa, V. I., Kabacoff, R. I., Deal, J., & Brown, H. (2007). Generational differences in leader values and leadership behaviors. *The Psychologist-Manager Journal, 10*(1), 47–74.

Smola, K. W., & Sutton, C. D. (2002). Generational differences: Revisiting generational work values for the new millennium. *Journal of Organizational Behavior, 23,* 363–382.

Stogdill, R. M. (1948). Personal factors associated with leadership: A survey of leadership. *Journal of Personality, 25,* 35–71.

Yammarino, F. J., & Bass, B. M. (1990). Long-term forecasting of transformational leadership and its effects among naval officers: Some preliminary findings. In K. E. Clark & M. B. Clark (Eds.), *Measures of leadership* (pp. 151–171). West Orange, NJ: Leadership Library of America.

Chapter 16
Leadership in VUCA Environment

Saniya Chawla and Usha Lenka

Abstract In changing times, leaders need to create new ideas and engage their teams in new beginnings. There are certain challenges that organizations face in order to help leaders move forward with new possibilities and choices available to them in VUCA world. By embracing volatile, uncertain, complex, and ambiguous environment and still remaining hopeful involves lot of confidence, positivity, courage, and creativity. This chapter aims to study the two different leadership styles, i.e., transformational and resonant leadership style highly suitable for developing private Indian higher educational institutes as learning organizations in order to survive in VUCA world. It shows the way and indicates about the best leadership style as predictor of learning organization in Indian context. Sample for this study consisted of 150 faculty members from 20 Indian higher educational institutes in National Capital Region, India. It has been found that both the leadership styles, i.e., transformational and resonant significantly impacted the learning organization in VUCA landscape. However, the impact on resonant leadership is higher than that of transformational leadership style to thrive well in VUCA world. Discussions and implications are further highlighted in the chapter.

Keywords Indian higher educational institutes · Learning organizations Resonant leadership style · Transformational leadership style · VUCA

16.1 Introduction

It is the era of rapid change and dynamic human development. A failure to meet challenges will leave many organizations behind and human capital potential of employee unfulfilled. Thus in changing times, leaders must encourage their

---

S. Chawla (✉)
Jagannath International Management School, Kalkaji, New Delhi, India
e-mail: chawla.saniya@gmail.com

U. Lenka
Indian Institute of Technology Roorkee, Roorkee, Uttarakhand, India

followers to bring fresh perspectives, challenge beliefs, create more empowering thoughts, develop flexibility, creativity and confidence in identity. These challenges faced by the organization have shifted our focus in engaging with uncertainty, and bringing higher levels of leadership agility to navigate through volatile, uncertain, complex, and ambiguous (VUCA) landscape (Dhir 2016). Thus, to overcome such challenges one of the strategies is to transform organizations into learning organizations in the VUCA world. Challenges faced in earlier times by the organizations have shifted our focus to learning organizations. Traditional organizations have faced a lot of problems such as bureaucratic structure, red-tapism, and top-down approach to name a few thereby creating barriers in effective learning during dynamic times. In contrast, learning organizations are considered to be significant source of competitive advantage. Learning organizations focus on organic structure, open communication, knowledge sharing, and experimentation that fosters learning. Organizational learning theory states that in a volatile environment, organizations change their actions through continuous learning to reach the desired goal (Argyris and Schön 1995). A key competence for organizational members is the ability to continuously learn. It is therefore important to facilitate learning practices throughout the organization at all the levels individual, team, and organizational level. Such organizations would then be termed as learning organizations that are able to survive in VUCA world. But transforming into a learning organization is not an overnight process. The organization has to surpass through several developmental stages in order to transform into a learning organization that requires accepting and embracing the change.

India is known for its highly skilled and educated workforce and has transformed its higher education sector. The country is recognized to be single largest provider of global talent and is presently in a development stage of becoming a hub of higher education. Indian higher education represents third largest in the world, next to USA and China (Choudaha 2013). Today there are more than 35,000 affiliated colleges and 700-degree-granting institutes in the country enrolling more than 20 million students every year. Though, the last few years, India has witnessed a significant increase in the number of higher educational institutes and student output, making it a complex and a large system. However, management programs across the country are losing some of their scintillation. All India Council for Technical Education (AICTE) shows 147 stand-alone B-schools and MBA programs offered by various engineering institutes across the country closed down in the academic year 2014–2015. Therefore, there is a need to overhaul the scenario of institutes offering management degrees. There are various problems faced by them in terms of lack of uniformity in the curriculum and indiscriminate admission policies. As a result, the institutes are not able to get best out of the students. Though, offer management degree but have a poor placement scenario. The reasons for poor employability skills of graduating students are lack of conceptual clarity and analyzing business problems to take effective decisions. Thus, there is an urgent need to upgrade the existing status quo of higher educational institutes by expanding its learning capacity. Learning organization would be a panacea for the impending problem of higher educational institutes as it makes organizations more meaningful, focused, and purposeful with involvement of every member in the system. There is an urgent need to make fundamental reforms in the status quo of the institutes, and the leader of the institute can only make that reform. Conventional leadership practices are no longer adequate. Organizations globally need next-generation leaders' competencies in order to address the challenges of VUCA business environment (Bawany 2016). Leading in VUCA not only provide a challenging environment for leaders to operate but also new range of strategies and competences to succeed. Therefore, it is requisite to endow higher educational institutes as learning organizations with emphasis on quality teaching, research, administration, consultancy, and student employability.

Thus, learning organization has emerged as an imminent requirement to develop human competence that can help an organization thrive in a VUCA world. A learning organization can improve relative position of an institute by promoting continuous learning of its members. To elevate the position of higher educational institutes as a provider of knowledge, the institutes need to adopt continuous improvement practices by promoting teaching and learning. Therefore, if the institutes have to prosper in the twenty-first century and to prevail in VUCA world, they must weed out such impediments in their way to transform into a learning organization.

To our knowledge, there is paucity of research on the comparative study of different leadership styles, i.e., transformational and resonant leadership styles that are best suited for a learning organization in Indian higher educational institutes. Therefore, this chapter aims to study these two leadership styles and predicts the best leadership style highly suitable for a learning organization in Indian higher educational institutes.

16.2 Literature Review

16.2.1 *Transformational Leadership Style (TLS)*

In an era of change, customers look for quality education and therefore are prepared for lifelong learning, problem-solving ability, critical thinking, communicate in international languages, be technologically skilled and become culturally responsible citizens. But this is highly influenced by role of system leaders and culture of the organization. System leaders have the capacity to improve the organizations performance by encouraging members to be actively involved in change process, creating a shared vision, learning in interactive networks, personal mastery, and information management system (Dhir et al. 2016). They are also trying to make an effort for collaborating the Asian universities with Western Universities to have better availability of resources, faculty development, and support for innovation (Hallinger 1998).

Thus, it is the role of the leader to take strategic actions and make interventions to ensure that learning occurs in the organization (Dhir and Mital 2012). Managers and leaders have managed their learning process by designing and continuously modifying various management practices and processes (Goh 1998). A transformational and supportive leader creates conditions necessary for promoting learning at all levels. It is the leader who acts as a primary change agent and shows confidence and commitment in promoting trust among members. Building a learning organization needs attention and time of the leader. It is working toward building a mindset, attitude, and behavior to live and lead in a VUCA world (Mustafa 2016). Therefore, leaders should focus on energy and talent to achieve learning excellence (Hiatt-Michael 2001). Extraordinary leaders are the form of transformational leaders that serve in educational settings (Kirby et al. 1992). Transformational leaders motivate followers through individual consideration, intellectual stimulation, idealized influence, and inspirational motivation (Avolio and Bass 1995). Individual consideration is the degree to which leaders listen to the followers concerns and needs. Intellectual stimulation is when leaders encourage the followers to be creative and innovative in accomplishing the task. Inspirational motivation is the degree to which leaders communicate the followers to be optimistic toward achieving organizational goals (Thekedam 2014). Idealized influence is the degree to which leaders values have been imbibed in the followers. A study conducted in Taiwanese school found that transformational leadership is a necessary condition for implementing organizational learning in schools because they provide dynamism and support to the members to create a school that learns (Lam et al. 2003).

Thus, leaders play a very significant role in promoting and nurturing learning in an organization (Antonoaie and Antonoaie 2010). As a transformational, visionary, and inspirational leader, their main responsibilities in promoting a learning culture are collective learning, knowledge sharing, influential networking, and developing learning climate. Their main challenge is to build organization ability for learning and adaptability across all the levels of an organization in order to thrive in VUCA world. Thus, creating a true learning organization requires powerful leaders at the top level that empowers the organizational members to engage in continuous learning. Therefore, we propose

H_1 Transformational leadership style will have a positive and predictive relationship with learning organization and thrive well in VUCA world.

16.2.2 Resonant Leadership Style (RLS)

Emotionally intelligent leaders inspire others by imbibing trust, cooperation, and satisfaction. Emotional intelligence accounts for 85–90% of the differences between an outstanding and average leader. It also affects the culture and climate that accounts for 30% of business performance (McKee 2011). Leaders with positive moods and emotions influence followers through perceived effectiveness thereby spreading positive vibes. Higher emotional climate in an organization results in idea generation, creativity, readiness to learn, and adaptability to learn and change. Therefore, leaders high on emotional intelligence are judicious decision-makers, work in teams, and contribute to effective team performance (Tran 1998). Primal leaders reflect positive emotions. A leader's primal task is to be emotionally strong for providing a positive direction to people (Khanra and Dhir 2017). Primal leaders are of two types: (a) resonant and (b) dissonant leaders. Resonant leaders develop resonance through mindfulness, hope, and compassion (Boyatzis and McKee 2005). Mindfulness requires individuals to remain in vigilance. Hope is when individual is able to frame a suitable future. Compassion is when individuals show tenderness. Resonant leaders handle pressure by controlling their emotions that send positive messages to their followers. Such leaders follow different approaches to leadership that creates resonance and boosts performance (Goleman et al. 2004). These approaches are: (a) visionary, (b) coaching, (c) affiliative, and (d) democratic. Visionary leaders set followers free to innovate, experiment, and take risks. Coaching helps followers to understand their strengths and weakness. Affiliative style of leadership promotes harmony and friendly interactions. Democratic leader facilitates teamwork, collaboration, and conflict management. Such approaches also help in bringing fresh perspectives in the situations that are faced by the individual, teams, and organisations thereby helping them turn challenges into opportunities. Resonant leaders have empathy and build long-lasting relationships with people, teams, and organizational culture. They inspire their followers by showing commitment, dedication, and concern for them. Emotions are contagious, and leader's emotions are drivers of their employee's moods that will affect their performance. But being a resonant leader is not so easy and sustaining it is even harder (Boyatzis and McKee 2005). These leaders are in a continuous state of sacrifice while helping out others. They give much time to their followers and not much is spent on cultivating new skills and practices for them. Leaders require the exercise of influence and power. With influence and power, comes greater responsibility and thus they experience great deal of stress. In this increasing pressure, leaders come under power stress and get trapped in a sacrifice syndrome. Here, dissonance comes into play that spreads across the organization and damages it. Dissonant leaders create havoc. They have volatile emotions, fear and are highly frustrated. They are completely unaware of the damage they are doing to the organization. They fuel negative emotions that hamper the team member's motivation, communication, and productivity. Therefore, in order to revive back to resonance position leaders undergo certain renewal steps by being mindful, hopeful, and compassionate. Thus being more compassionate and developing care toward followers, being more creative, experiencing less stress and moving with greater purpose can help thrive in VUCA world.

H_2 Resonant leadership style will have a positive and predictive relationship with learning organization and thrive well in VUCA world (Fig. 16.1).

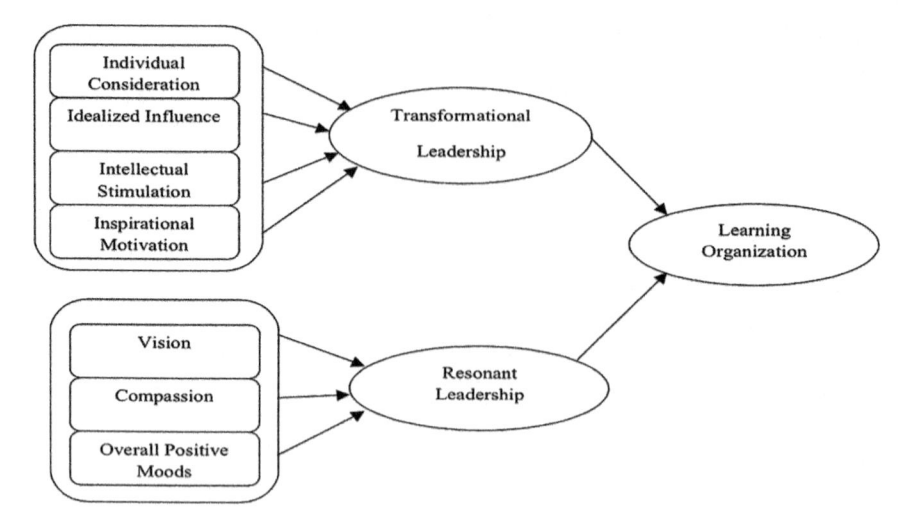

Fig. 16.1 Conceptual framework

16.3 Research Methodology

16.3.1 The Sample

Sample for this study consisted of 150 faculty members from 20 private Indian higher educational institutes in National Capital Region, India. The criterion that was kept during the survey was that the institute must have a minimum strength of eight faculty members, and the head of the institute must be holding the leadership position in that respective institute from at least one year.

16.3.2 The Measure

Survey for data collection was done using a self-designed instrument called as *"leadership survey for developing higher educational institutes as learning organizations."* The survey questions specific to the objectives of this study were chosen to capture the responses on various parameters of different leadership style. Questionnaire method is time-consuming and costly, but large amounts of information can be collected from large number of people with a higher response rate, and therefore, due to this reason it is selected for the present study. Data is collected during the period of January 2016 to February 2016. The questionnaire was short consisting of 15 questions on transformational leadership style and eight on resonant leadership style making the total to 23. There was no right or wrong answer to the items. The questionnaire takes approximately 5–7 min to complete.

16.3.3 Reliability of the Instrument

The reliability of the questionnaire is reported accurately for the purpose of maintaining integrity of the questionnaire. The reliability coefficients considerably higher than 0.60 thresholds commonly specified as minimally acceptable in the literature and support the internal consistency of the items. The questionnaire used reported the following reliability. Resonant and transformational leadership style renders the observation of faculty members in the behavior of their leader. As all the participants were holding key position profiles; hence, all total 23 items were there. Transformational leadership style is grouped into factors like individual consideration (three items), intellectual stimulation (three items), idealized influence (six items), and inspirational motivation (three items). The sample items are our head of the institute: "help us in our professional and personal development" (individual consideration), "enables us to think about the problems in newer ways" (intellectual stimulation), "feels that we are proud being associated with him/her" (idealized influence), "helps us finding meaning in our task" (inspirational motivation). Cronbach's alpha of the overall items and factors ranged between 0.69 and 0.82. Resonant leadership style was assessed using eight items. Total three factors, namely vision (two items), compassion (two items), and overall positive moods (three items) constitute this variable. The sample items are our head of the institute: "provides vision for teaching, learning and research excellence" (vision), "cares about our professional and personal development" (compassion), and "encourages interdisciplinary research to strengthen our knowledge" (overall positive moods). Cronbach's alpha of the overall items and factors ranged between 0.70 and 0.86. This established the reliability of the instrument.

16.4 Data Analysis and Results

The analysis was done using SPSS 21.0. The data was first checked for normal distribution, and it came out to be normal. The means and standard deviations were obtained to check the averages and variability of the data. Table 16.1 shows the average values of aggregated responses on each factor and variable.

To test the hypothesis, further correlation was performed. Table 16.1 also reports the results of correlation analysis. The variables, transformational and resonant

Table 16.1 Mean, SD, and inter-correlations among variables under study

	Mean	SD	TL	RL	LO
TL	3.29	0.99	1		
RL	3.90	0.87	0.214*	1	
LO	3.85	0.79	0.456**	0.641**	1

Notes $P < 0.01$, *RL*—resonant leadership, *TL*—transformational leadership, *LO*—learning organization, * denotes less significant values, ** denotes highly significant values

leadership style, were found to be significantly correlated ($p < 0.01$) with learning organization. However, transformational leadership was also found to have established a weaker relationship as compared to resonant leadership. The correlation analysis confirmed the relationship between resonant leadership and learning organization and between transformational leadership and learning organization. Therefore, our hypothesis H_1 and H_2 are partially accepted here.

To further affirm the hypothesis, the predictive ability of independent variables toward the dependent variables was tested using regression analysis. The level of significance was kept at 95% (0.05). Regression analysis was performed, and the model fit summary in form of percentages of variance explained by independent variable in the dependent variable (R square $= 0.30$) is reported.

The two independent variables, resonant leadership ($B = 0.56$, $t = 9.1$, $P < 0.05$) and transformational leadership ($B = 0.37$, $t = 7.4$, $P < 0.05$), significantly predicted learning organization and explained 38% variance and this provided partial acceptance of H_1 and H_2. Therefore, it can be said that resonant and transformational leadership style have been found to be significant predictors of learning organization in VUCA world.

16.5 Discussion

The prime aim of this study was to find out the comparative differences that existed between two different styles of leadership and to know if they are significant predictors of learning organization in VUCA world. The results confirmed the aimed relationship, and the discussion is as follows:

16.5.1 *Transformational Leadership and Learning Organization*

Results show that transformational leadership has an important role in developing an institute into a learning organization to face the challenges being imposed by VUCA environment. In this study, the construct transformational leadership consists of individual consideration, intellectual stimulation, idealized influence, and inspirational motivation. Leaders play an apparent role in promoting and nurturing learning in an organization. Transformational leaders stimulate the followers for team spirit, develop enthusiasm for work, and encourage them to be innovative and creative in providing new ways of working, and encouraging experimentation and risk-taking (Chawla and Lenka 2012). In this study, sample includes faculty members from Indian higher educational institutes who can best indicate about the leadership style of their leader. Individualized influence indicates the degree of trust, respect, and dedication toward the followers and acting as their role model. In a higher educational institute, the director ensures that his/her presence makes the faculty feel encouraged. She or he ensures there is a feeling of trust developed within faculty members, and they are proud to be associated with their director in every field of their task. However, this can only be achieved when the faculty feels highly motivated in the workplace. The director ensures that everyone in the institute find true meaning of the task they are accomplishing. These leaders provide them with common vision and inspire the faculty for interactive networking and collective learning. Such leaders also encourage the faculty to be innovative in various aspects of teaching and research practices. They focus on creating an atmosphere where creativity and innovation are practiced. She or he ensures faculty rethink their ideas and question on the present ways of working. This ensures them to think of the old problems in newer ways. The head of the institute also motivates the faculty to develop themselves professionally owing to multidisciplinary approach. Those faculties who are less involved in this approach, the director assigns them projects individually and focuses on their competency for developing them. It has been found that departmental leaders in higher educational institutions contribute for 80% of all administrative decisions made in colleges and universities (Knight and Holen 1985). Transformational leaders act as role models for the faculty members so that faculty members can walk on their path toward becoming role models for their own students. Thus, by carrying out their role as transformational leader, they set directions for the department and create policies that support faculty members for lifelong learning. However, this demands patience, common sense, and trust with uncertainty and complexity.

16.5.2 *Resonant Leadership and Learning Organization*

Our results show that resonant leadership has an extensive role in developing an institute into a learning organization since it counters VUCA through vision, compassion, and overall positive moods. Leaders are now adopting to resonant leadership style with more emotional closeness with their subordinates. Resonant leaders are always emotionally available, act with integrity, and understand the concern of their followers through vision, compassion, and overall positive moods (Lenka and Chawla 2015). In this study, sample includes faculty members from Indian higher educational institutes who can best indicate about the leadership style of their leaders. Vision is built by encouraging everyone to first build on their personal visions. This requires the commitment and connection with respect to that vision which will further provide learning for building a learning organization. According to goal setting theory, it is the motivation provided by the leader to derive their subordinates in the direction of high achievement of organizational goals (Locke 1968). In a higher educational institute, the director provides a vision for teaching, learning, and research excellence. She or he ensures that faculty member's involvement in teaching and research is aligned with institute's overall vision. She or he encourages them to develop action plan to attain the desired vision. Thus, faculty member's involvement in development and fulfillment of institute's goals is the extent to which the vision seems inspiring, long term, focused, and integrated. Such leaders are themselves hopeful with their vision statement. They are optimistic leaders who believe in their ability to embrace change. They see their future as realistic, feasible, and idealistic (Sushil 2010). However, the vision formed is in consideration to compassion trait of the resonant leader. Compassion means having an affinity and being considerate toward feelings of others. When resonant leaders care about their subordinates and work collaboratively, it results in long-term success. The leader ensures that she or he cares about faculty member's professional and personal development thereby generating a positive attitude in them. She or he also ensures that a constructive feedback to them will help them in improving their past experiences. When faculty members fear a degree of insecurity in their job, task, and delivering lectures, resonant leaders provide concern to them by removing their fear and involving them in learning activities so that they become more skillful. Resonant leaders are buoyant in their attitude by developing positive moods and sending positive messages to their followers. They ensure that faculty members promote harmony and friendly interactions. For this, they encourage interdisciplinary research to strengthen their knowledge. She or he praises them during official meetings and delegates administrative responsibilities. Such responsibilities do not act as burden on them instead broaden their task perspective (Chawla and Lenka 2015). Thus, resonant leaders are highly emotionally intelligent who create resonance by imbibing positive emotions in their followers. Such leaders are benevolent and work with everyone to create a meaningful workplace. Thus, leaders with high emotional intelligence are great performers and display a sense of organizational commitment. Such leaders owing to their competencies, better work, and enjoy doing every task (Brahma et al. 2004). They share ideas, information, power, and acknowledge the achievement of others. They create synergy and enhance other's self-admiration and build and sustain trust through regular communication. They emphasize organization building and behavioral processes to create a learning organization. Thus, resonant leaders themselves become comfortable and agile with VUCA environment by focusing on managing inconsistencies.

16.6 Conclusion

This chapter focused on two different leadership styles that would be best suited for a learning organization in a VUCA environment to build private institutes as learning organizations. From the findings and discussion, it has been found that both the leadership styles, i.e., transformational and resonant significantly impacted the transformation of institutes into learning organization during VUCA landscape. However, the impact on resonant leadership is higher than that of transformational leadership style. The main reason that accounts for the same is that in a rapid pace environment, where organizations have to continuously learn, adapt, and change, the leaders have been forced to change their leadership style of working. Transformational leaders recognize the need for change, create common visions, empower employees and raise them to higher levels of motivation by encouraging them to achieve the common goal (Chawla and Lenka 2012). However, such a leader is found to be bound toward organizational rules and regulations. Transformational leadership can be seen as a personal characteristic rather than a behavior in which people can be instructed. It is stiff and despotic because it gives the impression that the leader is acting independently of the followers (Northouse 2012). Moreover, a dyadic relationship exists between a leader and a follower. They build common vision and empower their followers to work toward attaining the vision. With this vision and energy, followers develop enthusiasm and are willing to adopt new roles and responsibilities. But this is only a short-term orientation and for any change to occur enquires long-term leadership with proper discipline and structure which is beyond the role of transformational leadership. Therefore, it can be said that resonant leaders visualize a brighter future and communicate that vision with resonance and compassion and pave the way by keeping their mood positive everlastingly (Chawla and Lenka 2015). These leaders focus on self-awareness, task reflexivity, and learning from past failures. They become resilient critical thinkers who embrace a mindset of change in the VUCA environment.

The main contribution of this work is for the academicians and researchers. Academicians can use this fact and practice the same to achieve higher forms of leadership style. Head of the institute is required to pay attention to resonant leadership style more than the transformational leadership style so as to ensure better learning practices in the institute in order to thrive well in VUCA world. Researchers can further take up this study through its in-depth exploration by considering different national culture settings.

However, the implications are subject to few limitations. The work is carried out in Indian higher educational institutes specifically private institutes. The sample collected was only from National Capital Region, India. Also, the study took into account only the faculty members as the respondents. Therefore, further research can be carried out by using significant sample size across the country to generalize the findings of the study. Also, the study can be conducted in schools and corporate sector. Comparative study on public and private Indian higher educational institutes can be done. Further, the study can take into account administrative staff and students as the respondents. Therefore, this study contributes to the existing body of knowledge and paves the way for future research.

References

Antonoaie, N., & Antonoaie, C. (2010). The learning organization. *Bulletin of the Transilvania University of Brasov. Series V: Economic Sciences, 3*.
Argyris, C., & Schön, D. (1995). *Organizational learning: A theory of action perspective, 1978*. Massachusetts: Addison-Wesley Publishing Company.

Avolio, B. J., & Bass, B. M. (1995). Individual consideration viewed at multiple levels of analysis: A multi-level framework for examining the diffusion of transformational leadership. *The Leadership Quarterly, 6*(2), 199–218.
Bawany, S. (2016). NextGen Leaders for A VUCA World.
Brahma, S., Macharla, S., Pal, S. P., & Singh, S. K. (2004, December). Fair leader election by randomized voting. In *International Conference on Distributed Computing and Internet Technology* (pp. 22–31). Berlin, Heidelberg: Springer.
Boyatzis, R., & McKee, A. (2005). *Resonant leadership: Renewing yourself and connecting with others through mindfulness, hope, and compassion*. Boston, MA: Harvard Business School Press.
Chawla, S., & Lenka, U. (2012). Role of transformational leaders in developing higher educational institutes as learning organizations-an Indian PERSPECTIVE. *Global Journal of Finance and Management, 5*(10), 30–33.
Chawla, S., & Lenka, U. (2015). A study on learning organizations in Indian higher educational institutions. *Journal of Workplace Learning, 27*(2).
Choudaha, R. (2013). Social media in international student recruitment. *Association of International Education Administrators (AIEA) Issue Brief*.
Dhir, S. (2016). Practice-oriented insights on creative problem solving. *Journal of Management & Public Policy, 7*(2).
Dhir, S., Mahajan, V., & Bhal, K. T. (2016). Himbunkar: Turnaround of a social public sector enterprise. *South Asian Journal of Management, 23*(4), 175.
Dhir, S., & Mital, A. (2012). Decision-making for mergers and acquisitions: The role of agency issues and behavioral biases. *Strategic Change, 21*(1–2), 59–69.
Goh, S. C. (1998). Toward a learning organization: The strategic building blocks. *SAM Advanced Management Journal, 63*, 15–22.
Goleman, D., Boyatzis, R. E., & McKee, A. (2004). *Essere leader*. Bur.
Hallinger, P. (1998). Educational change in Southeast Asia: The challenge of creating learning systems. *Journal of Educational Administration, 36*(5), 492–509.
Hiatt-Michael, D. B. (2001). Schools as learning communities: A vision for organic school reform. *School Community Journal, 11*(2), 113–127.
Khanra, S., & Dhir, S. (2017). Creating value in small-cap firms by mitigating risks of market volatility. *Vision, 21*(4), 350–355.
Kirby, P. C., Paradise, L. V., & King, M. I. (1992). Extraordinary leaders in education: Understanding transformational leadership. *The Journal of Educational Research, 85*(5), 303–311.
Knight, W. H., & Holen, M. C. (1985). Leadership and the perceived effectiveness of department chairpersons. *The Journal of Higher Education*, 677–690.
Lam, Y. J., Chan, C. M., Pan, H. L. W., & Wei, H. C. P. (2003). Differential developments of Taiwanese schools in organizational learning: Exploration of critical factors. *International Journal of Educational Management, 17*(6), 262–271.
Lenka, U., & Chawla, S. (2015). Higher educational institutes as learning organizations for employer branding. *Industrial and Commercial Training, 47*(5).
Locke, E. A. (1968). Toward a theory of task motivation and incentives. *Organizational Behavior and Human Performance, 3*(2), 157–189.
McKee, A. (2011). *Management: A focus on leaders*. London: Pearson Prentice Hall.
Mustafa, S. (2016). Leadership in VUCA World, What do you Need to Thrive?
Northouse, P. G. (2012). *Leadership: Theory and practice*. Sage Publications.
Sushil. (2010). From future market to future technology and business leader. *Global Journal of Flexible Systems Management, 11*(3), iii.
Tran, V. (1998). The role of the emotional climate in learning organizations. *The Learning Organization, 5*(2), 99–103.
Thekedam, J. S. (2014). Leadership and effective integration of information and communication technology for the age of restructuring. In M. K. Nandakumar, S. Jharkharia, & A. S. Nair (Eds.), *Organizational flexibility and competitiveness. Flexible systems management* (pp. 153–163). Springer: New Delhi.

Chapter 17
Why Do Small Brands Decline? A Perspective on Indian Apparel Market

Naveen Arora and Neelotpaul Banerjee

Abstract Economical success or failure of brands is not an outcome of one or two random variables, but it depends on the success of carefully planned and implemented array of marketing programs. This chapter aims to study the variables and factors, which play important role in the performance of small brands of clothing. In developing countries like India, small brands face more challenges than big brands. Marketers need to understand the factors or attributes, which are valued by consumers and then provide better value than competitors. Primary data has been collected from different channel partners like retailers, distributors, and wholesalers. Questions related to customer satisfaction, perceived quality, price, training and support to channel partners, terms and conditions of sales and payments, and replenishment policies have been asked. Factor analysis and confirmatory factor analysis have been used to group correlated variables or attributes and identify underlying dimensions. It is found that the marketing programs designed by the declined brands were not suitable and were inappropriate. Studied brands have been rated low on customers' perception of quality, price, durability, variety, and availability. Results, findings, and recommendations of the study can be helpful to entrepreneurs, managers, strategists, and academicians to understand Indian branded apparel market.

Keywords Apparels · Decline of brands · Factor analysis · Small brands

N. Arora (✉) · N. Banerjee
National Institute of Technology, Durgapur, West Bengal, India
e-mail: naveenarora_80@yahoo.com

N. Banerjee
e-mail: neelotpaul@gmail.com

© Springer Nature Singapore Pte Ltd. 2018
S. Dhir and Sushil (eds.), *Flexible Strategies in VUCA Markets*,
Flexible Systems Management, https://doi.org/10.1007/978-981-10-8926-8_17

17.1 Introduction

Role of small brands is very important in the development of a nation's economy and industries. Through technological innovations, new entrepreneurs and small companies introduce new technologies and innovative products (Acs and Audretsch 1990). Growing Indian economy is moving to be a free market economy. Though agriculture sector is still very important, other sectors are also crucial for economic growth. Clothing sector is one of those prominent sectors in India. It provides employment to a large number of skilled and non-skilled workers. Clothing industry also has significant contribution in gross domestic product (GDP) of India. Because of liberalization, privatization, and globalization (LPG), Indian economy has been experiencing a change in employment level, lifestyle, and demand pattern (Dhir 2016). Demand for branded products has increased significantly during past twenty years. In apparel segment, demand has been shifting from unstitched to readymade and from unbranded to branded. More importantly, this growth in demand for branded readymade garments is being experienced across all the income segments indicating growth in demand across different price levels. Entrepreneurs in India assessed this opportunity and launched their own, home-grown brands of apparels. In India, rapid emergence of quality-sensitive market for branded apparels like jeans, trousers, T-shirts, and shirts has also facilitated entry of established companies into branded clothing business (Ramaswamy and Gereffi 2000). While established players in clothing industry and big business houses had enough resources to invest in plants, machinery, inventories, supply chain, promotion and branding, new and small entrepreneurs lacked resources and in some cases, experience too. These micro- and small enterprises started operations in small scale and targeted few customer segments with regional approach (Garg and Jain 2008). Some of these small brands flourished with time and grew to be national brands, while some others could not acquire and retain a significant number of customers. Customer retention is important for a brand's growth as the cost of acquiring new customers is much higher than the cost of retaining existing customers (Rosenberg and Czepiel 1984). A large loyal consumer base also helps companies to grow by providing companies with valuable time to respond to competitors' actions (Aaker 1991). Growth and decline of brands have been crucial for marketers as it has financial implications for the company and is important for survival of a marketer. It has been established through researches that marketers' understanding of consumers' preferences significantly influences performance of brands.

The objective of the study in this chapter is to identify the attributes, which play important role in economical success of clothing brands. The study attempts to explore the importance of different factors for clothing brands. The study also attempts to get an insight into the marketing programs, which are not appropriate for small brands of clothing and could lead to decline of brands.

17.2 Literature Review

Small brands' role is critical for market contestability. Being source of competition, new entrepreneurial ventures help customers in getting better products at competitive prices (You 1995). However, the threat of small new entrants is not very prominent because these small firms operate on small scale and many disappear from the markets afterward (Geroski 1995). It has also been observed that individuals start small business as a last option rather than as first choice (Beck et al. 2005). Micro- and small companies are dependent on owners' funds for financial requirements. These entrepreneurs have low access to formal capital markets (Leff 1979). For further expansion of business, these companies rely on funds from friends, relatives, or other informal sources of financing (Kozan et al. 2006). Small brands face formidable challenges and find it difficult to grow or survive in competitive markets. As a result, entry of large companies into new business is more common than growth of small companies (Van Biesebroeck 2005). In developing countries, some of the most important challenges for small brands are limited financial resources, poor infrastructure, cost of transportation, inadequacy of suitable management resources, and sometimes the willingness to stay small and informal to avoid taxes and other formalities (Little 1987). The desire to stay small cannot be generalized for all micro- and small enterprises. In reality, there are some entrepreneurs with high aspirations and some with low aspirations (Autio 2008). So, the growth prospects of the brand might also depend on the entrepreneurs' aspirations to grow. As a result of homogenous product characteristics, marketers are also facing the challenge of shortening of product life cycles (Prasad et al. 2001).

Customer satisfaction, loyalty, and retention have been key factors for brands to grow. Brands, which acquire a significant number of new customers and lose customers on a normal rate, tend to grow, while the brands which lose customers at more than normal rate and fail to attract substantial number of new customers decline on medium to long term (Riebe et al. 2002). Customers tend to switch brands in case of breakdown of trust, poor performance by brand, or when marketer fails to reinforce consumer commitment or fails to keep promises (Fournier 1998). Brands, which are market leader, have more stable brand loyalty (Dekimpe et al. 1997).

Marketers of branded apparels are tending to outsource production and are focusing more on design and marketing of products (Ramaswamy and Gereffi 2000). In order to grow and survive in competitive market, the brands must listen to their customers and should be in a state of constant renewal. Customer feedback is very important and must be considered by the marketers for improvement in goods and services (Gerzema and Lebar 2008). Big companies having more products in their product line and multiple brands also take the advantage of evolving market opportunities and can react quickly with new products to any change or evolutions in market (Dhir and Mital 2013). Multiple offerings also provide opportunity to manage conflicting channels and categories (Keller and Lehmann 2006). Role of brand personality is important in customer satisfaction as customer satisfaction is influenced by the expectations built by the brand by projecting a brand image (Aaker et al. 2004).

Role of small brands is important in inclusive growth of a country, employment generation, economic development, and for idealistic market conditions. Clothing, being one of the largest product categories, significantly influences society and lifestyle in India. Consequently, it is important to determine the factors which influence performance of small brands of clothing. Brand performance largely depends on the marketers understanding of the market, design of marketing programs, and their effective implementation. Effective marketing programs cannot be generalized and should be formulated according to the type of industry, size of the company, target segment of customers in addition to other factors. While the study of successful brands provides valuable inputs to get an insight of the industry, study of brands which declined also contributes in having better understanding of the factors which could be important for small brands of clothing. The findings of the study shall be helpful in identifying the mistakes, which should be avoided by apparel marketers, and the factors, which are crucial and cannot be ignored for small brands.

17.3 Research Methodology

A comprehensive study has been conducted to explore and analyze various aspects of the decline of small brands of clothing in India. Brands which have evolved during the last 20 years had regional presence or limited product categories, low investments in plant (up to Indian rupees five crores), and promotions at the time of inception have been considered for the study.

Sales have been used as a determinant to evaluate effectiveness of marketing programs as the primary payoff from customers' opinions, feelings, and perceptions (Keller and Lehmann 2006). Increase in net sales represents growth, while drop in sales represents decline for apparel brands. Prowess, a software by Centre for Monitoring Indian Economy, has been used to acquire authentic historical data related to net sales, year of inception, and investments of marketers of apparel brands in India. For this study, four marketers of small brands have been chosen from the list of qualified brands on the basis of availability of channel partners for study. Structured interview has been used to collect primary data from fifty-six channel partners (dealers, distributors, multibrand retailers, exclusive stores, franchise outlets) of chosen brands of apparels. For this, a questionnaire has been used, consisting of questions related to channel partners' perception of marketer's support, promotions, sales promotion activities, employees' training, investments, replenishment policies, designs, supply chain, customers' perception of quality, price, durability, and satisfaction. Twenty statements have been rated in a scale of 1–5 by respondents. Rating 1 indicates 'strongly disagree,' while rating 5 indicates 'strongly agree.' Exploratory as well as confirmatory factor analysis has been used

Table 17.1 Indicators and sources

Construct	Number of indicators	Source
Quality, price, customer services, and design	4	Esquivias et al. (2013)
Advertising and customer perceived value	2	Smith and Amos (2004)
Sales promotions	1	Helsen and Schmittlein (1993)
Multiple channels	1	Keller and Lehmann (2006)
Stock replenishment	1	Abernathy et al. (2006)
Supply chain efficiency	1	Richardson (1996)
Sales persons' training	1	Frayne and Geringer (2000)
Comfort	1	Azevedo et al. (2008)

for data reduction and to bring intercorrelated variables together under one factor. Table 17.1 exhibits construction of scale and different indicators along with the sources.

17.4 Analysis

17.4.1 Factor Analysis

Principal component analysis has been applied for extracting factors. Varimax with Kaiser normalization rotation method has been employed as factors that are expected to be independent, and this method comes closest to satisfying the goal of simple structure (Aleamoni 1973).

Analysis of correlation coefficients in correlation matrix shows no values greater than 0.40. The value of determinant of correlation matrix is 0.000079, which is more than the required value of 0.00001 (Field 2000). Therefore, multicollinearity is not a problem for the data.

Value of KMO measure for sampling adequacy is 0.839, which is good and derives that the factor analysis is appropriate for this data. Bartlett's measure tests the null hypothesis that the original correlation matrix is an identity matrix. In the present study, Bartlett's test is highly significant ($p < 0.001$), and therefore, factor analysis is appropriate. According to Kaiser criterion, factors having eigenvalues greater than one have been retained and around 72% variance has been explained by five factors. Table 17.2 shows eigenvalues and explained variance.

Scree test is also recommended to be an appropriate criterion to determine the number of factors when the sample to variable ratio is not large (10:1) (Tucker et al.

Table 17.2 Total variance explained

Component	Initial eigenvalues			Rotation sums of squared loadings		
	Total	% of variance	Cumulative %	Total	% of variance	Cumulative %
1.	4.079	25.496	25.496	3.330	20.810	20.810
2.	2.506	15.665	41.161	2.601	16.255	37.065
3.	1.974	12.337	53.498	2.108	13.178	50.242
4.	1.610	10.061	63.559	1.812	11.324	61.567
5.	1.376	8.602	72.161	1.695	10.594	72.161

1969). Scree plot showing the eigenvalues from largest to smallest suggests that five factors can be considered for the study as the graph has a bend after five factors.

To improve reliability, psychological meaningfulness, and reproducibility of factors, factor rotation is used (Weiss 1976). In rotated component matrix, all the attributes with values less than 0.50 have been suppressed and sixteen attributes have been represented by five factors.

The factors have been named on the basis of attributes represented by them. These factors in order of relative strengths are:

(i) **Value for money** for attributes quality, price, comfort, durability, and latest trendy and fashionable products.
(ii) **Stock replenishment and variety** representing attributes return of unsold stock, variety, replenishment frequency, and consideration of customer feedback.
(iii) **Promotion** representing ads and promotions, celebrity endorsement, and store ambience.
(iv) **Brand image** for attributes customers' preference for big/national brands and preference for foreign brands.
(v) **Support to channel partners** for attributes sales team support and training to dealers' employees.

17.4.2 Confirmatory Factor Analysis (CFA)

Confirmatory factor analysis (CFA) provides information on confirmation of the measurement model with five factors revealed by the exploratory factor analysis method. This analysis provides clarity on variables, which are reflected in a given set of factors. The relationships have been assessed with the goodness of fit indices. Table 17.3 exhibits observed values of different indicators.

High values of GFI and AGFI as well as low value of SRMR (<0.08) indicate better model-data fit. Value of root mean square error of approximation (RMSEA)

17 Why Do Small Brands Decline? A Perspective on Indian ...

Table 17.3 Observed values of indicators

Indicator	Observed value	Acceptable value
NFI	0.952	≥ 0.95 (Bentler and Bonett 1980)
TLI	0.988	≥ 0.95 (Tucker and Lewis 1973)
CFI	0.990	≥ 0.95 (Bentler 1989)
GFI	0.917	≥ 0.90 (Jöreskog and Sörbom 1986)
AGFI	0.879	≥ 0.85 (Jöreskog and Sörbom 1986)
SRMR	0.032	<0.08 (Bentler 1995)
RMSEA	0.024	<0.06 (Steiger and Lind 1980)

is <0.06, and value of normed fit index (NFI), comparative fit index (CFI), and Tucker–Lewis index (TLI) is ≥ 0.95 which is an indicator of good fit.

Low values of correlation coefficients between different factors confirm that multicollinearity is not a problem for the data.

All the indicative items (variables) are expressing their latent constructs (factors) with a high degree of regression.

17.4.3 Validity and Reliability

Table 17.4 exhibits values of reliability and validity indicators.

Values of composite reliability (CR) are more than 0.7, and values of average variance extracted (AVE) are more than 0.5. As the value of AVE for each construct is also more than its maximum shared variance (MSV), so discriminant validity is supported.

17.4.4 Brands' Performance on Different Attributes and Variables

Availability: Brands under consideration are highly dependent on franchise outlets, while other channels of distribution are rarely used.

Table 17.4 Reliability and validity indicators

	CR	AVE	MSV
Brand image	0.903	0.833	0.086
Value for money	0.864	0.566	0.086
Stock replenishment and variety	0.817	0.533	0.062
Promotion	0.772	0.548	0.080
Support to channel partners	0.818	0.711	0.043

Structure of promotional offers: Most of the marketers are using multiple options for sales promotions, which include free units, discounts on maximum retail price (MRP), and consequential discounts. Around 78% respondents agree that the promotional offers continue throughout the year, while 20% mentioned that offers are available for 8–10 months a year.

Investments in distribution channels: According to 59% of the respondents, INR 5–8 lakh has been invested in company's products and for 41% of dealers, this amount is more than INR 8 lakh to INR 10 lakh. In 82% cases only, dealers have invested in company's stock.

17.5 Findings

It is found that the performance of small brands in apparel category is influenced by several attributes. These attributes can be represented by five factors, namely value for money, stock replenishment and variety, promotion, branding image, and support to channel partners. The study finds that brands under consideration do not have positive customer perception for quality, price, comfort, durability, and latest designs. The frequency of stock replenishment is low, and a very small proportion of unsold stock is taken back by marketers from dealers. This could be one of the reasons for unfavorable customer perception of variety. A very important finding establishes that the brands under consideration rely more on franchise outlets and do not practice multichannel retailing. This accords with earlier findings that a brand is rated higher if it is widely available (Keller and Lehmann 2006). Role of promotions and branding activities cannot be denied, and the study also indicates that the declining brands have not invested much in ads, promotions, and celebrity endorsements. It is found that the marketers of brands considered in the study have been rated low on attributes like sales teams' support to dealers and training to dealers' employees, while previous researches (Frayne and Geringer 2000) have established importance of these attributes in brands' performance. Though the brands have favorable credit policies for channel partners and profit margins for dealers are also fair, its positive impact is not significant. Unplanned and excessive use of sales promotion activities has also affected brands' performance negatively. It is observed that the brands under consideration offer multiple types of sales promotions throughout the year. The outcome of the study points out that dealers have deposited significant amount of money with marketers as security sales, but sales are remarkably low for the brands considered in the present study.

17.6 Conclusion

Economic success of a brand or firm is critical and is influenced by many factors. Growing brands certainly help marketers to formulate and implement marketing programs better than the brands which fail to grow and decline. In this chapter, clothing brands have been studied which declined after a few years of operations in Indian markets. The study distinctly depicts that some of the marketing activities adopted by the declined brands have not worked in a successful manner. The study identifies the factors important for small brands of clothing. As the brands under consideration failed to meet customers' expectations on those factors, they experienced decline in the highly competitive apparel market in India. The study provides valuable inputs on the mistakes that should be avoided by apparel brands to succeed.

References

Aaker, D. A. (1991). *Managing brand equity*. New York: The Free Press.
Aaker, J., Fournier, S., & Brasel, S. A. (2004). When good brands do bad. *Journal of Consumer Research, 31*(1), 1–16.
Abernathy, F. H., Volpe, A., & Weil, D. (2006). The future of the apparel and textile industries: Prospects and choices for public and private actors. *Environment and Planning, 38*(12), 2207–2232.
Acs, Z. J., & Audretsch, D. B. (1990). *Innovation and small firms*. MIT Press.
Aleamoni, L. M. (1973). Effects of size of sample on Eigenvalues, observed communalities and factor loadings. *Journal of Applied Psychology, 58*(2), 266–269.
Autio, E. (2008). *High- and low-aspiration entrepreneurship and economic growth in low-income economies*. Paper Presented at the UNU-WIDER Project Workshop on Entrepreneurship and Economic Development, Helsinki, Finland, 21–23 August.
Azevedo, S., Pereira, M. M., Ferreira, J. J. M., & Pedroso, V. (2008, November). *Consumer Buying Behavior in Fashion Retailing: Empirical Evidences*. MPRA 11908.
Beck, T., Demirguc-Kunt, A., & Levine, R. (2005). SMEs growth and poverty: Cross-country evidence. *Journal of Economic Growth, 10*(3), 199–229.
Bentler, P. M. (1989). *EQS structural equations program manual*. Los Angeles, CA: BMDP Statistical Software.
Bentler, P. M. (1995). *EQS structural equations program manual*. Encino, CA: Multivariate Software Inc.
Bentler, P. M., & Bonett, D. G. (1980). Significance tests and goodness of fit in the analysis of covariance structures. *Psychological Bulletin, 88*(3), 588–606.
Dekimpe, M., Steenkamp, J. E. B. M., Mellens, M., & Vanden Abeele, P. (1997). Decline and variability in brand loyalty. *International Journal of Research in Marketing, 14*(5), 405–420.
Dhir, S. (2016). Global competitiveness of informal economy organizations. In *Flexible work organizations* (pp. 209–224). India: Springer.
Dhir, S., & Mital, A. (2013). Asymmetric motives in Indian bilateral cross-border joint ventures with G7 nations: Impact of relative partner characteristics and initial conditions. *International Journal of Strategic Business Alliances, 3*(1), 69–92.
Esquivias, P., Knox, S., & Visser, J. (2013). *Fueling growth through word of mouth: Introducing the brand advocacy index*. Boston Consulting Group, Inc.

Field, A. (2000). *Discovering statistics using SPSS for windows*. London, Thousand Oaks, New Delhi: Sage Publications.

Fournier, S. (1998). Consumers and their brands: Developing relationship theory in consumer research. *Journal of Consumer Research, 24*, 343–373.

Frayne, C. A., & Geringer, G. M. (2000). Self management training for improving job performance: A field experiment involving salespeople. *Journal of Applied Psychology, 85*(3), 361–372.

Garg, R. K., & Jain, S. (2008). Impact of change management on competitiveness: A study of Small Scale Industry in Punjab. *Global Journal of Flexible Systems Management, 9*(2 & 3), 55–60.

Geroski, P. A. (1995). What do we know about entry. *International Journal of Industrial Organization, 13*(4), 421–440.

Gerzema, J., & Lebar, E. (2008). *The brand bubble: The looming crisis in brand value and how to avoid it*. A Wiley Imprint: Jossey-Bass.

Helsen, K., & Schmittlein, D. C. (1993). Analyzing duration times in marketing: Evidence for the effectiveness of hazard rate models. *Marketing Science, 11*(4), 395–414.

Jöreskog, K. G., & Sörbom, D. (1986). *LISREL VI: Analysis of linear structural relationships by maximum likelihood and least square methods*. Mooresville, IN: Scientific Software Inc.

Keller, K. L., & Lehmann, D. R. (2006). Brands and branding: Research findings and future priorities. *Marketing Science, 25*(6), 740–749.

Kozan, M., Oksoy, D., & Ozsoy, O. (2006). Growth plans of small businesses in Turkey: Individual and environmental influences. *Journal of Small Business Management, 44*(1), 114–129.

Leff, N. H. (1979). Entrepreneurship and economic development: The problem revisited. *Journal of Economic Literature, 17*(1), 46–64.

Little, I. M. D. (1987). Small manufacturing enterprises in developing countries. *World Bank Economic Review, 1*(2), 203–235.

Prasad, S., Tata, J., & Motwani, J. (2001). International supply chain management: Learning and evolving networks. *Global Journal of Flexible Systems Management, 2*(2), 31–36.

Ramaswamy, K. V., & Gereffi, G. (2000). India's apparel exports: The challenge of global markets. *The Developing Economies, 38*(2), 186–210.

Richardson, J. (1996). Vertical integration and rapid response in fashion apparel. *Organization Science, 7*(4), 400–412.

Riebe, E., Sharp, B., & Stern, P. (2002). An empirical investigation of customer defection and acquisition rates for declining and growing pharmaceutical brands. In *ANZMAC 2002 Conference Proceedings* (pp. 1441–1446).

Rosenberg, L. J., & Czepiel, J. A. (1984). A marketing approach to customer retention. *Journal of Consumer Marketing, 1*(Spring), 45–51.

Smith, P., & Amos, J. (2004). *Brands, innovation and growth—Evidence on the contribution from branded consumer businesses to economic growth*. London: PIMS Associates Ltd.

Steiger, J. H., & Lind, J. C. (1980). *Statistically based tests for the number of common factors*. Paper Presented at the Annual Meeting of the Psychometric Society, Iowa City, IA.

Tucker, L. R., Koopman, R. F., & Linn, R. L. (1969). Evaluation of factor analytic research procedures by means of simulated correlation matrices. *Psychometrika, 34*(4), 421–459.

Tucker, L. R., & Lewis, C. (1973). A reliability coefficient for maximum likelihood factor analysis. *Psychometrika, 38*(1), 1–10.

Van Biesebroeck, J. (2005). Firm size maters: Growth and productivity growth in African manufacturing. *Economic Development and Cultural Change, 53*(3), 545–583.

Weiss, D. (1976). Multivariate procedures. In M. D. Dunnette (Ed.), *Handbook of industrial/organizational psychology*. Chicago, IL: Rand McNally.

You, J.-I. (1995). Small firms in economic theory. *Cambridge Journal of Economics, 19*(3), 441–462.

Chapter 18
Non-tariff Barriers on International Trade Flows in India

Sanjay Kumar and Falguni Arora

Abstract Non-tariff barriers have a significant impact on regular trading activities. This study is conducted to determine a relationship between non-tariff barriers and international trade in India. Eleven such factors have been identified and thoroughly discussed in the Indian context. An empirical study has been conducted taking the opinion of experts through convenience sampling method. The primary data is analyzed through multiple linear regression, and results have been discussed. Most of the observed factors encourage trade creation.

Keywords Indian trade flows · International business · Non-tariff barriers (NTB) Trade creation · Trade diversion · World Trade Organization (WTO)

18.1 Introduction

International trade is affected by a wide variety of government measures including both tariff and non-tariff barriers (NTBs). Till the mid-1970s, international trade was distorted by tariff restrictions. Later, these tariff barriers were replaced by NTBs for the protection of the domestic country. In 1984, according to a study conducted for the World Bank (Finger and Olechowski 1987), approximately 15% of the import product categories of the major developed countries, accounting for 18% of the value of their imports, were subject of NTBs. There was an increase in import coverage of 2.4% as compared to 1981 (Baldwin 1989).

NTBs have had a great impact on the imports and exports of a country. They are a part of trade agreements formed after various rounds of meetings of the World Trade Organization (WTO) and General Agreement on Tariffs and Trade (GATT) (Dhir and Mital 2013). Recently, a meeting was conducted to discuss various

S. Kumar
Deloitte India, Delhi, New Delhi, India

F. Arora (✉)
Kirori Mal College, University of Delhi, Delhi, New Delhi, India
e-mail: falguniarora97@gmail.com

concerns about regulations on information and communications technology (ICT) and electronic products by the WTO Committee on Technical Barriers to Trade on November 10–11, 2016. (WTO, WTO: 2016 NEWS ITEMS, Technical Barriers to trade 2016; Böhm and Motschnig-Pitrik 2015).

Focusing on the Indian economy, the usage of NTBs like anti-dumping duties, countervailing duties began in early 2000s after a large reduction in tariff barriers from 87% in 1991–92 to 24.6% in 1996–97 (The World Bank 2011). The level and the coverage of products under these NTBs eventually increased over years eliminating quantitative restrictions and increasing the flow of trade. The most efficient use of these barriers has been seen in the year 2009 after the period of great depression. NTBs have played an integral role in the reviving of India from The Great Depression Period (The World Bank 2011).

NTBs are of various types like anti-dumping rules, voluntary export restraints (VERs), export subsidy, import policy barriers. They can largely be divided into three main categories, i.e., administrative barriers, technical barriers, and product standards. The objective of this study is to determine the impact of non-tariff trade barriers on the developing countries like India. For that purpose, NTBs can be categorized as independent variables and effect of these variables on international trade, i.e., trade creation or diversion, as the dependent variables. This study is focused on the Indian context.

It may be pointed out that there are not many studies on the effect of NTBs on the Indian trade. There are theoretical work about the developing countries in general, but nothing specific about India, hence the relevance of this study.

For this study, we have used first-hand data. The data is based on a questionnaire developed, and the survey was done on the basis of convenience sampling method, analyzed through hypothesis testing. The questionnaire was filled up by people having good knowledge of international business. After primary data collection and hypothesis building, statistical tool, Statistical Package for the Social Sciences (SPSS), was used for analysis; correlation and regression between the factors were figured out, and a conclusion was drawn.

18.2 Conceptual Background and Hypothesis Development

Various bureaucratic or legal issues often create hindrances to trade, known as NTBs (WTO, Understanding the WTO: The Agreements, n.d.). These barriers are present in all the three sectors of an economy, i.e., agricultural, industrial, and service sectors. But the way NTBs effect each sector is different. For instance, issues involving agricultural goods are usually behind the borders, and non-agricultural issues are normally due to domestic structural reforms.

Tariff and NTBs are negatively related to each other. Liberalization normally means free trade, and this basically entails tariff reduction. But decrease in tariff often accompanies imposition of NTBs to protect domestic market; correlation between tariff and NTBs is negative. NTBs, thus, are used as substitutes for tariffs.

18.2.1 Administrative Barriers

Disputes that involve custom and managements restrictions to trade are called administrative barriers (Dhir and Sushil 2017). They are concerned with the legal and organizational aspects of trading. Various administrative barriers are discussed below.

Voluntary Export Restraints (VERs)
VER is the most common NTBs to trade. It is an arrangement made by the government to protect domestic market. For this purpose, they persuade the authorities in a trading partner to restrict exports (Ethier 1991). The government of the importing country negotiates with the government of the exporting country to restrict the volume of latter's exports of various goods and services. This usually helps the country to comply with the international agreements as well as the domestic protection. As stated, VER is a result of extreme pressure from the importing country. It is entirely the choice of the exporting country whether to act toward this trade restriction or not.

From past two decades, these NTBs have been the most prominent protection mechanism for the domestic industry. It not only gives a chance to the large industries to grow, but also helps the local vendors to act as a useful human resource to the industry.

Hypothesis 1: *Voluntary export restraints have a negative impact on trading activities.*

Certification of Origin Requirements
This is a type of NTB which is concerned with the primary sector of an economy. In the agro-food sector, the certification of origin systems is usually based on the production rules, mainly yield restrictions. It also defines the territorial limits outside of which a producer cannot benefit from the official certification.

Certification of origin is different from VERs in some ways. Unlike VERs, certificate of origin involves both quantitative as well as qualitative restrictions. It may control the quantity of output produced along with the quality cost subsidies (Chambolle and Giraud-Héraud 2005). A certificate of origin may involve a certain level of standard benefits as well as a guarantee of quality. Hence, it is also a kind of cost subsidy which enhances the quality of the product as well as modifies the firm's quality investment. In other words, certification of origin or certification requirement is another version of VER which also includes quality cost subsidy.

Hypothesis 2: *Certification of origin requirements has a negative impact on trading activities.*

Anti-dumping (AD) Rules and Countervailing Duties

Anti-dumping duty is a protectionist tariff that the government puts on the imports when it believes that the price charged for the product is less than the fair price. It is one of the most important non-tariff restrictions to trade. WTO allows the government to act against dumping only when it feels that there is a genuine injury to the domestic market. The WTO's agreement on subsidies and countervailing measures does two things. Firstly, it defines the use of subsidies. Secondly, it explains what actions can be taken by the countries against the negative effects of subsidies. A procedure has to be followed in order to remove or withdraw the subsidy (WTO, Understanding the WTO: The Agreements, n.d.).

Most of the time, anti-dumping duties are used for the protection of industrial interest. Theoretically, very few instances have been noted where AD rules have been used by sound economic motives. They have a negative impact on the consumers' welfare and competition. Although AD and countervailing rules were formed for the benefit of developing and less-developed countries, they are not the only ones that have been benefited. The main objective of GATT is to promote free and secure foreign market so that the products can be exported without any fear and difficulty. There should be no unfair trade practices. But AD and countervailing rules have been a hindrance in achieving this objective. Harmful effects of AD and countervailing duties were taken as a matter of discussion in GATT negotiations 1947, and a solution was found out.

Hypothesis 3: *Anti-dumping (AD) and countervailing duties have a negative impact on trading activities.*

Bureaucratic Delays and Customs

There are various types of bureaucratic and legal issues that can lead to a reduction of import and export (Haldar et al. 2016). For example, import licensing as described by WTO should be simple, transparent, and predictable. The agreement of import licensing should clearly state why and how the license has to be taken by the traders. Even after such clear information, traders find it difficult to register and are unable to take the license. This acts as an obstacle in trading. This process is simple but tedious. The agreement of import licensing also states how the government of a country should inform the WTO when some new import licensing procedures are made.

Other than this, the Pre-shipment Inspection Agreement focuses on a further check on imports, the Rules of Origin Agreement focuses on where the product has been made, Custom Valuation Agreement aims for a fair, neutral, and uniform system for valuation of goods for the purpose of customs, and the Trade-Related Investment Measures Agreement outlays various measures that affect trade in goods (WTO, Understanding the WTO: The Agreements, n.d.).

Hypothesis 4: *Bureaucratic delays and customs have a negative impact on trading activities.*

Industrial Policy Resolutions (IPRs)

Industrial policy resolutions were adopted by the Indian government in the year 1956. It was a comprehensive statement for the development of industrial sector of the economy. This resolution promoted a socialistic pattern of the society. The control of social and economic development was handed over to the governmental machinery. Public sector was given much more importance than the private sector (Ministry of Industry 1956).

Hypothesis 5: *Industrial policy resolutions have a negative impact on trading activities.*

18.2.2 Technical Barriers to Trade (TBTs)

Besides administrative barriers, technical barriers have also gained importance in the past few decades. TBTs are the rules and standards that set out specific characteristics about the product that is being traded. Their main focus is to serve the legitimate goal of public policy, i.e., consumer protection, consumer safety, environment protection, (OECD, n.d.).

TBTs are different in different countries. The Technical Barriers to Trade Agreement is an agreement made by the WTO to ensure that the rules, regulations, standardizations, and certifications do not create unnecessary barriers to trade. Various TBTs are discussed below.

Export Subsidy

Export subsidy is a government policy which encourages the domestic producer to export goods rather than sell them domestically. This enhances the quality of international trade as a whole.

As we know, countries (other than members of the agreement) are always in competition with each other. They compete with the help of their products in the international market in order to make most profitable deals. In such a situation, export subsidies help the domestic firms to improve their relative position in the international market, compete with the foreign rivalries and expand their market share as well as gain profits. In short, export subsidies encourage exports. Since the demand for the subsidized good increases in the international market, its production expands leading to a decrease in cost of production (large scale production). Thus, the imports of the domestic country decrease because the product can be produced at much lower cost in the domestic market. This entire process when continues results in the reduction of flow of goods and services. Export subsidies, thus, act as a barrier to trade.

Hypothesis 6: *Export subsidies have a positive impact on trading activities.*

Labelling

It is a complex process, causing technical hitches for the developing countries and small businesses which are involved in trading activities. Labelling is done for the benefit of the consumers, i.e., to protect the consumer's interest. Labelling procedure and packaging vary from country to country. Due to its unique property, inventory and finished goods for each country have to be maintained separately. Marketing and advertisement requirements are also a part of labelling.

This NTB is less effective as compared to the other barriers. Labelling schemes are comparatively economical and consumer friendly. They are considered as "weak" barriers to trade.

Hypothesis 7: *Labelling has a negative impact on trading activities.*

Import Policy Barriers to Trade

Import quota is a quantitative restriction on imports. The government sets a physical limit on the quantity of goods that can be imported in a country within a given period of time. They can be expressed as an individual unit imported or as a total value of imports. Usually, quotas are set on yearly basis. Thus, during the initial months of the financial year, foreign firms make deals with the domestic firms so that their goods can be imported by the domestic firms before the quota is reached (Naumann and Lincoln 1991). Import quotas were created to protect the domestic market by importing less. Due to the import policy barriers, the demand for domestic products was increased.

Minimum import pricing is another type of import policy barrier to trade. The domestic price structure, when provided with a price floor, in order to increase the domestic firm's gross profits is called minimum import pricing restriction (Naumann and Lincoln 1991). Depending upon the required price level, the domestic firms can shift their marketing strategy emphasis to non-price elements.

Lack of access to suitable market channels also acts as an import restriction. In most of the countries, there is a requirement of close coordination between government and industries. This coordination results in the development of industries. Suitable markets are identified for the movement of goods, services, information, technology as well as people (Naumann and Lincoln 1991).

Hypothesis 8: *Import policy barriers have a negative impact on trading activities.*

Government Procurements

Government plays an important role in the modern economy. Goods and services purchased by the government sector constitute 10% of the GDP. Government machinery is the only body that makes a choice between purchasing overseas and favorite domestic suppliers and has a marked impact on international trade. Preferential government procurements affect several billion dollars' worth of trade each year.

This technical barrier was recognized by GATT in 1981. This barrier states the ways in which trade should be carried on by the government. Also, it ensures that the government procurement policies do not discriminate between the domestic and foreign products. GATT calls transparency of the laws and procedures of government procurement (McAfee and McMillan 1989).

Hypothesis 9: *Government procurements have a positive impact on trading activities.*

18.2.3 Product Standards

During the trading processes, a certain standard of product needs to be maintained. This standard is decided by a document that provides requirements, specifications, or guidelines that ensures the product is fit for the purpose (ISO Standards, n.d.). The product standards are of two types:

Sanitary and Phytosanitary Measures
This non-tariff barrier is concerned with the food safety and health conditions of animals and plants. The healthier the living creatures, the better will be the quality of the product.

The agreement on the application of sanitary and phytosanitary measures (the "SPS Agreement") came into existence on January 1, 1995, with the establishment of the WTO. The SPS agreement was discussed in the final act of Uruguay Round of Multilateral Trade Agreements.

The main aim of the agreement was to ensure that the food is safe for the consumers and no disease is caused among plants and animals (WTO, Understanding the WTO Agreement on Sanitary and Phytosanitary Measures 1998).

Hypothesis 10: *Sanitary and phytosanitary measures have a positive impact on trading activities.*

Maintaining the Quality of Goods
Product quality and technical standards are different in different countries. Product testing performed in one country may be of very little value or no value in another country. Thus, product testing should be done in home countries instead of foreign countries. This acts as a barrier in trade (Naumann and Lincoln 1991). The quality of products should be up to the mark. Better product quality enhances trade.

Hypothesis 11: *Maintaining the quality of goods has a positive impact on trading activities.*

18.3 Data and Method

For this study, we have used first-hand data. The data is based on a questionnaire developed, and the survey was done on the basis of convenience sampling method, analyzed through hypothesis testing. The questionnaire was filled up by approximately 65 people having good knowledge of international business. After primary data collection and hypothesis building, statistical tool, Statistical Package for the Social Sciences (SPSS), was used for analysis; correlation and regression between the factors were figured out, and a conclusion was drawn.

18.3.1 Dependent Variables

Two alternative situations are possible in case of dependent variables, that is, either there will be trade creation or trade diversion. In other words, an NTB can create trade or divert trade. They have been discussed below.

Trade Creation
When a free trade agreement (FTA) creates trade that would not have been created otherwise, then it is called trade creation. In such a situation, supply occurs from a more efficient producer of the product (Suranovic 1998). It replaces less efficient domestic production. The products produced domestically are sidelined in such a case.

Trade creation was basically a result of the formation of Preferential Trade Agreements (PTAs). Trade liberalization was in favor of non-discrimination among countries as mentioned in article I of GATT. This means that no WTO member is allowed to discriminate between trading partners; if an opportunity or favor is given to one, it has to be given to all. Later, Article XXIV of GATT introduced an exception to this principle (Nkuepo, n.d.). It allows the establishment of favorable trading condition by one WTO member to another of its own choice, without any compulsion to provide the same conditions to all the other members. This increases the participation of developing countries. This allowed the establishments of PTAs. It has helped developing countries to compete with the entire world (Nkuepo, n.d.).

Trade Diversion
When FTAs divert trade from a more efficient supplier toward a less efficient supplier within the free trade area, then it is called trade diversion. National welfare of a county can be reduced by trade diversion. But on the other hand, it can also improve trading country's national welfare (Suranovic 1998).

Let us take a look on an African country, Rwanda. Rwanda imports various products like steel, cement, machinery, foodstuffs from Kenya and Uganda. But their export partners are China and Belgium. Rwanda, itself being a part of East African Community (EAC), it imports goods from Kenya and Uganda because they also belong to EAC and not because they have a comparative advantage. Moreover, major products exported by Rwanda and Kenya are the same, that is, coffee, tea, and tin (Nkuepo, n.d.). Therefore, Rwanda is not in profit as it is exchanging goods from those countries which are struggling to produce; instead, it should be trading with those nations which have comparative or absolute advantage. This is bad for both countries. The rules of PTAs restrict profitable trading and should be revised. It seems like the developing countries will be in advantage when they enter into an agreement with the developed countries as trade directly fosters development. Increased trade with developing countries enhances their export earnings, promotes their industrialization, and encourages the diversification of their economies.

18.3.2 Independent Variables

Independent variables are those variables that influence dependent variables. In this study, there are 11 independent variables which are a part of NTBs. They have an impact on trade creation and trade diversion. These 11 variables have been studied thoroughly by the means of primary data gathered through convenience sampling method as well as the literature available. They are: (1) *voluntary export restraint*, (2) *certification of origin requirement*, (3) *anti-dumping rules and countervailing duty*, (4) *bureaucratic delays and customs*, (5) *industrial policy resolutions*, (6) *export subsidy*, (7) *labelling*, (8) *import policy barriers to trade*, (9) *government procurements*, (10) *sanitary and phytosanitary measures*, and (11) *quality of goods*.

18.4 Data Analysis

In this study, regression analysis is used for testing the hypothesis. Linear regression analysis is a way of predicting outcome variable (dependent variable) from one or more predictor variables (independent variables). Here, multiple linear regression analysis has been used having various predictor variables and one outcome variable (Field 2009). The data is collected from various people having good knowledge of international business. The data in this case is ordinal; that is, the responses have been received in ranks and Likert scale has been used for this purpose.

IBM SPSS Statistics 20 software package has been used to apply multiple regression and test the hypothesis. For data analysis in IBM SPSS Statistics 20 software package, all the independent variables were entered simultaneously into the model. Stepwise modeling was not considered as categorization of variables into different blocks was not feasible.

18.5 Results

Table 18.1 provides the paired correlation between all the variables along with its significances.

The hypothesis is accepted if the significant value is less than 1 or 5%.

Table 18.2 provides the model summary. The model summary table shows the estimates of R and R^2 for the data and model used. R^2 provides us with a good gauge of the substantive size of the relationship (Field 2009). The sample

Table 18.1 Correlation matrix

	Trade creation	Voluntary exchange restrains	Certification of origin requirement	Anti-dumping rules	Bureaucratic delays and customs	Industrial policy resolutions	Sanitary and phytosanitary measures	Import policy barriers	Labelling	Government procurements	Export subsidy	Quality of goods
Trade creation	1											
Voluntary exchange restrains	0.194	1										
Certification of origin requirement	0.251**	0.435*	1									
Anti-dumping rules	0.134	0.593*	0.219**	1								
Bureaucratic delays and customs	0.178	0.556*	0.362*	0.518*	1							
Industrial policy resolutions	0.479*	0.125	0.328*	0.411*	0.284*	1						
Sanitary and phytosanitary measures	0.357*	0.330*	0.331*	0.386*	0.584*	0.453*	1					
Import policy barriers	0.182	0.207**	0.350*	0.561*	0.516*	0.499*	0.289*	1				
Labelling	−0.041	0.143	−0.040	0.170	0.532*	−0.024	0.284**	0.145	1			
Government procurements	0.573*	0.325*	0.319*	0.296*	0.392*	0.355*	0.241**	0.504*	0.281**	1		
Export subsidy	0.146	0.216**	0.194	0.453*	0.453*	0.239**	0.047	0.657*	0.254**	0.352*	1	
Quality of Goods	0.226**	0.486*	0.263**	0.664*	0.609*	0.312*	0.434*	0.524*	0.152	0.195	0.356*	1

* Correlation is significant at the 0.01 level (one-tailed). ** Correlation is significant at the 0.05 level (one-tailed)

Table 18.2 Model summary

Model	R	R^2	Adjusted R^2	Std. error of the estimate	Sig. F change
1	0.790	0.624	0.547	0.760	0.000*

*$p < 0.01$

correlation coefficient, R, measures the strength of the relationship between the predictor and outcome variable. The higher the R, the stronger is the relationship. The stronger the relationship, the better is the model for the data. In this case, R represents a value of 0.79 which shows a simple correlation between various independent variables and a dependent variable. The model is a good fit for the given data. The value of R^2 is 0.624, telling us that 62.4% of trade is created by the various NTBs discussed above. In other words, 37.6% of the trade creation cannot be explained by the above-mentioned NTBs.

Table 18.3 provides the summary of unstandardized as well as standardized coefficients. The correlation coefficient provides us with a good estimate to the overall fit of the regression model (Field 2009). In this table, each variable's

Table 18.3 Coefficients

Model	Unstandardized coefficients B	Std. Error	Standardized coefficients Beta	t	Significance	
(Constant)	−0.828	0.752		−1.102	0.275	
Voluntary exchange restrains	0.016	0.217	0.011	0.074	0.941	Insignificant
Certification of origin requirements	−0.051	0.132	−0.042	−0.387	0.700	Insignificant
Anti-dumping rules	−0.288	0.161	−0.266	−1.788	0.079	Insignificant
Bureaucratic delays and customs	−0.272	0.272	−0.166	−0.999	0.322	Insignificant
Industrial policy resolutions	0.479	0.159	0.340	3.003	0.004	Significant ($p < 0.01$)
Sanitary and phytosanitary measures	0.322	0.133	0.297	2.424	0.019	Significant ($p < 0.05$)
Import policy barriers	−0.688	0.217	−0.497	−3.171	0.003	Significant ($p < 0.01$)
Labelling	−0.348	0.172	−0.229	−2.018	0.049	Significant ($p < 0.05$)
Government procurements	1.187	0.190	0.686	6.240	0.000	Significant ($p < 0.001$)
Export subsidy	0.249	0.111	0.275	2.235	0.030	Significant ($p < 0.05$)
Quality of Goods	0.410	0.158	0.337	2.600	0.012	Significant ($p < 0.05$)

Table 18.4 Hypotheses acceptance/rejection summary

Hypotheses	Outcome
Hypothesis 1: Voluntary export restraints have a negative impact on trading activities	Rejected
Hypothesis 2: Certification of origin requirements have a negative impact on trading activities	Rejected
Hypothesis 3: Anti-dumping (AD) and Countervailing Duties have a negative impact on trading activities	Rejected
Hypothesis 4: Bureaucratic delays and customs have a negative impact on trading activities	Rejected
Hypothesis 5: Industrial policy resolutions have a negative impact on trading activities	Accepted
Hypothesis 6: Export subsidies have a positive impact on trading activities	Accepted
Hypothesis 7: Labelling has a negative impact on trading activities	Accepted
Hypothesis 8: Import policy barriers have a negative impact on trading activities	Accepted
Hypothesis 9: Government procurements have a positive impact on trading activities	Accepted
Hypothesis 10: Sanitary and phytosanitary measures have a positive impact on trading activities	Accepted
Hypothesis 11: Maintaining the quality of goods have a positive impact on trading activities	Accepted

significance may be individually looked up and inferences on hypothesis acceptance or rejection could be made. The influence of each variable is shown through its coefficient denoted by beta. Government procurements with coefficient 0.686 denote that it is an important variable having the greatest influence on trade creation. Similarly, other variables, industrial policy resolutions (0.34), sanitary and phytosanitary measures (0.297), import policy barriers (−0.497), labelling (−0.229), export subsidy (0.275), and quality of goods (0.337) also influence trade creation. Rest of the variables, voluntary exchange restraints, certificate of origin requirements, anti-dumping rules, and bureaucratic delays and customs do not have an effective influence over trade creation. Instead, they promote trade diversion.

Table 18.4 represents whether the hypothesis has been accepted or rejected. In other words, the presumption made has been proved right or wrong.

18.6 Discussion and Implications

This study focused on the influence of various NTBs on international trade. NTBs discussed above are largely the important ones. But there are other NTBs also which create significant obstacles to trade in certain situations. Normally, these NTBs are not applied individually; they are applied in combination with a view to keep trade protection level high (Naumann and Lincoln 1991). For instance, industrial policy resolutions and import policy barriers mostly go hand in hand.

In order to test the influence of NTBs, empirical study was conducted in this study, having 11 hypotheses. Seven of these hypotheses were accepted, and four rejected. According to the hypotheses, there are eight NTBs which influence trade. Government procurement policies, as we found in the study, have a positive impact on international trade. The government machinery works for the benefit of the country. It encourages domestic market to increase trading activities in order to increase the foreign exchange in India resulting in trade creation. In other words, prioritizing domestic market to amplify trade is a successful measure taken by the government.

Certification of origin requirements, bureaucratic delays and customs are other factors which help to increase the adeptness and efficacy of trading activities because of the large amount of procedures involved. It may be a little time taking and tough for the first time, but the effectiveness increases eventually. This motivates the countries to escalate trading activities promoting simplified procedures and high level of proficiency.

Administrative barriers including VERs, AD and countervailing duties try to protect domestic industry from the foreign market attack. This presumption was neglected by the result of this empirical study. The study brings out the fact that VERs, AD and countervailing duties encourage trade by inspiring the domestic market to be strong and compete in the foreign market. The domestic firms are emboldened through export subsidies by the government. Export studies stimulate trade creation.

Lastly, products standards comprising of quality of goods, sanitary and phytosanitary measures need to be maintained in order to generate trade. The better the product standards, the more will be the demand for the products.

Besides this, there are certain NTBs that act as a hindrance in trade creation. Industrial policy resolutions as well as import policy barriers are prepared keeping in mind the development of domestic market. They are imposed when the domestic industries are seriously injured causing a reduction in trading activities. Another such NTB is labelling. Labelling procedures and packaging are unique for each county. Due to its unique property, inventory for each country has to be maintained separately, and accordingly, finished products should also be taken care of. This results in increasing of cost of production as well as efforts leading to reduction of trade creation.

Summing up, the NTBs differ from situation to situation. They can influence trade in a constructive sense as well as a diversionary sense. The former situation is called trade creation, whereas the latter is called trade diversion.

For academicians, the study contributes to the existing literature on the impact of NTBs on trading activities. The study gives a rigorous description of almost all important NTBs available in today's scenario. Unlike many research studies, this empirical study is based on primary data from people having good knowledge of international business. For practitioners, the study may be useful for international business managers to practically observe and understand the role of NTBs in the trading activities in the twenty-first century. For policymakers, the current opinions of experts visible in this study can be considered and policies can be modified accordingly. The policies to increase in the administrative plus technical work can be improved.

18.7 Conclusion

This study has been in the Indian context. It should not be generalized for different countries. The study is not specific to an industry rather presents a generalized view. Only eleven factors from a long list of NTBs were identified to influence international trade, but without difficulty it can be stated that there are other NTBs too which may influence the impact on trade. Formation of regional trade agreements plays a vital role in international business which has not been included in the study. For the collection of data, convenience sampling method has been used which can result in bias. Also, it would have been better if the sample size was larger. Multiple linear regression was applied as the preliminary tool.

The study should be replicated with a bigger sample to encompass different industries as well as different countries. Other factors influencing trade should be identified and added to the existing model.

References

Baldwin, R. E. (1989). Measuring Nontariff Trade Policies.
Böhm, C., & Motschnig-Pitrik, R. (2015). New research perspectives on managing diversity in International ICT Project Teams. In Sushil & Gerhard Chroust (Eds.), *Systemic flexibility and business agility. Flexible systems management* (pp. 21–31). Springer: New Delhi.
Chambolle, C., & Giraud-Héraud, E. (2005). Certification of origin as a non-tariff barrier. *Review of International Economics, 13*(3), 461–471.
Dhir, S., & Sushil. (2017). Flexibility in modification and termination of cross-border joint ventures. *Global Journal of Flexible Systems Management, 18*(2), 139–151.
Dhir, S., & Mital, A. (2013). Asymmetric motives in Indian bilateral cross-border joint ventures with G7 nations: Impact of relative partner characteristics and initial conditions. *International Journal of Strategic Business Alliances, 3*(1), 69–92.
Ethier, W. J. (1991). Voluntary export restraints. In A. Takayama, M. Ohyama, & H. Ohta (Eds.), *Trade, policy and international adjustments* (pp. 3–18). San Diego, California: Academic Press Inc.
Field, A. (2009). *Discovering statistics using SPSS* (3rd ed.).
Finger, J. M., & Olechowski, A. (1987). *The Uruguay round. A handbook on the multilateral trade negotiations*.
Haldar, A., Rao, S. N., & Momaya, K. S. (2016). Can flexibility in corporate governance enhance international competitiveness? Evidence from knowledge-based industries in India. *Global Journal of Flexible Systems Management, 17*(4), 389–402.
ISO Standards. (n.d.). Retrieved from International Organization for Standardization: http://www.iso.org/iso/home/standards.htm.

McAfee, R., & McMillan, J. (1989). Government procurement and international trade. *Journal of International Economics, 26,* 291–308.

Ministry of Industry. (1956). Industrial Policy Resolution.

Naumann, E., & Lincoln, D. J. (1991). Non-tariff barriers and entry strategy alternatives: Strategic marketing implications. *Journal of Small Business Management, 29*(2), 60–70.

Nkuepo, H. J. (n.d.). Preferential Trade Agreements, Trade Creation and Trade Diversion. Retrieved from World Trade Organization: https://www.wto.org/english/res_e/publications_e/wtr11_forum_e/wtr11_12july11_bis_e.htm.

OECD. (n.d.). Technical Barriers to Trade. Retrieved from Organization of European Economic Co-operation: http://www.oecd.org/tad/ntm/technicalbarrierstotrade.htm.

Suranovic, S. M. (1998). Countervailing duties in a perfectly competitive market. *International Trade Theory and Policy, 32*(1), 110–113.

The World Bank. (2011). *The great recession and import protection: The role of temporary trade barriers.* Washington, DC: London Publishing Partnership.

WTO. (1998, May). Understanding the WTO Agreement on Sanitary and Phytosanitary Measures. Retrieved from World Trade Organization: https://www.wto.org/english/tratop_e/sps_e/spsund_e.htm.

WTO. (2016, November). WTO: 2016 NEWS ITEMS, Technical Barriers to Trade. Retrieved from World Trade Organization: https://www.wto.org/english/news_e/news16_e/tbt_10nov16_e.htm.

WTO. (n.d.). Understanding the WTO: The Agreements. Retrieved from World Trade Organization: https://www.wto.org/english/thewto_e/whatis_e/tif_e/agrm9_e.htm.

Chapter 19
Employer Brand and Its External Perspective

Ruchika Sharma and Asha Prasad

Abstract The demand for qualified personnel is increasing faster than their availability in India as well as internationally. Intensified market competition has influenced both large and small companies to continuously update their hiring strategies in order to distinguish themselves from their competitors. With an aim of differentiating and creating a unique employment experience, employer branding is continuously gaining reputation as a strategic approach in the current scenario. The aim of this study is to find the various dimensions of employer brand that attracts the potential employees in IT sector. The research presented in this chapter involves both exploratory and conclusive aspects of research. The interviews were conducted with the final-year student placement coordinators of MCA and B. Tech studying in central, state and deemed universities in India. The themes identified through interviews along with Employer Attractiveness Scale developed by Berthon et al. (Int J Advertising 24(2):151–172, 2005) have been included in the final five-point Likert scale questionnaire with 34 statements defining employer brand. Confirmatory factor analysis and exploratory factor analysis have been used to analyse the data using SPSS and AMOS 2.0. The findings and conclusion have been presented depending upon empirical evidences.

Keywords CFA · EFA · Employer brand · India · IT · Prospective employees

---

R. Sharma (✉) · A. Prasad
B.I.T, Mesra, Ranchi, India
e-mail: ruchi.sharma0320@gmail.com

A. Prasad
e-mail: asha@bitmesra.ac.in

R. Sharma
VIPS, Delhi, India

R. Sharma
GGSIPU, Delhi, India

A. Prasad
B.I.T (Off Campus), Noida, India

© Springer Nature Singapore Pte Ltd. 2018
S. Dhir and Sushil (eds.), *Flexible Strategies in VUCA Markets*,
Flexible Systems Management, https://doi.org/10.1007/978-981-10-8926-8_19

19.1 Introduction

Brand is one of the most valued assets for any organisation, and its management is one of the key factors responsible for its success. Although the focus of organisations has always been on product branding, and its communication and maintenance, the concept has now spread its wings to management of human resource as well. The application of branding to human resource management is known as employer branding, wherein the employer brand itself can be seen as a 'good place to work in' for both the existing and prospective employees of the organisation. During the 1990s, organisations started realising the importance of gaining a competitive advantage over their rival organisations through their workforce (Dhir 2016). They comprehended the importance of attracting, hiring and retaining the best human talent for their organisations, and maintaining and developing their brand as a desired employer. This concept gained added momentum due to changing demographic and exclusive attitude of generation Y (youngsters born between 1977 and 1995) which is comprised of high maintenance, high self-interest and varied expectations of generation Y. The mid-1990s saw the advent of the organisational branding concept, which emerged in response to the changing needs of this generation, and was strategically introduced and defined in 1996 by various industries across different sectors. It was initially defined by Ambler and Barrow in 1996 as 'the package of functional, economic and psychological benefits provided by employment, and identified with the employing company' and was taken forward by many other subsequent researches. Conferring to American Marketing Association, any brand is defined as 'a name, term, sign, symbol or design, or combination of them which is intended to identify the goods and services of one seller or group of sellers and to differentiate them from those of their competitors'. Employer brand is the result of employer branding activities that are designed and followed by different organisations to differentiate themselves from their competitors. Backhaus and Tikoo (2004) define employer branding as 'a firm's efforts to promote, both within and outside the firm, a clear view of what makes it different and desirable as an employer'. Employer brand is thus a unique and identifiable brand identity, while employer branding is a process through which an employer brand is formed and communicated both internally and externally.

According to human resource practitioners and proponents of the intensive literature, employer branding is a process of three important steps. Firstly, the firm develops its 'value proposition' that covers all information about the organisation, including its culture, management style, type of product and services offered, and quality of the work life IT promotes, among other things. This value proposition lies at the heart of branding and the central message to be communicated to its current and prospective employees. The second step involves communicating the value proposition to both its existing and prospective employees. This communication concerning value proposition provides the central message that is conveyed by the brand to its employees and is also termed as 'external marketing'. The third and the last step of employer branding is internal marketing. This aspect pertains to the permanent incorporation of a communicated image in the culture of the organisation (Frook 2001). This three-step process comprehensively signifies the manner in which the concept of employer branding operates in attracting and retaining talent. This enables organisations to think and define their employment value proposition in a way that distinguishes the organisation from others as an employer and synchronises the employer brand with the product or corporate brand. The external marketing of an employer firm establishes it as an employer of choice for new recruits and also allows prospective candidates to create positive assumptions about the company before entering it as employees. These assumptions by the prospective recruits also facilitate their easy absorption into the existing culture of the firm. However, despite its significance for both employers and employees, the concept of employer branding and its relationship with other external aspects has not been extensively explored in the literature (Ewing et al. 2002).

Demographic trends are changing in most of the developed as well as developing economies (Dhir and Mital 2013). This dynamism has made companies to reconsider their responsibilities and roles as an employer in the labour market. They should understand that competition is not between the candidates to be hired with the right employer; rather, it is between the organisations to hire the right candidate. The role of human resource management is changing and adding a further responsibility of 'selling' the positions in the market. The organisations need to manage the various levels of people, process, technology and other business functions to support various business requirements and fight intensive competition in the market (Sushil et al. 2016).

Earlier organisations were less concerned about branding, and its various outcomes as both competition and employer choices were limited. However, with the phenomenal increase in the number of employers in the market, there has been a concomitant rise in employee turnovers due to the eagerness of employees to switch jobs. The intensive competition and rise in the number of firms across all sectors have fostered a new era of employment (Dhir and Sushil 2017). This has made it imperative for all businesses to understand the expectations of prospective employees and accordingly design their human resource policies in order to attract better talent.

The research presented in the current chapter is intended to explore the various dimensions of employer brand in Indian IT sector. Information Technology sector, being one of the major sectors contributing to the GDP of the nation and providing employment to large number of human resource, serves as the selected sector for the study.

19.2 Literature Review

Researchers have showcased the existence of different job- and organisation-related attributes that help produce employer attractiveness. These dimensions have the highest correlation with organisational as well as job attractiveness, thereby influencing decisions of various candidates to apply for or join any organisation.

Chapman et al. (2005) have stated that work environment is one of the major dimensions that define the employer's attractiveness. According to Ambler and Barrow (1996), in their research they assessed the possible application of branding techniques for better management of human resources. They concluded their study by mentioning the applicability of branding in employment situations. They also emphasised the relationship between the quality of product and services and quality of employees, and found them to be directly related to each other. Melin (2005) highlights the relationship between the internal and external brand images of a company. This study identifies five constituents of employer brand, namely compensation and benefits, product/company brand strength, work environment, work-life balance and the company environment and culture. Further, Moroko and Uncles (2008) have also supported his view that culture and ethics have an important part to play in making an employer attractive. Jain (2013) proposes four dimensions of employer branding through exploratory factor analysis, namely management of the organisation, perceived organisational prestige, transparency and leadership and organisation fit.

The younger generation of workers (especially from generation Y) have higher and different expectations regarding both job success and challenges; they wish for job promotions more quickly than baby boomer counterparts (Smola and Sutton 2002). This has resulted in the overall evolution of human resource practices. Students also think that the companies taking corporate social responsibility (CSR) initiatives are better employers due to the respect and reputation they earn in society (Albinger and Freeman 2000). According to previous studies, CSR moves also clearly effect the employees' commitment and loyalty towards organisation. The current generation can also be attracted to certain other factors, such as company is a fun place to work in, provides training opportunities, and whether or not perceived as an innovative company (Yadav et al. 2016; Bamel et al. 2017). It has also been observed that the attributes of 'innovative company' and 'offering the opportunity to grow' are important parameters over salary for attracting the current generation.

Mosley (2007) also states that many businesses are now trying to develop an 'ideal blueprint of employment to benchmark their own practices against those that have already been achievers and recognized as "Best Employers"'. Employer branding helps the organisation attract applicants with the right skill and desirable cultural fit and consistent experience of the employer (EB Insights 2011). In addition, Barrow and Mosley (2005) also have recognised various aspects of employer branding, which are employer centric, such as internal communication, corporate social responsibility, external reputation, senior leadership, team management, internal measurement system, service support, recruitment and induction, learning and development, reward and recognition, working environment and performance appraisal. They propose that companies should seriously consider these dimensions to effectively manage their brand. Sullivan (2004), on the other hand, proposes different parameters of employer branding: (i) a balance between good management and high productivity, (ii) a culture of sharing and continuous improvement, (iii) employees 'proactively' telling stories, (iv) obtaining public recognition ('great-place-to-work' lists), (v) becoming a benchmark firm, (vi) getting talked about, (vii) branding assessment metrics and (viii) increasing awareness of its best practices among prospective candidates. Albinger and Freeman (2000) present that social responsibilities initiatives taken by any organisation give it a competitive edge and project their image as attractive employer in the market (Chatterjee 2000).

Backhaus and Tikoo (2004) provide a strong direction on how employer branding and its several magnitudes such as customer orientation, corporate social responsibility, work-life balance are attracting the right candidates from the market. Backhaus et al. (2002) also demonstrated how the current generation is becoming concerned about the value system and CSR initiatives of the organisations while considering their employer of choice.

A number of researches, both theoretical and empirical, explore the dimensions of employer attractiveness that helps in building a successful and renowned employer brand in the market.

Table 19.1 represents all the studies conducted with regard to employer brand while also highlighting the sector undertaken for the study.

Table 19.1 Summary of employer branding literature (review of literature)

Author/Year	Sample used	Technique	Relationship identified
Ambler and Barrow (1996) The employer brand London	Twenty-seven semi-structured in-depth interviews Service sector (Consultancy)	CFA	Employer branding and employee attraction
Ewing et al. (2002) Employment branding in the knowledge economy Australia	Two hundred and eighty employees General sector	CFA	Employer branding dimensions and employee commitment
Lievens and Highhouse (2003) The relation of instrumental and symbolic attributes to a company's attractiveness as an employer Canada	Two groups of prospective applicants (275 final-year students and 124 bank employees) Service sector (Banking)	Multiple regression	Comparison of external and internal employer brand image
Backhaus and Tikoo (2004) Conceptualising and researching employer branding New York	Conceptual/theoretical paper General sector	Literature review	Employer branding and organisational career Management

(continued)

Table 19.1 (continued)

Author/Year	Sample used	Technique	Relationship identified
Miles and Mangold (2004) A conceptualisation of the employee branding process	One hundred and twelve engineers General sector	Conceptual paper	Employee and organisational fit, psychological contracts
Berthon et al. (2005) Captivating Company: dimensions of attractiveness in employer branding Australia	Six hundred and eighty-three students Service sector	SEM	Employer attractiveness and prospective employees
Knox, and Freeman (2006) Measuring and managing employer brand image in the service industry UK	Eight hundred and sixty-two students from 22 universities Service sector	Correlation, t test and mean analysis	Employer brand image and potential employees
Davies (2008) Employer branding and its influence on managers Europe	Eight hundred and fifty-four managers employed in seventeen organisations. Service, manufacturing sector	SEM	Brand personality and employees' affinity
Arachchige and Robertson (2013) Employer attractiveness: Comparative perceptions of undergraduates and postgraduate students Sri Lanka	Two hundred and twenty-one final-year business course students	Factor analysis	Students' perceptions and employer attractiveness
Agrawal and Swaroop (2009) Effect of employer brand image on application intentions of B-school undergraduates India	One hundred and twenty-four students from five diverse business schools General sector	Mean analysis and multiple regression	Early recruitment practices and employer brand
Srivastava (2010) An employer brand framework for prospective employees: Scale development and model testing India	Items were created through the literature review and exploratory study General sector	Principal component analysis	Employer attractiveness and prospective employees

(continued)

19 Employer Brand and Its External Perspective

Table 19.1 (continued)

Author/Year	Sample used	Technique	Relationship identified
Jain (2013) Employer branding and its impact on CSR, motivation and retention of employees using structural equation modelling India	Ninety employees working at three different levels of management: top, middle and junior. Taj Group of Hotels, ONGC and E&Y	Factor analysis, Pearson's correlation and Kruskal–Wallis test (SEM)	Employer
Hillebrandt and Ivens (2013) Scale development in employer branding Germany	Two hundred and twenty-three employees of German companies German companies	Exploratory factor analysis	Employer branding and its dimensions
Moroko and Uncles (2009) New Perspectives on Employer branding: an empirical investigation of scope, nature and success drivers Australia	Seventeen unstructured in-depth interviews with senior industry participants General sector	Four papers presented, each providing a new perspective	Employer branding and its dimensions
Melin (2005) Employer branding: Likeness and differences between external and internal employer brand images Sweden	Deductive approach with inductive element; survey of 3110 young professionals conducted by Universum Communications Swedish companies	Data analysed through Excel statistical tool and mean method	Internal and external employer brand image
Foster et al. (2010) Exploring the relationship between corporate, internal and employer branding UK	Literature review	Conceptual paper	Employer, internal and corporate branding
Kolle (2011) Alignment of internally and externally aimed employer branding efforts Denmark	Interview method, one interview from each strata of current, potential and employees with 8 or more years of experience Novo Nordisk, Denmark	Qualitative analysis through coding of questionnaire	External and internal employer brand image

(continued)

Table 19.1 (continued)

Author/Year	Sample used	Technique	Relationship identified
Arachchige and Robertson (2011) Business student perceptions of a preferred employer: a study identifying determinants of employer branding Sri Lanka	Two hundred and twenty-one students of final-year business course studying at Sri Lankan university General sector	Factor analysis along with mean standard deviation and correlation used for data analysis	Students' perceptions and employer branding

It can also be observed from Table 19.1 that major number of studies have been conducted outside India and that India particularly has not been the focus area for discussed subject. Since Information Technology (IT) sector is one of the growing sectors in India as well as abroad, it has been less considered for studies on employer brand. Both these facts can also be seen as jointly constituting the major reason for conducting a study on employer brand in India with the cities like Delhi and Hyderabad with the maximum number of IT giants.

19.3 Objective of the Study

The objective of this study was to determine various dimensions of employer brand in IT companies operating in India.

19.4 Research Methodology

The methodology is divided into two parts. In the first part, semi-structured interviews were conducted with 34 final-year placement student coordinators at central, state and deemed universities in India. These students were selected through convenience sampling and asked about what attracts them the most while selecting their employer, whenever a company comes for the campus placements what all factors students question for. On the basis of which factors students reject or accept a company's job proposal? The feedback collected through interviews was further added to the already developed scale of Berthon et al. (2005), the study conducted in Australia questing for the parameters that attracts prospective employees towards an employer.

In the second part of the study, using convenience sampling technique, a structured questionnaire inclusive of the parameters explored through interviews and adopted from the study of Berthon et al. (2005) was distributed to the final-year students of MCA and B. Tech studying at various central, state and deemed universities of India. The students were personally visited and given brief about the purpose of this research. The questionnaire was distributed to 950 students, and 791 completely filled in questionnaires were collected leading to the response rate of 83.2%. The percentages of male and female respondents were 47.9 and 52.1%, respectively, from deemed (21.6%), state (41.3%) and central (37.1%) universities in India.

The questionnaire was divided into three parts. First part of the questionnaire asked the students to think about their ideal employer and keep IT in mind while answering further questions. They were also presented an annual report of BT-PeopleStrong Survey 2015 to give them rational awareness of best IT companies to work for, namely Google India, Accenture, TCS, Microsoft India, IBM, Infosys Technologies, Wipro, and Genpact currently operating in India. This made it easier for them to think about their ideal employer and answer the questions in participative manner.

The second part of the questionnaire contained 34 statements on five-point Likert scale with 1 indicating strongly disagree and 5 strongly agree defining employer brand. The questionnaire concluded with demographics, name, course and university the student was studying in.

Exploratory factor analysis using SPSS version 21 and confirmatory factor analysis using AMOS version 21 were applied for analysing data and determining the various dimensions of employer brand in Indian IT Sector.

19.5 Data Analysis

19.5.1 Qualitative Analysis

Under the qualitative analysis, interview results were coded in the Excel sheet. All the responses given by the interviewees were recorded in the form of table irrespective of their relevance with the question. After the recording process, all the similar responses were clubbed together into the homogeneous groups supporting the common theme. The homogeneous groups were assigned a head or a code representing a construct associated with the expectations of prospective employees. Several important organisational characteristics that prospective employees look forward to while selecting an employer were missing in the scale opted for the current study. These characteristics were: employer should be an ethical organisation, and it should possess positive culture, must focus on personal welfare of employees, hold good brand image in the market, should provide easy job locations, focus on CSR, provide foreign assignments, better work-life balance, additional perks and benefits, training and development opportunities and should have a global presence. These aspects were added to the scale used for the current study and checked on reliability and validity concerns. None of these items was dropped during the analysis, and exploratory factor analysis clubbed them under different factors, namely growth and development opportunity, company's reputation, acceptance and belongingness, work-life balance and ethics & CSR with adequate factor loading.

19.5.2 Quantitative Analysis

Before conducting EFA and CFA, the data was purified and responses with missing values, redundancy, were deleted from the data set. Thus, 15 responses from the data set were deleted leading to the total sample size of 776.

19.5.2.1 Exploratory Factor Analysis (EFA)

The purified data was inserted into SPSS, and EFA was used to convert set of variables with the common characteristics into meaningful factors. Principal component analysis was used along with varimax rotation method with Kaiser normalisation to extract the factors. The adequacy of the data was checked through Kaiser–Meyer–Olkin (Kaiser and Rice 1974) which was found to be 0.874, greater than 0.6. Bartlett's test of sphericity also provided the satisfactory result with $p < 0.01$ indicating the multicollinearity within the variables. The PCA presented the presence of five factors explaining total variance of 66.751% and the total reliability of 0.86. Table 19.2 presents factors along with their factor loadings after exploratory factor analysis. EB29 was dropped due to the poor factor loading and was not considered in further analysis.

The variables with cross-loadings and with factor value less than 0.6 were not considered for further analysis.

19.5.2.2 Confirmatory Factor Analysis

CFA helps in assessing the unidimensionality and allows testing specific hypothesis (Fabrigar et al. 1999). The results of exploratory factor analysis were confirmed through confirmatory factor analysis using AMOS 21. Reliability and validity issues along with model fit were ascertained through CFA. Confirmatory factor analysis was run on individual construct and then final model. The validity and reliability concerns were checked for the model as well as for individual construct (results are presented in Table 19.3). Figure 19.1 presents the final model, and its fit indices are presented in Table 19.4. The indices signify good model fit with all the

19 Employer Brand and Its External Perspective

Table 19.2 Factors of employer brand after exploratory factor analysis (SPSS 20 Output)

Components	Items	Variables	Factor loadings
EBA Growth and development opportunity	The company provides good promotion opportunities	EB13	0.919
	The company provides training and development opportunities to its employees	EB34	0.900
	The organisation provides career enhancement opportunities	EB16	0.875
	The organisation provides opportunity for higher studies	EB27	0.866
	The company has positive culture	EB10	0.854
	It gives an opportunity to their employees to teach others what they have learned	EB5	0.839
	It provides job security to its employees	EB19	0.801
	This organisation gives more confidence and self-esteem	EB4	0.787
	Company has positive learning environment	EB22	0.784
	It gives chance to have hands-on interdepartmental experience	EB20	0.779
	The company provides foreign assignments	EB30	0.743
	The organisation values creativity among their employees	EB2	0.729
	The company provides a springboard for future employment	EB29	0.413
	It provides additional perks and benefits (e.g. excursion trips)	EB32	0.720
EBB Company's reputation	It provides an attractive overall compensation package	EB21	0.918
	It is a renowned brand in the market	EB24	0.904
	The company has global presence	EB33	0.870
	The company holds good reputation in the market	EB25	0.855
	The organisation is customer-oriented	EB18	0.840
	It is an innovative employer—novel work practices/forward thinking	EB9	0.836
	The organisation produces innovative products and services	EB12	0.821
	It is known as a good employer brand	EB1	0.775
EBC Acceptance and belongingness	Employees have good relationships with superiors in this organisation	EB6	0.933
	Employees have good relationships with colleagues	EB7	0.896
	It gives the feeling of acceptance and belongingness	EB17	0.803
	The leaders here are supportive and really encouraging	EB8	0.777

(continued)

Table 19.2 (continued)

Components	Items	Variables	Factor loadings
EBD Work-life balance	The company provides easy job locations to its employees	EB28	0.922
	The company provides flexibility (e.g. flexible working hours)	EB26	0.877
	It focuses on the personal welfare of its employees	EB15	0.869
	The organisation provides work-life balance	EB31	0.849
EBE Ethics & CSR	It is a humanitarian organisation—believes in giving back to society	EB14	0.852
	The organisation focuses on CSR	EB11	0.835
	It is an ethical organisation	EB23	0.794
	The organisation considers CSR as the part of its culture	EB3	0.771

Table 19.3 Reliability and validity statistics (Gakingston MS-Excel validity master output)

Indices	Criteria	Results
Chi-square		628
GFI	>=0.95	0.952
P value	<=0.05	<0.01
CFI	>=0.95	0.957
CMIN/df	<=3	1.875
AGFI	>=0.80	0.870
RMSEA	<=0.05	0.48
RMR	<=0.10	0.046

values under the desired limits. The model is free from convergent and divergent validity issues.

The organisation can attract prospective employees on the basis of five important factors which are growth and developmental opportunities, reputation of the company, the belongingness and association a candidate can expect from an organisation after becoming an important part of IT, the work-life balance and the ethical values an organisation holds. The confirmatory factor analysisconfirmed that these factors have major role in defining employer brand.

Due to less regression weight, EB16, EB34, EB5, and EB32 were dropped from the factor EBA and the indices have been modified wherever required in order to achieve a better model fit.

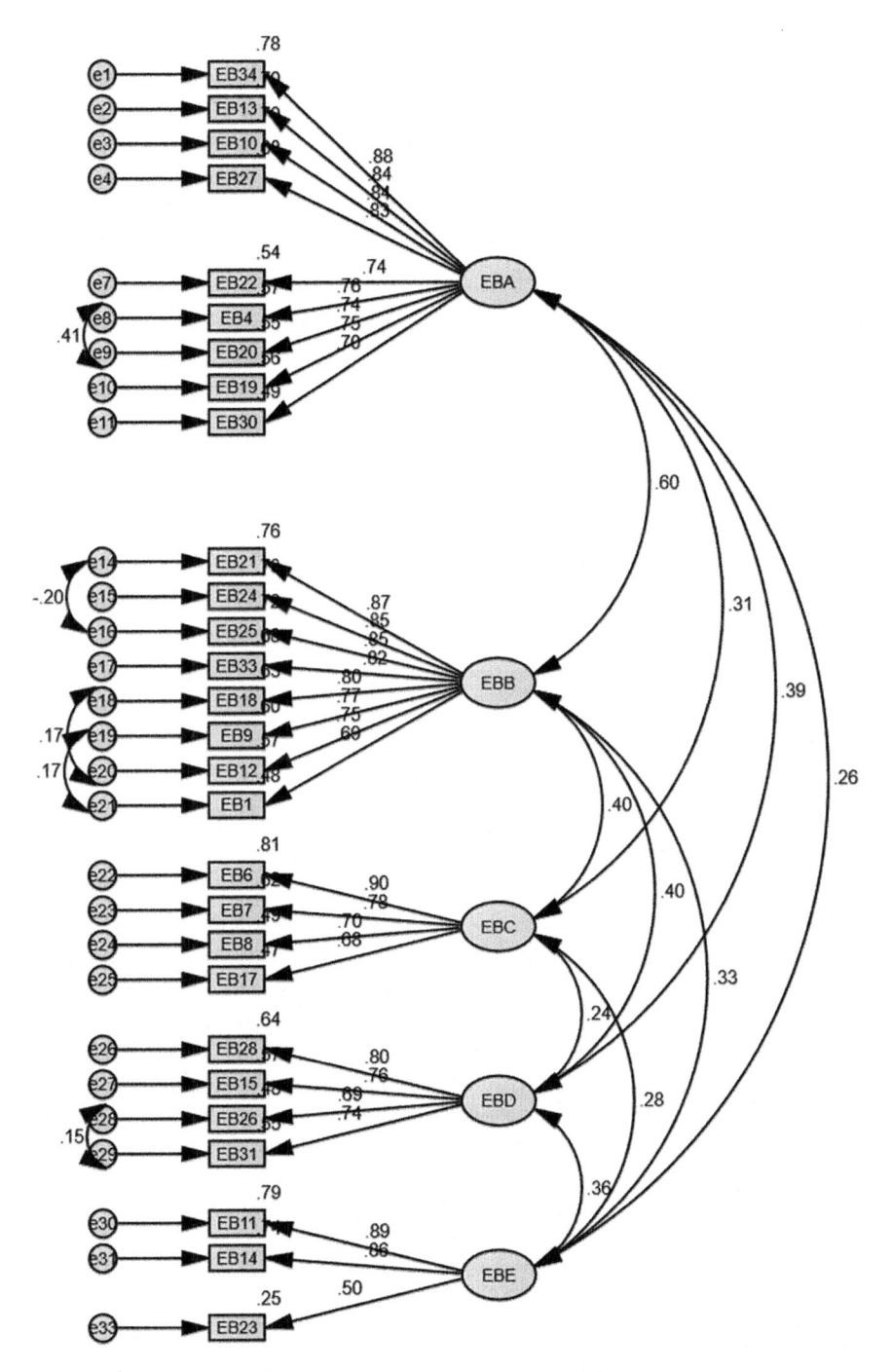

Fig. 19.1 First-order measurement model of employer brand (AMOS 21 Output). *Notes* EB3 and EB16 are deleted due to high covariance with two or more items

Table 19.4 Model fit indices (AMOS 21 Output)

	CR	AVE	MSV	ASV	Convergent validity	Discriminant validity
EBD	0.835	0.559	0.161	0.124	Yes	Yes
EBA	0.936	0.618	0.360	0.168	Yes	Yes
EBB	0.935	0.646	0.360	0.124	Yes	Yes
EBC	0.854	0.596	0.158	0.112	Yes	Yes
EBE	0.807	0.596	0.129	0.095	Yes	Yes

Table 19.5 Summary of dimensions of employer brand

Theoretical framework	Findings of present study
Ambler and Barrow (1996)	
Functional dimension	Growth and development; ethics and corporate social responsibility
Psychological dimension	Work-life balance; acceptance and belongingness
Economic dimension	Compensation and benefits
Berthon et al. (2005)	
Development value	Growth and development opportunity
Economic value	Company's reputation[a]
Interest value	
Social value	Acceptance and belongingness
Application value	CSR & ethics Work-life balance[a]

Note Prepared by Author
[a]New perspectives explored in the study

19.6 Discussion

Several important organisational characteristics that prospective employees look forward to while selecting an employer were missing in the scale opted for the current study. These characteristics were: employer should be an ethical organisation, and IT should possess positive culture, must focus on personal welfare of employees, hold good brand image in the market, should provide easy job locations, focus on CSR, provide foreign assignments, better work-life balance, additional perks and benefits, training and development opportunities and should have a global presence. These aspects were added to the scale used for the current study and checked on reliability and validity concerns. None of these items was dropped during the analysis, and exploratory factor analysis clubbed them under different factors, namely growth and development opportunity, company's reputation, acceptance and belongingness, work-life balance and ethics & CSR with adequate factor loading. The results were also consistent with the study conducted by Roy (2008) that explored the dimensions of employer brand in Indian context. This study presented seven clubbed dimensions defining the employer brand: application value where employees get to implement what they have learned; interest value where the employee grows in an exciting work environment with novel work practices, and given the chance to use creativity; ethical value where companies are ethical and have strong and clear cultures; economic value which includes overall compensation package, additional perks; social value that provides an enjoyable working environment, and worthy relationships with superiors and subordinates; psychological value which demonstrates the feeling of self-confidence being part of the organisation; and development value which includes job security.

Aspects similar to these have also been mentioned by Berthon et al. (2005). However, results of the current study differed on certain aspects from two major studies—Berthon et al. (2005) and Ambler and Barrow (1996). For instance, refer Table 19.5; Berthon et al. (2005) presented five major dimensions of employer attractiveness, namely application value, social value, interest value, development value and economic value. To compare with the identified dimensions of Berthon et al. (2005), the first factor (growth and development opportunity) is development value, second factor (company's reputation) is the combination of economic value and interest value, third factor (acceptance and belongingness) is social value and fifth factor (ethics & CSR) is application value. In contrary, work-life balance was found to be one of the important factors defining employer brand in the current context but was not highlighted in the research of Berthon et al. (2005).

Opposing to the research of Berthon et al. (2005), in the current study, students gave less preference for considering employer as the springboard for their future employment and selecting an employer which gives an opportunity to teach others what they have learned. In the referred study of Berthon et al. (2005), they were clubbed under development value but in present study they were eliminated due to poor factor loading. Employees differ in their strategies while selecting employer during their career. Some follow the strategy of 'local career strategy', wherein they stay with one or limited number of employers and others prefer changing employers frequently, i.e. 'Cosmopolitan Strategy' (Gouldner 1957). Newcomers tend to follow cosmopolitan strategy and consider their preliminary employer as an initial step taking them towards further opportunities (De Vos et al. 2009). This may be the reason for them considering their first employer a way to reach the next better employer.

19.7 Limitations and Scope for Future Research

Although the present research has important implications, yet it is not without limitations. First, the current study has been conducted in the IT sector and other sectors have not been included. Also, this research is restricted to students of MCA and B. Tech. Therefore, results of this study may not be applicable to other sectors and educational courses.

The current study adopts convenience sampling which has its own set of limitations. It is a sampling technique based on the convenience of researcher while choosing members of population to participate in the study. There is a scope of uncontrolled variability and bias in the estimates in such sampling technique. It has the highest probability of sampling error.

The current study considered the EmpAt scale of Berthon et al. (2005) to measure employer brand, whereas there are other scales also such as Roy (2008) to measure employer brand in Indian context which may be considered for other studies in future.

The expectations of Indian students may also be different from those studying in foreign universities. The universities considered for the study were limited to central, state and deemed universities of India. Other universities across other countries were ignored. Rosethorn (2009) argues that employer brand has been explored significantly in the context of recruitment and external aspects such as corporate branding, external employer branding, external marketing. Future studies may seek to explore the internal aspects of employer brand and their relevance in current scenario.

19.8 Conclusion

Employer brand has been an interesting area of research for many researchers, and there exists significant empirical evidence highlighting the importance of employer brand and its role in attracting human resources (e.g. Backhaus and Tikoo (2004), Berthon et al. (2005)). The present research has explored the various characteristics of employer brand that attract. The findings of the research presented in this chapter indicate that employer brand is composed of aspects such as growth and development opportunity, company's reputation, work-life balance, acceptance and belongingness and ethics & CSR. IT organisations can consider these characteristics while building their employer brand and designing their employer value proposition.

The current study seeks to provide a solution to the problem of talent acquisition being faced by organisations today. While organisations invest huge sums on recruitment and selection, marketing and projecting themselves as worthy employers in the market, it is important that they analyse the elements that may help them attract the right candidates. Organisation can hold attractive image in the market by focusing on certain important aspects explored under various studies, the current study being one of them.

Results of the current study and the developed scale can be managed and used by the current human resource managers to better understand the needs and desires of prospective employees. Expectations of employees keep on changing with respect to their demographics and external environment. This will also provide them better insight into changing expectations of future employees.

The organisations, after understanding the expectations of prospective employees, can embed them in their organisation culture and effectively communicate to employees intending to apply for a job. This will enhance person-organisation fit, and applicants would be in the better position to match their personal goal with that of the organisation.

References

Agrawal, R. K., & Swaroop, P. (2009). Effect of employer brand image on application intentions of B-school undergraduates. *Vision, 13*(3), 41–49.

Albinger, H. S., & Freeman, S. J. (2000). Corporate social performance and attractiveness as an employer to different job seeking populations. *Journal of Business Ethics, 28*(3), 243–253.

Ambler, T., & Barrow, S. (1996). The employer brand. *Journal of Brand Management, 4*(3), 185–206.

Arachchige, B. J., & Robertson, A. (2011). Business student perceptions of a preferred employer: A study identifying determinants of employer branding. *IUP Journal of Brand Management, 8* (3).

Arachchige, B. J., & Robertson, A. (2013). Employer attractiveness: Comparative perceptions of undergraduate and postgraduate students. *Sri Lankan Journal of Human Resource Management, 4*(1).

Backhaus, K. B., Stone, B. A., & Heiner, K. (2002). Exploringthe relationship between corporate social performance and employer attractiveness. *Business and Society, 41*(3), 292–318.

Backhaus, K., & Tikoo, S. (2004). Conceptualizing and researching employer branding. *Career Development International, 9*(5), 501–517.

Bamel, U. K., Paul, H., & Bamel, N. (2017). Managing workplace diversity through organizational climate. In T. P. S. Singh & A. J. Kulkarni (Eds.), *Flexibility in resource management, flexible systems management* (pp. 87–97). Singapore: Springer Nature.

Barrow, S., & Mosley, R. (2005). *The employer brand, bringing the best of brand management to people at work*. Chichester, England: Wiley Ltd.

Berthon, P., Ewing, M., & Hah, L. L. (2005). Captivating company: Dimensions of attractiveness in employer branding. *International Journal of Advertising, 24*(2), 151–172.

Chapman, D. S., Uggerslev, K. L., Carroll, S. A., Piasentin, K. A., & Jones, D. A. (2005). Applicant attraction to organizations and job choice: A meta-analytic review of the correlates of recruiting outcomes.

Chatterjee, J. (2000). Balancing external and internal flexibilities emerging strategy paradigms for Indian organizations. *Global Journal of Flexible Systems Management, 1*(1), 1–12.

Davies, G. (2008). Employer branding and its influence on managers. *European Journal of Marketing, 42*(5/6), 667–681.

De Vos, A., De Stobbeleir, K., & Meganck, A. (2009). The relationship between career-related antecedents and graduates' anticipatory psychological contracts. *Journal of Business and Psychology, 24*(3), 289–298.

Dhir, S. (2016). Global competitiveness of informal economy organizations. In *Flexible work organizations* (pp. 209–224). India: Springer.

Dhir, S., & Sushil. (2017). Flexibility in modification and termination of cross-border joint ventures. *Global Journal of Flexible Systems Management, 18*(2), 139–151.

Dhir, S., & Mital, A. (2013). Asymmetric motives in Indian bilateral cross-border joint ventures with G7 nations: Impact of relative partner characteristics and initial conditions. *International Journal of Strategic Business Alliances, 3*(1), 69–92.

EB Insights. (2011). Universum, Spring Edition. Retrieved from http://www.universumglobal.com/stored-images/81/81405691-a9bb-41e1-9b6b-afbff9af11d2.pdf.

Ewing, M. T., Pitt, L. F., De Bussy, N. M., & Berthon, P. (2002). Employment branding in the knowledge economy. *International Journal of Advertising, 21*(1), 3–22.

Fabrigar, L. R., Wegener, D. T., MacCallum, R. C., & Strahan, E. J. (1999). Evaluating the use of exploratory factor analysis in psychological research. *Psychological Methods, 4*(3), 272.

Foster, C., Punjaisri, K., & Cheng, R. (2010). Exploring the relationship between corporate, internal and employer branding. *Journal of Product & Brand Management, 19*(6), 401–409.

Frook, J. E. (2001). Burnish your brand from the inside. *B to B, 86*(8), 1–2.

Gouldner, A. W. (1957) Cosmopolitans and locals: Toward an analysis of latent social roles. *Administrative science quarterly*, 281–306.

Hillebrandt, I., & Ivens, B. S. (2013). Scale development in employer branding. In *Impulse für die Markenpraxis und Markenforschung* (pp. 65–86). Springer Fachmedien Wiesbaden.

Jain, S. (2013). Employer branding and its impact on CSR, motivation, and retention of employees using structural equation modelling. *Delhi Business Review, 14*(2), 83.

Kaiser, H. F., & Rice, J. (1974). Little Jiffy, Mark IV. *Educational and Psychological Measurement, 34*(1), 111–117.

Knox, S., & Freeman, C. (2006). Measuring and managing employer brand image in the service industry. *Journal of Marketing Management, 22*(7–8), 695–716.

Kolle, S. (2011). *Alignment of internally and externally aimed employer branding efforts—A case study of the novo nordisk employer branding programme 'Life changing careers'* (Bachelor Thesis). Retrieved from: http://pure.au.dk/portal-asbstudent/files/36182924/Bachelor_Thesis_FINAL.pdf.

Lievens, F., & Highhouse, S. (2003). The relation of instrumental and symbolic attributes to a company's attractiveness as an employer. *Personnel Psychology, 56*(1), 75–102.

Melin, E. (2005). Employer branding: Likenesses and differences between external and internal employer brand images.

Miles, S. J., & Mangold, G. (2004). A Conceptualization of the employee branding process. *Journal of Relationship Marketing, 3*(2–3), 65–87.

Moroko, L., & Uncles, M. D. (2008). Characteristics of successful employer brands. *Journal of Brand Management, 16*(3), 160–175.

Moroko, L., & Uncles, M. (2009). Employer branding. *Wall Street Journal, 23*.

Mosley, R. W. (2007). Customer experience, organisational culture and the employer brand. *Journal of Brand Management, 15*(2), 123–134.

Rosethorn, H. (2009). *The employer brand: Keeping faith with the deal*. CRC Press.

Roy, S. K. (2008). Identifying the dimensions of attractiveness of an employer brand in the indian context. *South Asian Journal of Management, 15*(4), 110–130.

Smola, K., & Sutton, C. D. (2002). Generational differences: Revisiting generational work values for the new millennium. *Journal of Organizational Behavior, 23*(4), 363–382.

Srivastava, P. (2010). *An employer brand framework for prospective employees: Scale development & model testing* (Unpublished Ph.D. Thesis). Management Development Institute, Gurgaon (India).

Sullivan, J. (2004). Eight elements of a successful employment brand, ER Daily, February 23.

Sushil, Bhal, K. T., & Singh, S. P. (2016). Managing flexibility: People, process, technology and business. In *Flexible systems management* (pp. 115–133). New Delhi: Springer.

Yadav, M., Rangnekar, S., & Bamel, U. (2016). Workplace flexibility dimensions as enablers of organizational citizenship behavior. *Global Journal of Flexible Systems Management, 17*(1), 41–56.

Index

A
Abnormal returns, 169–171, 173, 174, 189, 190, 192–194, 197
Academic environment conditions, 117, 118, 120
Academicians, 91, 113, 116, 120, 169, 223, 247
Acceptance and belongingness, 260, 261, 264–266
Accommodation, 83–86
Action management, 131
Administrative barriers, 236, 237, 239, 247
Advertising and Customer perceived value, 229
Age and leverage, 68
Anti-dumping (AD) rules and countervailing duties, 238, 246, 247
Apparels, 226–228
Assistive technologies, 83, 84
Attitude & behavior of authorities, 117–120
Attitude & behavior of students, 117–120
Attribute Check Sheet, 128, 129
Aurobindo Pharma, 37, 39

B
BEKK, 160
BEKK-GARCH, 163, 164
Big Five Personality, 204
Biocon Ltd, 37, 42
Biopharmaceutical companies, 32, 33, 37, 41, 45
Board, 7, 8, 11, 65–67, 69–72, 135, 140
Board busyness, 67
Board independence, 66, 69–71

Board leadership, 69–71
Board participation, 67, 69, 70, 71
Board size, 66, 69–71
BSE S&P Sensex (sensex), 160
Built-in environment, 83, 84
Bureaucratic Delays and Customs, 238, 239, 243–247

C
Case studies, 13, 92
Causal loop diagram, 145, 147, 148
Causes and effect diagram, 130
Certification of origin requirements, 237, 238, 245–247
Change in management, 188
Changing customer preferences, 151
Channel partners, 228, 230–232
Clinical trials, 34
Cluster, 50–56, 58, 59
Comfort, 146, 147, 229, 230, 232
Company's reputation, 260, 264–266
Compassion, 217, 219, 221–223
Compensation, 117–120, 254, 261, 264, 265
Competitive environment, 141
Complex and Ambiguous (VUCA) environment, 91, 103, 109, 215, 222, 223
Confirmatory Factor Analysis (CFA), 24, 206, 228, 230, 255, 259, 260, 262
Consolidation of holdings, 188
Corporate governance, 64, 65, 68, 69, 72
Corporate performance, 66
Corporate restructuring, 167, 168
Corporate strategies, vii

© Springer Nature Singapore Pte Ltd. 2018
S. Dhir and Sushil (eds.), *Flexible Strategies in VUCA Markets*,
Flexible Systems Management, https://doi.org/10.1007/978-981-10-8926-8

Creativity, 18–22, 214, 217, 221, 261, 265
Cross-border acquisitions, 168
Cross-sectional t-test, 171
Crude oil, 158–164
Crude oil prices and volatility spill over affect, 158
Cumulative average abnormal return, 171, 191
Customer buying behavior, 141
Customer satisfaction, 126, 147, 227, 228
Customer's buying behavior, 146
Customer's preference, 141
Customers' perception of quality, 228

D
Dark network, 90, 91, 103, 108, 109
Data collection, 22, 92, 127–129, 136, 218, 236, 242
DCC-GARCH, 159, 162, 163
Decline of brands, 226
Dependent variable, 55, 57, 68–71, 144, 150, 220, 243, 245
Descriptive statistics, 23, 56, 69, 117, 160, 161
Developing economy, 58
Development stages, 4–6, 11–15
Disability inclusion, 80, 82, 85, 86
Discipline, 101, 223
Discovery, 5, 11, 12, 14
Distributors, 53, 228
Diversity, 51, 80–83, 85, 86
Diversity management, 80
Dr. Reddy's Laboratories, 37, 38, 43
Drug discovery, 32, 33, 37
Durability, 228, 230, 232

E
Early recruitment practices, 256
Early stage startups, 6, 13
Economical success, 226
Economic and Customer Uncertainties, vii
Economic growth, 4, 178, 180, 181, 226
Economic instability, 151
Economic volatility, 140, 142, 143, 148, 150, 151
Economy and Financial Stability, 179
Economy, weather and political environment, 178, 179, 185
Efficiency/refine, 9, 64, 90, 91, 147, 178, 179, 182, 191, 248
EGARCH model, 159
Electricity utilities financial stability, 178, 180, 185
Emerging economy, 168
Emotional Intelligence (EI), 202–209

Employee accountability, 126
Employee and organizational fit, 256
Employee creativity, 19–24, 26, 27
Employee engagement, 126, 133, 135, 136, 202
Employee learning, 126
Employee reward and recognition, 126
Employer attractiveness, 253, 255, 256, 265
Employer attractiveness and prospective employees, 256
Employer brand, 252–259, 261, 263–266
Employer branding, 252–258, 266
Employer branding and employee attraction, 255
Employment experience, 252
Energy sector, vii
Entrepreneurship, 14
Ethics & CSR, 260, 262, 264–266
Event study, 170, 174, 189
Event window, 170–174, 190–195, 197
Exchange rate, 158–164
Exploratory Factor Analysis (EFA), 23, 230, 254, 257, 259–261, 264
Export subsidy, 236, 239, 243–246
External networking, 98
External perspective, viii

F
Facilities (i.e. fringe benefits), 113
Factor analysis, 151, 229, 256–258
Fair treatment, 83
Financial stability, 178–183, 185, 186
Financial stability index, 185
Flexibility in job, 83
Flexible work schedules, 83, 84

G
GARCH model, 163
Gender, 80, 95, 114–118, 120
Gender of Academicians, vii, 113, 118
Generalized sign test, 171
Gen X, 202
Gen Y, 202, 204
Gen Y employees, 201
Gen Z, 202
Geographical clustering, 50, 51, 53, 55, 56, 58, 59
Geographical clusters and subsidiary innovation, 52
Geographic clusters and innovation, 51
Globalization and economic reforms, 18
Government procurements, 240, 241, 243–246
Granger causality tests, 162

Index

Growth and development opportunity, 260, 261, 264–266
Growth and sustainability, 64

H
Human resource, 80, 82, 84, 85, 93, 127, 237, 252–254, 266
Human resource & personnel, 83

I
Idealized influence, 216, 219, 220
Import Policy Barriers to Trade, 240, 243
Improvement Adherence Action Plan, 134
Inclusion, 80–86, 192
India, 13, 18, 22, 32, 33, 35, 37–39, 43–45, 50, 51, 54, 56, 58, 59, 64, 80, 81, 86, 91–93, 95, 97–99, 127, 141, 142, 144, 157, 158, 168, 169, 174, 187, 190, 195, 202, 214, 218, 223, 226, 228, 233, 236, 247, 256–259, 266
Indian Apparel Market, viii
Indian Bio-Pharmaceutical sector, vi
Indian Cross-border Acquisitions, vii
Indian economy, 69, 226, 228, 236
Indian higher educational institutes, 215, 218, 220, 221, 223
Indicators, 11, 24, 35, 36, 38, 42, 43, 59, 229–231
Individual consideration, 216, 219, 220
Industrial Policy Resolutions (IPRs), 239, 243–246
Innovation, 18, 19, 21, 22, 27, 32, 35–37, 43–45, 50–56, 58, 59, 64–67, 163, 178, 179, 215, 221
Innovation in MNEs, 50
Innovation solution to uncertainty, 182, 185
Inspirational motivation, 216, 219, 220
Integrated system dynamic model, 148
Intellectual simulation, 142
Intensified market competition, 252
Internal networks, 51, 58
Internal networks and subsidiary innovation, 53
Internal security, 91
International business, 236, 242, 243, 247, 248
Interpersonal trust, 128, 136
IT, 64

J
Job satisfaction, 114–118, 120, 121
Johansen Co-integration test, 161, 162

K
Kaizen Sheet, 132
Key players, 35, 37
Key Result Area (KRA), 128, 129, 131–136
Knowledge spillover, 50, 53

L
Labelling, 240, 243–247
Leadership effectiveness, 202–209
Leadership in VUCA Environment, viii
Leadership styles, 215, 222
Learning organization, 214–217, 219–222
Legitimacy, 95–97, 104
Local knowledge spillover, 51, 55, 58, 59
Local knowledge spillovers and subsidiary innovation, 53
Lupin Limited, 38

M
Maintaining the quality of goods, 241, 246
Managerial implications, 26
Manufacturing, 4, 22, 23, 34, 37, 38, 45, 54, 82, 141, 145, 146, 172, 256
Market efficiency, 191
Marmer development stages, 5
Matching skills, 83
Mayer, Salovey and Caruso Emotional Intelligence Test (MSCEIT), 205
Measurement scales, 23
Mediating effect, 25, 26
Mediation, 25, 26
Mergers, acquisitions, and takeovers, 187
Military consolidation, 96
Millennial employees, 202
Motivation, 4, 21, 53, 99, 128, 135, 136, 217, 221, 223, 257
Multi-day event windows, 167
Multi-dimensional development model, 5, 13, 15
Multifactor Leadership Questionnaire (MLQ), 205
Multinational, 32, 33, 50, 52, 64, 81, 169
Multiple channels, 229

N
National Capital Region, India, 54, 218, 223
Non-tariff Barriers (NTB), 235, 237, 240–242, 247
NSE, 68, 159

O
Open offer, 187–195, 197

Organization, 4–13, 15, 18–23, 26, 27, 32, 34, 66, 83–86, 90–93, 95, 97–100, 103, 108, 109, 114, 115, 126, 127, 131, 133–136, 143, 179, 202, 208, 209, 214–217, 220, 222, 253, 261, 262
Organizational culture, 82, 83, 217
Organizational encouragement, 19, 20, 23
Organizational initiatives, 19, 22, 26, 27
Organizational innovation, 18, 19, 21–24, 26, 27
Organizational structure, 5, 93–95, 103–105
Organization competitiveness, 126
Organization design, 89
Organization flexibility, 93
Overall positive moods, 219, 221

P
Passenger car, 141, 142, 147, 150
Patent landscape, 34, 39, 44
Patents, 8, 32–45, 54–56, 59
Patents and Patent Citations, 52, 54
Payment consideration, 189, 191, 193, 195
People with disabilities, 80–86
Perceived leadership effectiveness, 205
Perceived quality, 225
Perceptions and feelings, 81
Perpetual challenging and employee creativity, 21
Policies & practices, 83
Policing, 90
Policy experimentation, 151
Policy issues and uncertainties, 181
Pre-recovery state, 144
Price, 34, 141, 144, 147, 150, 151, 157–164, 168, 170, 171, 174, 177, 178, 188–190, 193, 195, 197, 226, 228, 230, 232, 238, 240
Pricing mechanism, 188
Private University, 117, 118, 120
Process, Management and product, 18
Productivity, 36, 43, 45, 132–134, 178, 179, 182, 217, 254
Product-market fit, 3, 4, 6, 8, 10
Product standards, 236, 241, 247
Prospective employees, 252, 253, 256, 258, 259, 262, 264, 266, 267
Psychological contracts, 256
Public sector organizations, 81
Public University, 117

Q
QC Story Problem Solving Steps, 12
Quality, 36, 44, 45, 52–54, 56, 58, 59, 66, 84, 100, 101, 108, 126, 127, 130, 132–134, 141, 178, 182, 215, 226, 230, 232, 237, 239, 241, 243–247, 252, 2547
Quality of subsidiary innovation, 51, 53, 55, 57–59
Quality, Price, Customer services and Design, 229

R
R&D Intensity (RDI), 55, 57
Recruitment process, 99
Replenishment policies, 228
Research & Development facilities, 113
Research & Development Intensity, 68
Research and Development (R&D), 18, 22, 26, 32, 34, 36–39, 43–45, 52, 53, 55, 58, 59, 64–72, 118–120
Resonant leadership style, 216–219, 221, 223
Resources and financial uncertainty, 179
Retailers, 228
Role of co-worker, 83
Role of supervisor, 83
Rotated–factor–analysis, 146

S
Sales and payments, 225
Sales persons' training, 229
Sales promotions, 229, 232
Sampling, 22, 23, 81, 116, 229, 236, 241, 243, 248, 258, 265, 266
Sanitary and phytosanitary measures, 241, 243–247
Scale/grow, 5–7, 9–12, 23, 34, 116, 133, 141, 143, 146, 205, 226–229, 233, 237, 239, 243, 254, 256–260, 264, 266
Scaling Issues of Startups, vi
Sensex, 159–164
Service condition policies, 117, 119, 120
Shareholders' Wealth, 190
Small brands, 226–228, 232, 233
Startup ecosystem, 5
Startup lifecycle stages, 4
Stock market, 158, 159, 169, 174, 189
Stock market response, 167
Stock replenishment, 229–232
Strategic layers of the war, 96
Strategy, 18, 32, 35, 42, 50, 53, 90, 92, 95–97, 109, 126, 168, 169, 174, 185, 240, 265
Structural model, 25, 26
Subsidiary, 38, 50–56, 58, 59
Subsidiary Age (SA), 56, 57
Substantial acquisition of shares, 187, 188
Sun Pharma, 38, 42, 43
Supply chain efficiency, 229
Supply chain of passenger car firms, vii, 139

Index   273

Sustainability and inorganic growth, 187
Synergies, 109, 167
System dynamics, 142, 146, 149–151

T
Takeovers, 187, 190
Tax structures, 157
Teamwork, 126, 217
Technical Barriers to Trade (TBTs), 236, 239
Technological and informational needs, 117–120
Technology, 14, 18, 21, 35, 36, 50, 51, 53–55, 59, 64, 141, 178, 181, 182, 185, 202, 208, 236, 240, 253, 258
Technology diffusion, 182, 185
Terms and conditions, 225
Time Varying Conditional Correlation, vii
Top management attitude, 83
Top management leadership, 126
Total Employee Involvement (TEI), 126
Total Quality Management (TQM), 126
Trade creation, 236, 242–247
Trade diversion, 242, 243, 246, 247
Trainer Engagement, 128, 129, 135, 136
Trainer turnover ratio, 127–131, 134, 136
Training & career development, 83
Training and employee creativity, 20
Transformational and resonant leadership style, 220
Transformational leadership, 202, 203, 206–209, 216, 219, 220, 223
Transformational leadership style, 205, 215, 216, 218–220, 222, 223
TRIPS Agreement, 33

U
Unbalanced scaling, 4
Uncertain, 103, 109, 179, 180, 182, 183, 201, 214

Uncertainty, 6, 21, 64, 90, 91, 93, 95, 99, 104, 109, 141, 143, 146, 148, 149, 151, 178–181, 183–186, 214, 221
UNCTAD, 50, 64, 168
Utilization of resources, 82

V
Validation, 5, 11, 12, 14, 126, 128, 149
Value creation, 79, 168
Values & ethos, 83
Variable operationalization, 55
Variety and availability, 230
Vision, 95, 99, 208, 215, 219, 221–223
Volatile, 103, 109, 140, 151, 159, 161, 164, 168, 201, 214, 217
Volatile, uncertain, complex, and ambiguous environment, 89
Volatility, uncertainty, complexity, and ambiguity (VUCA) strategies, 90, 109, 201, 214, 215, 217, 220–222
Voluntary Export Restraints (VERs), 236, 237, 246, 247

W
Wholesalers, 225
Work life balance, 259, 260, 262, 264–266
Workforce, 80, 81, 86, 126, 135, 202, 208, 214, 252
Workforce diversity, 79, 80
Working environment conditions, 117–120
Workplace accessibility, 83–85
World Trade Organization (WTO), 33, 235, 236, 238, 239, 241, 242

X
5X scale, 205